WHAT WORKS NOW?

Evidence-informed policy and practice

Edited by Annette Boaz, Huw Davies, Alec Fraser and
Sandra Nutley

P

First published in Great Britain in 2019 by

Policy Press
University of Bristol
1-9 Old Park Hill
Bristol
BS2 8BB
UK
t: +44 (0)117 954 5940
pp-info@bristol.ac.uk
www.policypress.co.uk

North America office:
Policy Press
c/o The University of Chicago Press
1427 East 60th Street
Chicago, IL 60637, USA
t: +1 773 702 7700
f: +1 773-702-9756
sales@press.uchicago.edu
www.press.uchicago.edu

© Policy Press 2019

British Library Cataloguing in Publication Data
A catalogue record for this book is available from the British Library

Library of Congress Cataloging-in-Publication Data
A catalog record for this book has been requested

ISBN 978-1-4473-4548-0 paperback
ISBN 978-1-4473-4547-3 hardcover
ISBN 978-1-4473-4549-7 ePub
ISBN 978-1-4473-4550-3 Mobi
ISBN 978-1-4473-4552-7 ePdf

Cover design by Robin Hawes
Front cover image: istock
Printed and bound in Great Britain by CMP, Poole
Policy Press uses environmentally responsible print partners

To my family for helping me to keep a healthy sense of perspective
– AB

To my late father, with profound gratitude for a life well lived and
for always showing me the way – HD

To Dee, Bob, Melanie, Nina and Joe – AF

To my family – SN

Contents

Contents

Contents

List of tables and boxes

Tables

Boxes

List of abbreviations

AHRC	Arts and Humanities Research Council
ARC	Applied Research Collaboration
BCURE	Building Capacity to Use Research Evidence
BMJ	*British Medical Journal*
BPS	Better Public Services
CLAHRC	Collaboration for Leadership in Applied Health Research and Care
CPD	continuing professional development
CXC	ClimateXChange
DFID	Department for International Development
EBM	evidence-based medicine
EBPP	evidence-based policy and practice
EEF	Education Endowment Foundation
E4F	Education for the Frontline
EIF	Early Intervention Foundation
EIPP	evidence-informed policy and practice
ESRC	Economic and Social Research Council
EU	European Union
GRADE	Grading of Recommendations Assessment, Development and Evaluation
HTA	health technology assessment
IFS	Institute for Fiscal Studies
IT	information technology
NAO	National Audit Office
NERC	Natural Environment Research Council
NGO	non-governmental organisation
NHS	National Health Service
NICE	National Institute for Health and Care Excellence
NIHR	National Institute for Health Research
NIPH	Norwegian Institute of Public Health
NPM	New Public Management
NUBU	Norwegian Center for Child Behavioral Development
OECD	Organisation for Economic Co-operation and Development
OMB	Office of Management and Budget (US)
PART	Program Assessment Rating Tool
PbR	payment by results
QCET	Queensland Community Engagement Trial
QUERI	Quality Enhancement Research Initiative

R&D	research and development
RCT	randomised controlled trial
REF	Research Excellence Framework
RELU	Rural Environment and Land Use initiative
RIP	Research in Practice
RPP	research–practice partnership
SBU	Swedish Agency for Health Technology Assessment and Assessment of Social Services
SCIE	Social Care Institute for Excellence
SFI	Danish National Centre for Social Research
SIPR	Scottish Institute for Policing Research
Superu	Social Policy Evaluation and Research Unit
TLRP	Teaching and Learning Research Programme
tVM	the Vanguard Method
UK	United Kingdom
UN	United Nations
UPSI	Universities' Police Science Institute
US	United States
WWCCR	What Works Centre for Crime Reduction

Notes on contributors

Annette Boaz has spent more than 20 years exploring the relationship between research, policy and practice in the UK and internationally. She worked for a number of years in the UK Economic and Social Research Council-funded Centre for Evidence Based Policy. Until recently she edited the international journal *Evidence & Policy* with David Gough. She has supported a number of national and international initiatives aimed at increasing capacity for research use, including the National Institute for Health Research Knowledge Mobilisation Research Fellowship scheme, the Economic and Social Research Council (ESRC) Impact Prize, and the Irish Health Research Board Impact Prize. Recent projects have included the Medical Research Council-funded SEE-Impact study on stakeholder engagement in research. She is on the board of the UK Implementation Society and is a member of the World Health Organization European Advisory Committee on Health Research.

Jonathan Breckon has 15 years' experience in policy, research and public affairs. His expertise lies particularly in brokering relationships between decision-makers and researchers from across disciplines – social science, science and the humanities. He joined Nesta from the Arts and Humanities Research Council (AHRC), where he was Director of Policy and Public Affairs. He has also worked at the Royal Geographical Society, the British Academy and Universities UK and as a consultant developing quantitative skills in the social sciences. He is on the board of the Society for Evidence-Based Policing, and is Honorary Senior Lecturer at University College London.

Paul Cairney is Professor of Politics and Public Policy at the University of Stirling. His research interests lie in comparative public policy and his work has spanned comparisons on policy theories (*Understanding Public Policy*, 2012), methods associated with key theories (*Handbook of Complexity and Public Policy*, 2015), international policy processes (*Global Tobacco Control*, 2012) and comparisons of UK and devolved policy making. He has applied these insights to explain the use of evidence in policy and policy making in one book (*The Politics of Evidence-Based Policy Making*, 2016), several articles, and many blog posts on https://paulcairney.wordpress.com/ebpm/.

Carol Campbell is an Associate Professor of Leadership and Educational Change, and Co-Director of the Knowledge Network for Applied Education Research at the Ontario Institute for Studies in Education, University of Toronto. She is a member of the International Council of Education Advisers for the Scottish Government and a Board member of the International Congress for School Effectiveness and Improvement. Originally from Scotland, Carol has held education, academic and government roles in Canada, the UK and the US. Her recent co-authored books are: *Teacher Learning and Leadership: Of, By and For Teachers* (Routledge), *Empowering Educators in Canada* (Jossey-Bass) and *Empowered Educators: How High-Performing Systems Shape Teaching Quality Around the World* (Jossey-Bass). She is an active contributor on Twitter @CarolCampbell4.

Cynthia Coburn is Professor at the School of Education and Social Policy, Northwestern University. She studies the relationship between instructional policy and teachers' classroom practices in urban schools, the dynamics of school district policy making and the relationship between research and practice for school improvement. In 2011 she was awarded the Early Career Award from the American Educational Research Association in recognition of her contributions to the field of educational research in the first decade of her career. In 2015 she was elected Fellow of the American Educational Research Association, honouring 'exceptional contributions to and excellence in educational research'. She is a member of the California Collaborative for District Reform and the DREME network investigating coherence of early mathematics instruction. She has a BA in Philosophy from Oberlin College, and an MA in Sociology and a PhD in Education from Stanford University.

Huw Davies was a mathematician before working in public health, health services research and organisations research. Since 2001 he has been Professor of Health Care Policy and Management at the School of Management, the University of St Andrews, and Co-Director of the Research Unit for Research Utilisation (www.ruru.ac.uk). His research interests are in public service delivery, with a particular emphasis on quality and safety in healthcare, encompassing ideas of: evidence-informed policy and practice; performance measurement and management; and accountability, governance and trust.

Michael Di Francesco at the time of writing was Associate Professor in Public Sector Management at the University of New South Wales and the Australia and New Zealand School of Government, where he was also Case Program Director. Prior to this he held an academic post at Victoria University of Wellington, New Zealand. He has over a decade of senior advisory experience in central finance ministries, and international organisations such as the International Monetary Fund and World Bank. He has practice and research interests in decision rules in public financial management, evidence-based budget reform and public management policy design.

Kari Tove Elvbakken is Professor of Political Science at the Department of Administration and Organizational Theory at the University of Bergen, Norway (www.uib.no). Her doctoral thesis was on the institutionalisation of food control and food control legislation, and she has been a researcher and the research director at the Stein Rokkan Centre for social studies in Bergen. Her research interests include public health policy and institutions, comparative analyses of health and prevention policy, professionalisation processes and the activity and role of evidence-producing organisations.

Alec Fraser is Assistant Professor in Public Policy and Management at the Policy Innovation Research Unit at the London School of Hygiene and Tropical Medicine. His research interests focus on the relationship between evidence, policy making and practice in healthcare and other sectors in the UK and internationally. He has an MA in Public Policy and a PhD in Management, both from King's College London. Prior to entering academia, he worked in National Health Service administration and management.

Nicholas R. Fyfe has been researching and writing about policing for over 30 years, working on a diversity of topics including community engagement, organised crime, missing persons and police reform. Between 2006 and 2018 he was the founding director of the Scottish Institute for Policing Research, a pioneering collaboration between universities and the police focused on using research, knowledge exchange and professional education to contribute to policy and practice in policing. He is currently Dean of Social Sciences at the University of Dundee.

Deborah Ghate, formerly the director of the independent Policy Research Bureau in London and then the Centre for Effective Services in Ireland, is a researcher, analyst, consultant and organisational leader whose work has covered family social policy, childcare, youth justice and parenting, as well as evaluation methodologies. Since 2011 she has been chief executive of the Colebrooke Centre for Evidence and Implementation (www.cevi.org.uk), specialising in implementation science and practice in child and family services. She is chair of the UK Implementation Society (www.ukimplementation.org.uk) and was elected as a Fellow of the Academy of Social Sciences in 2016.

David Gough is Director of the EPPI-Centre at University College London (https://eppi.ioe.ac.uk/), which specialises in the development of methods of systematic review and in 'research on research use'. His particular interests are in the dimensions of difference between review methods, the mechanisms involved in linking research use to research production, the nature of What Works Centres and evidence standards for making justifiable evidence claims.

Hanne Foss Hansen has a PhD from Copenhagen Business School. She is a professor at the Department of Political Science, University of Copenhagen, where she is affiliated with the Centre for Results, Effects, Measurement and Evaluation (CRÈME; https://creme. polsci.ku.dk/english/researchers/). Her research interests concern public organisations, governance, public sector policy and reform, evaluation, evidence-based policy and practice and university reforms and organisation.

Brian Head has been Professor of Public Policy at the University of Queensland since 2007. He previously led a national non-governmental organisation in social policy and held senior roles in several Queensland government agencies, undertaking policy development, inter-governmental programmes and organisational evaluation. He is a national fellow of three professional bodies and assists the work of several leading social science journals. His research and publications focus on public policy issues, wicked problems, research utilisation and programme evaluation.

Bev Holmes is Chief Executive Officer of the Michael Smith Foundation for Health Research, a funding agency in British Columbia, Canada, and Adjunct Professor at the University of British Columbia (School of Population and Public Health) and Simon Fraser University (Faculty of Health Sciences). Her work focuses on the funding, production and uptake of health research evidence. Bev's research interests include knowledge translation, discourse analysis, health communication, risk communication, public involvement in health research and the science of science funding.

Rick Hood is a registered social worker with over 10 years' experience of statutory social work, mainly in child protection and with looked-after children. Since 2017 he has been Associate Professor in the Department of Social Work and Social Care at Kingston University and St Georges, University of London. His main research interests are in the applications of systems ideas to people-centred services, with a particular focus on complexity theory and socio-technical systems design.

Judith Hughes has spent over 30 years in healthcare practice, first as a clinical ophthalmologist and then in research and development in the pharmaceutical industry. Currently, she is an independent researcher who holds a PhD from the University of St Andrews, which examined the clinical guideline development process.

Gloria Laycock has a BSc and PhD in Psychology from University College London (UCL). She established and headed the Home Office Police Research Group and was founding director of the UCL Jill Dando Institute. She has carried out research and development in prisons, policing and crime prevention and has acted as a consultant and trainer on policing matters around the world. She is currently Professor of Crime Science at UCL and was director of research supporting the What Works Centre for Crime Reduction until 2016. She was awarded an OBE in the Queen's Birthday Honours 2008 for services to crime policy.

Graham P. Martin is Director of Research at The Healthcare Improvement Studies Institute, University of Cambridge. He has worked in healthcare and health policy research since 2001, holding various research and academic posts at Leicester and Nottingham and completing his PhD – a study of service-user involvement in the design and delivery of National Health Service service innovations – at Nottingham in 2009. His research takes critical and theoretically informed perspectives on contemporary healthcare issues, including professionalism, organisational change, quality and safety and public participation.

Laura Meagher has spent over 30 years working in the US and the UK with and within research and education institutions, along with industry and government, focusing on strategic change. She has frequently catalysed and facilitated novel initiatives, often multi-sector, interdisciplinary, interinstitutional and/or international, and so is keenly aware of challenges, issues and practical mechanisms. Through her consultancy, Technology Development Group, she has evaluated programmes and funding schemes promoting complex changes such as interdisciplinarity, knowledge exchange, societal impacts or economic development and capacity building. She provides expert advice, often conducting formative evaluation as a 'critical friend', to help project leadership teams, while also addressing accountability for funders. She shares knowledge through peer-reviewed publications, reports and masterclasses.

Anne Mette Møller holds an MSc degree in Sociology and a PhD in Political Science from the University of Copenhagen, Denmark. Prior to embarking on her PhD, she worked for several years in a private consultancy, where she conducted analyses and evaluations for public organisations at all levels of government. Her PhD research explores changing interpretations of evidence-based practice in the context of Danish child protection services, including the influence of this ideal on everyday knowledge mobilisation and decision-making practices in front-line organisations. Her broader research interests include public organisation and management, professional knowledge and practice and organisational ethnography.

Julie Nelson is a senior research manager at the National Foundation for Educational Research, where she directs a number of research studies on the topic of evidence-informed education. She is working with colleagues at the Education Endowment Foundation (EEF) to develop measures of teacher research engagement and also leads a number of knowledge mobilisation and scale-up evaluations on behalf of the Department for Education and the EEF. She recently co-edited a special issue of *Educational Research Journal* with Carol Campbell, University of Ontario, Canada, on the topic of evidence-informed practice.

Sandra Nutley is Emeritus Professor at the School of Management, University of St Andrews. She has published widely on research use and evidence-informed policy and practice, as well as contributing to the broad development of public policy and management. Prior to her academic career, she worked in local government. Since then, she has retained strong contacts with those working in public policy and service delivery, including through her role as a non-executive member of the Social Work Inspection Agency Board in Scotland (2005–11). She has advised several funding bodies on improving the use of research and the assessment of impact, including as Chair of the Scottish Funding Council's Public Policy Action Group (2006–09) and as a member of the Economic and Social Research Council's Evaluation Committee (2012–15). In 2011, she received the Campbell Collaboration's Robert Boruch Award for her distinctive contribution to research that informs public policy.

Mark Reed is a recognised international expert in impact research with over 150 publications, which have been cited more than 13,000 times. He holds a Research England and N8-funded chair at Newcastle University, is research lead for an international charity and has won prizes for the impact of his research. He collaborates and publishes across the disciplinary spectrum, from the arts and humanities to natural sciences, and he reviews research for funders around the world. He has been commissioned to write reports and talk to international policy conferences by the United Nations. Mark provides training and advice to universities, research funders, non-governmental organisations and policy makers internationally, and regularly works with business. He is author of *The Research Impact Handbook* and has trained more than 4,000 researchers from over 200 institutions in 55 countries through his company, Fast Track Impact. Find out more about his work at: www.profmarkreed.com or follow him on Twitter @profmarkreed.

Trevor A. Sheldon studied medicine, economics and medical statistics. He was founding director of the Centre for Reviews and Dissemination at the University of York, where he then took up the roles of head of the Department of Health Sciences and Deputy Vice-Chancellor, and was then Dean of the Hull York Medical School. His research interests include the effectiveness and cost-effectiveness of interventions to improve health and well-being and reduce inequalities, healthcare quality and health service performance, policy development and evaluation, resource allocation and research methods. He was elected Fellow of the Academy of Medical Sciences in 2000.

Ruth Stewart has worked to support evidence-informed decision making for over 20 years. Trained at the University of Cambridge and the University of London, she has worked at University College London's Evidence for Policy and Practice Information and Coordinating Centre (the EPPI-Centre) since 2000. Much of her work has been in collaboration with partners in Africa, and in 2012 she moved permanently to the University of Johannesburg, where she first led its Department for International Development-funded programme to Build Capacity to Use Research Evidence in African governments. In 2016 she founded the Africa Centre for Evidence, which supports the use of evidence to address poverty and inequality across the continent. Among other things she is chairperson of the Africa Evidence Network, and co-director of the Johannesburg Centre of the Collaboration for Environmental Evidence.

Sharon Straus is a geriatrician and clinical epidemiologist and trained at the University of Toronto and the University of Oxford. She is the Director of the Knowledge Translation Program and Interim Physician-in-Chief, St Michael's Hospital; Director, Division of Geriatric Medicine, University of Toronto; Vice Chair, and Professor, Department of Medicine, University of Toronto. She holds a Tier 1 Canada Research Chair in Knowledge Translation and Quality of Care and has authored more than 400 publications and three textbooks in evidence-based medicine, knowledge translation and mentorship. She is in the top 1% of highly cited clinical researchers as per Web of Science. She holds more than $57 million in peer-reviewed research grants as a principal investigator. She has received national awards for mentorship, research and education.

Vivian Tseng is the Senior Vice President, Programs at the William T. Grant Foundation, where she leads its grant-making programmes and initiatives to connect research, policy and practice to improve child and youth outcomes. In 2009 she launched the Foundation's initiative on the use of research evidence in policy and practice. To date the Foundation has invested $20 million in over 50 studies that have informed grant making among private and public funders across the United States. She received her PhD from New York University and her BA from University of California, Los Angeles, and was previously on the faculty in Psychology and Asian American studies at California State University, Northridge.

Oli Williams was awarded the NIHR CLAHRC West Dan Hill Fellowship in Health Equity, which he took up at the University of Bath. He later joined the SAPPHIRE Group at the University of Leicester as a research associate, before being awarded a THIS Institute post-doctoral fellowship based at King's College London. His research concerns health inequalities, co-production, patient and public involvement, knowledge translation, area-based and equitable intervention, obesity stigma and promotion of healthy lifestyles. He is an active promoter of health equity and social change and co-founder of the art collective Act With Love: www.actwithlove.co.uk.

Paul Wilson is a Senior Research Fellow at the Alliance Manchester Business School, University of Manchester. He previously worked for the Centre for Reviews and Dissemination, University of York, where he was responsible for translating the findings of systematic reviews for a wide range of professional audiences. His research interests are focused on the role and use of evidence in health decision making and methods to increase the uptake of research-based knowledge in practice and policy. Paul is deputy editor-in-chief of the journal *Implementation Science*.

Acknowledgements

This book would not have been produced without the generous contributions and support of many people and we would like to take this opportunity to record our heartfelt thanks for all the assistance provided. First and foremost, we are indebted to our contributing authors. This has been a collaborative project from the start, and our chapter authors have been involved throughout: commenting on the planned shape and content of the book; writing (and revising) their own contributions; commenting on the contributions of others; reacting with great patience as the editors reworked their prose in pursuit of consistency and coherence across the whole text; and helping to promote the book. Their involvement has gone above and beyond that usually expected of chapter authors and we are deeply grateful for their insights, commitment and forbearance. The collaboration has included several face-to-face meetings and we would like to record our thanks to the Research Unit for Research Utilisation at the University of St Andrews for organising and funding these meetings. Thanks are also due to the London School of Hygiene and Tropical Medicine for hosting a meeting for our contributors in London. We are also very grateful to The Nuffield Foundation, who organised and supported two wider meetings with those interested in researching and improving evidence use. These meetings enabled us to share, discuss and hone the book's main themes and findings with a wider group of stakeholders, whose helpful contributions we also acknowledge. More broadly than this, we would like to record our debt of gratitude to the many people – researchers, policy makers, practitioners, research funders and brokers – whose work and writings we have drawn upon when surveying the development of evidence-informed policy and practice since the late 1990s.

There are some specific individuals who have made key contributions at various points during this project. Special thanks go to Catherine Gray and her team at Policy Press who have encouraged and supported the production of this book. Thanks also to the peer-reviewers who gave us some excellent feedback on the manuscript. Particular thanks are also due to Catherine Grant and Benet Reid for their assistance and expertise in proofreading large parts of the manuscript.

Writers often rely on the encouragement and tolerance of their family and friends, and the editors are no different in this regard.

We would each like to record our sincere thanks for the on-going understanding and support of those who are dear to us.

Annette Boaz, Huw Davies, Alec Fraser and Sandra Nutley
January 2019

Foreword

This is an important time for the debates this book informs. Change and uncertainty in the policy and political landscape, both domestically and internationally, has led many to question the role of evidence and expertise. So, when considering the value placed on evidence-informed expertise, it is worth looking to three of the main audiences for the expert knowledge in question: policy makers, practitioners and the public. With respect to UK policy makers, we have recently seen a more significant injection of public funding into research than this country has experienced for many years. In tandem, practitioner groups such as teachers, social workers and healthcare professionals have increasingly been engaged in generating and using evidence in the delivery of front-line services. It is clear to those of us looking to fund excellent research that many in the policy and wider public service networks value evidence and are eager to engage. Finally, it is striking that a range of polling data suggest that public trust in experts has remained high and relatively stable over several decades.

To satisfy this appetite for evidence and its application, there is a need to identify new approaches to undertaking research, exploring policy challenges, evaluating interventions and getting that knowledge used. Such work will help us understand more and address better the range of complex questions and challenges we face about how to improve outcomes for the public. Progress has been made, but there is still much to be done and there remain many questions to address. For example: how do we improve economic and social opportunities for a wider range of people and groups? How do we support the maintenance of independence and social connections as people age? How do we develop resilience to a range of digital threats while benefiting from what these new technologies can offer? In addressing these and other questions there is a need to consider what claims can be made from various types and forms of evidence, and how best to include more of the relevant stakeholders in the creation of this evidence so that it is more likely to be relevant, useful and used. In this timely new book, the authors raise and discuss these issues and more, advancing how we think about this field and setting a constructive agenda for where we go next.

Professor Jennifer Rubin, Executive Chair of the UK Economic & Social Research Council (ESRC), and Champion for Equality, Diversity and Inclusion at UK Research and Innovation (UKRI)

1

What works now?
An introduction

Annette Boaz, Huw Davies, Alec Fraser and Sandra Nutley

Taking a fresh look at the evidence agenda

Evidence is integral to both the process and the evaluation of policy making, and evidence is also fundamental to both understanding and then improving practice. Beyond this, evidence also embodies claims to truth, and is thus imbued with import and power as well as being politically contested. In this book we take a fresh look at the relationships between evidence, policy and practice across different policy domains and different geographical jurisdictions. We appraise what we know about the use of evidence in policy and practice and consider the future direction of the field. Our focus and our starting point in doing so is the United Kingdom (UK), and especially UK public services. This is partly because this is where we, as editors, are based and the country we know best, and partly because this is where many of the debates have originated or been exemplified. That said, throughout the book we seek to look beyond these shores to see how new ideas have emerged in other jurisdictions or how existing themes are operationalised, with innovative twists, elsewhere. Thus the necessarily UK-centric nature of the analysis is balanced by a contextualisation in international practices and debates (while recognising that debates conducted in languages other than English have been less accessible to us).

We begin our explorations with an example to set the scene for the contributions that follow. In doing so, we tell the story of research conducted to inform the debate about food advertising aimed at children: one element of the policy response to tackling the obesity crisis. Through this example we show not only how evidence matters, but also how the relationship between evidence, policy and practice is nuanced, dynamic, political and contested.

The enduring interest in the role of evidence: an illustrative example

The dramatic rise in obesity rates across the world is a major concern for governments and healthcare professionals and has been for some time. Obesity impacts on people's capacity to live flourishing lives, reduces and potentially reverses gains in longevity and creates new challenges and costs for public services. In the meantime, many of the drivers of obesity (for example, ready access to calories, increasing sedentariness) are so woven into the fabric of our physical environment and our social and economic systems that these might properly be termed obesogenic. Unravelling these factors, and reforming these systems, is likely to be immensely complex – fraught with conflicting perspectives and competing interests. Obesity as a policy challenge, then, seems to be here to stay: unlikely to be resolved, and often to be re-examined for policy attention.

The impact of obesity has prompted governments to intervene to tackle the root causes, specifically in childhood. Policy initiatives have included healthy-eating campaigns (such as promoting fruit and vegetables), taxes on sugary drinks, changes to food labelling and education programmes aimed at parents. One further area identified for potential action is better control of food advertising aimed at children. In terms of stakeholder interests, this is perhaps one of the more contentious areas.

In order to understand this topic better the UK Food Standards Agency commissioned a review of the literature. Published in 2003, the review drew together a wide body of research evidence on food advertising (Hastings et al, 2003). The reviewers were careful to acknowledge that other factors were also likely to influence children's diets, and they drew attention to the limitations of the evidence base. However, this work caused some considerable controversy by concluding that there was evidence demonstrating the direct effect of food promotions on the food preferences, knowledge and behaviours of children. In 2004 a report commissioned by the Office of Communications, the UK communications regulator, came to similar conclusions (Livingstone, 2004).

The food and drinks industry responded by investing considerable time and effort in refuting the claim that there was any clear link between advertising and behaviour: critiquing the review on methodological grounds and going so far as to commission another review of the literature. However, restrictions on television advertising of unhealthy food and drink products directly to children were finally put in place in 2007, and these were extended to social media in 2017. The debate about the appropriateness of such restrictions rumbles on, and new consultations on the issue are planned by the UK government in 2018.

This example demonstrates a number of the challenges inherent in the relationship between evidence, policy and practice. A first challenge is linked to evidential quality. This is often particularly true of studies of complex social interventions that present a range of methodological difficulties, including uncertainty in demonstrating causation and the strictures of valid and reliable measurement. Such technical challenges pose fundamental questions about how we can truly 'know' anything, or adequately attribute outcomes to policy decisions. What is also interesting is how methodological concerns became a central battleground, with methodological shortcomings being used as a reason (or perhaps pretext) for discounting the evidence. This observation highlights the political power of some actors to actively seek to discredit knowledge so as to serve their own interests.

Second, there are challenges in presenting the nuanced findings of research and their subsequent interpretation. Even when there has been considerable effort to place research findings in context and to articulate the complexity of the key messages, a strong headline can jump out and take on a life of its own. This demonstrates the limitations of researchers to manage the messages that their work may be used to convey in the wider media. In the case of the study on food advertising, the conclusion that there was a link between food advertising and children's diets found its way onto the front page of a national newspaper (quite an achievement for a systematic review). Finally, this brief case demonstrates that when evidence is used there are always multiple interests at work, often drawing on discordant discursive techniques to frame policy implications in certain ways. In this case, the food industry found a clear statement of a link between food advertising and children's diets, shall we say, unpalatable.

The aims and scope of this book

It is the types of issues highlighted in the food advertising case above that prompted this book. It aims to revisit and build upon the picture presented in *What Works? Evidence-Based Policy and Practice in Public Services* (Davies et al, 2000), in which two of the current editors were involved. In asking 'what works now?' for evidence-informed policy and practice, we propose to take another look at the 'what works agenda' that sparked so much activity and interest from the mid-1990s.

We consider what is different, how much we now know about using evidence and what still needs to be done to develop the field. These questions are complex and challenging, but we consider them worth tackling due to the potential contribution that evidence can make to public services and to the welfare of society. With this in mind, the book has a particular emphasis on considering how debates and practices associated with the use of evidence in shaping public policies and service-delivery practices have evolved over the two decades since the late 1990s. We consider what this means for the various actors involved in these endeavours and also offer some thoughts on prospects and agendas for the future.

In this all-new text we are certainly still interested in the use of evidence to inform the design of policy and practice interventions (that is, to help us identify 'what works'). However, we are also concerned with the wider use of evidence to explore important issues and problems, and to examine the extent to which there is empirical evidence to support alternative explanations of the root causes of these problems, the ways they may be framed and the ways that they may be ameliorated. In addition, we are interested in the use of evidence to inform the making of policy and the improvement of practice. Reflecting this, the field as a whole has moved away from the language of evidence-based policy and practice (EBPP) and towards a more inclusive notion of evidence-informed policy and practice (EIPP). This framing also reflects a growing recognition that evidence alone is unlikely to dictate the direction of policy or practice but can, nonetheless, play an important influencing role alongside other forms of knowledge. So, the title of this book reflects both an interest in what works in policy and practice and also an interest in what works in supporting the broader goals and strategies of an inclusive EIPP.

The book is concerned with the debates, tensions, policies and practices associated with the aim of ensuring that evidence plays a role in public policies and practices. The tone of these debates, the main issues of concern and the shape of initiatives vary by sector and country. For example, whereas education has seen considerable interest in the development of practitioner-researchers and research–practice partnerships between universities and schools, other sectors, such as health, have continued to focus primarily on evidence generation, synthesis and more passive strategies regarding dissemination. In the United States (US), the debate about evidence use has continued to be largely dominated by questions about intervention and programme effectiveness, whereas in other geographical areas there are much wider concerns about which evidence is seen as being relevant. In some fields (such as the environment and international development) and in some places (such as Canada, Australia and New Zealand) there have also been important developments in terms of recognising and rectifying the absence of indigenous voices from processes of evidence generation and the setting of research priorities. And in many places, although to uneven extents, there is greater awareness of the need to include service users and the public in creating, interpreting and using evidence. The book seeks to reflect these field and geographic differences while also highlighting common themes and concerns. While the first half of the book is notably UK-centric in its purview (Section Two, especially), we later broaden our perspective by examining specific developments and their implications in other jurisdictions (Section Four).

One of the key debates about evidence use continues to be what counts (or should count) as evidence. This book, building on the earlier volume *Using Evidence* (Nutley et al, 2007), adopts an inclusive definition, recognising that evidence is a label that becomes attached by different actors to some types of knowledge and ways of knowing (see Chapter Eleven). At times, we focus primarily on research evidence – that is to say, evidence that is the result of systematic investigation, regardless of whether or not it emanates from a research setting (see Chapter Ten). But we take care to place this particular type of evidence in the wider knowledge context. Research-based knowledge can encompass any systematic and transparent gathering and analysis of empirical data, whether in explicit de novo research studies or through the careful exploitation of existing data sources. However, the different chapters reflect the diverse ways that various sectors define evidence, and their authors reflect on this in the text. We also recognise and explore how research evidence interacts with other forms of knowing, such as knowledge derived from experience and from professional practice. What counts as evidence is given extensive further consideration, then, in Chapters Ten and Eleven.

Of course, this book's subtitle is not just 'evidence', but 'evidence-informed *policy and practice*'. As we shall see, policy and practice are two of the most important arenas where evidence is marshalled and deployed, and these form the focus of our discussions. Again, we cast our net widely to include a variety of policies and practices as we aim to tease out the similarities and differences of the dynamics of evidence in these two arenas – albeit with an emphasis on those areas where government is a dominant player as both policy maker and service provider, either directly or indirectly.

A short history of the long debate on evidence use

Interest in the creation and use of evidence for policy and practice is not a new concern, and the underpinning aspects have long been studied in various ways through different academic disciplines. Scholars in the field of the sociology of knowledge or science and technology studies have been researching the role of scientific endeavour in society since the early 1960s. Key contributors such as Thomas Kuhn (with *The Structure of Scientific Revolutions*, in 1962) and Bruno Latour (with *Laboratory Life: the Social Construction of Scientific Facts*, in 1979) have challenged our understanding of how research or science create knowledge, and have had an impact way beyond their primary fields. Originating from rural sociology, Everett Rogers' conceptualisation of the adoption and diffusion of innovations was first published in 1962 and subsequent editions continue to be widely used (Rogers, 1962). In the 1970s Carol Weiss (1977; 1979) wrote a number of influential papers on the use of evaluation in policy that continue to resonate. Political scientists have also been long interested in questions of implementation, with key authors including Pressman and Wildavsky (1973), as well as Lipsky (1979) in the 1970s and Mazmanian and Sabatier (1983) in the 1980s.

At the time when the original volume on *What Works* was published (Davies et al, 2000), there was a tide of optimism around the role of evidence in shaping public policy and service delivery practice. It was epitomised in the UK by the New Labour 1997 general election mantra that 'what matters is what works', which some hailed as emblematic of a shift from ideology-based to evidence-based policy making (and a corresponding shift from professionally driven to evidence-based practices). Such trends were said to stem at least in part from widespread public mistrust of politicians and professionals, and signalled a move to a more technocratic era.

There was, however, already a considerable amount of scepticism about the possibility of post-ideological politics in 2000. There were also concerns about the desirability of evidence-driven policies and practices, due to unease about the quality of the evidence base itself, and there were worries that the limitations of evidence as a basis for decision making were being underplayed. Evidence does not substitute for a continuing need to adjudicate between differing sets of values (for example, on what matters), and there is an on-going need to exercise judgements that draw on experience and expertise alongside evidence.

There have been moments when lessons from the longer history of studying evidence use seem to have been lost. For example, in the early 1980s Maurice Kogan and Mary Henkel conducted ethnographic research in a UK government department and concluded that sustained interaction between scientists and policy makers was crucial if evidence was to play an active role in policy (Kogan and Henkel, 1983). We are only now rediscovering the importance of such fine-grained organisational accounts of evidence use and, indeed, of the critical role of sustained interactions.

However, the two decades since the late 1990s have seen a number of advances in the field of EIPP. In particular, there have been infrastructural developments on the supply side. These have included increased funding for evidence-generation activities, despite the climate of austerity. Difficult times often require cuts in public spending, but they have also led to calls for more evidence to inform the deployment of limited resources. In particular, in the UK there has been significant investment in the establishment of 'what works' centres (see Chapter Thirteen). The centres (and other similar initiatives internationally) have focused on the generation, synthesis and dissemination of evidence. Alongside and sometimes linked to these centres have been developments in evidence methodologies, such as systematic review techniques and the advancement of trial methodologies for complex interventions and of tools such as guidelines and toolkits to present evidence to practitioners in more accessible formats. At the same time, research impact assessment processes and reporting requirements introduced by government and funding bodies have led to increased interest within the academic community in the generation of policy and practice impacts from research.

On the demand side there have also been significant developments. In the UK there are now a set of expected skills and required practices for those working in policy-related roles. There are continuing professional development (CPD) and registration requirements linked to evidence use for various professional groups, including health professionals, teachers and social workers. There are also opportunities for professionals to complete more formal education, with support for masters-level courses and even PhD programmes in undertaking and understanding research. In healthcare there have been opportunities for health professionals to take on hybrid roles, where they can conduct research alongside their professional practice. While these opportunities were initially targeted at doctors, increasingly nurses and allied health professionals have also been encouraged to develop their capacity as researchers and research users.

Alongside the push that sometimes follows evidence production, and the pull generated by capacity-building initiatives, since the late 1990s there have emerged a large number of intermediary bodies that seek

7

to 'bridge the gap' between evidence supply and evidence demand. Some of these organisations explicitly label their activities as knowledge brokering, while others have adopted terms such as facilitating and liaison roles. For example, in Scotland the term 'knowledge brokering' is widely recognised and used, and there is a knowledge network and a programme of knowledge brokering training. Knowledge brokering has also been particularly popular in Canada (see Chapter Sixteen), where interactional relationships have been considered critical to promoting evidence use. In contrast, in England, 'Research in Practice' (see Chapter Five, Box 5.2) works to support the use of evidence in social care practice, but does not use the language of knowledge brokering. Across policy sectors internationally, there has also been a growing recognition that the public and service stakeholders could play a more active role in research. Such stakeholders may be given different labels, depending on the countries and sectors in which they are located; however, many different opportunities for engagement are identified, ranging from setting research agendas to supporting dissemination. There is also an active interest in engaging potential evidence users and service users more upstream, as co-producers of evidence (see Chapter Twelve for further discussion of co-production).

There have been a smaller number of initiatives that seek to achieve a more 'whole systems' approach to promoting evidence use. These ambitious initiatives build on an understanding that both social problems and related policy and practice responses have complex, multifaceted dimensions that require both intra- and inter-organisational action. These approaches have sought to address the multiple challenges to evidence use at different levels within organisations. Examples include developing a strategic approach to evidence use at a policy level. For instance, the Ontario education department has developed a Research and Evaluation Strategy (see Chapter Seven), and in the UK the Department for Environment, Food and Rural Affairs has introduced an Evidence Strategy. At a practice level in the health system, there has been an effort to bring together universities and hospitals in research collaborations (see Chapter Four), and in education in the US there have been similar attempts to build on-going research–practice partnerships to generate research agendas and co-produce evidence that is more suited to local use (see Chapter Seventeen).

However, while all this activity might be seen as constituting a partial shift in focus from linear, overly rational conceptualisations of evidence implementation to more nuanced understandings of the importance of the interactions between context and relationships within systems, there is still a dominant concern with developing the evidence base rather than ensuring that the evidence is used. This might be due in part to the continued dominance of the classic 'medical research model' in debates about evidence use. This model may be characterised in the following ways: it is based on a clear hierarchy of evidence (with systematic reviews and randomised controlled trials at the top); it demonstrates an orientation towards practice change rather than policy, with a 'pipeline' framing of the journey from evidence generation to application (often described as 'bench-to-bedside'); and it is supported by relatively bountiful resources, thanks to the traditional economic, social and political importance of the medical profession. These characteristics are not necessarily found in other sectors (such as education, social care or international development). In such sectors, what counts as good evidence is more contested, policy change tends to be viewed as at least as relevant as practice change and the research journey is often more iterative and occurs within heavily constrained resources. Given this, an architecture designed to serve the needs of the medical model is unsurprisingly poorly suited to most other sectors (and, indeed, for some areas of healthcare, such as mental health).

As we saw with the food advertising example at the start of the chapter, in key areas that have sought (at least initially) to embody an evidence-based approach to policy and practice (for example, Sure Start; No Child Left Behind; diagnostic and treatment pathways in healthcare; intelligence-led policing) the evidence-use story has been more complex, multifaceted and equivocal than the medical research model might imply. In many areas of application, we now have a broader understanding of what types of evidence might be of use, marking a shift from a narrow focus on what works to a wider interest in all the types of evidence that can help us to understand the world around us. As we have noted, the language used in the field has also evolved to reflect in particular a recognition that the routes that evidence takes are often circuitous, with as many dead ends as opportunities for influence, and that evidence is only one of the factors shaping policy and practice. However, the implications of these shifts – in terms of the many different types of evidence that might support change, and the skills and competencies needed to promote and use knowledge – are only now beginning to be fully recognised.

Locating the analysis in contemporary times

Despite widespread debates about the theory and practice of evidence use at the turn of the millennium (and in the years since then), including claims that policy-based evidence is more prevalent than evidence-based policy, this book is being written and published in a different social, economic and political climate than was evident in 2000. There is now much discussion about a rise in populism and a shift to post-truth politics, where claims are made with little regard to generally accepted facts. There is sometimes not just a mistrust of evidence and experts but a total dismissal of them. The politics of evidence use continues to preoccupy commentators, leading to a more sophisticated understanding of the interplay between evidence, policy and practice. However, regardless of the shifting context, evidence continues to have a role to play. For example, post-truth politics tends to relate to short-term, headline-grabbing issues, while much policy continues to emerge and evolve outside the glare of publicity. At present, away from the limelight, evidence is called upon and used in various ways by many different actors working at national and local levels on policy and practice issues. It is perhaps too early to see whether the shift to populism will lead to a broader shift in attitudes to evidence use.

As with the previous volume, the analysis presented in this book assumes two main groups of both users and shapers of evidence: policy makers and practitioners. However, we acknowledge that policy and practice happens at many different levels, including the development of policy in practice settings and the importance of recognising the practice of policy making. The delineation between policy and practice is not as clear cut as it might seem. We also recognise that there is a much wider body of potential users of evidence, including researchers themselves, service users, voluntary organisations and lobby groups. We do not intend to play down the importance of these stakeholder groups. On the contrary: there is a growing recognition in the field, and reflected in the chapters that follow, that diverse stakeholder groups have a significant role to play in promoting research use. Service users and individual citizens, in particular, have come to the fore in debates about evidence use. Methods currently advocated for co-creation and co-production of evidence promote an active role for different stakeholders throughout the research process. For this book, while we retain a focus on evidence use in both the official policy process and day-to-day service delivery, a wider group of stakeholders perhaps play a more visible role in the picture than they did in the late 1990s, and this is reflected in the text.

Outline of book structure and content

The book has four sections. After this introduction, Section One contains two chapters aimed at setting the scene for the rest of the book. These chapters outline the two key areas of focus for evidence-informed change: in policy arenas and in practice settings. These contributions come first because they provide an account of the settings where evidence use is expected to play out. Of course, distinctions between policy and practice may sometimes be too simplistically drawn, and many of the subsequent accounts in this book range seamlessly across both; nevertheless, the distinction is a practical one for our initial purposes.

The first of these chapters (Chapter Two) takes a critical look at evidence use in policy making. Drawing on insights from policy studies, it considers some of the conditions necessary for evidence use in policy making, advocating a shift in focus, away from normative discussions on how evidence *should* be used and towards more pragmatic discussions of how to respond to policy making in the real world, where evidence on its own is usually insufficient to bring about major policy change. The following chapter (Chapter Three) sees a move from evidence use in policy to evidence use in service delivery. It begins by exploring the deficiencies inherent in the top-down aspects of mandated evidence use in service-delivery organisations. The authors then advocate a more mixed approach that combines what they describe as 'outside in' approaches (where external evidence is pushed or pulled into service organisations to help reshape their services) with 'inside out' approaches (where locally sensitive knowledge is co-produced in situ and some efforts are made to share these experiences more widely).

Section Two discusses developments in four of the sectors that featured in the original *What Works* book (healthcare, social care, criminal justice and education), and also features two new sectors where there has been considerable activity and interest in the use of evidence to inform policy and practice (the environment and sustainability, and international development). The content of the first four chapters is mainly focused on developments in the UK, and also homes in on particular subsections of that policy field to illustrate the arguments. However, the chapters also draw out the generic and/or conceptual implications from their accounts, so that these accounts are lifted above and beyond the particular local or national developments. This approach is also true of the chapters on the environment and sustainability (Chapter Eight) and international development (Chapter Nine), although both of these necessarily engage with global as well as local issues.

Of course, the relationship between evidence and policy plays out in many other arenas than those covered here. While we have emphasised public services and the policies that support these, evidence is germane to many other topics of salience. Issues such as immigration, housing, violence, substance misuse, land use and economic development are all fertile areas for more evidence-informed approaches. Our hope is that the selections chosen in Section Two will be but a part of a broader and more inclusive analysis.

Following on from the sector-specific chapters of Section Two, we then step back to look at the key animator of the dynamics explored in those accounts: evidence and its influence. Section Three addresses three cross-cutting themes, moving from the particular accounts of Section Two to examine more thematic arguments. In turn, we explore: the types of research evidence available to support policy and practice; the key issue of evidential quality and labelling; and the use of evidence and how such use might be promoted and assessed.

In addressing the first of these issues, Chapter Ten begins by exploring systematic approaches to generating evidence in ways that answer important questions for policy makers, practitioners and other interested stakeholders. The chapter argues that diverse knowledge needs require a wide range of (complementary) methodological approaches. It considers the relative merits of these different approaches, before exploring methods of research synthesis and (more challenging) research integration. Chapter Eleven goes on to consider the important question of what counts as good evidence. In this chapter we explore some of the implications of technocratic approaches to this question, such as evidence hierarchies and methodology checklists. Nonetheless, what counts as good evidence is also concerned with knowledge needs, prior beliefs and contextual relevance, and we contend that the valuing of evidence must also take such issues into account.

The final chapter of this section (Chapter Twelve) picks up the debate to examine the ways in which evidence application is shaped. It considers what we mean by evidence use, influence, uptake and impact. The different connotations of these terms are analysed, alongside an exploration of the different ways in which we interpret what it is to be a 'research user'. Models of the research use process are also examined, from those that emphasise rationality and linearity, through those that explore a more complexity-informed, systems-based view. The chapter concludes by considering the effectiveness of activities designed to promote evidence use in various settings and the assessment of research impact more generally.

The final section (Section Four) considers important aspects of the international nature of the debates around EIPP through a series of international commentaries. These provide an opportunity to explore more widely the themes arising from the previous sectoral and cross-cutting chapters, most of which have a predominantly UK focus. Our authors here offer lively, sometimes idiosyncratic and necessarily partial contributions, frequently informed by the authors themselves being committed actors in the fields they describe. The purpose of these accounts is to spark recognition, insight and debates, rather than to offer systematic comparisons and analysis.

Five nations or wider geographical groupings are selected, primarily for their prominence in the debates about evidence, policy and practice. While some focus on individual countries (the US, Canada), others draw learning from across a wider geographical area (Scandinavia, the Antipodes). These are largely anglophone countries, reflecting the concentration of the evidence debate, although we see promising signs that this is beginning to shift. The opening chapter of this section takes a high-level, governmental perspective on the UK, providing a broader contextual backdrop to the sector-specific chapters in Section Two and some points of comparison with the other commentaries in this section.

The book concludes with a final chapter bringing together key learning points from across the various contributions. Here we reflect on a series of recurrent themes from the preceding chapters and expand on some of the recurring responses to those themes. In doing so we highlight the many and varied strategies open to those seeking to strengthen the role of evidence, whether in policy or in practice.

Although there is a rationale for the sequencing of the chapters in the book (outlined above), all chapters have been carefully constructed so as to stand alone. This should enable readers to dip into the book at will, without having to approach chapters or sections in any predefined sequence. For that reason, the chapters are extensively cross-referenced so that interested readers can follow up on arguments or exemplars in other chapters. This does mean that there is some recapitulation of the arguments at various points, but we hope that readers will find this helpful, especially as it allows separate chapters a completeness that would otherwise not be possible. Finally, each section of the book begins with a short overview to orientate the reader to the subsequent content and the emerging themes and issues.

Some intended audiences

This book is intended for a broad range of readers. We anticipate that those starting out on a research career (as undergraduates, postgraduates or early-career researchers) will be interested in exploring the role their research might play in policy and practice. For academics working in public policy research we anticipate that the domain-specific chapters in Section Two are likely to be attractive and useful. However, we hope that readers will also take the opportunity to read about other domains via the different chapters in that section or through the section introduction. We anticipate that the international chapters in Section Four will enable readers to learn from the interesting similarities and differences that have emerged across jurisdictions. In addition, we hope that Chapters Two and Three (on policy and practice) and Chapters Ten to Twelve (on evidence and its use) will provide some broader framing and thematic understanding of the issues, as well as pointing to some 'how to' advice for those interested in being participants in the field.

This is not just a book for researchers, however: it has much wider intent. We have also written this book with policy makers, practitioners, analysts and (especially) those working in voluntary and intermediary organisations in mind. With the growing recognition that service users and the public more widely are key actors in this field we also want this book to be a useful resource for interested (and committed) wider stakeholders and their representatives. We really hope that this book has something for everyone, and that at least some readers will go away inspired to advocate for more and better evidence use, while better understanding the challenges of so doing.

Some concluding remarks

Our knowledge of the use of evidence in policy and practice has developed considerably since the late 1990s. The chapters following in this book share a vast amount of learning spanning different sectors and jurisdictions. Chapter authors sometimes talk of this growing body of activity as a 'movement', or as an 'evidence idea'. Elsewhere it is described as an emerging 'evidence ecosystem'. There is now so much more activity, interest and learning around evidence use than we found in our first foray into this field in the late 1990s. There is also a deeper, richer understanding about evidence use beyond the original question of 'what works'. However, there still remain considerable gaps in what we know as the field develops. In particular, the contribution of some important changes in the landscape, such as the potential exploitation of big data and the role of new information and communication technologies, is not fully clear at the moment of writing and will require further interrogation over the coming years. Moreover, the excitement about knowledge co-production processes and a gradual dismantling of various category boundaries (for example, between researchers and the researched, or between research and practice) needs to be tempered by careful investigation into their utility. Authors comment on these challenges and opportunities in individual chapters, and they also form the focus of the discussion in the final chapter: the investigative work to understand these dynamics must go on if EIPP is to fulfil more of its promise.

References

Davies, H.T.O, Nutley, S.M. and Smith, P.C. (eds) (2000) *What works: evidence-based policy and practice in public services*, Bristol: Policy Press.

Hastings, G., Stead, M., McDermott, L., Forsyth, A., MacKintosh, A., Rayner, M., Godfrey, C., Caraher, M. and Angus, K. (2003) *Review of research on the effects of food promotion to children*, Food Standards Agency, http://www.foodstandards.gov.uk/multimedia/pdfs/promofoodchildrenexec.pdf.

Kogan, M. and Henkel, M. (1983) *Government and research*, London: Heinemann.

Kuhn, T. (1962) *The structure of scientific revolutions*, Chicago: Chicago University Press.

Latour, B. (1979) *Laboratory life: the social construction of scientific facts*, London: Sage Publications.

Lipsky, M. (1979) *Street level bureaucracy*, New York: Russell Sage Foundation.

Livingstone, S. (2004) *A commentary on the research evidence regarding the effects of food promotion on children*. Prepared for the Research Department of the Office of Communications, London: Media@LSE.

Mazmanian, D. A. and Sabatier, P. A. (1983) *Implementation and public policy*, Glenview Ill: Scott Foresman.

Pressman, J. L. and Wildavsky, A. (1973) *Implementation: How great expectations in Washington are dashed in Oakland*, California: University of California Press.

Rogers, E.M. (1962) *Diffusion of innovations*, New York: Free Press.

Weiss, C. H. (1977) *Using social science research in public policy-making*, Farnborough, Hants: D.C. Heath.

Weiss, C H (1979) 'The many meanings of research utilisation', *Public Administration Review*, 39, pp 426–431.

Section One
Policy and practice as arenas for evidence

It is commonplace to refer to evidence-informed policy and evidence-informed practice, and thereby to signal two different albeit related arenas where evidence may have influence. This distinction is reflected in the title of this book and in the content of this section. The distinction is not without foundation and it has some practical utility, but there are limitations to holding to any hard-and-fast delineation.

Broadly speaking, policy and practice *do* have distinct orientations and focus. The former is more about setting policy directions, priorities, budgets and directives, often through politically driven processes. The latter is more concerned with responding to such policy stipulations, managing and meeting service demands, and coping with local challenges within budgetary constraints. And then, as we get closer to 'the front line', practice is all about the delivery of everyday service: dealing with clients and managing any necessary supporting processes.

These discrete conceptions emphasise the roles played by different actors. A focus on policy draws attention to politicians, political advisors and government officials, and the much wider range of actors who seek to influence these. A focus on practice draws attention not only to managers and professionals (doctors, nurses, teachers, prison officers and so on), but also to the (often neglected) administrative and non-professional service personnel who are vital to the delivery of front-line services.

In addition, study of these two arenas is often carried out from distinct disciplinary perspectives that value and emphasise different aspects for analysis. For example, policy studies and political science may be the dominant viewpoints on the policy arena, emphasising the role of interests, ideas and ideology. Practice settings, in contrast, tend more often to be explored by management and organisation studies, or industrial and social psychology, looking at managerial and professional norms, cognitive processes, social identity and the like.

However, despite divergences between these two arenas, there is also a good deal of overlap in their foci of attention, key actors, shaping influences and the nature of their operations. For example, policy makers often become involved in detailed decisions about service delivery design (and are not purely concerned with setting broad directions of travel), and policy itself is made (explicitly and implicitly) at various levels, including in the very act of service delivery – what Lipsky (1979) called 'street-level bureaucracy'. Moreover, professional and managerial norms (articulated through representative bodies and influential individuals) may have a significant influence on policy directions in many service delivery areas, so the travel is not all one way from policy to practice, but may equally well be from practice to policy. In addition, academic explanations of the operation of both domains may usefully draw on many similar concepts and models (such as power relationships, the importance of networks of actors and the influence of institutional rules and norms).

Taken together, then, while the distinction between policy and practice is convenient for our purposes, this should not be over-emphasised: there is no hard boundary where policy stops and practice begins. One way of breaking down this distinction is to recognise that policy itself is composed of a set of practices carried out by different actors who inhabit delineated roles. Another way of breaking down the distinction is to focus on that which might be seen to sit between policy and practice. It is common to contrast evidence use in central government policy making with its individualised use by professionals (for example, doctors and teachers). However, this dual focus on what might be termed 'policy with a capital P' and on individual professional practice tends to underplay the importance of 'meso-level' service delivery organisations (for example, hospitals and schools and social work departments), which both enable and constrain the activities of individual practitioners: it is in these arenas where what might be termed 'small p policy' is formed – policies that reinterpret central diktats and set a context for local work. These local policies, procedures and routines are important because they condition the day-to-day work of *all* front-line staff – professional, semi-professional, administrative and support staff – who directly and indirectly interact with service users. They also influence and constrain the ambitions of 'policy with a capital P'.

Notwithstanding the above critique, this section continues with the convenience of separating out a discussion of evidence in policy making and evidence in practice in the two chapters that follow. These chapters tease out general concerns about how evidence plays out in these two arenas, and thus provide a foundation for considering the particularities of the arrangements in specific fields of application (in Section Two). The two chapters introduce many of the underpinning concepts, models and debates that have shaped our understanding of evidence use in each arena, and they begin to introduce not only the tensions inherent in prevalent ways of thinking about evidence use but also some of the ways in which these tensions may be, if not resolved, then perhaps ameliorated.

In Chapter Two an examination of evidence and policy begins with a debunking of the idea that traditional policy cycles provide useful insights into the relationship. Instead, a more complex picture is drawn of the policy networks and subsystems within which policy makers operate, and the short cuts and heuristics that they use while navigating these. The author concludes that policy-making systems are 'complex, not pathological', and identifies some of the more propitious ways in which those wishing to use evidence as an influencing factor can engage.

Turning to practice, in Chapter Three the authors highlight a number of reasons why 'top-down' evidence-based recommendations often fail to achieve traction at a service delivery level, including the fragility of the pathways from evidence to practice; the burden and complexity of professional practice; and practitioners embracing a professional stance in the face of creeping managerialism. The discussion then hinges around Gibbons et al's (1994) distinction between Mode 1 knowledge production processes (external, usually academic, context-free) and Mode 2 processes (local, co-productive and situated). In exploring the relative merits and dysfunctions of each, the authors conclude there is a need for a judicious mix of both approaches and explore some of the contingencies that support or hinder each.

Despite treating policy and practice separately, a number of themes emerge from each of these chapters with a degree of congruence. First, both accounts draw attention to the limitations of rational-linear models and approaches that emphasise centralised, top-down decision making. Such models and approaches provide neither an adequate description of evidence use nor good prescriptions for how evidence use could be improved. Instead, both accounts draw attention to the need to recognise that policy making and service delivery are shaped by networks of (often many, usually diverse) actors, who are interested (or have a stake) in how that policy or practice is shaped and who will draw on a wide variety of resources – evidence among them – to influence that shaping process.

Second, both chapters highlight the importance of a wide range of types and sources of evidence and other ways of knowing. Moreover, strength of evidence (however that is defined) is rarely the most important factor: the perceived relevance and actual use of evidence is mediated by ideology and values, and rules and norms, as well as power relationships. Ideas, stories and narratives – sometimes built from evidence, but not necessarily so – may have an equally important role.

Despite such caveats, the messages drawn from these chapters are fundamentally optimistic. Evidence can and does inform policy making and service delivery in subtle, sometimes indirect and often 'slow-burning' ways. There is a need therefore to appreciate and understand these subtle processes if we wish to improve the use of evidence. This is likely to involve recognising, encouraging and acting on often temporary but conducive environments – thus shaping and exploiting windows of opportunity for evidence influence.

These opening two chapters provide us with the concepts, tools and terminology to more readily describe and analyse what we see in an evidence-informed world. Collectively they articulate a grounding for those wishing to understand the arenas within which it is hoped evidence will have influence. Such an understanding allows us to see more clearly the generic patterns evident across the specific accounts provided in Section Two (sector-by-sector) and in Section Four (in different geographical jurisdictions).

References

Gibbons, M., Limoges, C., Nowotny, H., Schwartzman, S., Scott, P., and Trow, M. (1994) *The new production of knowledge*, London: Sage.

Lipsky, M. (1979) *Street level bureaucracy*, New York: Russell Sage Foundation.

2

Evidence and policy making

Paul Cairney

Introduction

The relationship between evidence and policy is far from straightforward. Perspectives range from the idealism of 'evidence-driven policy making' (where evidence sets the agenda and drives policy choices) to the pessimism of 'policy-based evidence' (where evidence is sought simply to legitimise pre-set policies). Viewing the evidence and policy relationship from either of these extremes tends to result in disillusionment: either the reality does not live up to the ideal, or evidence is considered as essentially tainted and self-serving. This chapter steers a course between these extremes by drawing on political science and policy studies to provide a more nuanced and pragmatic understanding of the relationship.

It begins with an account of idealised perspectives, and contrasts these with how things play out more typically. Idealised views tend to posit a combination of comprehensive rationality, in which policy makers can process all evidence and make consistent choices, within a policy cycle characterised by a series of well-delineated stages (Box 2.1). Policy scholars usually describe these idealised conditions to show how policy making does not really work. Instead, policy makers more typically face 'bounded rationality', and they respond by using rational and irrational short cuts to process information. They do so in complex policy environments that usually bear little resemblance to any idealised policy cycle.

With these points in mind, the chapter then turns to an overview of policy studies theories and concepts that help to describe and explain the complexity of real-world, policy-related activities (see Box 2.2 for a summary of some key concepts and terms). The argument is that insights from these theories and concepts have the potential to provide helpful guidance on how to understand the policy process and the use of evidence by policy makers.

These insights, and the guidance that flows from them, are then explored and expanded in two case studies: one on tobacco policy and the other on prevention and early-intervention policies. These case examples help to explain and illustrate why evidence alone is never sufficient to win the day: evidence may not even be necessary for major policy change, and it is certainly not sufficient.

Three conditions are identified as enabling evidence to be influential:

1. various actors are able to use evidence to persuade policy makers to pay attention to, and shift their understanding of, policy problems;
2. the policy environment becomes conducive to policy change; and
3. actors exploit these 'windows of opportunity' successfully.

To help produce these conditions, effective actors employ framing and persuasion techniques to generate policy-maker attention to evidence on problems and the effectiveness of solutions. These actors engage for the long term, form coalitions with powerful allies, identify the venues in which key decisions are made and learn the rules in each venue. Such strategies help to create and exploit opportunities for evidence-informed policy change.

Taken together, these insights illuminate the policy-making process and provide guidance for those seeking to promote better use of evidence in politics and policy making. The conclusion considers the implications of these insights, including the need to reflect on how far individuals should be willing to go to maximise the use of research evidence.

Idealised views of policy and evidence use

Comprehensive rationality

Models of rational action help us to understand the difference between idealised notions of policy making and messy, real-world action. In particular, the idea that policy makers and researchers should cooperate to use the best evidence to determine 'what works' in policy is reminiscent of post-war descriptions of synoptic or comprehensive rationality in policy making (Box 2.1). The key difference is that 'evidence-based policy making' is often described as a desirable ideal by researchers, who would like it to replace the more disappointing processes they find when they engage in politics (Cairney and Oliver, 2017). In contrast, in much of the policy studies literature 'comprehensive rationality' is seen more as an ideal-type (in a Weberian

Box 2.1: Key concepts and terms in public policy: rationality and policy cycles

Policy cycle. A model that depicts policy making as a set of clearly defined stages, for example: agenda setting; policy formulation; legitimation; implementation; evaluation; and policy maintenance/succession/termination (Hogwood and Gunn, 1984). The model is best seen as an idealised view, neither a good description nor a reasonable prescription for real-world policy making.

Comprehensive versus bounded rationality. *Comprehensive* rationality is also an idealised view that largely describes an ability to process all information and make consistent policy choices. *Bounded* rationality describes the real-world limits to policy-maker cognition and organisational action (Lindblom, 1959; Simon, 1976).

sense), used to illuminate what does not (indeed, cannot) happen and the practical implications of that impossibility.

The idealised view involves a core and central group of policy makers, directed by elected politicians, identifying the values or the problems they seek to resolve, translating policies into action to maximise benefits to society, aided by neutral organisations gathering all the facts necessary to produce policy solutions. There are inescapable limitations to this scenario because, in general, policy makers are unable to: separate their values from facts in any meaningful way; rank their policy aims in a logical and consistent manner; gather information comprehensively; or process that information effectively (Lindblom, 1959; Simon, 1976). Taken together, such challenges undermine the possibility of delivering on idealised views of policy making.

Instead, Simon (1976, p xxviii) suggests that policy makers deal with their 'bounded rationality' in two main ways: by using rules of thumb to limit their analysis; and by producing good-enough decisions. Further, our modern ability to get closer to the ideal of gathering evidence fully and systematically helps to address only one of the limitations of comprehensive rationality, and even then does not resolve debates on what evidence counts (see Chapter Eleven). The upshot is that policy makers will always need to make value judgements and use cognitive short cuts to understand and use evidence.

While this story of bounded rationality is central to policy studies, hopes for a more comprehensive rationality are still prominent in some discussions of 'evidence-based policy making'. Those discussions are often built on the notions that we can separate subjective policy-maker values from objective scientific facts (Douglas, 2009) and demarcate responsibilities between the elected policy makers identifying problems and analysts solving them (described by Pielke, 2007, and critiqued by Jasanoff, 2008). In practice, however, various actors use values and beliefs to generate research questions, concepts and measures, and they exercise power to set the agenda and secure resources in a mix of science and politics. Furthermore, evidence becomes relevant only when beliefs and values are engaged to make sense of that information in relation to policy problems and solutions. Choice is also necessary, because there is always competition to define important/unimportant problems and to decide the criteria used to determine the high or low effectiveness of solutions (Cairney, 2016, p 16).

In this context, attempts to set a policy agenda by focusing merely on the evidence of 'what works' are often based on misguided expectations (Botterill and Hindmoor, 2012), but may also be seen as pragmatic attempts to generate some academic–practitioner consensus. Yet, a pragmatic understanding of 'what works' relates as much to the *political feasibility* of solutions, based on values and power, as it does to technical feasibility based on research evidence (Kingdon, 1984). A policy has to 'work' for the elected policy makers, measuring success with reference to their future popularity and the ease in which they can generate consensus or deal with opposition when processing policy solutions, as much as the solution's long-term outcomes (McConnell, 2010).

Policy cycles

Hopes for evidence-based policy making are also often rooted in the idea of a policy cycle. Evidence advocates may be drawn to the idea of a linear and orderly policy cycle with discrete stages (summarised in Box 2.1) because it is an appealing model that offers clear guidance on how to engage (Oliver et al, 2014). Indeed, the stages approach began partly as a proposal to make the policy process more scientific, based on systematic policy analysis (Lasswell, 1956). It proposes how policy *should* be made: elected policy makers, aided by expert policy analysts, make and legitimise choices; skilful public servants carry them out; and policy analysts assess the results with the aid of research evidence (Everett, 2003, p 65; Jann and Wegrich, 2007, p 44).

Contemporary policy studies suggest that the policy cycle does not provide a good description of how policy is actually made (John, 2012; Sabatier and Weible, 2014). Policy making is generally not an orderly process with a clearly defined debate on problem definition, a single moment of authoritative choice and a clear chance to use evidence to evaluate policy before deciding whether or not to continue. At best, the cycle exists as a kind of story for policy makers to tell about their work, partly because it is consistent with the idea of elected policy makers being in charge and accountable (Everett, 2003, pp 66–8; Rhodes, 2013, p 486). Yet, some also question the appropriateness of a stages ideal, since it suggests that there should be a core group of policy makers making policy from the top down and obliging others to carry out their aims, which does not leave much room for the diffusion of power in multilevel systems or the use of localism to tailor policy to local needs and desires (Barrett and Fudge, 1981; Hill and Hupe, 2009).

Better explanations of real-world policy making

Modern policy theories provide better accounts of the policy process, but they are often more difficult to apply because they were developed to explain the process without necessarily recommending how to respond to it. Some of the key concepts and terms emerging from this literature are summarised in Box 2.2, and they are discussed in the remainder of this section by focusing on the ways in which policy makers (1) respond to bounded rationality and (2) adapt to their policy-making environment. The insights from these theories are then used to derive some pragmatic implications for those seeking to influence policy making.

Box 2.2: Key concepts and terms in public policy: policy makers and the policy environment

Framing. Policy makers often deal with bounded rationality by focusing on one 'policy image' and ignoring the rest. Problems may be multifaceted, but not all facets receive the same (or indeed any) attention. Policy actors exercise power by 'framing', or using information selectively to encourage one way to describe policy problems and draw attention to one policy image at the expense of others.

Policy environment. A shorthand term to describe the interaction between actors, institutions, networks, ideas, events and socioeconomic conditions. Some describe this policy-making environment as a 'complex system' from which policy outputs and outcomes emerge (Cairney, 2012b; and Box 2.3).

Actors and action. 'Actors' is a general term to describe any individual, organisation or collective group with the ability to act. It includes interest groups, policy makers and policy-making organisations. 'Action' covers the varied behaviours of actors.

Venues, arenas and levels. Venues are the arenas in which authoritative action takes place. Action can occur in many different places, not just central government. 'Levels' of government denote actions in international, supranational, national, regional and local government arenas, with some differences in descriptions (for example, federal, state and local action in the US). Studies also highlight a diffusion of power across venues at the same level (the 'horizontal' diffusion of power).

Networks and subsystems. 'Policy network' describes a relationship between policy makers and influencers (Cairney, 2012a, pp 178–9). Influencers can be interest groups, but the actors most likely to 'lobby' governments are other policy-making organisations (Jordan and Maloney, 2004). There are many ways to describe networks, reflecting academic debates on terminology (for example, some describe open and competitive networks as 'issue networks', and closed and exclusive networks as 'policy communities'). In the US, 'subsystem' describes the venues in which networks develop or where 'advocacy coalitions' compete, and 'policy community' is often used to describe an open network (Kingdon, 1984).

Institutions. These are the rules that actors use within organisations and networks, which have been studied in the literature on 'new institutionalism'. Some approaches describe rules as incentives for individuals, while others describe socialisation and norms. Some rules are formal, written and relatively easy to understand. Others are informal, unwritten, fluid and relatively difficult to understand and transmit (March and Olsen, 2006; Ostrom, 2007). For example, organisations may have standard operating procedures or routines to determine which types and sources of information count (see also Chapters Ten and Eleven).

Ideas. These can describe: (1) the well-established ways of thinking and communicating beliefs and values, described variously as paradigms, core beliefs, monopolies of understanding, world-views, ideologies and hegemons; and (2) the policy solutions proposed by actors (Hall, 1993).

Fast and slow thinking. Popularised by Kahneman (2012), 'fast thinking' refers to thought processes that are largely quick and automatic, often driven by emotions, stereotypes and (implicit or unconscious) heuristics. This is in contrast to 'slow thinking', which is deliberate, methodical, conscious, calculating and effortful. The use of evidence is too often targeted at the latter, to the neglect of the former.

Responding to bounded rationality

Policy theories describe the rational and irrational ways in which policy makers deal with bounded rationality, including their short cuts to identify 'good enough' sources of information, and the ways in which they use their beliefs, emotions, habits and familiarity with issues to identify policy problems and solutions quickly (Cairney and Kwiatkowski, 2017). Direct studies of individual and collective policy-maker psychology are relatively rare, but there is a larger body of policy studies inspired broadly by psychological studies of fast thinking (Box 2.2) and moral reasoning (Haidt, 2001; Kahneman, 2012). These studies prompt us to shift our focus from the supply of evidence to the demand for evidence, and to concentrate less on the use of evidence to reduce scientific uncertainty and more on the relationship between evidence and ambiguity, and the role of evidence in story-telling.

Ambiguity describes the potential for policy makers to understand and frame problems in many different ways, from many perspectives. For example, we can portray fracking (the search for shale oil and gas) as an economic boon, an environmental disaster or primarily a problem of regulation. Bounded rationality often limits policy-maker attention to a small number of key 'images' or understandings of a problem (Baumgartner and Jones, 1993, p 31; Zahariadis, 2007, p 66). Actors exercise power to focus attention on one image at the expense of others, drawing on basic psychological insights to, for example: understand how key actors see the world through the lens of their well-established beliefs or ideology; tailor the ways in which they combine a factual message with an emotional appeal; and/or tell stories with a hero or villain, plot and moral to provide a simple way to understand and seek to solve a complex problem (True et al, 2007, p 161; Weible et al, 2012; McBeth et al, 2014). In this process evidence is rarely conclusive enough to remove uncertainty, so persuasion, argument and narrative (rather than facts and analysis) are the key tools used by policy participants to address ambiguity (Cairney, 2012a, p 234).

Adapting to the policy-making environment

Policy thought and action takes place in complex policy-making environments or systems. In the place of policy cycles, modern policy theories posit a relationship between five main factors that constitute the policy-making environment (John, 2003, p 488; Cairney, 2016, pp 27–30). Each factor helps us to understand the role of actors and the use of evidence:

- **Many actors make and influence choices at many levels of government.** This image contrasts with that of the policy cycle in which an elite group of policy analysts work with a core group of policy makers at the centre. Many actors, including but not restricted to researchers, compete to present evidence and secure a policy-maker audience, and there are many venues or arenas in which authoritative discussions and decisions can take place.
- **A proliferation of institutions (rules and norms) occurs in many policy-making organisations.** These rules can be formal and well understood, or informal and difficult to grasp (Ostrom, 2007). They extend to the rules of evidence gathering, which means that support for particular 'evidence-based' solutions varies markedly, according to which organisation takes the lead and how its key actors understand problems and evidence (see, for example, Chapter Eleven).
- **Policy networks, or the relationships between policy makers and influencers, are pervasive.** They develop in subsystems and contain relatively small groups of specialists. Some networks are close-knit and difficult to access because bureaucracies have operating procedures that favour particular sources of evidence and participants. This can help certain evidence advocates if they are privileged insiders in some venues, but it can also hinder them, as relatively excluded actors, in other venues (Boswell, 2009, p 16).
- **There is a tendency for well-established ideas (the core beliefs of policy makers or the paradigms in which they operate) to dominate discussion** (Hall, 1993). These beliefs influence receptivity to new ideas in the shape of the policy solutions proposed to policy makers (Kingdon, 1984). In these circumstances, new evidence on the effectiveness of a policy solution has to be accompanied by successful persuasion to shift attention to a policy problem and to understand it in a new way.
- **Policy conditions and events can reinforce stability or prompt policy-maker attention to shift.** Social or economic crises or 'focusing events' (Birkland, 1997) can prompt lurches of attention from one issue to another, and evidence can be used to encourage that shift, but this outcome is by no means inevitable. The policy environment, then, is not static but dynamic, and opportunities for change can open up unexpectedly.

In addition, the ways in which evidence is used in policy making are also diverse. For example, evidence may be used for raising problem awareness, to aid problem reframing, and for identifying and ranking possible problem solutions. But evidence – or calls for more evidence – may also be used tactically to delay or deflect unwanted courses of action, and to sow uncertainty about the nature, extent and potential for amelioration of policy issues. Understanding this diversity can help us to see that 'evidence use' can accomplish many different things in these complex policy environments (see also Chapter Twelve).

Implications for pragmatic strategies to increase the influence of evidence

Although the above five elements of policy making, and the key concepts that underpin them, are far from straightforward, it is still possible to derive from them some pragmatic strategies to increase the influence of evidence. These include: being prepared to engage for the long term to develop a multilevel strategy; being in a position to learn how to influence policy by understanding 'where the action is'; identifying which policy makers matter; and understanding the rules of the game in different venues. Although this advice is broad, it is preferable to the alternative of identifying the key stages of policy making and the need to supply evidence to central policy makers.

It is also instructive to reflect on how theorists of complex systems describe policy environments, since they also give would-be influencers insights capable of application (Teisman and Klijn, 2008, p 288; Sanderson, 2009; Cairney, 2012b, p 349; Holmes et al, 2017). Box 2.3 summarises some of these insights and their implications. Many policy studies identify a tendency for policy to 'emerge' from systems, often at a local level, despite attempts by central governments and other actors to control or force certain outcomes. Such emergence makes it difficult to know how, and to whom, to present evidence, let alone to predict the impact of evidence (Cairney, 2016, p 9). In addition, it is clear that evidence advocates need to focus not only on attempts to reduce cognitive load (for example, by producing summary reports), but also on how policy makers use fast thinking to understand problems (see Box 2.2), with the associated need to frame the evidence in relation to that way of thinking (Cairney et al, 2016a).

The conditions under which evidence is influential

When we seek to identify the conditions under which evidence is influential in policy making, we find that evidence alone is almost never a complete game changer. Instead, many studies of policy identify the key explanatory role of ideas over evidence: ideas can change to

---

Box 2.3: Insights from considering policy-making environments as complex systems

Complex systems are characterised by the following.

Interconnectivity. Connections between actors and agencies may be many and varied, and of variable density. This can provide many opportunities to seek dialogue between disparate and perhaps previously unconnected parts of the system.

Self-organising capabilities. The lack of centralised control can allow for local emergence and pockets of opportunity, drawing on local capabilities and bottom-up actions.

Sensitivity to initial conditions. Linked to ideas of 'path dependency', complex systems can be very sensitive to initial starting conditions. Close consideration of these can be helpful in identifying more or less propitious times (and places) for action.

Feedback loops. The density and complexity of feedback loops across the system presents many opportunities for formative learning and adaptive change (for example, 'trial and error' policy making (Cairney, 2012b); prototyping and so on).

Distributed leadership. Weaker control from the centre allows for the emergence of distributed leadership and the potential to create local pockets of change that in turn may generate new knowledge about feasibility, acceptability and so on.

Locally and contextually situated knowledge. Complex systems tend to privilege Mode 2 knowledge production and application over Mode 1 (see extended discussion in Chapter Three).

Sources: Teisman and Klijn, 2008; Sanderson, 2009; Cairney, 2012b; Holmes et al, 2017; Rutter et al, 2017.

---

become relevant to policy agendas (Smith, 2013), or they can be seen to resemble viruses 'which mutate, take on a life of their own, and infect political systems' (Richardson, 2000, p 1019; Cairney, 2012a, p 223). Yet, if we take seriously the virus metaphor, we might assign most explanatory power to the host: the actors more or less receptive to new policy solutions and the political environments more or less conducive to policy change. By this logic, the following three conditions would seem to be necessary for evidence to win through:

1. Actors are able to use evidence to persuade policy makers to pay attention to, and shift their understanding of, policy problems;
2. The policy environment becomes broadly conducive to policy change;
3. Actors exploit high levels of attention to a problem, the availability of a feasible solution and the motive and opportunity of policy makers to adopt such solutions during (often brief) windows of opportunity (Cairney and Yamazaki, 2017, drawing on Kingdon, 1984).

In other words, evidence may be necessary, but it is usually insufficient on its own for major policy change. The role of evidence in these complex processes varies widely, as illustrated by the two policy examples that follow.

Evidence and tobacco policy in the UK

Tobacco policy serves as a model of hope, but also as a cautionary tale for evidence-informed policy change. On the one hand, tobacco policy is often treated as an exemplar case in which evidence has played a key part in policy making. On the other hand, this policy change took decades to achieve, long after evidence of the harmful effects of tobacco first became known.

The UK now has one of the most comprehensive sets of tobacco-control policies in the world. A period of post-war debate and limited policy change, in which the tobacco policy problem and solution were heavily contested, was followed by a generally accepted need for tobacco control, with the agenda shifting to solutions rather than problems. Part of the explanation for this shift is the emergence of the above three conditions necessary for evidence to be influential:

1. **Actors are able to use evidence to persuade policy makers to pay attention to, and shift their understanding of, policy problems.** It took decades to focus attention on the health effects of smoking, to reframe tobacco primarily as a public health epidemic (not an economic good) and to generate support for the most effective evidence-based solutions. Evidence from the 1950s on the health harms of smoking had a proportionate impact from the 1980s onwards, while evidence from the 1980s on passive smoking prompted bans on smoking in public places in the mid-2000s.

2. **The policy environment becomes conducive to policy change.** The new and dominant policy frame helped to give health departments a greater role. These departments fostered policy networks with public health and medical groups and marginalised the tobacco industry. They also emphasised the socioeconomic conditions supportive of tobacco control, including reductions in (a) smoking prevalence, (b) opposition to tobacco control and (c) perceived economic benefits of tobacco.

3. **Actors exploit opportunities successfully.** A supportive policy frame and policy environment maximised the chances of policy makers paying attention to this issue and provided the motive and opportunity for policy makers to select relatively restrictive policy instruments. However, the selection of policy instruments such as smoking bans was not inevitable, and occurred only when policy makers were willing and able to produce comprehensive legislation without fearing a public backlash (Cairney and Yamazaki, 2017).

So, evidence can be a helpful precursor and catalyst for major policy change, but key actors do not simply respond to new evidence: they use it as a resource to further their aims, to frame policy problems in ways that will generate policy-maker attention. It is also used to underpin technically and politically feasible solutions that policy makers will have the motive and opportunity to select. This remains true even when the evidence seems unequivocal to many people and the policy environment is relatively conducive to policy change.

Evidence and early-intervention policies in the UK

A second example is instructive as to why policy agendas sometimes do not progress even under seemingly propitious circumstances. Early intervention and preventative spending are terms used by many governments to describe an aim to address policy problems by intervening as early as possible in people's lives. The general argument is that too much government spending is devoted to services to address severe social problems at a late stage – including crime and antisocial behaviour, ill health and unhealthy behaviour, low educational attainment and unemployment. Instead, it is argued, these problems should be tackled sooner, pre-emptively, before they become severe and relatively expensive (Cairney et al, 2016b; and see Chapter Fourteen for a discussion of 'social investment' initiatives in New Zealand).

At an abstract level, prevention can generate consensus between the political left, seeking to reduce poverty and inequality, and the political right, seeking to reduce economic inactivity and the costs of public services (Billis, 1981, p 367). However, this apparent consensus has proved difficult to maintain when people make sense of prevention in different ways (Freeman, 1999) and emphasise different types of early intervention (Gough, 2013, p 3). For example, we can think of:

- **primary prevention** – to stop problems occurring by investing early and/or modifying the social or physical environment: a focus on the whole population;
- **secondary prevention** – to identify problems at an early stage, to minimise harm: that is, identify and focus on at-risk groups;
- **tertiary prevention** – to stop extant problems getting worse: hence, identify and focus only on affected groups.

For these reasons, a focus on prevention and early-intervention policy is useful in illustrating why policy agendas do not progress even when governments make a strong and highly visible commitment to policy change and there is much potentially relevant evidence. Part of the explanation for this lack of progress is that prevention and early-intervention policy does not support the emergence of the three conditions necessary for evidence to be influential (see previous), particularly when policy makers are seeking to make the shift from a general acceptance of the importance of prevention to implementing specific policy solutions (Cairney et al, 2016b). Three direct observations can be made:

1. **Prevention is a highly ambiguous term and actors have made sense of it in many different ways.** There has been no equivalent to the major shift in problem definition found in the tobacco-policy case study. There has also been little agreement on how to determine the most effective or cost-effective solutions.
2. **A supportive policy environment is far harder to identify or generate.** Prevention policy cuts across many policy-making venues at many levels of government, with little evidence of ownership by key actors. Consequently, there are many overlapping rules on how and from whom to seek evidence. Networks are diffuse and hard to manage. There is no dominant way of thinking about this across government. There are many socioeconomic indicators of policy problems, but there is little agreement on how to measure them or which measures to privilege (particularly when predicting future outcomes of prevention).

3. **There was perhaps a 'window of opportunity' for prevention policy, but the response of vague solutions to ambiguous problems provides a limited sense of direction.** Political enthusiasm for prevention/early-intervention policy (particularly in the late 1990s and early 2000s) provided opportunities for change, but the factors highlighted in (1) and (2) rather thwarted efforts to take advantage of this.

The absence of strong backing for an unequivocal way of thinking about prevention leaves policy change vulnerable to successful opposition, especially in areas where early intervention has major implications for resource redistribution (such as taking from existing services to invest in early-years policies) and personal freedom (encouraging or obliging behavioural change). The vagueness and long-term nature of preventive policy makes it uncompetitive with, and often undermined by, more specific short-term aims with a measurable pay-off, and it is too easy to reframe existing policy as preventative if the definition of prevention remains broad, fluid and ambiguous.

In such circumstances, various actors have proposed and used evidence in many different ways. In some instances, the use of evidence relates more to the dynamics of political systems than the type or quality of the evidence. For example, in the families policies of the UK government, evidence has been invoked in several ways in relation to prevention (Cairney, 2018):

- **Cynically, to define a problem and declare policy success.** The UK government used highly problematic proxies of risk to identify a large number of 'troubled families', and used self-evaluation of its solution to declare almost complete success (Levitas, 2012; Hayden and Jenkins, 2014; Crossley, 2015).
- **Dramatically, to bolster a policy agenda.** UK government reviews used images of the brains of 'normal' and 'extremely neglected' three-year-old children to support a 'now or never' story of early intervention before a child reaches three years old (Allen, 2011, p 1; Munro, 2011, pp 69–70). The images provided shock value without being backed by good-quality neuroscientific evidence (Wastell and White, 2012).
- **Optimistically, to base policy expansion on limited supportive evidence.** The UK government rolled out a model for family intervention projects from 2006, built on independent evaluations (using surveys and interviews with service users and practitioners, and case reports) that presented only very cautiously

optimistic accounts of prior pilot projects (Parr, 2009, p 1257; Nixon et al, 2010, p 306).

The willingness, then, of policy makers to (optimistically) support interventions based only on suggestive evidence of effect often depends on their ability to use this and other (sometimes highly problematic) forms of evidence somewhat cynically or dramatically (as in the first two categories above). This may reflect a need to provide short-term political cover through such usages in pursuit of longer-term aims.

In conclusion: making the most of evidence in policy

In political science and policy studies, phrases such as 'evidence-based' or even 'evidence-informed' policy making and 'what works' are often analysed as political slogans rather than as good descriptions of the policy process and the role of evidence in it. Consequently, many debates about what should count as good evidence, and how we should measure the effectiveness of policy solutions, can seem less relevant than studies of how policy makers actually use evidence. The latter shifts the focus away from normative discussions on how evidence should be used, and towards more pragmatic discussions of how to respond to policy making in the real world.

This chapter has discussed some of the insights from policy studies, which suggest that those interested in using evidence to influence policy making need to identify and adapt to both rational and irrational thought when thinking about how to engage in complex policy environments. This involves understanding the conditions under which evidence becomes influential and then fostering a policy environment that is conducive to evidence-informed policy change. Success tends to involve making persuasive cases to help prompt increasing levels of attention to one way of understanding a policy problem, and then exploiting windows of opportunity to prompt action that is in line with this way of framing the problem and how it might be addressed. This making of persuasive cases necessarily involves a sophisticated understanding of: policy networks and communities; the complex (formal and informal) rules under which these operate; and the many venues and levels where such interactions occur.

However, in making persuasive cases, there is also a need to reflect on how far it is appropriate to go in seeking to ensure that evidence informs policy. Policy studies tell us how the world works and how we could respond effectively, but not how to combine our aims, values and ethics when choosing to act. Crucially, there are many principles of good policy making that do not conceive of policy as being evidence-driven, referring instead to: the value of pragmatism and consensus building; combining research advice with public values; improving policy delivery by generating ownership of policy among key stakeholders; and sharing responsibility with elected local policy makers (Cairney, 2016, pp 127–9). So, it is important for all evidence advocates to consider how far they are (or should be) willing to go to promote the use of research evidence in policy making when there are so many other ways to justify action in political systems. Further, when promoting evidence, evidence advocates need to identify the blurry line between positive persuasion and manipulation. For example, if policy makers and the public are emotional decision makers, should evidence advocates seek to influence policy thinking by using simple stories with heroes and villains, and clear (but simplistic) moral messages? Current guidance on using evidence to influence policy making rarely addresses such questions, but it is clear that evidence advocates need more than the evidence on 'what works' to help them to engage appropriately in policy making and politics.

Finally, it is tempting to bemoan the lack of strong 'evidence-based' policy making (where it is clear that evidence has had a determining influence on policy making), but the message of this chapter is that a nuanced understanding of politics and the policy-making process helps us to appreciate the subtle ways in which evidence can and does influence policy making over time. Policy makers deal with bounded rationality, not total irrationality. Policy-making systems are complex, not pathological. There are opportunities for evidence-informed policy, and many people are ready and waiting to work collaboratively to exploit these. Therefore, a positive response is for researchers and other evidence advocates to draw on modern policy-process theories and concepts to help them to engage effectively within this process. Evidence matters, but has influence only when backed by effective policy action.

References

Allen, G. (2011) *Early intervention: smart investment, massive savings*, London: HMSO, https://www.gov.uk/government/uploads/system/uploads/attachment_data/file/61012/earlyintervention-smartinvestment.pdf.

Barrett, S. and Fudge, C. (eds) (1981) *Policy and action*, London: Methuen.

Baumgartner, F. and Jones, B. (1993) *Agendas and instability in American politics*, 1st edn, Chicago, IL: Chicago University Press.

Billis, D. (1981) 'At risk of prevention', *Journal of Social Policy*, 10 (3), pp 367–79.

Birkland, T. (1997) *After disaster: agenda setting, public policy and focusing events*, Washington, DC: Georgetown University Press.

Boswell, C. (2009) *The political uses of expert knowledge*, Cambridge: Cambridge University Press.

Botterill, L. and Hindmoor, A. (2012) 'Turtles all the way down: bounded rationality in an evidence-based age', *Policy Studies*, 33 (5), pp 367–79.

Cairney, P. (2012a) *Understanding public policy*, Basingstoke: Palgrave.

Cairney, P. (2012b) 'Complexity theory in political science and public policy', *Political Studies Review*, 10 (3), pp 346–58.

Cairney, P. (2016) *The politics of evidence based policy making*, London: Palgrave Springer.

Cairney, P. (2018) 'The UK government's imaginative use of evidence to make policy', *British Politics*, early view doi: 10.1057/s41293-017-0068-2.

Cairney, P., Oliver, K. and Wellstead, A. (2016a) 'To bridge the divide between evidence and policy: reduce ambiguity as much as uncertainty', *Public Administration Review*, 76 (3), pp 399–402.

Cairney, P., Russell, S. and St Denny, E. (2016b) 'The "Scottish approach" to policy and policy making', *Policy and Politics*, 44 (3), pp 333–50.

Crossley, S. (2015) *The troubled families programme*, London: Centre for Crime and Justice Studies, https://www.crimeandjustice.org.uk/sites/crimeandjustice.org.uk/files/The%20Troubled%20Families%20Programme,%20Nov%202015.pdf.

Douglas, H. (2009) *Science, policy, and the value-free ideal*, Pittsburgh, PA: University of Pittsburgh Press.

Everett, S. (2003) 'The policy cycle: democratic process or rational paradigm revisited?', *Australian Journal of Public Administration*, 62 (2), pp 65–70.

Freeman, R. (1999) 'Recursive politics: Prevention, modernity and social systems', *Children and Society*, 13 (4), pp 232–41.

Gough, I. (2013) *Understanding prevention policy: a theoretical approach*, London: New Economics Foundation, http://eprints.lse.ac.uk/47951/1/Understanding%20prevention%20policy%20(lsero).pdf.

Haidt, J. (2001) 'The emotional dog and its rational tail', *Psychological Review*, 108, (4), pp 814–34.

Hall, P. (1993) 'Policy paradigms, social learning, and the state: the case of economic policy making in Britain', *Comparative Politics*, 25 (2), pp 275–96.

Hayden, C. and Jenkins, C. (2014) 'Troubled Families' Programme in England: "wicked problems" and policy-based evidence', *Policy Studies*, 35 (6), pp 631–49.

Hill, M. and Hupe, P. (2009) *Implementing public policy*, 2nd edn, London: Sage.

Hogwood, B. and Gunn, L. (1984) *Policy analysis for the real world*, Oxford: Oxford University Press.

Holmes, B.J., Best, A., Davies, H.T.O., Hunter, D., Kelly, M.P., Marshall, M. and Rycroft-Malone, J. (2017) 'Mobilising knowledge in complex health systems: a call to action', *Evidence & Policy*, 13 (3), pp 539–60.

Jann, W. and Wegrich, K. (2007) 'Theories of the policy cycle', in F. Fischer, G. Miller and M. Sidney (eds), *Handbook of public policy analysis*, London: CRC Press.

Jasanoff, S. (2008) 'Speaking honestly to power', *American Scientist*, 6 (3), pp 240.

John, P. (2003) 'Is there life after policy streams, advocacy coalitions, and punctuations: using evolutionary theory to explain policy change?', *The Policy Studies Journal*, 31 (4), pp 481–98.

John, P. (2012) *Analysing public policy*, 2nd edn, London: Routledge.

Jordan, G. and Maloney, W. (2004) 'Defining interests: disambiguation and the need for new distinctions?', *British Journal of Politics and International Relations*, 6 (2), pp 195–212.

Kahneman, D. (2012) *Thinking fast and slow*, London: Penguin.

Kingdon, J. (1984) *Agendas, alternatives and public policies*, 1st edn, New York: Harper Collins.

Lasswell, H. (1956) *The decision process: seven categories of functional analysis*, College Park, MD: University of Maryland Press.

Levitas, R. (2012) 'There may be trouble ahead: what we know about those 120,000 "troubled" families', *Poverty and Social Exclusion*, Policy Response Series 3, http://www.poverty.ac.uk/system/files/WP%20Policy%20Response%20No.3-%20%20'Trouble'%20ahead%20(Levitas%20Final%2021April2012).pdf.

Lindblom, C. (1959) 'The science of muddling through', *Public Administration Review*, 19 (7), pp 9–88.

McBeth, M., Jones, M. and Shanahan, E. (2014) 'The narrative policy framework', in Sabatier, P. and Weible, C. (eds), *Theories of the policy process*, 3rd edn, Chicago, IL: Westview Press.

McConnell, A. (2010) *Understanding policy success: rethinking public policy*, Basingstoke: Palgrave Macmillan.

March, J. and Olsen, J. (2006) 'Elaborating the "new institutionalism"', in R. Rhodes, S. Binder. B. Rockman (eds), *The Oxford handbook of political institutions*, Oxford: Oxford University Press.

Munro, E. (2011) *The Munro Review of child protection final report*, London: Department for Education.

Nixon, J., Pawson, H. and Sosenko, F. (2010) 'Rolling out anti-social behaviour families projects in England and Scotland', *Social Policy and Administration*, 44 (3), pp 305–25.

Oliver, K., Lorenc, T. and Innvær, S. (2014) 'New directions in evidence-based policy research', *Health Research Policy and Systems*, 12, 34, http://www.biomedcentral.com/content/pdf/1478-4505-12-34.pdf.

Ostrom, E. (2007) 'Institutional rational choice', in P. Sabatier (ed), *Theories of the policy process*, 2nd edn, Cambridge, MA: Westview Press.

Parr, S. (2009) 'Family intervention projects', *British Journal of Social Work*, 39 (7), pp 1256–73.

Pielke Jr, R. (2007) *The honest broker: making sense of science in policy and politics*, Cambridge: Cambridge University Press.

Rhodes, R. (2013) 'Political anthropology and civil service reform: prospects and limits', *Policy & Politics*, 41 (4), pp 481–96.

Richardson, J.J. (2000) 'Government, interest groups and policy change', *Political Studies*, 48, pp 1006–25.

Rutter, H., Savona, N., Glonti, K., Bibby, J., Cummins, S., Finegood, D.T. and White, M. (2017) 'The need for a complex systems model of evidence for public health', *Lancet*, 390 (10112), pp 2602–4.

Sabatier, P. and Weible, C. (eds) (2014) *Theories of the policy process*, 3rd edn, Chicago, IL: Westview Press.

Sanderson, I. (2009) 'Intelligent policy making for a complex world: pragmatism, evidence and learning', *Political Studies*, 57, pp 699–719.

Simon, H. (1976) *Administrative behavior*, 3rd edn, London: Macmillan.

Smith, K. (2013) *Beyond evidence based policy in public health: the interplay of ideas*, Basingstoke: Palgrave Macmillan.

Teisman, G. and Klijn, E. (2008) 'Complexity theory and public management', *Public Management Review*, 10 (3), pp 287–97.

True, J.L., Jones, B.D. and Baumgartner, F.R. (2007) 'Punctuated equilibrium theory', in P. Sabatier (ed), *Theories of the policy process*, 2nd edn, Cambridge, MA: Westview Press.

Wastell, D. and White, S. (2012) 'Blinded by neuroscience', *Families, Relationships and Societies*, 1 (3), pp 397–415.

Weible, C., Heikkila, T., deLeon, P. and Sabatier, P. (2012) 'Understanding and influencing the policy process', *Policy Sciences*, 45 (1), pp 1–21.

Zahariadis, N. (2007) 'The multiple streams framework', in P. Sabatier (ed), *Theories of the policy process*, Cambridge, MA: Westview.

3

Evidence and service delivery

Graham P. Martin and Oli Williams

Introduction

The opening two decades of the 21st century can arguably be characterised as a period of continued technocratic consensus about the need for a better articulation between evidence and public services, alongside rising contestation about how that relationship should be realised. This has been accompanied by an increase in the range of data that are amenable to analysis, synthesis and use (see Chapter Ten) and a broadening of notions of evidence that are seen as legitimate (see Chapter Eleven). At the same time, however, there has been some disillusionment − itself informed by a growing body of knowledge − about the feasibility of a straightforward path from evidence generation, through policy formation (the challenges of which are articulated in Chapter Two) and into implementation in service delivery (the focus of this chapter).

We explore these developments with a particular emphasis on evidence-informed service delivery. First, we describe traditional 'top-down' approaches to the dissemination and implementation of evidence. Despite rhetoric to the contrary, these approaches remain important in many public services, backed by sometimes rigid and powerful regimes of audit, inspection and rating. However, their limitations are increasingly acknowledged, and the second section outlines critiques of such approaches and describes 'bottom-up' alternatives that rely on more localised evidence generation and utilisation, often with a view to incorporating wider forms of knowledge. In the third and fourth sections we consider approaches to the sharing of knowledge and evidence within and across public service organisations, and the challenges in so doing, and then highlight a number of cross-cutting challenges to the use of evidence in service delivery. In the final section we consider the future relationship between evidence and public service practice, especially in what some suggest is a world where expertise and evidence are becoming devalued currencies (see also Chapters One and Eighteen).

By way of introducing the first two of these sections, we note that a distinction is sometimes made between two 'modes' of knowledge production (Gibbons et al, 1994). The first of these (denoted Mode 1), emphasises traditional, sequential approaches to research and its implementation, whereby research and practice are seen as separate endeavours and the task of implementation is the effective transfer of knowledge from one sphere to the other. The second, receiving greater attention over recent decades (and denoted Mode 2), posits that there are no hard boundaries between the production and utilisation of knowledge, and suggests that innovation is the product of close, continued interaction among practitioners and researchers. This binary distinction is of course a simplification that masks a variety of intermediate points (for example, Weingart, 1997), but it is nonetheless a useful heuristic for understanding the predominant approaches to evidence use in public services, and their associated advantages and disadvantages. The thinking behind it shapes our discussion in the following two sections.

Research *into* practice: top-down evidence implementation

Mode 1 knowledge production, in which research is the stuff of dedicated experts in universities and other evidence-generating organisations, tends to be associated with a linear and often 'top-down', didactic approach to knowledge translation, whereby evidence is gathered and synthesised by some central authority (for example, a government agency) and then turned into recommendations (or mandates) for practice, which those delivering services (individual practitioners or public service organisations) are expected to assimilate and account for in their day-to-day work. The advantages of such top-down approaches to the incorporation of evidence into organisational and professional practice are fairly clear: in principle, they should secure rapid and equal uptake of high-grade, carefully appraised evidence across a sector, ensuring uniformity of practice and speedy introduction of evidence-based innovations.

A good deal of the evidence that public service professionals and service delivery organisations contend with can broadly be placed into this category. In the UK, an early innovation of the Blair government from 1997 onwards was the creation of 'institutes of excellence' at arm's length from government, charged with bringing together the best evidence. The most notable of these are in healthcare (the National Institute for Health and Care Excellence – NICE) and social care (the Social Care Institute of Excellence – SCIE). Indeed, formal guidelines produced by NICE in relation to treatments and some aspects of service organisation are binding on healthcare organisations, supported by a range of mechanisms for checking and enforcing compliance (Abraham, 2009). Further discussion of these and similar institutions takes place in many later chapters.

In other fields of public service delivery such institutes have been slower to emerge – perhaps reflecting the qualitatively different nature of their evidence bases (and the rather more context-specific, contingent nature of evidence about, say, social housing design, as compared to drug effectiveness). However, this does not mean that these fields are not subject to similarly directive approaches to the implementation of research evidence. The field of education, for example, has seen a range of government prescriptions in relation to both curricular content and pedagogic technique both in the US (see Chapter Seventeen) and in the UK (see Chapter Seven), based in varying degrees on research – albeit often contested and inconclusive evidence. Despite the absence of an independent body for appraising the evidence base and formulating recommendations, the expectations on service delivery organisations and staff are frequently highly prescriptive. For an example of this, on the use of synthetic phonics to teach literacy, see Box 3.1.

The case of synthetic phonics throws into sharp relief the potential dark side of top-down approaches to integrating evidence into the practice of public service organisations and professionals. Even discounting the contested nature of the evidence base, it is clear that an approach to implementation based on strict mandates, with punishments for those falling short, risks resulting in a rather mechanistic, unreflective approach to evidence adoption that leaves no space for adaptation: an approach that can even undermine professional responsibility for judiciously integrating evidence into practice. As Ellis and Moss (2014, p 252) put it, such an approach is 'destructive of forms of professionalism that accept responsibility for reflecting on and adjusting professional practice in the light of research evidence and practitioner experience'.

There is thus a risk that top-down approaches might give rise to 'implementing a set of treatment principles rather than an on-going quest to be evidence-based practitioners', as Nutley and Davies (2000, p 109) argue in relation to the probation service. Similar concerns have been expressed in other fields, from minimum sentencing guidelines in criminal justice (Fitz-Gibbon, 2016) to implementation of NICE

Box 3.1: Top-down policy making and contested evidence bases

Early-years literacy education in the UK has been an area of sustained policy-maker interest, and the setting for a contested relationship between research, policy and practice. Ellis and Moss (2014) recount how a very narrow approach to teaching young children to read – synthetic phonics – made its way from a series of experimental studies in one Scottish region into national government policy and teaching practice. Although the quality of the evidence and its relevance to teaching practice was hotly contested, in 2012 the government made synthetic phonics the mandatory approach to literacy education for all state primary schools. This mandate was backed by incentives for uptake and penalties for non-compliance: teacher training courses were required to teach the government-mandated approach alone; school inspections focused exactingly on how synthetic phonics was taught; only CPD courses that toed the mandated line were eligible for accreditation. Yet Ellis and Moss (2014) note that the evidence base for synthetic phonics comes primarily from (basic) psychology research, not from (applied) educational research; evidence in real-world classrooms suggested a more mixed picture in terms of the effectiveness of synthetic phonics, and a need for judgement and flexibility on the part of teachers in catering for children of all abilities.

guidelines in healthcare (Harrison and McDonald, 2003): whether the evidence base itself is seen as solid or shaky, top-down implementation is often characterised as a crude approach that has multiple unintended and negative consequences.

Critiques of the top-down approach to evidence implementation reflect wider concerns about regimes of performance management imposed on public service organisations by governments, and about the rule-following and compliant behaviours that such regimes incentivise. The approach risks encouraging instrumental game playing to hit narrow targets while neglecting policy makers' broader intentions (Bevan and Hood, 2006; and for an example, see Toffolutti et al, 2017 and Box 3.2).

In the UK, increasing public concern about the unintended consequences of government-by-target has led to an apparent softening of the regime, with (compulsory) targets in some fields replaced by (advisory) 'standards', accompanied by a reassertion of the values of professionalism over managerialism (Martin et al, 2015). However, the extent to which this shift has resulted in any greater discretion at

Box 3.2: Instrumental game playing in service delivery

The narrow interpretations of policy targets that can result in public services 'hitting the target but missing the point' are not limited to professional activity. Indeed, outsourced services that are governed by tight contractual specifications can be especially prone to this kind of behaviour. Toffolutti et al (2017) demonstrate how hospitals in the UK that outsource cleaning services are susceptible to 'gaming' the system of targets and performance monitoring in public services in relation to infection control and cleanliness. Staff awareness of imminent inspections led to significantly higher levels of cleanliness around the time of inspection periods, as compared to the months that preceded and followed.

the coalface of service delivery is debatable, not least because of the continued regime of audit and inspection that applies in many fields and the increasingly overt ways in which the outcomes of such inspections are used to manage performance and encourage public scrutiny.

Bodies such as the Care Quality Commission (CQC, in health and social care) and the Office for Standards in Education (Ofsted, in education and children's services) incorporate compliance with (policy-mandated) evidence into their inspections. Their findings are used to rate public service organisations on scales ranging from 'inadequate' to 'outstanding' and are deployed in comparison websites and league tables oriented towards 'consumers', not just internal stakeholders: parents, patients and others (notwithstanding the very limited evidence that citizens actually wish to take up the mantle of consumers in a public service market place – Clarke et al, 2007).

Mechanisms such as professional revalidation and performance-related pay similarly incentivise individual practitioners to follow (certain specific, centrally mandated forms of) evidence. This kind of scrutiny, with an explicit focus on the performance management of organisations and professionals, can have a chilling effect on locally led innovation and on any deviation from formally approved evidence bases (Currie and Lockett, 2007).

To this extent, the top-down approach to incorporating evidence into organisational and professional work might be expected to achieve 'evidence-based practice' of a rather particular kind: a stifled, obedient compliance with officially mandated evidence, at the cost of using alternative sources of evidence more creatively (such as practitioner knowledge, or professional experience and intuition – see Box 3.1).

Yet there is another, quite different reason for doubting the efficacy of top-down approaches to implementing evidence: whatever their ambitions, central government approaches to direction and surveillance of professional practice can never achieve full coverage; in between inspections and appraisals, there will always be gaps where deviation from policy prescriptions can flourish (see also Box 3.2).

There are several reasons why day-to-day professional practice might deviate from policy-prescribed 'evidence-based' recommendations. One is the simple, long-documented overwhelming burden of professional practice and the mismatch between demand and available resources, which necessitates 'street-level' decisions about which rules to apply in which circumstances (Lipsky, 1980). A second is the enduring application of the professional ethic in spite of the pressures of managerialism and inspection: a refusal to follow guidelines and an insistence on the importance of professional judgement or client-centred practice (Martin et al, 2015). A third, though, is the fragility of the pathway by which policy prescriptions are expected to transfer into practice, and the ease with which core messages about evidence can be lost in translation or ignored, especially in relation to more complex programmes and politically divisive issues (Pressman and Wildavsky, 1974).

A telling example of this third limitation is the policy response to global and national evidence on the social determinants of health (Commission on Social Determinants of Health, 2008; Marmot Review, 2010). While a strong evidence base links so-called lifestyle choices (for example, physical activity, diet, tobacco consumption) to biomedical measures of good health, there is also a clear inverse social gradient in compliance with health-promoting behavioural interventions: those further down the socioeconomic scale are less likely to adhere to the norms of a 'healthy lifestyle'. Moreover, there has been a tendency for policy to 'start off recognising the need for action on upstream social determinants of health inequalities only to drift downstream to focus largely on individual lifestyle factors' (Popay et al, 2010, p 148). Therefore, this 'lifestyle drift' in local public health practice may achieve the opposite of what is intended by policy, exacerbating health inequalities, as compared to a focus on the upstream 'causes of the causes' of ill health and related inequalities (Marmot Review, 2010).

This phenomenon of lifestyle drift illustrates how the top-down model for evidence implementation can be vulnerable to conceptual slippage at the local level. For example, research with local council staff in Australia found that, despite relatively high levels of agreement on ideas about the social determinants of health, the majority of participants identified simple lifestyle choices as having the greatest effect on health – rather than 'upstream' intervention in relation to socio-structural determinants (Lawless et al, 2017). Research in the UK has shown that local decision makers are restricted by established systems and structures, particularly pressure to deliver outcomes and demonstrate value for money in a short-termist culture that can neglect the longer-term efforts needed to address health inequalities (Blackman et al, 2012). This incongruence can ultimately lead to ineffective local action, with interventions that can even run counter to stated policy intentions. For example, lifestyle interventions are liable to reproduce the 'inequality paradox', whereby interventions exacerbate rather than reduce health inequalities, further disadvantaging target groups (Williams, 2017). Such unintended consequences illuminate the limits of the top-down model for translating evidence into local action, while simultaneously identifying good reasons for challenging the status quo through alternative approaches.

Research *in* practice: bottom-up evidence generation and use

Perhaps unsurprisingly, given the increasingly acknowledged limitations of top-down approaches to realising evidence-based practice, there has been a growing focus in research and practice communities on the potential of locally driven evidence generation (sometimes called Mode 2). Arguably *more* surprising – given its global reach and positivist science underpinnings – is that much of this work is to be found in healthcare. In part, the rise of this movement in healthcare might be understood as a reaction to the more mechanistic aspects of the predominant approaches to 'implementing evidence' that have arisen worldwide following the birth of the evidence-based medicine movement in the 1980s and 1990s – approaches that have been promoted through both government sanction and the intervention of private insurance companies (see Chapter Four). As we have seen, top-down approaches to securing compliance with evidence bases are often seen as bureaucratic, overly financially driven and sometimes incompatible with patient- or client-centred care.

The rise of localised approaches to evidence generation (and use) can also be seen as a response to a growing awareness of the often slow and patchy impact of new evidence on practice, and of the paucity of evidence-based models for achieving implementation. This is exemplified by the development of new subfields of academic activity under the rubric of 'improvement science'. These developments might best be characterised as an effort to find locally sensitive approaches to implementing established evidence bases by learning about the strengths and weaknesses of current practice and innovating in response to this – rejecting both indiscriminate professional autonomy and inappropriate managerial imposition.

A range of 'quality management' and 'quality improvement' methodologies has been advocated for this 'organisational learning' form of evidence generation and use, largely deriving from approaches developed in the manufacturing industry over many years. Most prominent in healthcare is the 'Model for Improvement' promulgated by the US Institute for Healthcare Improvement, which comprises small cycles of change that involve gathering information about current practice, implementing changes to address shortfalls, analysing data to understand impact and then adjusting or building on the changes made as appropriate (see, for example, Institute for Healthcare Improvement, 2003). The approaches used to make sense of the data produced in the course of these 'plan-do-study-act' (PDSA) cycles derive ultimately from the ideas of early US industrial engineers such as Walter Shewhart and W. Edwards Deming (Nicolay et al, 2011).

Other approaches adopted from various parts of the manufacturing sector, such as Lean (originally developed by the car manufacturer Toyota) and Six Sigma (whose origins can be traced to the electronics company Motorola), similarly advocate: data collection; critical self-examination around the strengths and weaknesses of current practice; intervention to improve effectiveness, efficiency or reliability; and on-going monitoring of data to inform continued improvement. Quality-management techniques have also been applied in areas of public service such as local government (McNary, 2008) and social services (Neubeck et al, 2014), although to a less pervasive extent than in healthcare, perhaps because of critical differences in professional culture, the structure of work activities and the availability of data (Neubeck et al, 2014).

However, the evidence base for the effectiveness of these approaches is itself contested (Powell et al, 2009). For example, the PDSA approach to structured experimentation for organisational learning and improvement is easily violated in environments characterised by production pressures, and by hierarchical power relationships that inhibit its ethos of empowerment (Reed and Card, 2016). Similarly, studies of Lean in practice suggest that it may act to reinforce top-down preoccupations and improvement priorities rather than genuinely involving front-line practitioners in generating data, creating evidence for improvement and putting it into practice (Waring and Bishop, 2010).

More broadly, a growing body of literature has begun to question the appropriateness of adopting techniques from *manufacturing* industry in public services – particularly when the private sector *service* industry has its own menu of approaches to generating and acting on evidence for improvement (Osborne, 2010). A particularly important implication of such analyses is that, unlike the manufacture of electronics components or car parts, the output of a service (whether the provision of catering or the curation of a museum or the education of a child) is produced, to greater or lesser extent, by the professional and the 'client' *working together*: that is, it has the potential to be co-produced. This reframing has important consequences for both how to maximise the quality of public services and how to produce the evidence that might inform such improvement. In particular, it implies that the evidence to be used in informing service improvement should derive from a wider range of sources, most notably directly from those who use and deliver services (Batalden et al, 2016).

In some fields, the rhetorical shift towards acknowledging the importance of sources of evidence and ways of knowing that were previously silenced by dominant actors has been quite profound. In sustainability work and in international development, for example (see Chapters Eight and Nine), a growing critique has emerged of approaches to intervention that uncritically apply evidence bases developed largely in economically developed countries, side-lining locally produced knowledge. Such approaches are increasingly seen as questionable on grounds of ethics and efficacy, giving rise to a call for development partnerships that incorporate both scientific-professional and traditional-local evidence bases into their activity (Pigg, 2001).

In public service organisations, approaches such as 'experience-based co-design' provide a framework for gathering and acting upon evidence from a variety of sources in a collaborative, participatory manner so that front-line staff and service users are 'actively contributing to the design' of services (Donetto et al, 2015, p 234). However, these approaches too can be inhibited by the asymmetric relationships that characterise public services, not just between senior and junior staff, but perhaps more importantly between staff and service users, with staff struggling 'to move between their familiar "expert" and "decision-maker" role and that of partner and colleague required by co-design work' (Donetto et al, 2015, p 239).

Besides such innovations in generating and utilising data from novel sources, recent developments in information technology (IT) have sparked interest in the potential for harvesting and deploying large sets of routinely collected data to provide insight into performance and resources for improvement. 'Big data' offers the enticing prospect of 'near real-time' evidence generation and responsive service delivery (explored further in Chapter Ten), while open data sources have the potential to democratise access to evidence, unlocking the control of evidence-informed improvement to anyone with the requisite time, inclination and IT skills: front-line staff, citizens and entrepreneurial consultants, to name just some (Clarke and Margetts, 2014).

Real-world examples of such activity are so far scarce; again, healthcare has been a relative trailblazer, particularly in the US, where sophisticated information-management systems required for billing also provide a resource for monitoring activity, benchmarking among similar organisations and targeting improvements. The healthcare experience also points towards the potential dangers inherent in the bottom–up use of such data to inform organisational learning and improvement: data collected for professionally led improvement can readily be appropriated for more managerialist purposes, such as comparisons of performance and associated sanctions (Hersh et al, 2013). Enabling locally led efforts at compiling and harnessing evidence, then, may require its 'insulation' from external influences that can undermine such efforts.

In sum, the potential to open up notions of evidence to a wider diversity of voices, methods and sources, and the scope to better integrate knowledge production with knowledge application and use, offer an exciting counterbalance to more traditional knowledge-transfer approaches (discussed further in Chapters Ten to Twelve). This has in turn led to more innovative thinking about the challenges of knowledge sharing, within and between service delivery organisations.

Sharing knowledge within and between service organisations

A long-standing concern within private and public sector bodies alike has been how best to ensure that the 'asset' of knowledge is appropriately shared within an organisation. It is one thing to invest in the generation of evidence, but how best to ensure that it is exploited towards organisational advantage? This question has been a key preoccupation in the management studies literature since the 1990s, with the development of the 'knowledge-based view of the firm', which holds that the possession of knowledge, the ability to create new knowledge and (crucially) the ability to apply it are central to an organisation's competitive advantage (Alavi and Leidner, 2001).

The challenge, of course, is that moving knowledge between different parts of an organisation, and ensuring that different members of an organisation have the capacity to apply it, is far from straightforward.

First, knowledge itself is mercurial. It can take different forms, such as tacit and explicit and individual and collective (Nonaka, 1994). Translating knowledge between these forms is difficult, and many of these forms do not readily lend themselves to storage or communication. Second, injunctions to 'pool knowledge' for the greater organisational good face technical, political and social barriers: there may actually be benefits in hoarding knowledge rather than sharing it, particularly in competitive environments where it can offer gains to individuals or social groups (Currie and Suhomlinova, 2006).

A widespread approach to sharing knowledge within organisations has been the introduction of knowledge management systems, often IT-based. The promise of such systems is in their ability to extract knowledge and thus contribute to the preservation of organisational memory, reducing reliance on individuals who may hoard, forget or depart (Hendriks and Vriens, 1999). However, a key limitation is that knowledge management systems, by their very nature, render knowledge 'an objective, portable and manageable commodity' (Swan and Scarbrough, 2001, p 915) – and thus neglect the more tacit, subjective and social dimensions of knowledge and knowing (Nonaka, 1994). These systems are much more adept at storing and transferring some forms of knowledge (for example, information) than others (for example, know-how). Thus, while knowledge management systems have some potential for rapidly disseminating new evidence-informed guidelines, they are likely to be much less effective in spreading the 'know-how' that is required for putting such ideas into practice; these remain largely the purview of interpersonal exchange, often through membership of professional communities (see, for example, Gabbay and Le May, 2004).

Partly in acknowledgement of the limitations of IT-based knowledge management systems, alternative approaches to encouraging the sharing of knowledge within and across organisations have emerged, premised on fostering social rather than technologically mediated exchange. A prominent example is the 'community of practice'. Originally developed as part of Lave and Wenger's (1991) theory of social learning, the community of practice is seen as a key means to secure both the sharing of existing knowledge (subjective know-how as well as objective information) and the development of new highly contextualised knowledge.

In giving space to individuals with a common concern to interact and share practical wisdom on how they go about their daily routines and tackle the challenges they face, communities of practice are seen as a source of innovation as well as knowledge sharing. For Cox (2005, p 535), they 'offer a plausible solution to many classic knowledge management problems in that such groups are a social instrument to create, share and steward knowledge, including tacit knowledge'. However, while communities of practice may overcome the reductivist tendencies of IT-based approaches, they face certain barriers as well. For example, they can be plagued by unequal power relationships and knowledge asymmetries: for those who already possess knowledge and power, what incentive is there to share or face challenge?

Wider trends – such as outsourcing, frequent organisational restructurings and increasing reliance on casual labour and short-term contracts – may further undermine the sense of trust built up over repeat interaction that is fundamental to the operation of communities of practice (Cox, 2005). Public services are far from immune to such pressures, especially in times of financial austerity. Public service professionals may also be more inclined to share knowledge *within* rather than *across* professional boundaries (Ferlie et al, 2005), and it is worth recalling that Lave and Wenger's (1991) original theory pertained to apprenticeship largely within professional communities (so the ideas may not travel well to other, less professionalised, settings or across different professional groups).

Efforts to encourage the sharing of knowledge and evidence *across* public service organisations face similar challenges, sometimes further exacerbated by contradictory pressures from government that inhibit collaboration – for example, market-based reforms that encourage competition, or performance management that demands a narrow focus on specific measures rather than collaboration across fields.

Injunctions to collaborate with third-sector organisations in the delivery of public services face similar challenges. Collaborations can be undermined by an 'emphasis on competitive contracts and centrally driven frameworks' (Milbourne, 2009, p 277), while the distinctive views that third-sector organisations can bring, imbued by service-user experience, are often overshadowed by more pressing productivity concerns (Martin, 2011). All in all, policy makers' efforts to encourage knowledge sharing between organisations can be undermined by competing pressures, some of them deriving from policy makers themselves (Box 3.3).

Box 3.3: Encouragement to share knowledge between public service organisations

The late 1990s and 2000s saw the introduction of 'Beacon' schemes in English public services, including local government and education. The identification of Beacons was intended to highlight and reward good practice, as well as to develop an evidence base from which other organisations might learn. In local government, the scheme included programmes of events to showcase the activities of the Beacon councils and allow others to discuss their approaches and consider how they might apply them. However, Rashman and Hartley (2002) note several impediments to these commendable ambitions. The events themselves were driven more by formal presentations than by informal dialogue, with an emphasis on explicit evidence and little scope for conveying tacit 'know-how'. Moreover, in rendering councils as competitors as they sought to achieve Beacon status, the scheme risked discouraging exchange altogether, or reinforcing the notion that any knowledge transfer should be unidirectional: a matter of identifying good practice and encouraging others to mimic it, rather than a more socialised notion of evidence generation that would emphasise the benefit of dialogue in producing understanding, and of learning from mistakes as well as successes.

With budgets for learning and knowledge-sharing initiatives dwarfed by those of regimes of audit, inspection and performance management, Rashman and Hartley (2002, p 539) argue that such schemes are likely to remain the 'poor cousin', their good intentions overshadowed by the more pressing task of demonstrating compliance with central government mandates. Hartley and Benington (2006, p 102) summarise the conundrum neatly: 'the emphasis in audit and inspection has primarily been on compliance to a national standard, rather than local learning, knowledge-sharing and innovation. The emphasis on performance targets and league tables implies that what constitutes "best practice" [or indeed "what works"] is already known and is agreed.' Debates, then, about evidence for service improvement always seem to circle back to what counts as evidence in what context (see Chapter Eleven). What seems to be key is developing a judicious mix of 'outside in' approaches (where external evidence is pushed or pulled into service organisations to help reshape their services), while not neglecting 'inside out' approaches (where locally sensitive knowledge is co-produced in situ, and some efforts are made to share these experiences more widely; see also Chapter Twelve).

Persistent cross-cutting challenges: a theoretical perspective

Despite the diversification of both the available sources of evidence and the approaches to achieving evidence-informed public service practice, the overview above highlights a number of common challenges that complicate the relationship between evidence and practice. Frequently, the consequence seems to be a fall-back to a more traditional, linear conception of the relationship, whereby 'canonical' evidence endorsed by a powerful authority, such as a national government or international agency, is prioritised by local service delivery organisations and their staff. The reasons for this are several, but they are perhaps best conceptualised through the lens of institutional theory (Powell and DiMaggio, 1991).

Institutional theory seeks to elucidate the influences that enable and constrain organisations' behaviour in a given field of social activity. It highlights how what organisations can and cannot reasonably do in a particular field (for example, local government or education) is governed by a range of rules and norms, including not only formal laws but also implicit expectations and internalised assumptions about what constitutes 'appropriate' behaviour. These rules and norms are relatively durable and resistant to change because they are reproduced through the behaviour of the individual and organisational actors within the field, particularly the more powerful actors. The result is that, within a field, behaviour tends to be relatively uniform, as different organisations are subject to the same regulatory pressures, have broadly similar understandings of what constitutes appropriate behaviour and imitate each other's actions in order to minimise risk and maintain their legitimacy (Powell and DiMaggio, 1991).

In the field of public service provision, and especially in developed democracies, the state is a particularly influential actor, stemming in large part from the relationship of resource dependency between most service organisations and the state. The state's expectations about organisational behaviour will have a strong influence, often reinforced by financial and reputational carrots and sticks. The development of 'targets and terror' (Bevan and Hood, 2006) attaches particular importance to the achievement of certain objectives, such as financial balance or expected throughput of clients, to the neglect of others. Because some objectives are so explicitly prioritised in this way, they will take precedence over others, even if these too are nominally encouraged by the state. Therefore certain forms of evidence (for example, around the use of synthetic phonics in early literacy education

– see Box 3.1) will likely trump others, and certain priorities may lead to the neglect of some forms of evidence altogether (for example, targets around waiting times in hospital emergency departments, which continue to be prioritised despite concerns from the medical profession that they are not well founded in evidence and can give rise to perverse clinical consequences – Bevan and Hood, 2006).

Although particularly powerful, the state is not the sole determinant of the norms and rules of an institutional field. In fields characterised by strong professional groups (such as law and healthcare, and to a lesser extent education and social work), the professions too are strongly influential on what constitutes appropriate behaviour. Indeed, the field of healthcare is sometimes characterised as being dominated by a 'pact' (or perhaps a stand-off) between the state and the medical profession (Salter, 2004). Doctors thus have a strong role both in determining the evidence base mandated by national bodies such as NICE and in turning this evidence into practice in local service delivery organisations. In other parts of the public sector, professionals may not hold quite the same sway as doctors, yet they are influential nonetheless.

The hierarchical relationship between different professional groups *within* organisations also means that some groups are more powerful than others when it comes to developing and acting on local evidence bases (for example, through data collection for quality improvement), and in determining what evidence is legitimate and what is not. This means that evidence deriving from certain sources – for example, subordinate professional groups, and particularly clients of public services – may be devalued and delegitimised in favour of more conventional sources of knowledge, especially in fields such as social care or mental health, where there are steep authority gradients between clients and professionals (Hodge, 2005). The boundaries between professional groups can also impede the flow of knowledge between them, such that parallel knowledge bases may emerge between professions and organisations, with little scope for transfer between them (Ferlie et al, 2005).

In all, the consequence of these institutional forces is that the strength of the evidence is not the sole, or even the major, determinant of its influence on practice; rather, more powerful actors hold considerable sway in determining what (and indeed whether) evidence is used (see also Chapter Two on why evidence is a sometimes necessary but largely insufficient condition for major policy change). In this light, the relative durability of top-down evidence implementation in the face of an increasing array of alternative modes of evidence generation and use is readily explicable. However, this does not mean that there is no deviation from institutionally prescribed behaviours.

Human agents are often creative in the way that they find space for discretion and innovation in the face of apparently overwhelming institutional forces. One of the key early insights of institutional sociology was that there is often a mismatch between what is expected within the field and what is needed to accomplish an organisation's tasks. This can result in a 'decoupling' between the public image projected by an organisation and the reality of behaviour within it (Meyer and Rowan, 1977). From a policy maker's perspective, such practice might look like unwarranted variation from a well-founded, mandated evidence base. But it could equally represent the exercise of professional judgement, or the use of alternative sources of evidence, or innovation that might produce new evidence. At any rate, when examining the uptake and use of evidence in public service organisations, we should not assume that the public representation of compliance with government-dictated 'evidence-based standards' tells the whole story.

In conclusion: future prospects for evidence and service delivery

We began this chapter by claiming that the first two decades of the 21st century have seen a continuation of a technocratic consensus about the proper relationship between evidence and service delivery, albeit one increasingly disturbed by contestation and diversification of approach. In recent years the rise of populist politics across large swathes of the economically advanced world has seen evidence-based claims and expert knowledge readily questioned. However, government policies that run counter to broadly accepted evidence bases are nothing new. Politics is about more than evidence (see Chapter Two).

There is no doubt that a more nakedly ideological politics can have direct implications for public service organisations charged with putting policy into practice. Undoubtedly, a more polarised, contested and public debate about evidence, policy and practice, fuelled by greater data transparency and the rise of social media, does complicate the task for professionals and organisations wishing to enact evidence-informed practice. Moreover, prescriptive but ineffective top-down models of evidence dissemination, or bottom-up models that are more tokenistic than empowering, fuel distrust in the usefulness of evidence, and scepticism in experts and their capacity to identify and implement what works.

All of these challenges speak to the need to develop, justify, advocate for *and evaluate* approaches to evidence-informed services that are fully cognisant of the limitations and pitfalls outlined in this chapter. The decisions of service delivery organisations are more open to scrutiny than ever before, and the nature of the knowledge(s) of which they are expected to take account is more plural and contested. Organisations and professionals can expect to be held accountable for their activities in relation to evidence to an increasing number of audiences, and according to a broader range of criteria. Hence there is likely to be considerably more turbulence yet in public services as we seek to exploit the benefits of evidence for public good.

References

Abraham, J. (2009) 'Partial progress: governing the pharmaceutical industry and the NHS, 1948–2008', *Journal of Health Politics, Policy and Law*, 34 (6), pp 931–77.

Alavi, M. and Leidner, D.E. (2001) 'Knowledge management and knowledge management systems: conceptual foundations and research issues', *MIS Quarterly*, 25 (1), pp 107–36.

Batalden, M., Batalden, P., Margolis, P., Seid, M. et al (2016) 'Coproduction of healthcare service', *BMJ Quality and Safety*, 25 (7), pp 509–17.

Bevan, G. and Hood, C. (2006) 'What's measured is what matters: targets and gaming in the English public health care system', *Public Administration*, 84 (3), pp 517–38.

Blackman, T., Harrington, B., Elliott, E., Greene, A. et al (2012) 'Framing health inequalities for local intervention: comparative case studies', *Sociology of Health and Illness*, 34 (1), pp 49–63.

Clarke, A. and Margetts, H. (2014) 'Governments and citizens getting to know each other? Open, closed, and big data in public management reform', *Policy and Internet*, 6 (4), pp 393–417.

Clarke, J., Newman, J., Smith, N., Vidler, E. et al (2007) *Creating citizen-consumers*, London: Sage.

Commission on Social Determinants of Health (2008) *Closing the gap in a generation*, Geneva: World Health Organization.

Cox, A. (2005) 'What are communities of practice? A comparative review of four seminal works', *Journal of Information Science*, 31 (6), pp 527–40.

Currie, G. and Lockett, A. (2007) 'A critique of transformational leadership: moral, professional and contingent dimensions of leadership within public services organizations', *Human Relations*, 60 (2), pp 341–70.

Currie, G. and Suhomlinova, O. (2006) 'The impact of institutional forces upon knowledge sharing in the UK NHS: the triumph of professional power and the inconsistency of policy', *Public Administration*, 84 (1), pp 1–30.

Donetto, S., Pierri, P., Tsianakas, V. and Robert, G. (2015) 'Experience-based co-design and healthcare improvement: realizing participatory design in the public sector', *The Design Journal*, 18 (2), pp 227–48.

Ellis, S. and Moss, G. (2014) 'Ethics, education policy and research: the phonics question reconsidered', *British Educational Research Journal*, 40 (2), pp 241–60.

Ferlie, E., Fitzgerald, L., Wood, M. and Hawkins, C. (2005) 'The nonspread of innovations: the mediating role of professionals', *Academy of Management Journal*, 48 (1), pp 117–34.

Fitz-Gibbon, K. (2016) 'Minimum sentencing for murder in England and Wales: a critical examination 10 years after the Criminal Justice Act 2003', *Punishment and Society*, 18 (1), pp 47–67.

Gabbay, J. and Le May, A. (2004) 'Evidence based guidelines or collectively constructed 'mindlines'? Ethnographic study of knowledge management in primary care', *British Medical Journal*, 329, (7473), pp 1013–16A.

Gibbons, M., Limoges, C., Nowotny, H., Schwartzman, S. et al (1994) *The new production of knowledge*, London: Sage.

Harrison, S. and McDonald, R. (2003) 'Science, consumerism and bureaucracy: new legitimations of medical professionalism', *International Journal of Public Sector Management*, 16 (2), pp 110–21.

Hartley, J. and Benington, J. (2006) 'Copy and paste, or graft and transplant? Knowledge sharing through inter-organizational networks', *Public Money and Management*, 26 (2), pp 101–8.

Hendriks, P.H.J. and Vriens, D.J. (1999) 'Knowledge-based systems and knowledge management: friends or foes?', *Information and Management*, 35 (2), pp 113–25.

Hersh, W.R., Weiner, M.G., Embi, P.J., Logan, J.R. et al (2013) 'Caveats for the use of operational electronic health record data in comparative effectiveness research', *Medical Care*, 51 (8 Suppl 3), pp S30–S37.

Hodge, S. (2005) 'Participation, discourse and power: a case study in service user involvement', *Critical Social Policy*, 25 (2), pp 164–79.

Institute for Healthcare Improvement (2003) *The breakthrough series*, Cambridge, MA: IHI.

Lave, J. and Wenger, E.C. (1991) *Situated learning*, Cambridge: Cambridge University Press.

Lawless, A., Lane, A., Lewis, F., Baum, F. et al (2017) 'Social determinants of health and local government: understanding and uptake of ideas in two Australian states', *Australian and New Zealand Journal of Public Health*, 41 (2), pp 204–9.

Lipsky, M. (1980) *Street level bureaucracy*, New York: Russell Sage Foundation.

McNary, L.D. (2008) 'Quality management in the public sector: applying lean concepts to customer service in a consolidated government office', *Public Administration Quarterly*, 32 (2), pp 282–301.

Marmot Review (2010) *Fair society, healthy lives*, London: The Marmot Review.

Martin, G.P. (2011) 'The third sector, user involvement and public-service reform: a case study in the co-governance of health-service provision', *Public Administration*, 89 (3), pp 909–32.

Martin, G.P., Armstrong, N., Aveling, E.-L., Herbert, G. et al (2015) 'Professionalism redundant, reshaped, or reinvigorated? Realizing the "third logic", in contemporary health care', *Journal of Health and Social Behavior*, 56 (3), pp 378–97.

Meyer, J.W. and Rowan, B. (1977) 'Institutionalized organizations: formal structure as myth and ceremony', *American Journal of Sociology*, 83 (2), pp 340–63.

Milbourne, L. (2009) 'Remodelling the third sector: advancing collaboration or competition in community-based initiatives?', *Journal of Social Policy*, 38 (2), pp 277–97.

Neubeck, T., Elg, M., Schneider, T. and Andersson-Gäre, B. (2014) 'Prospects and problems of transferring quality-improvement methods from health care to social services: two case studies', *The Permanente Journal*, 18 (2), pp 38–42.

Nicolay, C.R., Purkayastha, S., Greenhalgh, A., Benn, J., Chaturvedi, S., Phillips, N. and Darzi, A. (2011) 'Systematic review of the application of quality improvement methodologies from the manufacturing industry to surgical healthcare', *British Journal of Surgery*, 99 (3), pp 324–35.

Nonaka, I. (1994) 'A dynamic theory of organizational knowledge creation', *Organization Science*, 5 (1), pp 14–37.

Nutley, S. and Davies, H. (2000) 'Criminal justice: using evidence to reduce crime', in H.T.O. Davies, S.M. Nutley and P.C. Smith (eds), *What works?* Bristol: Policy Press, pp 93–116.

Osborne, S.P. (2010) 'Delivering public services: time for a new theory?', *Public Management Review*, 12 (1), pp 1–10.

Pigg, S.L. (2001) 'Languages of sex and AIDS in Nepal: notes on the social production of commensurability', *Cultural Anthropology*, 16 (4), pp 481–541.

Popay, J., Whitehead, M. and Hunter, D.J. (2010) 'Injustice is killing people on a large scale – but what is to be done about it?', *Journal of Public Health*, 32 (2), pp 148–9.

Powell, A.E., Rushmer, R.K. and Davies, H.T.O. (2009) *A systematic narrative review of quality improvement models in health care*, Edinburgh: Quality Improvement Scotland.

Powell, W.W. and DiMaggio, P.J. (1991) *The new institutionalism in organizational analysis*, London: University of Chicago Press.

Pressman, J.L. and Wildavsky, A.B. (1974) *Implementation*, Berkeley, CA: University of California Press.

Rashman, L. and Hartley, J. (2002) 'Leading and learning? Knowledge transfer in the Beacon Council Scheme', *Public Administration*, 80 (3), pp 523–42.

Reed, J.E. and Card, A.J. (2016) 'The problem with plan-do-study-act cycles', *BMJ Quality and Safety*, 25 (3), pp 147–52.

Salter, B. (2004) *The new politics of medicine*, Basingstoke: Palgrave Macmillan.

Swan, J. and Scarbrough, H. (2001) Knowledge management: concepts and controversies', *Journal of Management Studies*, 38 (7), pp 913–21.

Toffolutti, V., McKee, M. and Stuckler, D. (2017) 'Evidence points to "gaming" at hospitals subject to National Health Service cleanliness inspections', *Health Affairs*, 36 (2), pp 355–61.

Waring, J.J. and Bishop, S. (2010) 'Lean healthcare: rhetoric, ritual and resistance', *Social Science and Medicine*, 71 (7), pp 1332–40.

Weingart, P. (1997) 'From "Finalization" to "Mode 2": old wine in new bottles?', *Social Science Information*, 36 (4), pp 591–613.

Williams, O. (2017) 'Identifying adverse effects of area-based health policy: an ethnographic study of a deprived neighbourhood in England', *Health and Place*, 45, pp 85–91.

Section Two
Fields of policy and practice intervention

Although many parts of the public sector in the UK have been exploring wider and better uses of evidence, the debates within these different areas of policy and practice have not always unfolded along similar lines. Indeed, there has been a growing recognition of important variations when it comes to the strategies and practices of using evidence. Moreover, evidence use has typically been explored somewhat separately in each sector and this has sometimes led to missed opportunities for cross-sectoral learning. This section teases out some of these similarities and differences through detailed explorations of the nature of evidence and evidence use in six sectors. In doing so it surfaces new learning not only for the individual fields, but also for the wider enterprise of promoting the role of evidence in policy and practice. Our focus in this section is very much the UK, reflecting our own and our contributors' knowledge and interests, but also shining a light on a national context that has seen much innovation and activity in the realm of evidence.

Evidence use is considered in six fields of policy and practice intervention: health and healthcare; social care; criminal justice; education; the environment and sustainability; and international development. The first four of these have been selected because they are the 'big ticket' items of health and human services, areas of policy and practice where the state has typically taken a major role and where large amounts of public money are expended. A continued focus on these four fields is justified not only for these reasons but also because of the high visibility of evidence in policy and practice debates in these fields and a substantial investment in an architecture to support evidence use. In addition, a renewed look at the unfolding of evidence debates in these fields provides a degree of continuity with the foray into cross-sector comparisons in our earlier book (Davies et al, 2000).

This section also includes chapters on two new fields where evidence is being applied – on environmental and sustainability issues and in international development. Developments in both these fields have unfolded somewhat differently from those in sectors that are the mainstays of health and human services, and there has been less interplay of debates from (for example) healthcare into these fields. An examination of evidence and evidence use in these two additional settings adds a fresh perspective and extends the debates into new terrain with an interesting international dimension.

In choosing these six fields of policy and practice intervention we have sought a blend of the familiar and the new. This is not to say that considerable developments around evidence have not occurred in other areas of policy making. For instance, there is an on-going debate about the use of evidence in housing policy and in the development of social welfare, and evidence too might be sought to enlighten over issues such as immigration, violence and substance misuse. The response to the Grenfell Tower disaster in London in 2017, for example, has highlighted the role of research evidence in housing policy, drawing attention once again to the centrality of housing to social well-being and the interconnectedness of housing and migration issues (Lund, 2016). Turning to social welfare, there have been a number of high-profile, government-sponsored randomised controlled trials (RCTs) conducted on aspects of the UK Welfare to Work programme (Greenberg and Morris, 2005). Both of these examples have demonstrated that debates about the sorts of evidence that policy makers find compelling are as alive here as anywhere. While space limitations have precluded the casting of our net wider than the six selected fields, we nonetheless anticipate that the arguments built through reviewing the included areas will provide relevant transferable learning for fields of policy and practice not explored in detail in this book. We also hope that the book as a whole will stimulate debate about evidence use in other sectors, and we encourage experts in those sectors to develop accounts of the dynamics in similarly grounded ways.

As noted, the content of the first four chapters is mainly focused on developments in the UK. Yet, devolution has led to differences in public services in England, Scotland, Wales and Northern Ireland, and our authors recognise these differences and try to be clear about where arguments apply to the UK more broadly and where they are relevant to particular countries within the UK. Readers unfamiliar with the UK context are encouraged to refer to Chapter Thirteen first as a means of understanding the broader political and governmental backdrop against which these field-specific developments play out. Albeit briefly, and where such comparisons prove illuminating, some authors also draw attention to parallel developments overseas, but the bulk of the international commentary in this book is located later, in Section Four. The last two chapters in this section, on environment and sustainability and on international development, necessarily engage with global as well as local issues, and so their reach is broader.

Our authors also home in on particular subsections of their policy fields to illustrate and particularise the arguments. For example, the education chapter focuses on school-based education, the social care chapter is orientated towards services for children and families and the chapter on the criminal justice system focuses especially on policing. Such particularising of the arguments reflects the need for specificity in the accounts as well as the interests and knowledge of our contributors. It is also worth noting that many of our contributors are or have been active players in some of the developments and debates, so the accounts are grounded in experience as well as scholarship. While providing detailed and fine-grained accounts, the chapters also draw out the generic and/or conceptual implications, so that these accounts are lifted above and beyond particular local or national developments.

What is clear from across the chapters in this section is the considerable increase in activity relating to promoting evidence use in the UK over the 20 years since the late 1990s. There are a wide range of initiatives designed to promote evidence acquisition, collation and use. These activities form a spectrum ranging from investments in producing, synthesising and disseminating evidence (such as the Education Endowment Foundation, the National Institute for Health Research, and the Cochrane and Campbell Collaborations), to initiatives designed to build capacity for evidence use (such as the Senior Command Course for UK police leaders, discussed in Chapter Six), through to the development of networks to support evidence use (such as the Africa Evidence Network, discussed in Chapter Nine). There are also examples of more systems-level interventions such as the national programme of Applied Research Collaborations (ARCs, formerly CLAHRCs; see Chapter Four), designed to foster joint working between healthcare providers and universities conducting healthcare research. Together these activities start to look like the beginnings of an infrastructure or ecosystem to support evidence use, although the extent to which the various elements join up varies. The wide variety of approaches to evidence use (and their interconnections) is discussed in more detail in Chapter Twelve.

The six fields included in this section have typically approached questions of evidence generation and implementation in different ways. For some (particularly in healthcare) there continues to be a strong focus on the primacy of evidence from RCTs and systematic reviews of these studies. For others, evidence-informed policy and practice (EIPP) involves a wider range of not just research but also diverse sources of knowledge (see, for example, evidence for the environment, sustainability and international development). Often, competing views coexist, sometimes uneasily, within the same field of application, leading to tensions and disputes. These arguments, recurring across the next six chapters, are developed in depth in Chapter Eleven, where we consider what counts as good evidence. Reading across these accounts, though, there seems to be a growing maturity and confidence in many fields about the positive contribution of evidence to policy and practice. Yet, bubbling away beneath the surface there is still on-going debate about what type of research evidence is being talked about when evidence use is promoted.

Investment in evidence creation, promotion and use varies considerably between fields. It can be argued that this has always been the case: indeed, other sectors often feel (and perhaps are) the 'poor relations' of healthcare, which has seen focused attention and determined investment around evidence use since the early 1990s. Moreover, the prominence of debates about evidence in healthcare, and the formulation and promotion of evidence-based medicine (EBM) in particular, has had some unfortunate consequences with spillover onto other sectors. It has reinforced, for example, a linear framing of the 'journey' from evidence to policy or practice, and it has often promoted the primacy of one type of evidence (that from RCTs) over other, more diverse sources of knowledge.

The centrality of trial evidence in healthcare has also led to a strong discourse (if not always the actual delivery) of standardised practices, again with spillover for debates in other sectors. Yet, randomised trials are much more rarely conducted in areas of service delivery that are less well resourced than healthcare, and there is greater disputation than in healthcare as to whether they should be. Moreover, professional hierarchies (as seen, for example, by the professional dominance of doctors in healthcare and the associated power imbalances with other occupational groupings) are less pronounced in some sectors than others, and this too has implications for more inclusive and dialogical approaches to evidence. Taken together, these observations suggest that normative arguments about evidence derived from experiences in healthcare are questionable, at least. Finally, the hegemony of healthcare thinking has sometimes squeezed out some of the valuable learning that lies nestled in other fields (see, for example, the work in international development about the importance of networks, and in social care on co-production).

However, in lots of ways the factors that unite the fields come out most strongly, reinforcing the scope for cross-sectoral learning and the potential for avoiding duplication of effort. The on-going commitment to evidence use and the plethora of approaches being tried (and sometimes even tested) present a cause for optimism, which is echoed later in the international commentaries in Section Four. The cross-cutting commitment to building better stakeholder engagement in research (including service users, policy makers and practitioners) also feels like a positive development with important ramifications. Different fields of public policy are faced with similar challenges in terms of making the most of over-stretched resources and making sure that evidence has a role to play in complex policy and practice decisions. An additional common challenge is to ensure that evidence plays an active role in a global context that requires both multilateralism in particular areas of policy such as the environment and international development, and at the same time localism in the context of national and international fragmentation.

This section of the book, then, builds on the broad ideas introduced in Section One and grounds them in specific areas of policy and practice. It highlights similarities and differences in evidence use across different fields. It identifies and develops cross-cutting themes for further exploration and analysis in Section Three and in the concluding chapter (Chapter Eighteen) and it fleshes out the predominantly UK developments for later international comparison in Section Four.

The chapters in this section all follow broadly the same structure to aid cross-reading and comparison. Each chapter provides an introduction to evidence use in a specific field of policy and practice. The authors go on to discuss the nature of evidence in that policy and practice field and the ways in which this has developed over recent years. There is then an overview of the structures and systems for the production and synthesis of research-based knowledge, followed by a discussion of key approaches to encouraging and enabling evidence use. The chapters conclude with brief reflections, based largely on developments in the UK, and they also look ahead to possible future directions in their specific fields.

Taken together, these six chapters provide a detailed and particularised analysis of developments in the UK. This allows us to begin to map the contours of the evidence debates across services, looking back and looking forward, with a view to expanding awareness and sharing insights.

References

Davies, H.T.O., Nutley, S.M. and Smith, P.C. (eds) (2000) *What works: evidence-based policy and practice in public services*, Bristol: Policy Press.

Greenberg, D.H. and Morris, S. (2005) 'Large-scale social experimentation in Britain', *Evaluation*, 11 (2), pp 223–42.

Lund, B. (2016) *Housing politics in the United Kingdom: power, planning and protest*, Bristol: Policy Press.

4

Using evidence in health and healthcare

Paul Wilson and Trevor A. Sheldon

Introduction to evidence use in health and healthcare

While for many fields of practice 'what works' thinking was a relatively new phenomenon back in 2000, the field of health and healthcare could already look back on over a quarter of a century of debate about the challenges of using evidence in service delivery and improvement (Davies and Nutley, 2000). Systematic study in healthcare had found large and unjustified variations in clinical practice (Wennberg et al, 2016), significant levels of inappropriate care (Brook, 1994) and evidence of over-medicalisation and treatment-induced ill health (Illich, 1974). Questions were being asked about both the effectiveness and the cost-effectiveness of care (Cochrane, 1972). The development of Evidence Based Medicine (EBM) was one major response to these concerns, a development that has an interesting and well-documented history (summarised in Box 4.1).

This chapter considers the on-going development and influence of this dominant discourse relating to evidence use. It discusses: the evolution of EBM; the importance of the nature and quality of evidence within EBM; the structures and systems that have emerged for the production and synthesis of research; and the development of key approaches to encouraging and enabling evidence use in medicine specifically and in healthcare more broadly. While evidence in healthcare has come to mean so much more than just clinical evidence, EBM remains the normative model against which other applications of evidence are so often compared.

The EBM approach and the evidence-based movement associated with it can be regarded as a *disruptive technology* – a new way of doing things that sought to overturn previous practices. It was radical, in that it challenged standard practice or policy and, more fundamentally, the assumed authority of the clinical professional and the centralised policy-making apparatus. Moreover, by making the process of putting the evidence base together more explicit and transparent (for example, through systematic reviews) it had (and retains) the potential to democratise decision making by making research evidence available for everyone.

Box 4.1: A short history of evidence-based medicine

Sackett and colleagues in Canada promulgated clinical epidemiology as a practical approach for clinicians (Sackett et al, 1996). This challenged the tradition of medicine, where clinical practice had largely reflected the authority of experts, rather than any systematic engagement with research evidence. The groundwork was laid then for what came to be called 'evidence-based medicine': a philosophy and an approach that expanded (although not without some persistent contestation) to cover all aspects of healthcare and (increasingly) health policy and healthcare management.

The EBM 'movement' was fuelled by a variety of technical advances, including: a rapid expansion in new diagnostic and therapeutic technologies; increasing amounts of robust evaluative research; the new era of information technology, which transformed the ability to host, organise and search for information; and the conduct of systematic reviews of the evidence to take stock of, appraise and summarise the growing knowledge base.

During the 1990s, the UK invested in the infrastructure for healthcare evidence as part of the new NHS research and development (R&D) programme (Sheldon and Chalmers, 1994). In 1992 the UK Cochrane Centre was established as a base for promoting and coordinating reviews of trials, leading to the global Cochrane Collaboration. Subsequently, Sheldon and colleagues developed the *Effective Health Care* bulletins, a bimonthly series of systematic evidence reviews, in order to inform the decisions of healthcare purchasers. This led to the establishment of the Centre for Reviews and Dissemination at the University of York, a more methodologically pluralist centre than Cochrane, and one charged with synthesising and disseminating the best available evidence to inform NHS policy and practice.

The evidence-based movement was given a further boost when Sackett established the Centre for Evidence-based Medicine at Oxford (in 1995), and with the establishment of NICE in 1999. Other UK centres for evidence-based practice in other professional areas, such as nursing, have followed (Cullum et al, 2008).

As the movement grew in clinical practice, it was increasingly recognised by policy makers and managers that they too could use scientific evidence to identify the most effective services, and that the evidence-based approach was a potentially useful framework for handling (often exaggerated) claims about innovations and new technologies. We have seen policy makers intervening more, with attempts to reform and restructure the delivery of care and to promote health through public health initiatives. Evidence, of various forms, has figured increasingly prominently in these debates.

So, while the origin of the evidence-based movement was focused on clinical care, the principles of the approach have been extended to public health policy and to the organisation and management of healthcare systems and their component parts, such as healthcare teams, service delivery models, service settings, packages of care and ways of managing change. Moreover, as the term 'evidence-based' became a 'primary currency in health care rhetoric', it was also gradually adopted as a prefix in wider policy debates and in the media (Rychetnik, 2008).

However, health policy making is never likely to be as open to the use of evidence as that seen in clinical practice (see Chapter Two). Research is only one of several knowledge sources, and policy makers have goals other than effectiveness and efficiency. They are often driven by ideology, political motives and other, sometimes short-term, factors. Indeed, even where an explicit policy commitment to follow the findings of a systematic review is made (as in the case of water fluoridation, for example), prior beliefs and policy intent can override the inconvenient truth of contrary findings (Wilson and Sheldon, 2006).

A more recent example is the debate about whether there is a real 'weekend effect' raising mortality rates for emergency admissions to National Health Service (NHS) hospitals. The Department of Health used a study published in the *British Medical Journal* (*BMJ*) to claim that many thousands of patients die because of understaffing of hospitals at weekends, and hence to justify major changes in NHS working and contracts for junior doctors (McKee, 2016). More careful analysis suggested that much of the so-called 'weekend effect' arises from sicker patients being admitted at the weekend (Meacock et al, 2016). Perhaps unsurprisingly, when a study was published in *BMJ Open* in 2017 suggesting a much larger number of premature deaths associated with constraints on health and social care spending (that is, politically motivated austerity) (Watkins et al, 2017), this piece of evidence did not receive nearly so much attention from policy makers.

Evidence-based approaches, then, have proliferated and become normalised as part of clinical practice and (perhaps more selectively) in policy and management. Large numbers of evidence summaries, guidelines and disseminating initiatives have been launched, with varying degrees of rigour and success. Such is the volume of new research and the proliferation of evidence sites that many clinicians now rely on intermediaries or proxies (such as NICE) or commercial products (such as UpToDate or Map of Medicine) to assemble and assess evidence and produce guidelines. This can mean that front-line professionals are more distant from the original research studies, as they are using predigested and codified knowledge in the form of guidelines and other policies.

Despite these advances, as with any movement that questions authority and autonomy, early initiatives often met with stiff opposition: from some professionals (as authorities were challenged); from the pharmaceutical industry (when the results did not support their products); and from government (when findings contradicted current policy or escalated costs). Evidence-based medicine in particular has seen significant critique, and sometimes even disillusionment from early enthusiasts (Greenhalgh et al, 2014; Ioannidis, 2016) (Box 4.2). EBM is seen to have resulted in a glut of guidelines that are difficult or impossible to assimilate, with much of the research evidence being generated by trials sponsored by companies with large resources (principally, the pharmaceutical industry), which can bias the knowledge base. There is also some antagonism to the primary focus on quantification, alongside the accusation of over-standardising care resulting in 'cook book medicine'.

Concerns also arise about the over-emphasis on following algorithmic rules (for example, through decision support systems) and a creeping managerialism, threatening to turn medicine into a 'depersonalized, industrial process' (Borg, 2016) – critiques echoed more broadly in Chapter Three. Moreover, the evidence base, which is often focused on one disease or condition, is often a poor fit for patients who increasingly have several conditions (multi-morbidity). Critics have called for a 'renaissance in EBM' (that is, a return to its founding principles) or for 'real EBM', an approach that is more individualised, that values judgement as well as numbers and that is better aligned to professional relationship-based care (Greenhalgh et al, 2014).

Many of these criticisms are well founded. They focus attention on the original purpose of EBM and highlight some of the distortions due to the 'over-enthusiasm and reductionism from those who fail to recognise EBM's practical and methodological limitations' (Liberati

Box 4.2: Common criticisms of evidence-based medicine

• Has too many guidelines, unsuited for local application.
• Objectifies medicine: used as a control tool and erodes the professional role.
• Evidence base is overly influenced by commercial interests.
• Much research is of poor quality.
• Too many published findings turn out to be false or non-replicable.
• Remaining gains from forced implementation are now only marginal.
• Cannot deal adequately with complexity of comorbidities.
• Lacks applicability to the local context.
• Does not sufficiently incorporate patient preferences.

and Vineis, 2005). However, some criticisms reflect concerns that long precede the rise of EBM and can sometimes seem overplayed. For example, fears that individual patients are dealt with in highly generic ways that devalue professional expertise were expressed nearly 30 years ago (Mechanic, 1991). Medical research has also been dominated by commercial interests for a long time (Liberati and Vineis, 2005) but, as a result of evidence-based approaches, awareness of the biases from commercially sponsored trials or researchers is now more widely recognised (Ahn et al, 2017), and moreover this has stimulated the funding of more research by public agencies such as the NHS Health Technology Assessment (HTA) programme. Guidelines, too, have been around for many years, but historically they mostly reflected opinion or professional consensus without explicit incorporation of the evidence.

Building on the gains of EBM, then, there are other sorts of knowledge and information that should also influence decision making, including values and resource constraints, clinical experience, patient experience and information from the local context (Rycroft-Malone et al, 2004). The challenge, in the practice of evidence-based healthcare, is to find ways to take proper account of such diverse knowledge(s). This has possibly been the least developed part of the evidence-based 'project'. For example, one of the challenges of the evidence-based approach has been how to incorporate patients' views into the decision-making process, and hence avoid simply shifting authority from the clinical expert to the evidence expert. More recently, research has focused on how shared decision making can help clinicians to use evidence, integrate it with their expertise and reflect patients' values, preferences and circumstances (Hoffmann et al, 2014). The evidence-based and shared decision-making agendas have been brought together by NICE in an initiative to highlight the importance of incorporating patients' needs and wishes in guidelines and the development of patient decision aids (Stacey et al, 2017).

In exploring these developments we will first expand on perspectives on evidence in healthcare, before turning to the institutional arrangements that support evidence creation and use.

The nature of evidence in health and healthcare

The fundamental feature of the evidence-based approach is that clinical and public health practice, as well as healthcare management and healthcare policy, should be informed by scientific evidence. That is, reliable empirical evidence of, for example, the extent to which a policy choice, public health intervention or treatment improves (aggregate) outcomes is central: intuition, or extrapolation from clinical or policy experience, theory or pathophysiological principles, are insufficient grounds for decision making (Liberati and Vineis, 2005).

Those proposing a more explicit use of evidence in clinical practice (and in healthcare more generally) put great store on the reliability of that evidence, focusing on: internal validity (that is, the degree to which the results of studies are likely to be unbiased) and external validity (that is, the degree to which the results are likely to be relevant to populations or persons beyond those in the specific study). A key feature of the evidence-based approach, therefore, is the appraisal of primary research studies for the quality and strength of the evidence they contain (see Chapter Eleven). This appraisal depends initially on the appropriateness of the study design (related to the questions being addressed; see Chapter Ten), and then on how well the study has been conducted and analysed. These are the key criteria for the substantiation of evidence claims: *the rules of evidence.* And they have led to a plethora of methodological hierarchies, critical appraisal guides and checklists to help with this task (see extensive discussions in Chapter Eleven).

When it comes to evidence in healthcare, then, there is an emphasis on: (1) making appropriate methodological choices; (2) assessing methodological quality; (3) weighing up the collective evidence in a transparent way; and (4) increasingly, considering whether policy choices or interventions constitute good value for money. We now explore each of these in turn.

Making appropriate methodological choices

The optimal design for assessing the effectiveness of interventions (perhaps the most common clinical and policy question) is generally a randomised controlled trial (RCT). This is because, through random assignment of individuals (or clusters or areas) to comparison groups, both known and unknown confounders are (likely) to be distributed evenly between the groups (see also Chapter Ten). Thus, differences in outcome can be more confidently attributed to differences in the interventions between the groups. There are numerous examples of policies or practices that might appear to be beneficial but, when evaluated using randomised trials, have been shown to be of doubtful value or even harmful (Ogundeji et al, 2016). As a result, randomised trials (and especially systematic reviews of all of the available high-quality randomised trials) have come to be seen by many as the 'gold standard' for judging whether an intervention does more good than harm (for example, Cullum et al, 2008).

This focus on randomised trials has been criticised from a variety of professional disciplines and by some social scientists for being reductionist and for ignoring other useful forms of evidence (Pawson, 2013; and see extended discussion in Chapter Eleven). And indeed it is hard to argue against the view that a more broadly based social science approach to evaluation (for example, incorporating more ethnography and process evaluation) would often improve the capacity of experiments to inform important health service and policy questions (Oakley, 2000; and see Chapter Ten). Yet randomisation remains key to making unbiased assessment of treatment effects and remains at the heart of EBM.

Assessing methodological quality

One of the beneficial spin-offs of the evidence-based approach was that it shone a light on the quality of primary research. Critical appraisal of studies has meant that large swathes of research papers, which hitherto might have been taken at face value, were now seen as inadequate, due to badly-specified research questions, inadequate design, poor conduct and reporting, lack of replication and commercial bias (Ahn et al, 2017). The attention drawn to these issues has contributed to a general improvement in the quality of research expected by healthcare journals and led to an enhancement in the quality, transparency and reporting of health research. This is true not just of trials but also of a very wide range of methodologies (for example, the EQUATOR Network is an international initiative promoting wider use of methodological reporting guidelines).

There has also been more thought given to the quality of evidence from wider research traditions, and the need for frameworks against which qualitative research especially can be assessed (respectful of epistemological differences) (Popay and Williams, 1998). As methodological pluralism is embraced, variations in the standards of reporting and underlying research quality remain a concern, particularly with regard to mixed-methods approaches. This needs to be addressed if anxieties as to the usability and policy relevance of wider social research are to be assuaged (Whitty, 2015).

Evaluating individual studies remains important if the expanding research base is to have value, but assessing the overall weight of evidence requires more. For this we need careful review work.

Weighing up the collective evidence

While systematic reviews of 'treatment effects' had been developed in other fields, they really took off in the context of healthcare. Mulrow (1987) showed that traditional reviews were often written by experts who reflected their biases by being selective in the literature they included. Such reviews were neither transparent nor systematic in the ways that they summarised the evidence. The following three decades saw enormous effort put into creating structured, systematic, transparent and replicable review methodologies, together with a supporting infrastructure to ensure that reviews were maintained and updated. The combined efforts of systematic review and meta-analysis have undoubtedly revolutionised the quality of evidence on effectiveness that is available to the healthcare sector, especially in medicine.

However, decision makers must address many more complicated questions than just those about aggregate treatment effects. For example, they need information and advice on: the nature and significance of the problem to be addressed; the nature of proposed interventions; their differential impacts; and their feasibility, cost-effectiveness and acceptability. So, systematic reviews of research with a narrow focus on summarising RCTs are rarely sufficient (Whitty, 2015). The need to address questions beyond 'what works' and to include questions of how it works, for whom and in what circumstances is now being recognised (Petticrew, 2015). Policy makers require access to high-quality syntheses of such evidence that will include a wider range of study designs and that likely incorporate both qualitative and quantitative research findings (Mays et al, 2005). Social scientists have long argued that proponents of the evidence-based approach often neglect the need to synthesise the wider range of evidence that might legitimately contribute to decision making (Popay and Williams, 1998).

Hence, relevant healthcare evidence is not restricted to randomised trials and syntheses of these. It involves tracking down the most appropriate evidence to answer the question of interest, in all its breadth and variety (Petticrew, 2015). As more evidence is sought to inform macro and meso decision making rather than just clinical practice, so other forms of evaluation are increasingly being used. RCTs are more difficult to conduct when evaluating policy and management interventions (for example, in public health and in service redesign), and a range of quasi-experimental approaches to evaluation are available that, under the right circumstances, can provide robust estimates of effect (Craig et al, 2017). Interrupted time series analysis, for example, testing statistically for a change in outcome between the period before and after implementation of a policy/programme (Penfold and Zhang, 2013), is becoming more feasible and powerful as larger, linked routine data sets are constructed. What counts as evidence, therefore, continues to evolve and has led to a flowering of research on ways to combine quantitative and qualitative data. Of growing importance in such comprehensive evaluations is a consideration of costs alongside benefits.

Trading off costs and benefits

Evidence-based approaches encourage a structured approach to making recommendations based not just on best outcomes but (at least implicitly) on the trade-off of costs and benefits. A comprehensive approach here would also include an assessment of disbenefits (such as side-effects) as well as costs (both direct and indirect). For example, the GRADE approach (Burford et al, 2012) assesses the quality of evidence relative to the specific context in which it is to be used, and the confidence in the estimate of effects (see further discussion in Chapter Eleven). It challenges decision makers to explicitly take into account all outcomes of importance to patients and the public, and the resource use needed to achieve those outcomes. The strength of a recommendation, then, reflects the extent to which one can be confident that the desirable effects of an intervention outweigh the undesirable ones, and at acceptable cost.

Health economics has also had a distinctive role to play in the development of evidence-informed healthcare (Drummond et al, 2015). A variety of approaches are available, with a particular emphasis on cost utility analysis (Box 4.3). This approach, taken by NICE, expresses differential costs per Quality Adjusted Life Year (QALY) when comparing interventions.

> ## Box 4.3: Types of economic evaluation in evidence-based healthcare decision making
>
> **Cost-benefit analysis** measures costs and benefits in monetary terms; a 'net' benefit results where monetary benefits exceed the costs.
>
> **Cost-effectiveness analysis (CEA)** compares the relative costs and effects (for example, outcomes such as deaths avoided or life-years gained) of two or more alternative interventions; which represents the best value for money can then be compared in terms of the ratio of cost per unit of effectiveness.
>
> **Cost utility analysis** is a type of CEA where cost inputs are examined for their impacts on standardised but non-monetary outcome measures. This incorporates not just cost inputs and outcome utilities, but also some assessment of their variance over time. The **Quality Adjusted Life (QALY) and Disability Adjusted Life Year (DALY)** are standardised units against which relative costs can be compared across diverse interventions. For example, NICE uses incremental cost-per-QALY, with a specific threshold range of £20,000–£30,000 per QALY in its treatment approvals, but this approach is not without some controversy (Claxton et al, 2015).

Looking across these discussions, it can be seen that the nature of acceptable evidence in healthcare involves some complex and technical arguments over methodology, as well as more values-based debates over ontological and epistemological differences and stakeholder inclusion. While these debates ebb and flow, significant investments have been made to strengthen and enlarge the production and synthesis of research–based knowledge for policy and practice.

Production and synthesis of research-based knowledge in health and healthcare

Adopting a more evidence-based approach to healthcare has required the creation of supporting evidence infrastructures. In the US, the Agency for Health Care Policy and Research (AHCPR) was established in 1989 to enhance the quality, appropriateness and effectiveness of healthcare services and to improve access to care. It was to do this by conducting and supporting research, demonstration projects and evaluations, and by developing guidelines. However, the AHCPR was significantly weakened as a result of producing guidelines that conflicted with the financial interests of certain professional groups and related companies. In 1999 the Agency was reauthorised by statute, the name was changed to the Agency for Healthcare Research and Quality and it survived only with a much reduced budget. This illustrates the uncomfortable truth that when even high-quality evidence meets vested interests, evidence may not prevail. Thus, investments in evidence architecture may fail to provide full return.

In the UK, the NHS (initially via the R&D programme and latterly via the National Institute for Health Research, NIHR) has seen a significant investment in infrastructure to support the production, synthesis and translation of research to inform healthcare decisions and patient choices. The NIHR funds a broad portfolio of research programmes that support evidence synthesis across a range of fields. This includes: capacity for horizon-scanning emerging technologies in healthcare; a policy research programme to deliver timely but rigorous evidence to ministers and arm's-length agencies; a programme to cover the wide range of interventions relevant to public health; and a health services and delivery research programme focused on evidence to improve the quality, accessibility and organisation of health services. To that end, NIHR has funded three evidence synthesis centres to conduct reviews in broad areas such as workforce, equity and access, new models of care/service redesign, quality and safety of services and management, leadership and efficiency.

HTA, the systematic evaluation of the effectiveness and cost-effectiveness of treatments, devices, procedures and ways of working, has become a mainstay of global health systems. Alongside the NHS HTA programme there are now over 50 similar HTA agencies across the world. The investment in HTA activity has been complemented by a similar global investment in evidence synthesis centres, the most prominent of which remains the Cochrane Collaboration, which now involves contributors from over 120 countries. Much of the global HTA and synthesis infrastructure is publicly funded to support national and international guideline-development processes. In supporting this work, the Guidelines International Network represents over 100 organisations involved in the development, appraisal and implementation of clinical practice guidelines worldwide.

Assembling reliable evidence, then, has seen considerable organisation and investment, with national approaches building on, contributing to and drawing from international collaborations. Yet, ensuring a ready supply of evidence is one thing: making it count for policy and/or service change can be quite another.

Encouraging and enabling evidence use in health and healthcare

The early period of the evidence-based 'movement' focused on producing and curating reliable evidence, making it more available and usable. There was interest in getting evidence into practice, but understanding of how to do this was relatively basic and tended to assume a general receptiveness to implementation. Timely dissemination of synthesised evidence *can* have impact, particularly when there is a single clear message and there is awareness by recipients that a change is required (Murthy et al, 2012); however, knowledge-push alone is rarely sufficient to implement and sustain change in health systems.

'Getting research into practice' has long been recognised as a persistent challenge (see Chapters Three and Twelve for a more general discussion). Addressing this challenge, a new academic endeavour known as 'implementation science' has emerged. Grounded in applied health research methods, implementation science is the study of methods to promote the systematic uptake of evidence-based interventions into healthcare practice and policy (Wilson et al, 2017b). It includes the study of professional, patient and organisational behaviour change, and it has championed increased use of theoretical approaches to understanding, guiding and evaluating the processes of translating research into practice (Nilsen, 2015; and see extended discussion in Chapter Twelve). Many of the theoretical and methodological developments that have emerged through implementation science have permeated back into mainstream health services research, particularly in shaping the evaluation of complex interventions (for example, Craig et al, 2008).

One strategy for encouraging the uptake and application of research has been the emergence of legislative frameworks that have sought to embed research use as a core function of the commissioning arrangements of the NHS. The Health and Social Care Act (2012) mandated those responsible for commissioning health services to promote the use of evidence obtained from research. However, the extent to which this is being acted upon has been questioned: studies suggest that health service commissioners appear to be well-intentioned but rather ad hoc users of research (Wilson et al, 2017a). Indeed, formal operational guidance for commissioners focuses on leadership, financial and performance management, planning and delegated functions – but not, generally, on making use of research evidence.

In the UK, guideline recommendations from NICE have been given statutory status in the Health and Social Care Act (2012). NICE also uses statutory power to promote/incentivise the uptake of evidence in primary healthcare though Quality Standards and general practitioner incentive payment schemes (the Quality Outcomes Framework), although criticism has been levelled at the quality of the evidence underpinning the indicators (Foy et al, 2013), and others have seen this as incentivising processes of care at the expense of clinically meaningful outcomes (Roland and Guthrie, 2016).

Where the NHS has been relatively slow is in its development of systems to identify and then disinvest from those interventions found to be of low or no clinical value (Prasad and Ioannidis, 2014). So there is an asymmetry between processes to recommend the use of new and existing interventions and those supporting disinvestment. This partly reflects the practical challenges in identifying and contextualising research evidence to inform these processes. Even so, awareness of NICE 'do not do' recommendations among commissioners has been found to be low, as have been the skills necessary to support disinvestment activity at a local level (Wilson et al, 2017a). Other countries, notably Australia (Elshaug et al, 2012) have developed approaches to tackle disinvestment at a local level, such as the Systems Sustainability in Health Care by Allocating Resources Effectively programme (Harris et al, 2017).

Other approaches to getting research into practice seek to close the distance between research production and research use: while the notion of 'two communities' (that is, research producers and research users) remains prevalent, there is growing recognition of the need for these two communities to work much more closely together (Walshe and Davies, 2013). Active and continuous participation in the creation and application of research-based knowledge is viewed as essential to the development of truly 'learning health systems' (Lessard et al, 2017). An early example of this – the Improving Cancer Outcomes initiative in response to the Calman–Hine report – broke new ground for evidence-informed service redesign (Haward and Eastwood, 2001). More recently, starting in 2008, the NIHR funded Collaborations for Leadership in Applied Health Research and Care (CLAHRCs, subsequently renamed Applied Research Collaborations or ARCs; Box 4.4). These build in part on the US experience of the Quality Enhancement Research Initiative (QUERI) of the US Veterans Health Administration (Box 4.5). Collectively, these initiatives highlight the potential gains, but also the significant challenges, of more integrated research and implementation processes. Increasingly, the role and importance of patients, carers and the public as stakeholders are also being recognised, with funders supporting active involvement throughout the research process (see Chapter Three).

Box 4.4: The Collaborations for Leadership in Applied Health Research and Care (CLAHRCs)

In 2008, the NIHR funded nine CLAHRCs as collaborative partnerships between universities and their surrounding NHS organisations, focused on improving patient outcomes through the shared conduct and application of applied health research. Subsequent refunding in 2013 led to 13 CLAHRCs across England, each developing independently within a local context, but each having a high degree of collaborative and partnership working.

CLAHRC goals could be summarised as follows:
• to carry out more and better targeted applied health research;
• to foster more rapid uptake and implementation of applied research findings;
• to create increased local capacity for responding to research-based knowledge.

External evaluation of the early CLAHRCs focused on their formative partnerships, vision(s), values, structures and processes, looking at their boundary-spanning and hybrid roles, the deployment of knowledge brokering and the nature and role of institutional entrepreneurship (Lockett et al, 2014; Scarbrough et al, 2014; Rycroft-Malone et al, 2015; Soper et al, 2015).

While they are an exciting development, the relative lack of comprehensive data about the impact of CLAHRCs on healthcare provision or outcomes is notable (Kislov, 2018). Nonetheless, a renewed round of funding from NIHR was made available in 2018, under a revised title of ARCs.

At a policy level, too, there is growing interest in building better linkages between research and policy worlds through knowledge-broker roles (Cooksey, 2006). Current thinking highlights the fragility of such intermediary roles being dependent on individuals, and suggests instead that, if the impact of research on policy is to be maximised, a more collective process of brokering supported at the policy level will be required (Kislov et al, 2017). These types of processes also need to consider the 'fundamentally ... ideological nature of policy making' (Smith, 2013; and see more general discussion in Chapter Two). Indeed, the extent to which policy makers engage with and use evidence is often a reflection of their willingness to act (Marmot, 2004), the pre-existing direction of policy travel (Wilson and Sheldon, 2006) and/or where there is a need to strengthen the legitimacy of decisions (Ettelt et al, 2014). In this space, *ideas* (perhaps informed by research) are likely to have as much or more purchase than *evidence* alone (Smith, 2013: and see also Chapter Two).

Box 4.5: The Quality Enhancement Research Initiative (QUERI)

Established a decade before the CLAHRCs, the QUERI initiative in the US Veterans Health Administration (VHA) also involved close collaboration between research users and producers that has impacted on the quality of care delivered. QUERI used the collaborations to identify and develop evidence-based best practices and to embed these into routine practice across the VHA system (Stetler et al, 2008). In contrast to some CLAHRCs (subsequently ARCs), the key feature of QUERI has been a strong focus on rigorous comparative-effectiveness research, particularly through the evaluation of implementation strategies to support uptake and spread (Atkins et al, 2017).

Finally, rather than driving the use of evidence to inform service delivery, there is often instead a policy climate that explicitly incentivises unevaluated innovation and integration. The 2011 White Paper *Innovation Health and Wealth* asserted (but did not evidence) that identifying and applying innovative approaches to delivering healthcare would dramatically improve the quality of care in the NHS and strengthen its role as a wealth creator for the UK economy (Department of Health, 2011). The subsequent Health and Social Care Act (2012) made innovation in the provision of health services a statutory duty, and since then 50 new care models, known as 'vanguards', have been rolled out, supported by a £200 million transformation fund from NHS England. Some elements of these initiatives have been pursued despite limited or contradictory evidence, such as integrating funding arrangements to promote integrated care and reduce costs (Goddard and Mason, 2017) or the widespread promotion of social prescribing to alleviate pressures on general practice (Bickerdike et al, 2017). There is, therefore, an inherent tension within the health system that, on the one hand, continues to make significant investments in the production and synthesis of research-based knowledge and, on the other hand, actively promotes pursuit of 'innovative' but often untested approaches.

Reflections and conclusions

Healthcare has been one of the most dynamic areas for the development of the evidence-based approach, especially in clinical practice. Several countries have seen a transformation from *eminence*-based to the general acceptance of (at least) evidence-*informed* healthcare, part of a more general shift in many areas of professional life in response to calls for accountability and value for money. The uptake of evidence (for example, via use of guidelines and standards) has helped to reduce variability of care and contain costs, although formal evaluations of its impact on patient and population outcomes are sparse.

Evidence-based (or evidence-informed) healthcare supports attempts to improve services through optimal use of properly evaluated intervention strategies. From an initial focus on what works in individual treatments, interest has broadened out to encompass more diverse questions and an increasing openness to a wider range of evidence, and to embrace ways of incorporating patient and public preferences. Despite this, concerns remain with some that evidence, unthinkingly applied, can be a blunt instrument, insensitive to inter-individual variability and neglectful of context. Worries about a creeping managerialism have led some early enthusiasts to assert that EBM has in effect 'been high-jacked' (Ioannidis, 2016). Initially a radical programme, as it has matured the evidence-based approach has become institutionalised and part of mainstream thinking. Yet, through becoming mainstream it may be that evidence has had more impact on practice and policy than if it had remained on the margins.

Much time, effort and money has been spent on strengthening the applied health-research base (for example, through the NIHR), on synthesis of that knowledge (for example, through the Cochrane Collaboration) and on further integration with wider voices, with a view to making recommendations (for example, through NICE). It remains considerably less clear how to achieve impact with that evidence on policies, day-to-day practice or, most importantly, health outcomes, and new models that more closely link knowledge generation and use are both emerging and evolving (for example, CLAHRCs/ARCs). Such initiatives are, however, in need of proper testing.

Fundamentally, evidence-based healthcare has the potential to improve societal health and well-being, both through technocratic application of evidence *and* by democratising knowledge and increasing transparency and accountability. Capitalising on a productive tension between these two processes is key. However, this potential can be fully realised only if the evidence generation and publication process is relevant, transparent, honest and reliable, and its application and use reflects the needs of patients and the public more generally. Moreover, unless we can unlock the transformative potential of evidence in policy and practice arenas, upstream investments in research, synthesis and guidance will yield only disappointing returns. The lesson from healthcare over recent decades is that this final puzzle is a tough nut to crack.

References

Ahn, R., Woodbridge, A., Abraham, A., Saba, S., Korenstein, D., Madden, E., Boscardin, W.J. and Keyhani, S. (2017) 'Financial ties of principal investigators and randomized controlled trial outcomes: cross sectional study', *BMJ*, 356.

Atkins, D., Kilbourne, A.M. and Shulkin, D. (2017) 'Moving from discovery to system-wide change: the role of research in a learning health care system: experience from three decades of health systems research in the Veterans Health Administration', *Annual Review of Public Health*, 38, pp 467–87.

Bickerdike, L., Booth, A., Wilson, P.M., Farley, K. and Wright, K. (2017) 'Social prescribing: less rhetoric and more reality. A systematic review of the evidence', *BMJ Open*, 7, (4), e013384.

Borg, H. (2016) 'The evidence-based transformation of American medicine', *Journal of American Physicians and Surgeons*, 21, pp 70–73.

Brook, R.H. (1994) 'Appropriateness: the next frontier', *BMJ*, 308, pp 218–19.

Burford, B.J., Rehfuess, E., Schünemann, H.J., Akl, E.A., Waters, E., Armstrong, R., Thomson, H., Doyle, J. and Pettman, T. (2012) 'Assessing evidence in public health: the added value of GRADE', *Journal of Public Health*, 34 (4), pp 631–5.

Claxton, K., Sculpher, M., Palmer, S. and Culyer, A.J. (2015) 'Causes for concern: is NICE failing to uphold its responsibilities to all NHS patients?', *Health Economics*, 24, pp 1–7.

Cochrane, A. (1972) *Effectiveness and efficiency: random reflections on health services*, London: Nuffield Provincial Hospitals Trust.

Craig, P., Dieppe, P., Macintyre, S., Michie, S., Nazareth, I. and Petticrew, M. (2008) 'Developing and evaluating complex interventions: the new Medical Research Council guidance', *BMJ*, 337, a1655.

Craig, P., Katikireddi, S.V., Leyland, A. and Popham, F. (2017) 'Natural experiments: an overview of methods, approaches, and contributions to public health intervention research', *Annual Review of Public Health*, 38, pp 39–56.

Cullum, N., Ciliska, D., Haynes, R.B. and Marks, S. (eds) (2008) *Evidence-based nursing: an introduction*, Oxford: Blackwell Publishing.

Davies, H.T.O. and Nutley, S.M. (2000) 'Healthcare: evidence to the fore', in H.T.O. Davies, S.M. Nutley and P.C. Smith (eds), *What works: evidence-based policy and practice in public services*, Bristol: Policy Press.

Department of Health (2011) *Innovation health and wealth: accelerating adoption and diffusion in the NHS*, London: Department of Health.

Drummond, M.F., Sculpher, M.J., Claxton K., Stoddart, G.L. and Torrance, G.W. (2015) *Methods for the economic evaluation of health care programmes*, 4th edn, Oxford University Press.

Elshaug, A.G., Watt, A.M., Mundy, L. and Willis, C.D. (2012) 'Over 150 potentially low-value health care practices: an Australian study', *Medical Journal of Australia*, 197, pp 556–60.

Ettelt, S., Mays, N. and Allen, P. (2014) 'The multiple purposes of policy piloting and their consequences: three examples from national health and social care policy in England', *Journal of Social Policy*, 44, pp. 319-337.

Foy, R., Locock, L., Purdy, S., O'Donnell, C., Gray, N., Doran, T. and Davies, H.T.O. (2013) 'Research shapes policy: but the dynamics are subtle', *Public Money and Management*, 33, (1), pp 9–14

Goddard, M. and Mason, A.R. (2017) 'Integrated care: a pill for all ills?', *International Journal of Health Policy Management*, 6 (1), pp 1–3.

Greenhalgh, T., Howick, J. and Maskrey, N. (2014) 'Evidence based medicine: a movement in crisis?', *BMJ*, 348, g3725.

Harris, C., Green, S., Ramsey, W., Allen, K. and King, R. (2017) 'Sustainability in health care by allocating resources effectively (SHARE) 1: introducing a series of papers reporting an investigation of disinvestment in a local healthcare setting', *BMC Health Services Research*, 17, pp 323.

Haward, R. and Eastwood, A. (2001) 'The background, nature and role of the national cancer guidance', *Clinical Oncology*, 13, pp 322–5.

Hoffmann, T.C., Montori, V.M. and del Mar, C. (2014) 'The connection between evidence-based medicine and shared decision making', *JAMA*, 312, pp 1295–6.

Illich, I. (1974) *Medical nemesis*, London: Calder and Boyars.

Ioannidis, J.P.A. (2016) 'Evidence-based medicine has been hijacked: a report to David Sackett', *Journal of Clinical Epidemiology*, 73, pp 82–6.

Kislov, R., Wilson, P. and Boaden, R. (2017) 'The "dark side" of knowledge brokering', *Journal of Health Services Research Policy*, 22(2), pp 107-112.

Kislov, R., Wilson, P.M., Knowles, S., and Boaden, R. (2018) 'Learning from the emergence of NIHR Collaborations for Leadership in Applied Health Research and Care (CLAHRCs): a systematic review of evaluations', *Implementation Science*, 13, p 111.

Lessard, L., Michalowski, W., Fung-Kee-Fung, M., Jones, L. and Grudniewicz, A. (2017) 'Architectural frameworks: defining the structures for implementing learning health systems', *Implementation Science*, 12, p 78.

Liberati, A. and Vineis, A. (2005) 'Defining a proper background for discussing evidence-based medicine', in R. Ter Meulen, N. Biller-Andorno, C. Lenk, and R. Lie (eds), *Evidence-based practice in medicine and health care: a discussion of the ethical issues*, Berlin and Heidelberg: Springer-Verlag.

Lockett, A., El Enany, N., Currie, G., Oborn, E., Barrett, M., Racko, G., Bishop, S. and Waring, J. (2014) 'A formative evaluation of Collaboration for Leadership in Applied Health Research and Care (CLAHRC): institutional entrepreneurship for service innovation', *Health Services and Delivery Research*, 2, p 31.

McKee, M. (2016) 'The weekend effect: now you see it, now you don't', *BMJ*, 353, p i2750.

Marmot, M.G. (2004) 'Evidence based policy or policy based evidence?', *BMJ*, 328, pp 906–7.

Mays, N., Pope, C. and Popay, J. (2005) 'Systematically reviewing qualitative and quantitative evidence to inform management and policy-making in the health field', *Journal of Health Services Research and Policy*, 10, pp 6–20.

Meacock, R., Anselmi, L., Kristensen, S.R., Doran, T. and Sutton, M. (2016) 'Higher mortality rates amongst emergency patients admitted to hospital at weekends reflect a lower probability of admission', *Journal of Health Services Research and Policy*, 22, pp 12–19.

Mechanic, D. (1991) 'Sources of countervailing power in medicine', *Journal of Health Politics, Policy and Law*, 16, pp 485–98.

Mulrow, C.D. (1987) 'The medical review article: state of the science', *Annals of Internal Medicine*, 106, pp 485–8.

Murthy, L., Shepperd, S., Clarke, M., Garner, S., Lavis, J. and Perrier, L. (2012) 'Interventions to improve the use of systematic reviews in decision-making by health system managers, policymakers and clinicians', *Cochrane Database Systematic Reviews*, 12, p CD009401.

Nilsen, P. (2015) 'Making sense of implementation theories, models and frameworks', *Implementation Science*, 10, p 53.

Oakley, A. (2000) *Experiments in knowing: gender and method in the social sciences*, Cambridge: Polity.

Ogundeji, Y.K., Bland, J.M. and Sheldon, T.A. (2016) 'The effectiveness of payment for performance in health care: a meta-analysis and exploration of variation in outcomes', *Health Policy*, 120, pp 1141–50.

Pawson, R. (2013) *The science of evaluation: a realist manifesto*, London: Sage.

Penfold, R.B. and Zhang, F. (2013) 'Use of interrupted time series analysis in evaluating health care quality improvements', *Academic Pediatrics*, 13, pp S38–S44.

Petticrew, M. (2015) 'Time to rethink the systematic review catechism? Moving from "what works" to "what happens"', *Systematic Reviews*, 4, pp 36.

Popay, J. and Williams, G. (1998) 'Qualitative research and evidence-based healthcare', *Journal of the Royal Society of Medicine*, 91, pp 32–7.

Prasad, V. and Ioannidis, J.P. (2014) 'Evidence-based de-implementation for contradicted, unproven, and aspiring healthcare practices', *Implementation Science*, 9, p 1.

Roland, M. and Guthrie, B. (2016) 'Quality and outcomes framework: what have we learnt?', *BMJ*, 354, p i4060.

Rychetnik, L. (2008) *Concepts of evidence in medicine and public health*, Riga: VDM Verlag.

Rycroft-Malone, J., Burton, C., Wilkinson, J., Harvey, G., McCormack, B., Baker, R., Dopson, S., Graham, I., Staniszewska, S., Thompson, C., Ariss, S., Melville-Richards, L. and Williams, L. (2015) 'Collective action for knowledge mobilisation: a realist evaluation of the Collaborations for Leadership in Applied Health Research and Care', *Health Services and Delivery Research*, 3, p 44.

Rycroft-Malone, J., Seers, K., Titchen, A., Harvey, G., Kitson, A. and Mccormack, B. (2004) 'What counts as evidence in evidence-based practice?', *Journal of Advanced Nursing*, 47, pp 81–90.

Sackett, D.L., Rosenberg, W.M.C., Gray, J.A.M., Haynes, R.B. and Richardson, W.S. (1996) 'Evidence based medicine: what it is and what it isn't', *BMJ*, 312, pp 71–72.

Scarbrough, H., D'andreta, D., Evans, S., Marabelli, M., Newell, S., Powell, J. and Swan, J. (2014) 'Networked innovation in the health sector: comparative qualitative study of the role of Collaborations for Leadership in Applied Health Research and Care in translating research into practice', *Health Services and Delivery Research*, 2, p 13.

Sheldon, T. and Chalmers, I. (1994) The UK Cochrane Centre And the NHS Centre for Reviews and Dissemination: Respective roles within the information systems strategy of the NHS R&D programme, coordination and principles underlying collaboration, *Health Economics*, 3, pp 201–3.

Smith, K. (2013) *Beyond evidence based policy in public health*, Basingstoke: Palgrave Macmillan.

Soper, B., Hinrichs, S., Drabble, S., Yaqub, O., Marjanovic, S., Hanney, S. and Nolte, E. (2015) 'Delivering the aims of the Collaborations for Leadership in Applied Health Research and Care: understanding their strategies and contributions', *Health Services and Delivery Research*, 3, p 25.

Stacey, D., Legare, F., Lewis, K., Barry, M.J., Bennett, C.L., Eden, K.B., Holmes-Rovner, M., Llewellyn-Thomas, H., Lyddiatt, A., Thomson, R. and Trevena, L. (2017) 'Decision aids for people facing health treatment or screening decisions', *Cochrane Database of Systematic Reviews*.

Stetler, C.B., McQueen, L., Demakis, J. and Mittman, B.S. (2008) An organizational framework and strategic implementation for system-level change to enhance research-based practice: QUERI series', *Implementation Science*, 3, p 30.

Walshe, K. and Davies, H.T.O. (2013) 'Health research, development and innovation in England from 1988 to 2013: from research production to knowledge mobilization', *Journal of Health Services Research and Policy*, 18 (Supp 3), pp 1–12.

Watkins, J., Wulaningsih, W., Da Zhou, C. et al (2017) 'Effects of health and social care spending constraints on mortality in England: a time trend analysis', *BMJ Open*, 7:e017722, doi: 10.1136/bmjopen-2017-017722.

Wennberg, J., McPherson, K. and Goodman, D. (2016) 'Small area analysis and the challenge of practice variation', in A. Johnson and T. Stukel (eds), *Medical practice variations*, Boston, MA: Springer US.

Whitty, C.J. (2015) 'What makes an academic paper useful for health policy?', *BMC Medicine*, 13, pp 301.

Wilson, P.M., Farley, K., Bickerdike, L., Booth, A., Chambers, D., Lambert, M., Thompson, C., Turner, R. and Watt, I.S. (2017a) 'Effects of a demand-led evidence briefing service on the uptake and use of research evidence by commissioners of health services: a controlled before-and-after study', *Health Services and Delivery Research*, 5, p 20.

Wilson, P.M., Sales, A., Wensing, M., Aarons, G.A., Flottorp, S., Glidewell, L., Hutchinson, A., Presseau, J., Rogers, A., Sevdalis, N., Squires, J. and Straus, S. (2017b) 'Enhancing the reporting of implementation research', *Implementation Science*, 12, p 13.

5

Using evidence in social care

Deborah Ghate and Rick Hood

Introduction to evidence use in social care

Social care in the UK covers a wide spectrum of caring services provided by a mixed economy of organisations, including central and local government alongside non-governmental organisations, both commercial and not-for-profit. In local authority social services departments, where the legal responsibilities largely reside, social care now generally refers quite narrowly to the services regulated by statute such as out-of-home care for adults and children, including fostering and residential care, child protection services (safeguarding) and in-home care (for example, for elderly or other vulnerable people). However, a broader, non-technical and more holistic understanding would include the wide range of services aimed at promoting the downstream well-being of local communities, including in particular early intervention, prevention and support and development work in the community with children, young people and their families. This chapter uses a wide definition of social care, with examples from children's services including early intervention and prevention, and adult and child social work services.

We begin by outlining some significant features of the social, political and policy contexts in which social care and related services are situated. We note the increasingly interdisciplinary influences on how practice is shaped and how evidence is deployed, including the development of more nuanced understandings and discourses about complexity alongside a drive for clarity and simplification. We describe some case examples of how practice has been using evidence in different settings, drawing out the different perspectives that underpin these efforts. We also highlight recent institutional approaches to building an infrastructure for evidence use in social care policy and practice in the UK. We conclude with reflections on how the field could be strengthened now and for the future.

Three key contextual challenges face social care: the underfunded and undervalued nature of the sector; perennial complexity and turbulence; and the challenges of an increasingly managerial culture. First, social care has always been considered a poor relation to the better-funded, higher-status NHS in the UK (Thane, 2009; Glendinning, 2012). Training and qualifications to become a social care professional have long been regarded as less demanding relative to those required to practise medicine, for example. Caring has been, by tradition – and continues to be seen as – low-status work, with social care jobs disproportionately occupied by lesser-educated, lower-paid, female and immigrant workers (National Audit Office, 2018). It is also work with high levels of personal risk: when something goes wrong, political and public hostility both to social work as a profession and to social-work staff as individuals can reach extreme levels (Jones, 2014). Yet, while medical staff and some other professions have powerful lobbying associations, the political leverage of the social care workforce is minimal.

Second, social care – like other fields of public service – exists within a turbulent environment that has been described as being characterised by volatility, uncertainty, complexity and ambiguity (or VUCA, in military vocabulary; Ghate et al, 2013). For years there has been talk of a 'burning platform' in local authorities; diminishing resources, due to policies of public austerity, and spiralling demand are placing heavy pressure on local social care budgets (All Party Parliamentary Group for Children, 2017). Budgetary constraint means less plentiful or less comprehensive service provision, and a workforce that feels over-burdened, exploited and demoralised (National Audit Office, 2018; Webb and Bywaters, 2018). The sense of turbulence has been exacerbated by significant staff turnover and shortages, and widely reported scandals and lapses in basic quality of care.

A third challenge for social care is the managerial culture of public administration (Seddon, 2008) and the accompanying preoccupation with performance measures (Hood, 2018). Social care (in line with other public services) has become subject to a regime of process measurement and performance targets and indicators: how many cases processed/resolved/unresolved within what time-scale; how many forms completed; how many meetings held within what period; and so on. Social workers have found themselves increasingly diverted from direct work with clients in favour of office-based work, creating a climate of dissatisfaction. An influential government-commissioned report (Munro, 2011) noted this and recommended reform, including a reaffirmation of the importance of professional judgement and autonomy in social work practice. What was needed, it was suggested, was a focus not on 'doing things right', which might equate to 'doing the wrong things righter', but rather an emphasis on 'doing the right thing'. These concerns may have been exacerbated by well-intentioned moves to 'outcomes-based' performance frameworks, which were introduced to improve the quality and effectiveness of children's services: including, in England and Wales, *Every Child Matters* (HM Treasury, 2003) and the *Integrated Children's System* (DCSF, 2007), and, in Scotland, *Getting it Right for Every Child* (Scottish Government, 2008). Some of these frameworks, while outcomes based, have been criticised for also introducing onerous process reporting requirements.

All the above features of the social care landscape have implications for evidence and evidence use in the sector. Moreover, there have also been substantial fluctuations in the funding and prominence given by central government to social care innovation and research since the early 1990s. Children's services, for example, particularly around care and early intervention, enjoyed a period in the limelight and some generosity of funding during the years of New Labour (1997–2010). The Labour administration made a point of emphasising its credentials regarding evidence-based policy (Wells, 2007; and see Chapter Thirteen), and there was increased spending on policy research and innovation, particularly in children's services.

New Labour was criticised for paying lip-service to the idea of evidence-based policy in social care, often commissioning and using research selectively to buttress apparently predetermined decisions and making 'policy-based evidence' rather than evidence-based policy (Hammersley, 2005; Crossley, 2015). However, a number of coherent and influential programmes of research were commissioned during the New Labour years, such as the national evaluation of Sure Start (see below). Think-tanks also came to prominence during this period, including, for example, the Institute for Public Policy Research and Demos, and these too urged government and localities to show greater respect for, and use of, evidence. There was at the same time a significant political push towards diversification in providers of research on care, with the voluntary, social enterprise and commercial sectors all jostling with the academy to contribute.

There have also been some notable, proactive (if generally top-down) approaches to generating and disseminating evidence to improve services within the social care field, dating from before the original *What works?* book was published (Davies et al, 2000) and continuing in the intervening period. For example, at the Departments of Health and then Education (the central government departments with responsibility for children's social services over this period) a number of policy-focused, synthesised digests of knowledge (known as *Messages from Research*) were produced, based on a distillation of specific messages drawn from specially commissioned and carefully integrated suites of empirical research on existing services (for example, HMSO, 1995; Quinton, 2004; Davies and Ward, 2012; Thomas, 2013). Some of these were highly influential on subsequent practice and policy.

From the late 1990s until the end of the then Labour administration in 2010, major funding streams were provided from central government to local areas. These funds were earmarked for the design, delivery and evaluation of 'promising', innovative and large-scale (programmatic) preventive approaches to community-based services for families. These approaches included flagship programmes such as Sure Start (a huge national initiative, beginning with a budget of £452 million in 1999 for its first three years alone, and inspired by the US Head Start programme), the Children's Fund and On Track (also inspired by a US programme). Although these programmes were mostly derived from overseas experience, they were distinctively 'home grown' in their design. Some concerns were raised about this design process; one account described the programmes as 'designed, by and large, on the basis of informed guesswork and expert hunches, enriched by some evidence and driven by political and other imperatives' (Coote et al, 2004, p 47). Most significantly for the growth of the UK evidence industry, each programme was accompanied by a substantial national (and centralised) research budget, as well as a devolved budget for local evaluation.

From 2010 onwards, however, national resources were much less plentiful and the focus of commissioning in relation to evidence use shifted to less expensive forms of literature synthesis and secondary analysis and away from expensive programmes of indigenous empirical research. Possibly also influenced by a degree of general disappointment in the results of the national preventive programmes noted above, commissioners in government became more interested in the learning from successful international preventive and therapeutic intervention models, and in 'translational' work to distil key messages applicable to the sector at home that might eventually enable their roll-out and scaling up in the UK. The What Works Centres (WWCs) and the focus on so-called 'evidence-based programmes' (EBPs) can to some extent be viewed as an outgrowth of this trend (see later in this chapter).

Against this dynamic backdrop we can now begin to consider the nature of evidence (and its contestation) in social care, before we move on to examine the production and synthesis of that evidence and strategies to encourage its use.

The nature of evidence in social care

The place of evidence in social care in the UK links to changes in the global 'evidence landscape' and the nature of intellectual debate on human services more generally. In this section we highlight some key trends and developments nationally and internationally that have influenced how evidence is conceptualised and operationalised in social care in the UK.

As in other fields, like education and criminal justice (see Chapters Seven and Six), the construct of evidence and what currently 'counts' as useful and credible evidence for social care has been shaped over the last two or three decades or so by the pursuit of scientific method as the basis for identifying and designing effective services (see Section Three of this book). Globally, we have seen the emergence of intervention and prevention science in social care, incorporating evidence from human development including the fields of neuroscience, genetics and forensic psychiatry. Within these fields, there is often a marked division of expertise between those establishing the evidence base (seen as a scientific activity often carried out by independent researchers) and those delivering services (seen as a pragmatic activity often carried out by practitioners and managers).

The discourses of prevention and intervention science, in particular, have been dominated by the idea that effectiveness can be optimised if only services are designed and delivered according to a particular set of scientific principles, which we summarise in Box 5.1 based on our reading of a wide literature on effective social programmes over the past 20 years or so. The scientific approach privileges quantifiable data above other forms of evidence, tending to result in a narrow focus on what can be measured (Campbell, 1979).

Another related feature of the recent evidence landscape in social care and prevention has been the development of the ideal of Evidence Based Programmes (Dick et al, 2016). Firmly coupled to the pursuit of scientific method, this term is often used to describe a small number of 'model' programmes of intervention approved by (mainly American) clearing houses with reference to the amount of experimental (RCT) evidence in support of their effectiveness. These programmes have been promoted as examples of using science to address the big social problems of the day (poor parenting, youth marginalisation and antisocial behaviour, violence prevention, child abuse and neglect, crime and mental health problems, community exclusion and so on). Many of the programmes have been promoted alongside cost–benefit analyses of the likely future public savings per head of population treated (for example, Drake et al, 2009).

Box 5.1: Scientific principles for intervention design, implementation and assessment

The following 'core principles' can be discerned from an examination of the debate and discourse surrounding the design and testing of interventions in social care, especially from those contributions that approach the issues from a positivistic science perspective.

1 The design of services or interventions (that is, content, curriculum) should be based on theory informed by knowledge about root causes and past evidence of effective solutions.
2 A predetermined theory of change (a summative articulation of the theory that also sets out an expected causal pathway and makes clear the logical connections between the intervention activities and the outcome) is vital to help to guide stakeholders in delivery and evaluation.
3 A degree of linearity between cause and effect can be modelled; and therefore, if the service is well designed and well delivered, desired outcomes should logically follow.
4 Practitioners on the ground must deliver the intervention 'as designed', observing standards of treatment and adherence to the curriculum as laid down by the developers (known as fidelity).
5 Evaluation using the most robust methods of quantification available (that is, RCTs) is the most desirable way to assess outcomes. Moreover, if an RCT returns neutral or even negative results, and if Principle 3 (above) is satisfied, this means that the intervention should be discontinued.
6 If the RCT returns positive results, replication in other settings should be possible, with minimal adaption to context (and scaling up becomes almost a moral imperative).
7 Interventions in this model should ideally follow a developmental pathway through theory-based design, testing for so-called efficacy in 'ideal' settings (thus testing internal validity or proof of concept), and finally testing for so-called effectiveness in wider, more varied community settings (thus testing for external validity).

Local authorities across the UK have been funded and actively encouraged by national government to try out these interventions and to evaluate their performance, often with considerable fanfare and excitement about being at the cutting edge of science-into-practice. Programmes have typically had firm curricula to which the delivering agencies and practitioners are contractually obliged to adhere; programme developers operate licensed delivery models, supported by manuals and detailed guidance. Programme developers more or less offer firm promises of guaranteed outcomes. Indeed, such has been the degree of confidence in the probability of programme success that financial investment vehicles have been designed around them: such as 'social impact bonds', where socially motivated individuals and organisations invest money in the services in return for the equivalent of dividend payments if pre-specified results are achieved (Edmiston and Nicholl, 2017; Albertson et al, 2018). EBPs have therefore tended to be highly attractive both to funders and to providers, seeming to promise certain results and substantial returns on investment.

The degree of standardisation of these programmes made them easier to evaluate using experimental methods. Although not remotely comparable with the level of funding for RCTs in health, alongside the introduction of EBPs came funding for the first wide-scale use of social care trials in the UK (Davies and Ward, 2012; Ghate, 2015). This was particularly from 2010, when the Conservative–Liberal Democrat coalition government appeared to be more persuaded by the promise of experimental methods than were prior administrations. Several major and some more minor RCTs were commissioned in the social care field in the period 2010 to 2017 (for example, Fonagy et al, 2018; Cottrell et al, 2018; Forrester et al, 2018; Humayun et al, 2017; Robling et al, 2015; Little et al, 2012; Biehal et al, 2010). Many of these UK studies have found that the evidence-based innovations do not confer measurable advantages over case management as usual. Thus, very few of the programmes have reliably delivered on their promises, some failing at considerable scale. There are heated debates on which of a complex range of factors might account for this, but, given the costs, it may be that the wave of enthusiasm for imported EBPs and their expensive research infrastructure has peaked for the time being (Ghate, 2018).

Alongside debate about the use of scientific methods and imported EBPs in social care, there continues to be an active stream of more locally situated evidence generation. In local social services many other factors, apart from the scientific quality of evidence, influence what is commissioned. An absence of experimental evidence has not necessarily been a hindrance to the implementation of a range of evidence-*informed* (if not evidence-*based*) approaches. For example, the evaluation of Signs of Safety (Box 5.2), a model of child protection casework that is being adopted in a range of jurisdictions, has largely continued the tradition of 'client opinion studies, pre-test-post-test or post-test only designs' (MacDonald, 2000, p 120). Furthermore, social care has a number of localised and network-based models of knowledge production, dissemination and use (such as Making Research Count and Research in Practice) that promote a diverse range of types of evidence aligned to local learning needs.

This section has considered the rise of evidence-based social care as an opportunity and a challenge for the field. It has looked at some of the implications of a focus on measurement in a complex field of service delivery with hard-to-measure outcomes. It has noted a preoccupation with innovative programmes and specific packages of practices (particularly, named or branded interventions or programmes). These have tended to be prioritised over improving the standards of basic practice as usual (Davies and Ward, 2012). This has led commentators to conclude that, while rigour has an important role to play, it must be balanced by considerable flexibility in a field like social care (Ghate, 2015). The next section will consider another development in the field: the shift in emphasis from research production to research synthesis.

Production and synthesis of research-based knowledge for social care

The review and synthesis of existing international research for social care has become a major area of funding in the UK since the late 2000s. This has been prioritised (with some notable exceptions) over the generation of new empirical evidence via primary research. There has been, both nationally and globally, a substantial growth in the infrastructure for sifting and synthesising research-based knowledge in social care and related fields. The infrastructure comprises research groups within existing institutions, independent research groups and specialised organisations occupying a space somewhere between the scholarly production of reviews and the interface between evidence and policy (with the latter sometimes being described as evidence intermediaries). Originally, synthesis work was mainly conducted in academic and independent research centres, before moving out to intermediary organisations such as the Social Care Institute for Excellence (SCIE). From 2013 the UK WWCs have been a centrepiece of this growth in review and synthesis capacity (see Chapter Thirteen). A new WWC for Children's Social Care was commissioned in 2017.

Box 5.2: The Signs of Safety approach to child protection

Background. Signs of Safety is an approach to child protection casework, originally developed in Western Australia in the 1990s (Turnell and Edwards, 1999) and adopted in many other countries. Its principles are based on solution-focused brief therapy (Woods et al, 2011) and are designed to create a general framework rather than a prescriptive methodology for practice.

Key features. Signs of Safety emphasises partnership working, critical thinking and a grounding in everyday practice. Core elements include understanding the perspective of every family member, searching for exceptions to maltreatment, identifying strengths and resources, focusing on goals, measuring progress through the use of scaling questions and assessing willingness, capacity and confidence (Bunn, 2013).

Evidence. The literature on Signs of Safety includes a series of evaluations, undertaken mainly in Australia, the US and the UK (Skrypek et al, 2012; Bunn, 2013; Idzelis Rothe et al, 2013; Baginsky et al, 2017). Most of these studies have been observational and interpretative, employing a cross-sectional or longitudinal design. Findings suggest that the approach is consistently rated positively by practitioners and service users and leads to improvements in aspects of casework and safety planning that correspond to the model's theory of change (see Baginsky et al, 2017). The literature on Signs of Safety also has the merits of discussing contextual factors that affect implementation, such as reorganisations and staff changes (Baginsky et al, 2017).

Implementation. Implementation generally involves a series of training sessions for front-line practitioners and managers, along with additional input on supervisory and organisational processes. Only licensed trainers and consultants are able to undertake this work, and so implementation will generally involve commissioning services from the private consultancy that owns the Signs of Safety trademark. In England, 10 pilot local authorities were provided with government funding through the Children's Social Care Innovation Programme to implement the programme in their child protection services (Baginsky et al, 2017). This combination of public funding and private enterprise is increasingly common in the sector, reflecting the growing diversity and marketisation of social care provision (Jones, 2015).

WWCs are to some extent modelled on US Clearing Houses (see Chapter Seventeen), although there is variability in form, structure, focus and ways of working across the four nations, reflecting the differing priorities of devolved governments and the fact that some centres (such as NICE) have become WWCs after their initial establishment as something else (see Chapter Thirteen). WWCs are centrally funded bodies set up in specific practice areas to focus on reviewing high-quality evidence and sharing it with practitioners. The UK WWCs' activities (conferences, meetings and so on) and their online resources (websites, interactive lists of interventions and so on) have added substantially to the accessibility of certain kinds of research evidence. Many of the centres promote the principle of evidence and accountability for outcomes as an integral duty of care in the provision of effective services, and they have set out to promote a discourse at local and national levels about how evidence may be woven into decision making and action. These centres have also supported a growth in evaluation activity as a routine part of practice development, although they themselves do not fund it. In emphasising the importance of outcomes, WWCs contribute to reasserting the importance of 'value for service users', which ought to lie at the heart of professional, organisational and political debates about service development.

However, the typical role of clearing houses is mostly to repackage or translate evidence into usable products and formats rather than to move that evidence more actively into practice (Breckon and Mulgan, 2018). This model has distinct limitations. Implementation science literature, for example, shows us that while dissemination and repackaging can increase knowledge it does not usually and by itself tend to change practitioner behaviour (Joyce and Showers, 2002). For this, other, more active and interactive methods to encourage evidence use are required (Meyers et al, 2012). What these active methods might look like in social care is the focus of the next section.

Encouraging and enabling evidence use in social care

The structure of social care, funded through local budgets and locally delivered, gives evidence use a distinctively local flavour in the UK. This has allowed for the emergence of a wide local variety of approaches to services and to evidence. However, alongside this, governments in the four UK nations have also played a major role in shaping how and when evidence is used in social care policy and practice, and what kind of evidence is seen as most important at the local level.

Beyond a central emphasis on evidence review and dissemination, via the clearing-house model, there are only a few organisations in the UK that have moved into the space of actively encouraging and enabling evidence use in social care. There has been much less funding for more bottom-up approaches to encouraging evidence use, as opposed to top-down approaches (see Chapter Three). One example of a largely bottom-up approach is Research in Practice (RIP; Box 5.3), which for many years not only has disseminated research knowledge relevant to improving social work for adults and children, but also has been working locally to encourage the use of this research (while at the same time valuing and drawing on local data and experience, as well as professional knowledge). Sometimes this has been achieved through the co-creation of change projects with partner organisations. RIP has successfully used a subscription model to provide a sustainable funding format for their work on research use (see Box 5.3). SCIE has similarly supported a wider notion of what counts as relevant knowledge in social care (Pawson et al, 2003); and it has also been active in supporting the co-production of knowledge and evidence with service providers and service users (see Chapters Eleven and Twelve).

Despite these local initiatives, active support for organisational change has largely been left to private sector consultancies (whose focus is often on strategy and the management of processes rather than on front-line practice change) and some small non-profit intermediary organisations. There has been some additional support for specific programme-related changes in front-line practice, for example, where EBPs such as multi systemic therapy and multi-treatment foster care have been introduced. This assistance has usually been provided by the implementation support teams associated with the different EBPs.

In the US, and anywhere that implementation science-led approaches are gaining traction, attention is being paid to how to build more generalist implementation teams that can provide hands-on support for practitioners to improve their daily practice in evidence-informed ways (for example, Metz et al, 2017). The emphasis here is on practice in a wide sense, not just on the specific practices associated with a particular brand of intervention. This more generalist approach emphasises the importance of multidisciplinary support teams working alongside service providers and their staff in their daily settings. It is argued that these teams need to be well versed in implementation and improvement science as well as being familiar with the details of the intervention or front-line practice in question. People within these teams are also said to need expertise in data and information management, so that decision making is data informed (often considered as a key weakness

Box 5.3: Research in Practice (RIP)

Since 1996, Research in Practice (RIP) has worked to bridge the gaps between research, practice and service users' lived experiences. The goal of the organisation is to improve practice and, ultimately, outcomes for children and families. RIP brings together researcher and practitioner expertise to build capacity in the social care sector to deliver evidence-informed practice. RIP achieves this aim through a variety of activities, the production of knowledge resources and tailored support. RIP is funded via a subscription model, where organisations pay to become members and, as members, access resources, professional development and tailored support. Priority topics for events and resources are identified in consultation with the members. Tailored support to member organisations might take the form of workshops, help with strategy development, research syntheses and evaluations. There is a sister organisation to support evidence use in adult social care: RIPfA (Research in Practice for Adults).

in social care organisations). The personnel involved in these teams would thus straddle the worlds of research and practice. They offer the promise of being able to help service providers to use evidence on what works by making thoughtful adaptations for context, when necessary, without undermining the basic components of effectiveness (Ghate, 2015).

The UK has yet to establish such generalist implementation teams at scale, although, as the model crystallises elsewhere and as we learn more about the extent to which it improves outcomes and cost-effectiveness, we can hope to see interest develop. The underpinning philosophy for these teams resonates with the idea of 'consultant social workers' suggested by Munro (2011) and others. The latter are senior and experienced practitioners able to mentor and coach less experienced colleagues and (in multidisciplinary teams) to make cross-system connections with professionals in other areas. Where the generalist implementation team model is distinctive is in that the expertise of these teams is based in implementation and improvement science as well as in established practice.

Another development in approaches to encouraging and enabling research use has been a growing interest in the scope for understanding improvement and learning in social care from a systems perspective. A brief account of the ideas and implications of systems thinking is provided in Box 5.4. The notion of social care as a complex adaptive system is likely to be fundamental to our ability to generate useful

Box 5.4: Understanding social care from a complex adaptive systems perspective

The wide literature on systems thinking and complexity, and in particular the literature on socio-technical systems design (STSD) (for example, Ashby, 1956; Trist, 1981), that draws strongly on complexity science and systems thinking, can support an understanding of social care and the role of evidence in supporting improvement. The underlying premise of STSD is that most work in advanced societies involves a complex interaction between people, technology and other factors in the environment. Innovations in social care do not stand alone, but are innovations that are being introduced into a system (Ghate, 2015). A complex adaptive or responsive system is defined by its properties of emergence and, therefore, unpredictability (Mowles, 2014). It is also self-organising (Meadows, 1999, 2008), learning from experience and adapting its behaviours accordingly in order to survive. It is affected by the individual actors within the system and their ability to exercise choice and respond to the actions of others (Stacey, 2006).

evidence to tackle complex problems in the future. There are parallels here with Best and Holmes's (2010) third generation of knowledge-into-practice 'systems thinking' (see Chapter Twelve), and connections into a wide interdisciplinary literature on social change.

Despite the promise of systems thinking for surfacing and working with the complexity of social care, there have been relatively few illustrations of these ideas being used to encourage and enable evidence use. However, one example is provided by the Vanguard Method, which uses systems thinking to inform improvement in services (Box 5.5). Rather than seeking to implement tried and tested evidence-based interventions, this approach focuses on the needs of the local system. It taps into local knowledge and draws together learning to support local, systems-focused solutions. The shift to understanding social care as a complex adaptive system has potentially significant implications for the future development of the field, which will be discussed as part of the final section of this chapter.

Box 5.5: The Vanguard Method (tVM)

Background. The Vanguard Method (tVM) is an approach to organisational systems redesign, developed by John Seddon (2003; 2008) and delivered by Vanguard Consulting. It draws on business management ideas and is closely related to the principles of socio-technical systems design (STSD). Since 2010 tVM has been applied in both child and adult social care.

Key features. The theory behind the approach is critical of 'industrial' approaches to delivering services, which tend to involve a high degree of standardisation and specification of discrete activities and tasks. With this approach, managers are encouraged to move away from trying to control what their workers do and focus instead on developing 'requisite variety' in the system. To begin with, this means understanding demand from the end-user's perspective and studying how the current design meets that demand. Managers then use this knowledge to redesign their system against demand, using measures that are derived from overall purpose rather than tasks and processes. Often the result is a reduction in the number of unnecessary steps, assessments and handovers that service users have to go through before they get a service, which in turn reduces costs in the system as a whole.

Evidence. Evaluation of tVM presents some difficulties, since it is a methodology for redesign rather than an intervention or model of provision in its own right. However, it does have the advantage of incorporating empirical measures into the check-and-redesign process, which lends itself to case studies and action research. In children's social care, a study by Gibson and O'Donovan (2014) found that redesign using tVM led to large reductions in failure demand and 'end-to-end times' for resolving family problems. The Vanguard approach currently lacks independent evaluation or comparative longitudinal study.

Implementation. tVM is an interesting case of implementation because the codification of method is mainly geared towards discovering what it is that should be implemented. Whereas conventional evidence-based approaches suggest that a pre-specified set of problems should be matched to a tried-and-tested solution, tVM highlights the contingent nature of problems and solutions alike.

Reflections and conclusions

A key theme in the social care chapter in the original *What Works* book (MacDonald, 2000) was the tendency of social care – and social work as a profession within social care – to be in some respects resistant to the 'evidence-based' paradigm inherited from the medical sciences. In part, this was described as arising from lack of agreement about what constitutes evidence and, in particular, hostility to the idea that certain types of data (especially quantitative data) were inherently more valuable than others. Yet, that resistance also indicated a more fundamental critique of the underpinning assumptions of the 'evidence-based' paradigm – that is, that 'science' (separated from practice and generated by external and independent professionals) could be a better or more reliable way of knowing than practice wisdom (the accumulated experience and know-how of those doing the work on the front line) and locally generated research.

The evidence landscape for social care services in the UK continues to be challenging: social care services are widely considered to be underfunded, and there is only limited funding available for the collation of fresh evidence on the effectiveness of those services. The turbulence of social care has often made it quite difficult to research, especially at large scale or by using methods that require standardisation. However, since the late 1990s resistance to the idea of evidence-informed practice has become less pronounced and there have been some investments in infrastructure to support such practice. There has also been increasing cross-disciplinary elaboration of the knowledge and evidence base for social care (and even more so for early intervention). This has been gleaned using a wide variety of sources, approaches and methods.

There have been largely top-down attempts to introduce the kinds of evidence-based interventions that would not look unfamiliar to a clinical scientist. This includes policy interest in rolling out evidence-based programmes and their accompanying research infrastructure. Alongside this, there has been a proliferation of groups and organisations whose focus is to identify and promote 'what works' in social intervention. Yet, perhaps because of the inherent limitations of the 'science-based' rather than 'complexity-based' perspective, the pace towards widespread adoption of practices for which there is strong evidential support remains slow and is confined largely to pockets of innovation that do not achieve sustainable scale-up. This is true internationally as well as in the UK (for example, Mitchell, 2011). There has been disappointment that the introduction of formally defined evidence-based interventions in social care has so far produced few results that inspire confidence in their long-term sustainability. This is despite a considerable investment of funds, local effort and political energy in supporting the implementation of these interventions. It has been acknowledged that this 'crisis of replication' is not unique to social care (Grant and Hood, 2017; and see also Chapter Ten).

There is, therefore, a need to consider more carefully the complexity of services and of the contexts in which they operate, and then to work to ensure that the methods used to gather and use evidence are more sensitive to that context. The world of social care is not simple, and any simple answers to complex questions are likely to be simplistic. Complexity science, systems thinking and some more recent developments in the implementation and improvement sciences provide some clues as to how to raise the game in this regard (Cooke and Tönurist, 2016).

In order to mobilise evidence *in practice* (in contrast to simply moving evidence *into practice*), there is a need for more active approaches to supporting social care organisations and practitioners: enabling them to draw on, adapt and contribute to knowledge about best practices in their daily work (not just telling them 'what works'). Active implementation and improvement support structures are needed that intellectually and physically mobilise knowledge both within and into practice settings. This will mean some new investment in developing a cadre of professionals with sufficient expertise to support evidence use in social care. These professionals will require a new combination of skills and expertise, knowledge of both evidence and practice and an ability to apply that knowledge in environments characterised by volatility, uncertainty, complexity and ambiguity. It also perhaps means placing less emphasis on innovation (and the introduction of new evidence-based programmes) and more on improving basic practice and 'business as usual' in the work of social care. Currently, however, there are only a few organisations in the UK that begin to show what can be done to promote an evidence-informed agenda at a local level. Moving forward, social care needs more integrative approaches that understand and respond to complexity and seek to improve existing practice alongside providing support for innovation.

References

Albertson, K., Fox, C. O'Leary, C. and Painter, G. with Bailey, K. and Labarbera, J. (2018) *Payment by results and social impact bonds: outcome-based payment schemes in the UK and US*, Bristol: Policy Press.

All Party Parliamentary Group for Children (2017) *No good options: report of the inquiry into children's social care in England, March 2017*, London: NCB, https://www.ncb.org.uk/sites/default/files/uploads/No%20Good%20Options%20Report%20final.pdf.

Ashby, W.R. (1956) *An introduction to cybernetics*, London: Chapman and Hall.

Baginsky, M., Moriarty, J., Manthorpe, J., Beecham, J. and Hickman, B. (2017) 'Evaluation of signs of safety in 10 pilots', London: Department for Education.

Best, A. and Holmes, B. (2010) 'Systems thinking, knowledge and action: towards better models and methods', *Evidence and Policy*, 6 (2), pp 145–59.

Biehal N., Dixon J., Parry E., Sinclair I., Green J., Roberts C., Kay C., Rothwell, J., Kapadia K., and Roby, A. (2010) *The Care Placements Evaluation (CaPE) Evaluation of Multidimensional Treatment Foster Care for Adolescents (MTFC-A)*, London: Department for Education DfE RR, p 194.

Breckon, J. and Mulgan, G. (2018) Blog for the Alliance for Useful Evidence, 19 January, https://www.alliance4usefulevidence.org/celebrating-five-years-of-the-uk-what-works-centres/.

Bunn, A. (2013) 'Signs of Safety in England, an NSPCC commissioned report on the Signs of Safety model in child protection', London: NSPCC.

Campbell, D.T. (1979) 'Assessing the impact of planned social change', *Evaluation and Program Planning*, 2, pp 67–90.

Cooke, J.W. and Tönurist, P. (2016) 'From transactional to strategic: systems approaches to public service challenges', OECD/Observatory of Public Sector Innovation, https://www.oecd.org/media/oecdorg/satellitesites/opsi/contents/images/h2020_systemsthinking-fin.pdf.

Coote, A., Allen, J., and Woodhead, D. (2004). *Finding out what works. Building knowledge about complex, community-based initiatives*, London: Kings Fund.

Cottrell, D.J., Wright-Hughes, A., Collinson, M., Boston, P., Eisler, I., Fortune, S., Graham, E.H., Green, J., House, A.O., Kerfoot, M., Owens, D.W., Saloniki, E.C., Simic, M., Lambert, F., Rothwell, J., Tubeuf S., and Farrin, A.J. (2018) 'Effectiveness of systemic family therapy versus treatment as usual for young people after self-harm: a pragmatic, phase 3, multicentre, randomised controlled trial', *Lancet Psychiatry*, 5 (3), pp 203–16.

Crossley, S. (2015) 'The Troubled Families Programme: the perfect social policy?', Centre for Crime and Justice Briefing 13, November, https://www.crimeandjustice.org.uk/sites/crimeandjustice.org.uk/files/The%20Troubled%20Families%20Programme%2C%20Nov%202015.pdf.

Davies, H., Nutley, S. and Smith, P. (2000) *What works? Evidence-based policy and practice in public services*, Bristol: Policy Press.

Davies, C. and Ward, H. (2012) *Safeguarding children across services: messages from research*, London: Jessica Kingsley Publishers.

DCSF (Department for Children, Schools and Families) (2007) *The Integrated Children's System*, http://webarchive.nationalarchives.gov.uk/20100520112419/http://www.dcsf.gov.uk/everychildmatters/safeguardingandsocialcare/integratedchildrenssystem/abouttheintegratedchildrenssystem/about/.

Dick, A.J., Rich, W. and Waters, T. (2016) *Prison vocational education policy in the United States: a critical perspective on evidence-based reform*, New York: Palgrave Macmillan.

Drake, E.K., Aos, S. and Miller, M.G. (2009) 'Evidence-based public policy options to reduce crime and criminal justice costs: implications in Washington State', *Victims and Offenders*, 4, pp 170–196, doi: 10.1080/15564880802612615.

Edmiston, D. and Nicholl, A. (2017) 'Social impact bonds: the role of private capital in outcome-based commissioning', *Journal of Social Policy*, doi: 10.1017/S0047279417000125.

Fonagy, P., Butler, S., Cottrell, D., Scott, S., Pilling, S., Eisler, I., Fuggle, P., Kraam, A., Byford, S., Wason, J., Ellison, R., Simes, E., Ganguli, P., Allison, E., and Goodyer, I. (2018) 'Multisystemic therapy versus management as usual in the treatment of adolescent antisocial behaviour (START): a pragmatic, randomised controlled, superiority trial', *Lancet Psychiatry*, 5(2), pp 119–133.

Forrester, D., Westlake, D., Killian, M., Antonopoulou, V., McCann, M., Thurnham, A., Thomas, R., Waits, C., Whittaker, C. and Hutchison, D. (2018) 'A randomised controlled trial of training in Motivational Interviewing for children protection', *Children and Youth Services Review*, 88, pp 180–190.

Ghate, D. (2015) 'From programs to systems: deploying implementation science and practice for sustained real-world effectiveness in services for children and families', *Journal of Clinical Child and Adolescent Psychology*, 45 (6), doi: 10.1080/15374416.2015.1077449.

Ghate, D. (2018) 'Developing theories of change for social programmes: Co-producing evidence-supported quality improvement', *Palgrave Communications*, 4(90), https://www.nature.com/articles/s41599-018-0139-z

Ghate, D., Lewis, J. and Welbourn, D. (2013) *Systems leadership: exceptional leadership for exceptional times*, Nottingham: The Staff College, http://thestaffcollege.uk/wp-content/uploads/VSC_Synthesis_complete.pdf (accessed 21 March 2018).

Glendinning, C. (2012) 'Home care in England: markets in the context of under-funding', *Health and Social Care in the Community*, 20 (3), pp 292–9.

Grant, R. and Hood, R. (2017) 'Complex systems, explanation and policy: implications of the crisis of replication for public health research', *Critical Public Health*, 27(5), pp 525–532.

Hammersley, M. (2005) 'Is the evidence-based practice movement doing more harm than good? Reflections on Iain Chalmers' case for research-based policy making and practice', *Evidence and Policy*, 1 (1), pp 85–100.

HMSO (1995) *Child protection: messages from research*. London: HMSO.

HM Treasury (2003) *Every Child Matters*, https://www.gov.uk/government/publications/every-child-matters.

Humayun, S., Herlitz, L., Chesnokov, M., Doolan, M., Landau, S., and Scott, S. (2017) 'Randomised controlled trial of Functional Family Therapy for offending and antisocial behaviour in UK youth', *Journal of Child Psychology and Psychiatry*, 58 (9), pp 1023–32.

Idzelis Rothe, M., Nelson-Dusek, S. and Skrypek, M. (2013) 'Innovations in child protection services in Minnesota – research chronicle of Carver and Olmsted Counties', St Paul, MN: Wilder Research.

Jones, R. (2014) *The story of Baby P: setting the record straight*, Bristol: Policy Press.

Joyce, B. and Showers, B. (2002) *Student achievement through staff development*, 3rd edn, Alexandria, VA: Association for Supervision and Curriculum Development.

Little, M., Berry, V., Morpeth, L., Blower, S., Axford, N., Taylor, R., Bywater, T., Lehtonon, M., and Tobin, K. (2012) 'The impact of three evidence-based programmes delivered in public systems in Birmingham UK', *International Journal of Conflict and Violence*, 6 (2), pp 260–272.

MacDonald, G. (2000) 'Social care: Rhetoric and reality', in H. Davies, S. Nutley and P. Smith (eds), *What works? Evidence-based policy and practice in public services*, Bristol: Policy Press, pp 117-140.

Meadows, D.H. (1999) 'Leverage points – places to intervene in a system', The Sustainability Institute, https://groups.nceas.ucsb.edu/sustainability-science/2010%20weekly-sessions/session-112013–11.22.2010-managing-for-sustainability-speaker-pamela-matson/supplemental-readings-from-the-reader/Meadows.%201999%20Leverage_Points.pdf/view.

Meadows, D. (2008) *Thinking in systems – a primer*, White River Junction, Vermont: Chelsea Green.

Metz, A., Louison, L., Ward, C., Burke, K. et al (2017) *Global implementation specialist practice profile: skills and competencies for implementation practitioners*, http://www.effectiveservices.org/downloads/Implementation_specialist_practice_profile.pdf.

Meyers, D.C., Durlak, J.A. and Wandesman, A. (2012) 'The Quality Implementation Framework: a synthesis of critical steps in the implementation process', *American Journal of Community Psychology*, doi: 10.1007/s10464–012–9522-x.

Mitchell, P.F. (2011) 'Evidence-based practice in real world services for young people with complex needs: new opportunities suggested by recent implementation science', *Children and Youth Services Review*, 33, pp 207–16, http://www.sciencedirect.com/science/article/pii/S0190740910003373.

Mowles, C. (2014) 'Complex, but not quite complex enough: the turn to complexity sciences in evaluation scholarship', *Evaluation*, 20 (2), pp 160–75.

Munro, E. (2011) *The Munro Review of child protection – final report: a child-centred system*, London: Department for Education.

National Audit Office (2018) *The adult social care workforce in England: report by the Comptroller and Auditor General*, House of Commons, 5 February, https://www.nao.org.uk/wp-content/uploads/2018/02/The-adult-social-care-workforce-in-England.pdf.

Pawson, R., Boaz, A., Grayson, L., Long, L. and Barnes, C. (2003) *Types and quality of knowledge in social care*, Bristol: Social Care Institute for Excellence/Policy Press, http://www.scie.org.uk/publications/knowledgereviews/kr03.pdf.

Quinton, D. (2004) *Supporting parents: message from research*, London: Jessica Kingsley Publishers.

Robling, M., Bekkers, M.J., Bell, K., Butler, C.C. and others (2015) 'Effectiveness of a nurse-led intensive home-visitation programme for first-time teenage mothers (Building Blocks): a pragmatic randomised controlled trial', *Lancet Online,* 14 October, http://dx.doi.org/10.1016/ S0140-6736(15)00392-X

Scottish Government (2008) *Getting it Right for Every Child (GIRFEC)*, http://www.gov.scot/Topics/People/Young-People/gettingitright (accessed 21 March 2018).

Seddon, J. (2008) *Systems thinking in the public sector*, Exeter: Triarchy Press.

Skrypek, M., Idzelis, M. and Pecora, P. (2012) 'Signs of Safety in Minnesota: parent perceptions of a Signs of Safety child protection experience', St Paul, MN: Wilder Research; https://www.gov.uk/government/uploads/system/uploads/attachment_data/file/175391/Munro-Review.pdf.

Stacey, R. (2006) 'Learning as an activity of interdependent people', in *Complexity and organization: readings and conversations*, London and New York: Routledge, pp 237–46.

Thane, P. (2009) 'Memorandum submitted to the House of Commons' Health Committee Inquiry: Social Care', October, http://www.historyandpolicy.org/docs/thane_social_care.pdf (accessed 21 March 2018).

Thomas, C. (2013) *Adoption for looked-after children: Messages from research*, London: BAAF.

Trist, E. (1981) *The evolution of socio-technical systems: a conceptual framework and an action research programme*, Toronto: Ontario Quality of Working Life Centre.

Turnell, A. and Edwards, S. (1999) *Signs of Safety: a solution oriented approach to child protection casework*, London: W.W. Norton.

Webb, C.J.R. and Bywaters, P. (2018) 'Austerity, rationing and inequity in children's social care – trends in children and young people's services expenditure in England between 2010 and 2015', *Local Government Studies*, February, doi: 10.1080/03003930.2018.1430028.

Wells, P. (2007) 'New Labour and evidence-based policy-making: 1997–2007', *People, Place and Policy Online*, 1 (1), pp 22–29 https://extra.shu.ac.uk/ppp-online/new-labour-and-evidence-based-policy-making-1997–2007/.

Woods, K., Bond, C., Humphrey, N., Symes, W. and Green, L. (2011) 'Systematic review of Solution Focused Brief Therapy (SFBT) with children and families', Department for Education Research Report 179, London: Department for Education.

6

Using evidence in criminal justice

Nicholas R. Fyfe and Gloria Laycock

Introduction to evidence use in criminal justice

Criminal justice covers a range of policy and practice areas. Agencies in this field are typically responsible for enforcing the law (including the prevention, disruption and detection of crime), prosecuting offenders (which requires appropriate prosecution and defence authorities and court services), dealing with convicted offenders (which involves prisons, probation services and staff who might deal with a wide range of alternative disposals) and supporting the victims of crime (which involves developing victim support groups and treatment services). The configuration of these arrangements in individual countries varies.

This chapter primarily describes the use of research evidence in criminal justice as it pertains to the UK (and mainly England and Wales, but with some reference to Scotland). Here there are a mix of national and local agencies, including a National Crime Agency and national prison and prosecution services, local police forces in England and Wales (but now a national force in Scotland) and a myriad of local public, private and voluntary organisations working with offenders and victims. Policy development is divided between a group of agencies, including (in England and Wales) the Ministry of Justice, the Home Office, the National Fraud Office and the Crown Prosecution Service. These policies inform the work of practitioners, who might be police officers, those working in courts services, the National Offender Management Service (which includes prison and probation officers), aftercare staff and a plethora of medical or social service staff who are to varying extents involved in the treatment and care of offenders and victims.

In the original *What Works* book (Davies et al, 2000), the criminal justice chapter focused on interventions with convicted offenders, particularly the services provided by the probation service and its What

Works Project (Nutley and Davies, 2000). That project was concerned with identifying and implementing some key principles for achieving effective practice. While Nutley and Davies welcomed the opportunities created by this interest in evidence of what works, they warned of the dangers of rushing ahead with wide-scale implementation of tentative effectiveness principles, and commented that the concomitant call for routine evaluations might lead to a proliferation of poorly conceived, small-scale studies that add little to the existing evidence base.

Two decades on, the extent to which the various elements of the criminal justice system in the UK are involved in evidence-informed policy and practice initiatives varies widely across the different institutions and organisations. Since 2000, not only has the probation service undergone significant restructuring (resulting in a greater fragmentation of approach) but the police have emerged as arguably the most active criminal justice agency in terms of embracing evidence-informed approaches. This has been driven by a combination of factors, including: commitments to the greater professionalisation of policing; significant budget cuts since the mid-2000s, which have prompted reflection on issues of efficiency and effectiveness; and greater engagement with the academic community in the form of strategic partnerships and collaborations. Other sectors of the criminal justice system are either comparatively small (like the courts services), heavily fragmented (like the partially privatised and heavily stretched prison and probation services) or closely connected with other elements of the evidence-based movement (such as drugs treatment agencies with close connections to health services). This chapter therefore concentrates on evidence in the context of policing policy and practice.

To understand the use of evidence in policing it is important to consider both the shifting characteristics of professionalism within police organisations and changes in the nature of policing research, and then how both of these developments have influenced each other and have shaped interactions between police organisations and the research community. In the latter half of the 20th century there were significant attempts by police organisations (particularly in the UK and US) to move from an 'old' police professionalism that dominated police departments in the 1960s and 1970s to a 'new' professionalism, elements of which began to emerge in the late 1990s and early 2000s (Stone and Travis, 2011). Under old professionalism, crime fighting and law enforcement were central tasks and these were viewed as essentially technocratic activities that required little engagement with either the public or researchers (Kelling and Moore, 1988). A limited repertoire of tactics were deployed in tackling crime, including the retrospective investigation of crime rather than upstream preventative approaches. By the late 1990s, there were significant pressures on both sides of the Atlantic to change this approach, due to a continuing rise in crime and catastrophic breakdowns in the relationships between the police and sections of the black and ethnic minority communities (particularly in the US). In addition, research evidence was increasingly challenging the effectiveness of police tactics, which were often deemed to lack evidential support (Reiner, 2010). According to Stone and Travis (2011), these pressures gradually brought about a shift towards a new type of professionalism characterised by three key elements: increased accountability; a greater focus on legitimacy; and moves towards evidence-informed practice.

Alongside these changes, there have also been shifts in the nature of policing research. For much of the 20th century policing research was 'on' and 'about' the police, particularly the contours of a complex police sub-culture. Much of this research was highly critical, raising concerns about racist and sexist behaviours as well as weak forms of accountability and governance. The evidence gathered was largely qualitative and, perhaps unsurprisingly, there was little interest from either the research community or police organisations in a dialogue around the policy and practice implications of research findings.

There were some attempts to develop a research agenda that was more orientated to working with the police, and to offer them evidence about their (in)effectiveness in tackling crime. Within England and Wales, the Home Office Research Unit (HORU) was established in 1957 to carry out (or fund) research of relevance to criminal justice policy and practice. HORU had variable success in this aim, but became more influential from the 1970s onwards, particularly with the establishment of the British Crime Survey (now the Crime Survey for England and Wales), which helped to reorient government policy towards the care of victims and their greater involvement in the criminal justice process. HORU was also instrumental in demonstrating the importance of the situational environment as a focus for crime-prevention activities and, from around the early 1980s, Home Office policy began to emphasise the importance of crime prevention as a neglected area of policy and practice (Jones et al, 1994).

Since the 2000s there has been a significant expansion of applied policing research (Reiner, 2015). Part of this expansion has revolved around the development of an 'evidence-based policing movement', which has gathered considerable momentum since the late 1990s. Initial ideas about what this entails in practice have, over time, extended from a preoccupation with 'the processes or products of evaluating police practices' to also include consideration of 'the translation of that knowledge into digestible and useable forms and the institutionalization of that knowledge into practice and policing systems' (Lum and Koper, 2017, p 4). From this broader perspective, evidence-informed policing encompasses everything from evaluations of policing interventions to reflections on research knowledge at a managerial level, and from use of crime analysis to guide the deployment of police resources to the use of risk instruments to identify problematic situations.

Against this background, we next discuss debates about the nature of evidence for policing policy and practice. This is followed by consideration of the structural arrangements for producing and synthesising research-based evidence for policing. The penultimate section outlines some of the difficulties in encouraging and enabling evidence use in policing and how these are being addressed. We conclude by commenting on the experiences of other countries and highlight some of the continuing challenges around the integration of evidence into criminal justice policy making.

The nature of evidence for policing

The very term 'evidence' comes loaded with established meanings and assumptions within the criminal justice arena. Indeed, the notion of evidence is central to much of what criminal justice practitioners do. In policing, this ranges from engaging in different forms of evidence gathering (from obtaining forensic evidence from crime scenes through to taking witness statements) to weaving that evidence together into a narrative that will form the basis of prosecution within the court system, where the evidence will be contested by defence lawyers and judged by a jury. However, the term is used in a different sense in this chapter, where the central concern is the use of research-based evidence to inform policy and practice, albeit alongside other considerations and ways of knowing such as organisational priorities, professional experience and public expectations. In line with the discussion of evidence use terminology in Chapter One, the generic phrase 'evidence-informed policing' is used in this chapter. Exceptions are made when referring to the official names of centres promoting evidence use and when contrasting a somewhat purist 'evidence-based' approach with a more inclusive 'evidence-informed' stance.

One of the most significant champions of evidence use in policing, Larry Sherman of Cambridge University, argues that 'police practices should be based on scientific evidence of what works best' (Sherman, 1998, p 2). He highlights two requirements of an 'evidence-based' police organisation. First, it should use the results of rigorous evaluations of policing tactics and strategies to guide decision making; and, second, it should generate and apply analytical knowledge derived from police data on crime problems and other issues. However, there have been strong (and occasionally acrimonious) debates about what kinds of research evidence should underpin police policy and practice. Taking their lead from Sherman (1998) and his argument that the police need to base their practice on scientifically developed evidence (echoing developments in evidence-based medicine – see Chapter Four), the evidence movement in policing has tended to promote experimental and quasi-experimental methodologies as the best basis for generating good evidence. The Maryland Scientific Method Scale (developed by Sherman and colleagues – see Chapter Eleven) defines acceptable methodologies for research on a five-point scale, with RCTs as the 'gold standard'.

However, the above view of 'best evidence' has been hotly disputed. Cockbain and Knutsson (2015, p 3), for example, argue in favour of a 'more pragmatic and inclusive stance on evidence' that embraces the benefits of other approaches such as case study methods and action research. There is also the view that there is a fundamental incompatibility between the experimental methods championed by the evidence movement and the operational realities of police work (Sparrow, 2016). The former is said to be too slow in generating useful knowledge, it also narrows the range of solutions available to the police by advocating only those approaches that have been 'scientifically' tested and is too focused on macro-level issues rather than the details of particular problems (Sparrow, 2016, pp 137–45). In line with the need to better understand problems and how interventions work, Pawson and Tilley (1997) had earlier emphasised the importance of identifying mechanisms (how initiatives achieve their effect) and how they interact with contexts (on the basis that what works in one place or at one time does not necessarily work in another). This 'realist' view of what counts as good evidence is now at the centre of a major initiative to provide the police with evidence of what works in crime reduction (see Box 6.3 in the next section). The methodological approaches advocated by Pawson and Tilley have also now found favour in many other settings (see Chapter Ten).

The nature of evidence needed to inform policing policy and practice remains a contentious issue, then, and this has implications for the arrangements for producing and synthesising research-based knowledge.

Production and synthesis of research-based knowledge in policing

As noted in the introduction, Home Office researchers have played an important role in facilitating the production and synthesis of research-based knowledge for policing. A key development was the establishment of the Home Office Police Research Group (PRG) in 1992 (directed by one of the authors, Laycock). This group had a remit to carry out and fund policing research relevant to policy and practice. A particular aim of the PRG was to improve the relationship between researchers and police, and to foster the view that experimentation and information derived from research could be useful, pragmatic and timely (Laycock, 2001). The programme of work around the notion of repeat victimisation (although observational rather than experimental) was particularly influential in this regard (Box 6.1).

Box 6.1: Research on repeat victimisation and its impact

An early burglary prevention project in the north of England showed high rates of repeat burglary and demonstrated that, by focusing on repeat victims and protecting them, burglary could be reduced significantly. This led to a programme of work demonstrating the relevance of repeat victimisation across a range of offences (Farrell and Pease, 1993). Despite the success of this programme there were no clear signs that the police were aware of this research or were changing their practices to take account of it. The Home Office's response included: providing advice on how to measure repeat victimisation; a series of 'roadshows' around the country to promote the ideas; small, non-technical research reports describing the relevant research; and introducing a staged set of performance targets intended to focus police thinking (Laycock, 2001). The effect of these activities, particularly the performance targets, was measured by Farrell et al (2000, p vi), who concluded that:

> the degree and speed of progress made suggests that the impact of the performance regime was considerable. By May 1999, all police forces in England and Wales claimed to have strategies in place to address repeat victimisation and it is unlikely that this universal response would have resulted from the diffuse process of research dissemination.

The lesson taken from this experience was that research, no matter how well conducted or relevant to policing, is unlikely to affect policing practice unless additional steps are taken to address its implementation.

The establishment of the Jill Dando Institute in 2001 also emphasised the need to produce relevant and rigorous research. It advocated a 'crime science' approach characterised by three main features: a focus on ways to reduce crime; the use of scientific methods and knowledge; and a multidisciplinary approach.

A further milestone in the development of an infrastructure for synthesising policing research was the establishment of the Campbell Collaboration's Crime and Justice Group in 2000. This is an international network of researchers that prepares and disseminates systematic reviews of high-quality research on methods to reduce crime and delinquency and improve the quality of justice. It has become a major repository of systematic reviews on what works in criminal justice (including in policing).

In general, the architecture for promoting evidence-informed policing, including the generation of applied research, has centred on the development of collaborations between police organisations and university researchers. In the UK this was pioneered by the Cambridge University Institute of Criminology (and its director, Larry Sherman). In 1996 the Institute became the university academic partner on the UK's Strategic Command Course – the programme that all aspiring senior police officers need to take in order to progress to the most senior ranks. Since then, the Institute has played a significant role in the training of senior police officers, who each have an option to complete a research project as part of a masters-level degree. This programme has promoted the idea of research and experimentation among a key group of senior police officers, with the effect of creating high-level 'evidence champions' across UK police forces.

Other partnerships between police organisations and universities have since been developed and extended. Indeed, even a cursory glance at the contexts in which evidence for policy and practice is being produced indicates a growing range of innovative activity aimed at establishing dialogue between police and research communities. Special issues of journals such as *Police Practice and Research: an International Journal* (see Johnston and Shearing, 2009; Cordner and White, 2010; Fyfe, 2012), alongside edited collections (such as Cockbain and Knutsson, 2015), all point to increasing interaction between policing researchers and practitioners. Such collaborations are said to depend on building relationships of trust, openness and honesty; establishing good personal relationships between 'the right people' (Foster and Bailey, 2010; Marks et al, 2010); and developing a strategy of continuous negotiation and communication (Fleming, 2010). These collaborations can also take a variety of forms: Engel and Henderson's (2014) typology distinguishes between critical partnerships (where the aim is to contribute to the general knowledge base about policing and inform high-level decision making rather than directly alter police practices); policy partnerships (which focus on practically relevant research that affects policing); and fully collaborative partnerships (which range from individual researchers working directly with police agencies, to researchers from across several academic institutions working with multiple police agencies).

The UK provides two good examples of full-collaborative partnerships: the Scottish Institute for Policing Research (SIPR – Box 6.2) and the What Works Centre for Crime Reduction (Box 6.3, and see further discussion in Chapter Thirteen). The SIPR approach has also been adopted and adapted in other places in the UK: the N8 Policing Research Partnership brings together eight universities with 11 police forces in the north of England; the East Midlands Policing Academic Collaboration involves seven universities and five police forces; and the Universities' Police Science Institute involves the South Wales Police, Cardiff University and the University of South Wales. The long-term success of these police–academic partnerships in developing policing research and evidence use depends on a combination of factors. An independent evaluation of SIPR, carried out 10 years after it was established, identified the following factors as playing a part in SIPR's positive impact on developing a research-informed environment for Scottish policing: the joint role of police and academics within the governance and management infrastructure of the Institute; strong collaborative communities of academics and practitioners at a grassroots level; focused communication and networking activities; and high-quality and committed leadership by both senior academics and senior police officers (SFC, 2017).

These and a number of other more modest partnership initiatives are now fairly common across the UK. They are a snapshot of what is happening at the time of writing, and it would be reasonable to expect development and innovation to continue. There is a real sense that the accessibility and use of research evidence is being actively encouraged across the police field, particularly among some of the new recruits who are either selected with a university degree or encouraged to take academic qualifications and CPD throughout their careers. In 2010, for example, a group of police officers were instrumental in the establishment of the Society of Evidence Based Policing in the UK, which is open to police and academics and is active in promoting the approach. Sister organisations have now been established in Australia, the US and Canada.

Box 6.2: Partnership working in the Scottish Institute for Policing Research (SIPR)

SIPR was established in 2007, with one of the authors (Fyfe) as director. It brings together 14 universities working in partnership with Scotland's national police force (Police Scotland) and national governance body (the Scottish Police Authority). SIPR has created institutionalised arrangements in which chief police officers and senior academics meet on a regular basis to discuss the research needs of the police service and opportunities for collaboration. There is regular and routine engagement around the nature and value of the research evidence base for policing, helping to secure a culture of engagement and a commitment to the co-production of research between the police and academic communities. Such an infrastructure is crucial because the wider literature on strategies for encouraging research use emphasises the importance of social interaction and the benefits of leveraging social influence via senior practitioners.

Further details: Fyfe and Wilson, 2012; Henry, 2017.

The developments traced thus far represent an encouraging picture of policing becoming a more evidence-informed profession. However, it is important not to overstate these developments, or underestimate the need to find new ways of encouraging and enabling evidence use in policing. Indeed, some observers have noted the paradox of 'successful failure' wherein, despite the expansion of policing research and police–academic partnerships, the impact of research on policy and practice remains limited (Fyfe, 2017). It is to these issues that we now turn.

Encouraging and enabling evidence use in policing

Many of the barriers that tend to limit the use of research are not specific to policing. Research findings are often messy, ambiguous and contradictory; there may be a lack of autonomy to implement findings from research and a lack of support for research-based change; and there may be cultural resistance to research and its use (Nutley et al, 2007). All these barriers are relevant in understanding the constraints that limit the integration of research evidence into policing. Bullock and Tilley (2009) highlight how, within policing, there is often disagreement about what counts as evidence of effective practice, there are issues about the accessibility of evidence to practitioners and there is a lack of support for practitioners to engage with research that might be seen as a threat to professional expertise (see also Chapter Three). Similarly, Lum et al (2012, p 65) highlight an organisational culture and system of promotions that focus on 'rewarding knowledge of procedures and reactivity [and so] help strengthen barriers to using research that promotes proactivity and problem solving'.

Against this background, it is vital to find ways of ensuring that research evidence becomes part of the conversation about policy and practice. It is also important to reflect on some of the main ways in

---

Box 6.3: Partnership working in the What Works Centre for Crime Reduction (WWCCR)

The WWCCR was established in 2013 under the aegis of the UK government's What Works programme (see Chapter Thirteen). The Centre is based in the UK College of Policing. One of its first initiatives, in collaboration with the Economic and Social Research Council (ESRC), was to fund a consortium of eight universities, led by University College London, to carry out a programme of work that included systematic reviews of crime-reduction topics; the development of an online toolkit to improve access to and understanding of research on the impacts of different interventions to reduce crime (Box 6.4); and the design and delivery of a training programme for police officers on how to use the toolkit to inform their decision making (Bowers et al, 2014a; 2014b; Fleming and Wingrove, 2017).

The role of the College of Policing in supporting evidence use in policing goes beyond simply hosting the What Works Toolkit. It also acts as a conduit for Home Office funding and manages the bidding process for a wide range of projects throughout England and Wales designed to enhance police/research interactions via what is termed the Police Knowledge Fund. These relationships are expected to support the police in carrying out their own research programmes and they also facilitate access to police data and other systems by academics who may wish to carry out research that has relevance to policing. Information on the projects funded in this way, as well as those supported in the normal course of academic practice, can be submitted to the College and published in the form of a 'research map' on its website. Again, this is intended to facilitate dissemination of applied research. In addition, the College provides training opportunities designed to increase police familiarity with academic output and it has experimented with different methods for doing this. There is also a network of 'evidence champions' in police agencies, who are expected to disseminate research evidence and act as a first point of contact where necessary.

---

which this challenge is being approached. Here we focus on four approaches to encouraging evidence use in policing practice: better tailored dissemination; support for research-informed practitioners; embedding research-based recommendations in policing routines; and shifting the culture of policing organisations.

Tailored dissemination

Tailored dissemination involves thinking carefully about how research is 'packaged' for practitioners and policy makers in ways that increase research awareness and encourage its use. The What Works Toolkit, mentioned in Box 6.3, illustrates an increasing commitment to tailored dissemination (see Box 6.4 for further details). A similar approach to tailoring dissemination activities has been developed in the US at the Center for Evidence-Based Crime Policy at George Mason University and comprises an online toolkit known as the 'evidence-based policing matrix'. This categorises experimental and quasi-experimental research

---

Box 6.4: Targeted dissemination and the College of Policing What Works Toolkit

The What Works Toolkit was developed by an academic consortium in partnership with the College of Policing (based in various locations across England and Wales). It enables the police to access research findings on different aspects of interventions to reduce crime. The design of the toolkit embraces the importance of recognising 'local conditions' as a key aspect of presenting evidence to practitioners. Simply providing evidence of the crime-reduction effect of an intervention was deemed insufficient for developing practical plans for police action. The toolkit therefore provides advice about the mechanisms through which an intervention might work and the contexts (or moderators) that might impact on outcomes. It also provides advice about implementation (because some interventions might require coordinated action by several organisations and not just the police) and about the cost of implementing an intervention locally (given that this might outweigh the benefits). The toolkit organises the presentation of research evidence around these themes referred to by the acronym EMMIE: Effect (on reducing crime); Mechanism (how an intervention works); Moderator (where the intervention works); Implementation (what is needed to make it happen); and Economics (what is the cost-effectiveness).

The crime reduction toolkit is available on the College of Policing website, and for further information see Johnson et al (2015).

---

on policing and crime reduction in order to allow practitioners as well as other researchers to rapidly determine those policing approaches that appear most promising in reducing crime (Lum et al, 2011).

Support for research-informed practitioners

In Nutley et al's (2007) model of the 'research-based practitioner', it is the role and responsibility of individual practitioners to be aware of research and to use it to inform their day-to-day practice. One example of this is the SIPR Practitioner Fellowship programme. This typically involves police officers or members of police staff being mentored by an academic in relation to a piece of research that the practitioner is undertaking as part of their professional role. The academic is able to provide information about other relevant research in the field as well as advising on research design and methodology in situations where primary data collection is also involved.

There are important connections between the research-based practitioner model and tailored dissemination. For example, work undertaken by Fleming et al (2016) trained officers in the use of the What Works Toolkit (see Box 6.4) and used the research-based practitioner model to frame the training. Focusing on the EMMIE themes within the toolkit (see Box 6.4), officers were informed about the importance of 'Thinking EMMIE' (that is, considering research-based interventions), 'Applying EMMIE' (that is, implementing an intervention based on information contained within the toolkit) and 'Evaluating EMMIE' (by undertaking an assessment, perhaps with support from researchers at a local university, of whether the intervention had the anticipated impact).

Embedding research findings in policing procedures

Although tailored dissemination and the research-based practitioner model have much to commend them, there is an underlying assumption that practitioners have relatively high levels of autonomy in their day-to-day practice. Another model of improving research use in practice is what Nutley et al (2007) refer to as the 'embedded research model'. Unlike tailored dissemination and the research-based practitioner approaches, this model does not require practitioners to directly engage with research. Rather, 'research enters practice by becoming embedded in service systems and processes, through mechanisms such as national and local policies and procedures, intervention programmes and practice tools' (Nutley et al, 2007, p 210).

Within a policing context, there are an increasing number of examples where research-based strategies and tactics are being embedded in policing routines. In terms of routine encounters between police and citizens, for example, ways have been developed to embed procedural justice principles into these interactions as a way of improving levels of public trust and confidence in police actions. This was pioneered in Australia in the Queensland Community Engagement Trial (Mazerolle et al, 2014), which tested the impact of police engaging with citizens by operationalising key aspects of procedural justice in short, high-volume police–citizen encounters (Box 6.5). Another example is the development of research-based temporal and spatial profiles to aid missing persons investigations. These profiles are based on a range of research-based predictive variables (including age, gender and mental health) that are used to predict likely outcomes (such as distance

---

Box 6.5: Embedding research findings in scripts of routine encounters: the Queensland Community Engagement Trial (QCET)

In this trial the research team, in consultation with the police, developed key components of procedural justice into a special script that was delivered by officers during random breath tests of drivers. The script contained four key procedural justice elements that were provided on a postcard-sized aide memoire, emphasising the following.

- **Neutrality** – police conveyed that they were pulling drivers over at random.
- **Trustworthy motives** – police emphasised they were worried about people drink-driving and hurting themselves and others.
- **Voice** – citizens were encouraged to talk with the police about how to improve crime prevention.
- **Respect** – officers were polite and drivers were thanked for their time.

The results of the QCET study (Mazerolle et al, 2014) showed that the way citizens perceive the police can be influenced by the way in which police interact with citizens during routine encounters, and demonstrated the positive benefits of police using the principles of procedural justice. Drivers who were stopped by the police and who received the specially designed script reported significantly stronger perceptions of procedural justice than did drivers who received the standard police encounter.

---

travelled by a missing person and likely locations). These profiles are now systematically used by police agencies throughout the UK (Woolnough et al, 2017).

As these examples illustrate, an important difference between the embedded research model and the research-based practitioner model is that responsibility for ensuring research-informed practice lies not with the individual practitioner but with policy makers and service delivery managers who translate key messages from research into guidance and practice tools. This approach therefore overcomes some of the limitations of the research-based practitioner model because it does not rely on practitioners having the time and interest to engage with the research, or the autonomy to act upon findings.

Shifting the culture of police organisations

Policy makers and service delivery managers can also play an important, strategic role in fostering a research-minded culture within organisations, which Nutley et al (2007) refer to as the 'organisational excellence model'. This broader perspective on evidence use is exemplified by the police–academic collaborations, discussed earlier, where the focus is not simply on the instrumental use of research knowledge but on developing an increased appetite and capacity for police organisations and researchers to work together. The independent assessment of the 10-year impact of the SIPR partnership draws attention to 'a key culture change in relationship between academics and the police in Scotland' and a fundamental change in police and academic attitudes to each other's roles and responsibilities (SFC, 2017, p 17). An important consequence of this is not only collaborative and co-produced research on high-profile and sensitive topics (such as missing persons and stop and search) but also more strategic use of research to inform long-term policy. For example, the joint 10-year policing strategy developed by Police Scotland and the Scottish Police Authority (*Policing 2026*) was informed by a series of commissioned evidence reviews on key issues, including prevention, performance and partnership working (SIPR, 2017).

Reflections and conclusions

The relationship between policing and policing research in the UK has changed since the 1990s. This has been facilitated by the increasing expectation that academic research will have some practical impact, which has encouraged academics to work *with* practitioners rather than simply *on* them. In addition, falling policing budgets and shifting notions of what professionalism means in policing have increased expectations that police organisations and police officers will be aware of research on what works and involve themselves in the further development of this evidence base. All this is very positive but, as already mentioned, there remain concerns about the relatively limited extent to which research findings are having an impact on policing policy and practice.

UK policing is not alone in embracing a greater commitment to evidence-based policy and practice in policing, but there are some differences as well as similarities in approach. In Australia and New Zealand, strategic partnerships between police organisations and higher education institutions, similar to those in the UK, have been established. In 2017, the New Zealand Police formed a research partnership with the University of Waikato to establish a Centre for Evidence Based Policing, while in Australia the Centre for Excellence in Policing and Security brought together four universities working collaboratively with the Australian Federal Police, Queensland Police Service and Victoria Police. In the US, there are also local examples of police–academic collaborations that involve integrating evidence into discussions around policing policy and practice, including the Center for Evidence-Based Crime Policy at George Mason University and the University of Cincinnati Center for Police Research and Policy. However, looking at the highly complex and fragmented US law enforcement landscape as a whole, US policing researchers have highlighted the scale of the challenge of developing a more evidence-based approach. Lum and Koper (2017, p 5) observe that 'adjusting the philosophy and culture of policing to embrace a more scientific approach may require fundamental changes in long standing practice deeply embedded within the organization'.

Similar observations have been made in a European context. Mouhanna (2017, p 27) observes how in France there has been a 'persistence of mistrust and even fear of researchers among police forces, especially at the highest level', with practitioners dismissing researchers for not having an understanding of the problems and challenges faced by police officers. This lack of engagement is attributed to a concern among the police in France that researchers are not under their control and are able to provide an alternative perspective on policing that threatens the notion of a well-functioning organisation. In other parts of Europe, notably Scandinavia, the connections between research, policy and practice in policing are much more established. Norway and Finland, for example, both have Police University Colleges where research, education and training are all closely integrated within a single institution operating in the context of national policing structures.

Looking to the future, important challenges remain in relation to the use of research evidence in policing, and these have wider relevance for the criminal justice sector as a whole. There are differences and debates within the research community around support for 'evidence-based' versus 'evidence-informed' approaches, and more fundamentally on what counts as evidence. Those pressing for evidence-based policies and practices tend to take a purist approach and argue that experience is no substitute for 'hard scientific fact'. Evidence-informed advocates argue that, particularly given the present state of knowledge in the field and the need to take account of the context and mechanisms, better policies and practices will be determined through a melding of diverse evidence and local experience. Moreover, the available evidence base is still weak in many areas, such as cybercrime, counter terrorism and tackling vulnerability through partnership working. There is therefore a real threat to the credibility of a hard-push approach to promoting the use of existing evidence, especially when there is often little or no research evidence to draw upon. Finally, wider considerations of professionalisation frame many of the current debates and developments around research use in the criminal justice sector. Drawing some inspiration from the health sector (and particularly nursing), some criminal justice agencies (notably police and prisons) are exploring new professional models founded on academic qualifications and the ability to interpret and apply research relevant to their practice (see also the discussion in Chapter Three). These professional models challenge strongly held views about the importance of craft and experience-based knowledge, as compared to more academic, research-informed understandings. The future of evidence use in the criminal justice sector will undoubtedly be shaped by the contours of these challenges and debates.

References

Bowers, K.J., Johnson, S.D., Tilley, N., Tompson, L.A. and Belur, J. (2014a) *Protocol for Work Package 1: Identifying Existing Systematic Reviews of Crime Reduction*, London: UCL Department of Security and Crime Science, http://discovery.ucl.ac.uk/id/eprint/1462098.

Bowers, K.J., Tompson, L. and Johnson, S.D. (2014b) 'Implementing information science in policing: mapping the evidence base', *Policing: A Journal of Policy and Practice*, 8 (4) pp 339–52, doi: 10.1093/police/pau052.

Bullock, K. and Tilley, N. (2009) 'Evidence-based policing and crime reduction', *Policing: A Journal of Policy and Practice*, 3 (4), pp 381–7.

Cockbain, E. and Knutsson, J. (2015) 'Introduction', in E. Cockbain and J. Knutsson (eds), *Applied police research: challenges and opportunities*, London: Routledge.

Cordner, G. and White, S. (2010) 'Special issue: the evolving relationship between police research and police practice', *Police Practice and Research: An International Journal*, 11 (2), pp 90–94.

Davies, H., Nutley, S. and Smith, P. (eds) (2000) *What works? Evidence-based practice and policy in public services*, Bristol: Policy Press.

Engel, R. and Henderson, S. (2014) 'Beyond rhetoric: establishing police–academic partnerships that work', in J. Brown (ed), *The future of policing*, London: Routledge.

Farrell, G. and Pease, K. (1993) *Once bitten, twice bitten: repeat victimisation and its implications for crime prevention*, Crime Prevention Unit, 46, London: Home Office Police Research Group, http://eprints.whiterose.ac.uk/97486/.

Farrell, G., Edmunds, A., Hobbs, L. and Laycok, G. (2000) *RV snapshot: UK policing and repeat victimisation*, Crime Reduction Research Series Paper 5, London: Home Office.

Fleming, J. (2010) 'Learning to work together: police and academics', *Policing: A Journal of Policy and Practice*, 4 (2), pp 139–45.

Fleming, J. and Wingrove, J. (2017) '"We would if we could … but not sure if we can": implementing evidence-based practice. The evidence-based practice agenda in the UK', *Policing: A Journal of Policy and Practice*, 11 (2), pp 1–12.

Fleming, J., Fyfe, N.R. and Wingrove, J. (2016) *Evidence-informed policing: an introduction to EMMIE and the crime reduction toolkit. A pilot training evaluation*. Report submitted to the College of Policing (copy available from authors).

Foster, J. and Bailey, S. (2010) 'Joining forces: maximising ways of making a difference in policing', *Policing: A Journal of Policy and Practice*, 4 (2), pp 95–103.

Fyfe, N.R. (2012) (ed) 'Special issue: police-university collaborations', *Police Practice and Research: An International Journal*, 13 (4), pp 299–401.

Fyfe, N.R. (2017) 'Paradoxes, paradigms and pluralism: reflections on the future challenges for police science in Europe', in D. Nogala, J. Fehervary, H-G. Jaschke and M. den Boer (eds), *European Police Science and Research Bulletin – Special Conference Edition: Police Science and Police Practice in Europe*, 2nd edn, Luxembourg: European Union Agency for Law Enforcement Training, pp 309–16.

Henry, A. (2017) 'Reflexive academic collaboration with the police', in S. Armstrong, J. Blaustein and A. Henry (eds), *Reflexivity and criminal justice: intersections of policy, practice and research*, Basingstoke: Palgrave, pp 169–90.

Johnson, S.D., Tilley, N. and Bowers, K.J. (2015) 'Introducing EMMIE: an evidence rating scale to encourage mixed-method crime prevention synthesis reviews', *Journal of Experimental Criminology*, 3, pp 459–73, doi: 10.1007/s11292-015-9238-7 .

Johnston, L. and Shearing, C. (2009) 'Special issue: new possibilities for policing research and practice', *Police Practice and Research: An International Journal*, 10 (5–6), pp 415–22.

Jones, T., Newburn, T. and Smith, D. (1994) *Democracy and policing*, London: Policy Studies Institute.

Kelling, G. and Moore, M. (1988) 'The evolving strategy of policing', *Perspectives on Policing* No 4, Washington, DC: National Institute of Justice.

Laycock, G. (2001) 'Hypothesis based research: the repeat victimization story criminal justice', *International Journal of Policy and Practice*, 1 (1), pp 59–82.

Lum, C. and Koper, C. (2017) *Evidence-based policing: translating research into practice*, Oxford: Oxford University Press.

Lum, C., Koper, C. and Telep, C.W. (2011) 'The evidence-based policing matrix', *Journal of Experimental Criminology*, 7 (1), pp 3–26.

Lum, C., Telep, C.W., Koper, C. and Grieco, J. (2012) 'Receptivity to research in policing', *Justice Research and Policy*, 14 (1), pp 61–94.

Marks, M., Wood, J., Ally, F., Walsh, T. and Witbooi, A. (2010) 'Worlds apart? On the possibilities of police/academic collaborations', *Policing: A Journal of Policy and Practice*, 4 (2), pp 112–18.

Mazerolle, L., Sargeant, E., Cherney, A., Bennett, S., Murphy, K., Antrobus, E. and Martin, P. (2014) *Procedural justice and legitimacy in policing*, Cham, Switzerland: Springer.

Mouhanna, C. (2017) 'Colliding views of police reality – science vs politics of policing', in D. Nogala, J. Fehervary, H-G. Jaschke and M. den Boer (eds), *European Police Science and Research Bulletin – Special Conference Edition: Police Science and Police Practice in* Europe, 2nd edn, Luxembourg: European Union Agency for Law Enforcement Training, pp 27–34.

Nutley, S. and Davies, H. (2000) 'Criminal justice: using evidence to reduce crime', in H. Davies, S. Nutley, and P. Smith, (eds), (2000) *What works? Evidence-based practice and policy in public services*, Bristol: Policy Press.

Nutley, S., Walter, I. and Davies, H. (2007) *Using evidence: How research can inform public services*, Bristol: Policy Press.

Pawson, R. and Tilley, N. (1997) *Realistic evaluation*, London: Sage.

Reiner, R. (2010) *The politics of the police*, Oxford: Oxford University Press.

Reiner, R. (2015) 'Revisiting the classics: three seminal founders of the study of policing: Michael Banton, Jerome Skolnick and Egon Bittner', *Policing and Society*, 25 (3), pp 308–27.

SFC (Scottish Funding Council) (2017) *Impact review: the Scottish Institute for Policing Research*, Edinburgh: Scottish Funding Council, http://www.sipr.ac.uk/downloads/SFCCP012017_Impact_Review_Scottish_Institute_for_Policing_Research.pdf (accessed 10 July 2017).

Sherman, L. (1998) 'Evidence-based policing', Ideas in American Policing, Washington, DC: Police Foundation, http://www.policefoundation.org/content/evidence-based-policing.

Sparrow, M. (2016) *Handcuffed: what holds policing back and the keys to reform*, Washington, DC: The Brookings Institute.

Stone, C. and Travis, J. (2011) *Towards a new professionalism in policing*, Cambridge, MA: Harvard Kennedy School and National Institute of Justice.

Woolnough, P.S., Stevenson, O., Parr, H. and Fyfe, N.R. (2017) 'Geography of missing adults', in K. Shalev Greene and L. Alys (eds), *Missing persons: a handbook of research*, London: Routledge, pp 123–34.

7

Using evidence in education

Julie Nelson and Carol Campbell

Introduction to evidence use in education

This chapter considers the nature of evidence in education and discusses the effectiveness with which it is produced, shared and used within and across different elements of the system. It focuses on mainstream school education – that is, the system that supports children and young people though their years of compulsory school learning. It is based primarily on the English context, but also includes illustrations and developments from other UK countries. It also provides some comparative illustrations from the province of Ontario in Canada, which has a relatively well-developed system supporting educational evidence use in policy and practice.

Education is compulsory in England from the ages of five to 18 (a young person must remain in some form of learning, either academic or work based, between the ages of 16 and 18). Education is a critical gateway to young people securing economic independence in adulthood, progressing in their careers and ambitions and contributing to society as effective citizens. Education has an essential role to play in creating the conditions for social mobility and equity by enabling young people to reach their full academic and personal potential and by reducing economic and social inequality. Yet there remains a stubborn and persistent 'attainment gap' between young people from affluent and disadvantaged backgrounds, which typically widens as they progress through their school careers (see, for example, Andrews et al, 2017). In terms of evidence, there is much that is not yet fully understood about how best to support every child to succeed, although, as we outline later, the evidence base is improving. There remain gaps in the evidence base for education about 'what works', 'what works best', 'what works for who' and 'what works in what contexts'.

At the turn of the millennium, Fitzgibbon (2000) described the key challenges facing the supply of educational research, in the predecessor to this volume (Davies et al, 2000). Fitzgibbon drew particular attention to a paucity of experimental research in the UK and a consequent lack of robust 'what works' evidence to inform educational practice. A great deal has changed in the intervening period, including a combination of conceptual, policy and practice developments around the desired purpose, actions and outcomes of integrating evidence and education.

In addition to infrastructure developments (such as the establishment of the What Works Centres and networks; see Chapter Thirteen), ideas about how to get evidence into policy and practice have been changing. While the term evidence-based policy and practice (EBPP) is still used (for example, Jones and CEBMa, 2016), there is now increasing focus on evidence-*informed* policy and practice (EIPP). The terminology of EIPP assumes that a range of evidence (not just research evidence) must interact with professional judgement to influence policy and practice. It also denotes the inclusion of a wider range of types of research than those typically associated with EBPP.

A number of research studies have indicated that when schools use evidence to inform their practice this can contribute to effective education systems (CUREE, 2011; Mincu, 2014; Greany, 2015). Understanding is also increasing about how research evidence can inform those systems (Sharples, 2013). In parallel, there has been a growth in educator demand for evidence, illustrated in England by the recent rise of grassroots initiatives such as researchED, the Research Schools Network and the launch of the Chartered College of Teaching (Nelson and Sharples, 2017). In Scotland, teacher networks and use of social media, for example, Pedagoo and ScotEdChat on Twitter, have emerged to enable teachers to lead and engage in dialogue about evidence and practice.

In this chapter we focus not only on 'supply-side' issues related to the production of educational research but also on 'demand-side' issues related to schools', teachers' and policy makers' priorities in accessing, understanding and/or applying educational research in their daily practices. Our interest is not only in the relative merits of different types of evidence but also in the factors – at system, policy, school and individual educator levels – that enable or hinder the incorporation of evidence into day-to-day policy making and practice. EIPP is not simply a technical activity: it is influenced by personal and professional values and beliefs, and it is affected by political and educational contexts, policies and developments. While the supply of educational research must be as robust and relevant as possible, such research can easily fail to gain traction within schools, with teachers and inside government. Effective mediating processes can help to overcome this by engaging those whom researchers ultimately seek to inform and support. Hence, in subsequent sections we also consider the mediating processes that exist (or are needed) to support the flow of evidence from production through to practical application, and (equally important) from professional knowledge and practice back into the evidence base.

The nature of evidence in education

Educators in schools have a variety of evidence sources at their disposal that they can draw on to support decision making and/or pedagogy. Some of these are practice-based (for example, teacher assessments, professional judgement and/or the results of professional enquiry), some are research-based (for example, meta-analyses or syntheses, research studies and/or evaluation results) and some are data-based (for example, pupil-performance and/or school management data). Evidence-informed practice occurs at the intersection between these different forms of evidence and is envisaged to be most effective when all sources and forms are used in tandem. As Sharples comments (2013, p7), evidence-informed practice is about 'integrating professional expertise with the best external evidence from research to improve the quality of practice'. Research is a core element of EIPP, but it does not provide the sum total of evidence needed for EIPP.

There is also an important role that classroom data (in the form of teacher observations and assessments) can play in EIPP (LaPointe-McEwan et al, 2017). Formal quantitative assessments of pupil performance tend to dominate decision making in schools; however, research illustrates the importance of educators taking a broader view of classroom data (incorporating summative, formative, quantitative, qualitative and observational data; LaPointe-McEwan et al, 2017). This necessitates educators developing wide-ranging data-literacy skills and learning to triangulate across different data sources in developing well-balanced decisions.

Turning now to the *research* component of EIPP, there are continuing debates about the relative robustness and value of different research methodologies, including experimental and quasi-experimental studies, qualitative studies and mixed-methods approaches (see also Chapter Ten). Experimental research studies, such as RCTs, still represent only a small proportion of all educational research studies in England, and they remain controversial. Some have expressed concern that they reduce the notion of relevant research to a preoccupation with 'what works', to the exclusion of broader questions such as 'what matters' (see, for example, Bredo, 2006; Nutley et al, 2013). However, while RCTs and quasi-experimental studies cannot answer all relevant research questions, they do add an important dimension to EIPP. The paucity of experimental studies is being addressed by the growth in funding for them, particularly since the inception of the Education Endowment Foundation (EEF) in England. The EEF is an independent charity established in 2011 with a £125 million founding grant from the UK Department for Education. It funds the development and trial of promising education programmes and approaches; provides free evidence-based summaries and practical tools; and supports schools in implementing evidence-based guidance.

There is also disagreement about the value of practice-generated research, which has sometimes been dismissed as small scale, anecdotal or non-replicable (Borg, 2010; CUREE, 2011; Wilkins, 2012). However, advocates such as Bryk et al (2011) have argued that fine-grained practice-generated knowledge (sometimes termed practice-based evidence) can be applied formatively to support professional learning and student achievement. Such disagreements hinge around the intended *purposes* and *uses* of practice-based evidence. Arguably, there is a clear role for practice-based evidence where it enables and contributes to professional learning and reflection to inform knowledge and practice – it is important for educators to be scholarly, enquiring professionals. But caution may need to be exercised when it comes to scaling up practitioner findings within or across schools, especially where the work was small scale or not generalisable.

Production and synthesis of research-based knowledge for education

There is often a lack of coherent and systemic research-based evidence linked to the current needs of educators and/or policy makers (Cooper et al, 2009). Academic research is not necessarily linked to, or funded for, addressing day-to-day problems of practice for teachers or for current policy issues. A UK-based programme that aimed to improve the production and dissemination of educational research was the Teaching and Learning Research Programme (TLRP) (Box 7.1). While seemingly promising in principle, and despite large-scale funding, this programme is considered to have failed to achieve many of its key objectives (Pollard, 2011), drawing into question its impact and value for money. Educational research is still often conducted in small-scale

Box 7.1: The Teaching and Learning Research Programme (TLRP)

The TLRP was an ESRC-funded programme that attracted over £40 million in funding between 1999 and 2012. It was developed to support leading-edge research to inform teaching and learning throughout the UK and to build research capacity to that end within UK universities. Although the programme attempted to build collaborations between schools and researchers, its central focus was encouraging better links between universities and academics – in other words, improving the supply of high-quality educational research.

Practitioner communities that were directly involved in the TLRP had high levels of awareness of the programme and its outputs, but evaluations of the programme showed that there was very little *wider* awareness of the TLRP among the teaching profession. Where schools were involved in shaping the TLRP *inputs*, their awareness and appreciation of the programme and its outputs was high. In contrast, where schools were only in receipt of the TLRP *outputs* (this was the case in the majority of schools), awareness of the programme, and its offer, was very low (Parsons and Burkey, 2011; Pollard, 2011).

and somewhat isolated projects, without developing a cumulative body of evidence on persisting issues for educational policy or practice.

Nevertheless, in spite of some disappointing attempts at improving the supply and relevance of educational research over recent years, current developments are beginning to change this picture. There are now many more providers of educational research and producers of evidence summaries and syntheses in England and elsewhere. By early 2016, the EEF had funded 121 evaluations of promising practices in 6,200 schools across England. The results of these evaluations are summarised, together with the results of other relevant research, in the EEF's Teaching and Learning Toolkit. This is an online resource that collates and synthesises the results of research studies on issues relevant to teaching five- to 16-year-olds. At the time of writing, the toolkit is organised into 34 issue 'strands', including extending school time, homework, peer tutoring and reducing class size. For each strand there is an assessment of likely impact, cost and the strength of evidence (for example, reducing class size is found to have moderate impact, for high cost, based on moderate evidence). The EEF also provides actionable guidance for teachers on a range of high-priority issues. Around two-thirds of school senior leaders were reported by the EEF to have used the Teaching and Learning Toolkit during 2014–15.

There are a number of other independent research organisations that aim to connect the worlds of research and practice through providing practical syntheses, summaries and tools. Examples include the Centre for the Utilisation of Research Evidence in Education (CUREE), the Institute for Effective Education (IEE) and the National Foundation for Educational Research (NFER). These are helpful developments, as Borg (2010) suggests that research summaries, digests or research-based guidelines are more likely to be useful to educators than research reports or journal articles. In a recent study of evidence-based teaching in schools in England, Coldwell et al (2017) note that teachers and school leaders increasingly use social media to support their professional learning and to access evidence – a move that again emphasises the need for summaries and translations of research.

The infrastructure for producing and synthesising educational research needs to be viewed in the context of wider developments. The notion of an evidence ecosystem has been presented by a number of authors (Gough et al, 2011; Sharples, 2013). Indeed, Gough et al (2011) have developed a typology of an 'evidence production-to-use system'. In addition to a focus on evidence production, mediation and use, the model includes stakeholder engagement and a whole-system focus. The authors explain that an evidence-informed system is 'qualitatively different from examining the components on their own. It emphasises the importance of coordinated and effective interventions with the readiness and sufficient capacity for both the production of effective policy-relevant evidence, the mediation between policy and evidence, and the successful use of evidence by policymakers' (Gough et al, 2011, pp 23–4).

This conceptualisation helps us to understand that the infrastructure for EIPP in education should not be developed in isolation from its policy and practice environment; and that the evidence ecosystem should not be regarded as a series of individual components but, rather, as an entire and interconnected *system*.

While ecosystem models provide a helpful means of conceptualising a complex process, they also present two key issues. First, primacy tends to be ascribed to evidence produced by universities, government or research organisations. Research or enquiry undertaken or produced by educators (see, for example, Atkinson, 2017) tends not to feature so strongly in these models. Second, research production tends to be seen as the starting point for the system. However, there are other points where the process could usefully begin. Durbin and Nelson (2014) argue that educators' questions about daily challenges and issues requiring resolution in their schools could be an alternative starting point, influencing the commissioning and production of future research.

In examining EIPP in education across Europe, Gough et al (2011) found that the majority (66%) of evidence-informed policy activities were found to have been initiated by government. Yet the authors found evidence of very few fully developed whole-system approaches. In their study of 269 activities to support EIPP across 30 European countries, only 4% of these activities 'focused on making changes to the entire evidence-to-policy system' (Gough et al, 2011, p 8). Such system-level changes require concerted action by governments in partnership with research producers and users, including educators. This is immensely challenging and requires substantial political will.

One non-European example of a whole-system approach can be found in the province of Ontario, Canada. Here an attempt has been made to develop a system-wide culture and capacity for EIPP through the Ministry of Education's Ontario Research and Evaluation Strategy (Box 7.2). Analysis of the strategy indicates the development of six main forms of evidence for EIPP (Campbell and Fulford, 2009): literature reviews and syntheses; school-based enquiry and research projects; research across multiple sites to identify 'effective', 'successful' and 'promising' practices; research to investigate a policy question or concern; data analysis and information tools; and policy and programme evaluations. However, the production of evidence is insufficient on its own: there is also a need for knowledge mobilisation, mediation strategies and capacity building to support evidence use.

In sum then, while there are high levels of activity in the production and synthesis of evidence in education, there is still work to do in developing systems to encourage and enable the use of that evidence. This is the focus of the next section.

Encouraging and enabling evidence use in education

A complex set of actions need to take place at policy, research, school and individual teacher levels if meaningful systemic change is to be achieved. EIPP generally requires some form of 'transformation' or 'translation' process, which sits between the production of research and the use of that research in policy or practice. Becheikh et al (2009) have identified four different forms of 'evidence transformation'. Each involves different levels of input from research producers (such as academics or professional researchers), intermediaries (such as professional bodies, local government or training providers) and

Box 7.2: The Ontario Ministry of Education Research and Evaluation Strategy

The Ontario Ministry of Education Research and Evaluation Strategy incorporates a host of initiatives that have been resourced to develop the Ministry's capacity for EIPP, as well as to support school districts, schools, school leaders, teachers and educational support workers' use of evidence in their practices. The strategy comprises:

• **leading** the Ministry's research agenda to coordinate and manage Ministry research activities to support provincial educational goals;
• **applying** research and evaluation to support evidence-based policy and programme decisions and practices;
• **building** individual and organisational capacity to access, use and conduct research;
• **fostering** research collaboration through networking and partnerships between and among Ministry staff researchers and educators across Ontario, to address priority research needs;
• **communicating** information about existing and new research activities and findings; and
• **contributing** to the provincial, national and international body of research knowledge about educational policies, programmes and practices.

Interviews with Ontario Ministry of Education policy makers indicated that they considered the following elements as key to the success of the strategy:

• **access** to research with content highly relevant to policy makers;
• **clear communication and mobilisation** strategies to make such research accessible in a timely way;
• **development of capacity** among government officials to understand how to access, interpret and apply research, and also to build the capacity of researchers to navigate within policy processes; and
• **collaboration** between research and policy communities to interact and to influence and develop shared knowledge.

Sources: Ontario Ministry of Education, not dated; Campbell and Fulford, 2009, p 13.

educators (including multi-academy trusts, schools and/or individual teachers). Their four identified forms of transformation are as follows:

1. **Research, development, diffusion** – research producers disseminate their research through a variety of channels.
2. **Problem solving** – educators identify their priorities and challenges and use researchers as 'technicians' to help them find answers.
3. **Linkage** – intermediaries help to translate research evidence into usable guidance for practice and support change in schools.
4. **Social interaction** – researchers and educators work together as 'co-creators' and users of research evidence.

If taking a diffusion approach, then providing clear messages about what works, in what contexts and at what costs, is important. Evidence has greatest practice relevance when its messages are accessible and timely, objective, easy to understand and implement and relevant to current school-level problems or matters of professional practice (Gough, 2013; Sharples, 2013; Nelson and O'Beirne, 2014; Coldwell et al, 2017). However, the provision of clear and relevant evidence needs to be complemented with a range of activities to encourage and enable evidence use.

Another of Becheikh et al's (2009) forms of evidence transformation is the 'problem solving' approach, where teachers identify their problems and use researchers as 'technicians' to help solve these. This is a relatively rare approach (but see the US Research Practice Partnerships described in Chapter Seventeen), not least because many academics prefer to retain independence in the generation of ideas and knowledge, but also because school funding structures rarely provide sufficient budgets for schools to draw on academics or researchers in this way. However, an initiative in England, Evidence for the Frontline (E4F), is helping to put teachers in control of the questions to be asked and then matching these to relevant research evidence (Box 7.3).

Another fundamental enabler of evidence use is the development of on-going social interaction between researchers, policy makers and practitioners (Becheikh et al, 2009). In many of the examples already discussed there is a supply–demand relationship, mediated to lesser or greater degrees by individuals or organisations who help to translate the evidence and support its use in practice. Examples of all parties working together to co-construct and apply evidence are much rarer, however.

One attempt to develop a system-wide interaction strategy is the Knowledge Network for Applied Education Research (KNAER), which operates in Ontario, Canada. The first phase of KNAER

Box 7.3: Evidence for the Frontline (E4F)

First initiated by the Coalition for Evidence-based Education, E4F is an online forum that enables teachers to submit questions related to their practice and then directs them to relevant research, researchers or schools with the right experience to help them answer those questions. E4F was available to just over 30 schools in England during a trial of the project. The E4F initiative is funded by the EEF, the service is based at Sandringham School in St Albans (England) and it is supported by the Institute for Effective Education.

An independent evaluation of the pilot phase of E4F, undertaken by NFER, found early indications of promise in the service (Lord et al, 2017c). Teachers and school leaders engaged positively with E4F, asking a range of questions and valuing the quality of answers provided. They also appreciated the fact that the service provided them with opportunities to discuss research with colleagues, and believed that it had enhanced their enthusiasm for, and schools' uses of, research evidence. However, it was too early to say whether there had been wider benefits in terms of pupils' learning outcomes.

funded 44 projects, involving over 150 partners, which produced over 1,000 outputs to connect research and practice knowledge (products and activities). While an evaluation of the first phase of KNAER concluded that there had been growth in a culture of knowledge mobilisation between and among researchers, practitioners and policy makers collaborating in partnership (see Campbell et al, 2014; 2017), more effort was needed to achieve a fully system-wide approach and to demonstrate improved practices and outcomes in education. The renewed KNAER involves system-wide leadership from lead partners (Ontario Ministry of Education, University of Toronto and Western University) and funding for four large, province-wide thematic networks in the areas of mathematics, equity, well-being and indigenous knowledge. Each network is hosted by capable and credible organisations and provides support for local 'communities of practice' to facilitate and enable research use connected to the problems of practice for educators and communities (see also Chapter Two).

Despite a growing range of activities that aim to improve the production, sharing and use of evidence in policy and practice, we still know very little about the relative effectiveness (and cost-effectiveness) of different ways of mobilising education research knowledge, such as those described in this chapter. Additionally, in spite of many positive developments in the production, synthesis and mobilisation of research evidence, recent evidence shows that research is still having only a small to moderate influence on school-level decision making relative to other sources, despite teachers generally reporting a positive disposition towards it (Nelson et al, 2017). In 2014 the EEF launched a fund to test a series of pilot projects exploring the most effective means of translating research findings into changes in the classroom. Funded projects contained a variety of enabling approaches, both passive (based on various models of research diffusion) and active (drawing on various forms of light-touch linkage and interaction). Results of the three-year evaluations that ran alongside these developments indicate that attempts to increase research use by teachers do not necessarily result in improved educational attainment for students, especially when they do not include scaffolding and/or in-depth support structures for teachers (Lord et al, 2017a; 2017b).

There is no straightforward means of ensuring that evidence plays a useful role in educational practice or policy. It relies on the combination of multiple factors including: high educator demand; supportive school and policy climates; the availability of accessible, relevant and timely evidence; and, in some cases, appropriate mediation or brokerage (for examples of brokerage, see Box 7.4). Teacher motivation is central to effective evidence use. Edwards (2011) claims that, if educators do not believe in the value or trustworthiness of evidence, they are unlikely to turn to it in support of their practice. Evidence is much more likely to be used by educators if it has been provided in response to an articulated need and is compatible with school or teacher goals (Shiell-Davis et al, 2015). CUREE (2011) note the value of co-construction, a model in which educators and researchers work as partners; Edwards (2011) stresses the importance of researchers and educators working together to find a *shared language* to describe and evaluate the key components of practice.

In addition, evidence use does not occur in a vacuum. In England, the school system is increasingly devolved, with reduced local authority control and much of the impetus for school improvement resting with individual schools and senior leadership teams. Within this climate, teachers' evidence use is in large part dependent on the opportunities or support provided by individual leadership teams or, on occasion, partnerships of schools.

Researchers have conducted extensive research exploring the school- and school leader-level conditions that create a fertile environment for evidence use to flourish. For example, research by Brown and colleagues (Brown et al, 2016; Brown and Zhang, 2016) has identified

Box 7.4: Current brokerage initiatives

The Education Endowment Foundation (EEF): The EEF is currently funding large scale-up programmes based on evidence of best practice in the deployment of teaching assistants and the pedagogy of effective literacy provision. Both programmes contain a component in which place-based 'advocates' (practice partners) work directly with networks of schools to help them understand, use and embed evidence-based guidance produced by the EEF and other prominent researchers. These campaigns are being independently evaluated, the first by the Institute for Fiscal Studies and Sheffield Hallam University, and the second by the NFER and the University of Nottingham. At the time of writing, results were not in the public domain.

The Research Schools Network. The Research Schools Network involves hundreds of schools. The intermediaries in this case are research schools themselves, which work with networks of other schools to disseminate evidence-based guidance, provide training on evidence-based practices and support innovation across their networks. This is a peer-to-peer linkage model that, according to the Research Schools Network website, 'provides school-led support for the use of evidence to improve teaching practice'. The work of the Network is being independently evaluated by the University of Nottingham, but again, at the time of writing, results were not in the public domain.

The Education Media Centre. The Education Media Centre is an independent charity, staffed by journalists with expertise in the education system. It helps journalists to access important research evidence and connects them with academic experts on topics of public and policy interest. It also helps educational researchers to make the most of their research, so that it can make a difference across the education system. The media centre provides training, advice and support for educational researchers who wish to reach a national audience.

important 'transformational' and 'learning centred' aspects of leadership, in which school leaders provide both the vision for, and the resources and structures to support, EIPP. Features of school leadership and school conditions to support EIPP include:

- **Creating a trusting and innovative learning environment** through a climate in which informed risk taking is encouraged and 'failure' is not chastised. Brown et al's (2016) study found that 'trust' was the most statistically significant factor impacting on schools' research use.

- **Providing open and collaborative learning opportunities** and encouraging colleagues to have an 'enquiry habit of mind' or an openness to 'self-study' (Kroll, 2006; Stoll, 2015), supported via professional learning communities or joint practice development opportunities (Galdin-O'Shea, 2015; Roberts, 2015). In the most research-engaged schools, senior leaders often acted as 'evidence brokers', signposting colleagues to relevant and useful research and resources (Coldwell et al, 2017).
- **Providing resources**, in the shape of time, funds and protocols to support colleagues to access, read and apply evidence and to engage in joint practice development. There is also evidence that providing resources for a designated within-school research champion or research lead can support effective evidence use across the school.
- **Modelling effective evidence use** by demonstrating to colleagues how data and research can be used wisely and precisely to support change, and by encouraging a disciplined approach to monitoring and evaluation of new initiatives and approaches.

These insights provide many clues as to how evidence use can be encouraged locally, but the wider educational climate is also important. Governments, educational representation bodies and educational service providers all have a role to play in creating a climate for evidence use. Central to this is a need for better educator training and development in research methodologies and in the interpretation of data and research. This is often referred to as data or research 'literacy' (Sharples, 2013; Nelson and O'Beirne, 2014; Roberts, 2015; Brown and Zhang, 2016; Coldwell et al, 2017). There have also been calls for more effective leadership training in data and research literacy (CUREE, 2011; Sharples, 2013). Indeed, Campbell (2016) has argued that teaching is a knowledge-based profession where it is a professional responsibility for teachers to engage in and with evidence.

The 2015 Carter review of Initial Teacher Training (ITT) in England called for more attention to be given to research literacy training in ITT programmes, and the 2016 standard on Teachers' Professional Development (PD) recommended that PD should be underpinned by robust evidence and expertise. The Chartered College of Teaching also has a commitment to supporting evidence-based professional development and evidence-informed policy. While there is clearly growing policy-level encouragement for educators to use evidence in their practice, in a climate in which the influence of universities in ITT is diminishing and the majority of CPD remains unregulated, this remains a challenging goal.

Taken together, then, there are many exciting developments in encouraging and enabling evidence use in education, but sustaining and scaling up the insights gained from these initiatives remains a challenge.

Reflections and conclusions

The use of evidence in policy and practice is complex and challenging, explaining in part why, after many decades of effort, there is still some way to go to achieve a more evidence-informed education system in England and elsewhere. Since 2000, interest and activity concerning evidence in education have accelerated. There have been shifting conceptions about evidence-*informed* education to take account of a range of evidence and processes of professional judgement. There have been attempts to fund large-scale research programmes focused on teaching and learning, funding for 'what works' trials, evaluations, summaries and toolkits and concerns to improve the overall supply and quality of educational research linked to priority policy and practice needs.

However, perhaps even more prevalent is the growing interest in how to mediate, broker, transfer and/or mobilise research and professional knowledge between and among researchers, educators, policy makers, stakeholders and the wider public (Cooper, 2014). Many of these activities have focused on the creation of products, events and networking opportunities to bring together research, policy and practice in accessible ways. Nevertheless, which approaches are more or less effective for actually connecting research, policy and practice are not yet fully known. The further development of evaluation and research on EIPP processes, outputs and outcomes seems critical to developing the field further.

The Teaching and Learning International Survey (OECD, 2014) indicated that only 27% of respondents (teachers and head teachers) in England reported participating in individual or collaborative research. Not all educators will necessarily engage in conducting primary research; however, it is an appropriate professional expectation and responsibility that all educators will engage *with* research through accessing, appraising, adapting and potentially applying external evidence in their work (Nelson and O'Beirne, 2014). Developing the individual and collective capacity of educators to engage in and with research requires further development, from initial teacher training, through continuing professional learning and development, to opportunities for teacher-led research and enquiry, to school leaders facilitating and enabling a school-wide culture and capacity for evidence use.

Ultimately, the goal of EIPP is to improve educational practices and outcomes in schools and for students. Encouragingly, a systematic review published by CUREE (2011) concluded that practitioner engagement with and in research is becoming a more mainstream element of professional learning and development in England. CUREE's (2011, p 33) systematic review identified the benefits of engagement in and with research for teachers' pedagogical knowledge, skills and practices, and for 'enhanced professional growth [and] greater teacher confidence', as well as benefits for students' outcomes. Support for educators' capacity to access, understand, share and apply research, combined with other forms of professional knowledge and evidence, is considered to be a work in progress (CUREE, 2011).

More broadly, the development of an overall evidence-informed system in education remains an important, although not yet realised, goal. Consideration of how to identify, leverage, share and potentially scale up existing promising local practices is developing. At the same time, government funding and support to create the enabling conditions for a culture and infrastructure for EIPP are required. Developing a truly evidence-informed education system requires supporting and engaging the capacity of all those involved. It means maximising the accessibility of existing evidence as well as prioritising needs for new research and evidence. And it also means supporting multiple processes and products to encourage the mobilisation and co-creation of evidence and professional knowledge. Finally, monitoring and evaluation are vital to identify 'what works now' for the purposes, processes, outputs and outcomes of EIPP.

References

Andrews, J., Robinson, D. and Hutchinson, J. (2017) *Closing the gap: trends in educational attainment and disadvantage*, London: Education Policy Institute, https://epi.org.uk/report/closing-the-gap/# (accessed 30 November 2017).

Atkinson, D. (2017) 'Embedding research activities in school', *Impact: Journal of the Chartered College of Teaching*, Interim Issue, May, pp 21–2.

Becheikh, N., Ziam, S., Idrissi, O., Castonguay, Y. and Landry, R. (2009) 'How to improve knowledge transfer strategies and practices in education? Answers from a systematic literature review', *Research in Higher Education Journal*, 7, pp 1–21.

Borg, S. (2010) 'Language teacher research engagement', *Language Teaching*, 43 (4), pp 391–429.

Bredo, E. (2006) 'Philosophies of educational research', in J.L. Green, G. Camilli and P.B. Elmore, with A. Skukauskaitė and E. Grace (eds), *Handbook of complementary methods in education research*, Washington, DC: American Education Research Association; Mahwah, NJ: Lawrence Erlbaum Associates, pp 1–30.

Brown, C. and Zhang, D. (2016) 'Is engaging in evidence-informed practice in education rational? Examining the divergence between teachers' attitudes towards evidence use and their actual instances of evidence use in schools', *British Educational Research Journal*, 42 (5), pp 780–801.

Bryk, A., Gomez, L. and Grunow, A. (2011) 'Getting ideas into action: building networked improvement communities in education', in M. Hallinan (ed.), *Frontiers in sociology of education, frontiers in sociology and social research*, Dordrecht: Springer, pp 127–62.

Campbell, C. (2016) 'Supporting teachers as a profession of knowledge developers and mobilisers', *Education Today*, 66 (2), pp 5–20.

Campbell, C. and Fulford, D. (2009) 'From knowledge generation to knowledge integration: Analysis of how a government uses research', paper presented to American Educational Research Association Annual Meeting, San Diego, CA.

Campbell, C., Pollock, K., Briscoe, P., Carr-Harris, S. and Tuters, S. (2017) 'Developing a knowledge network for applied education research to mobilise evidence in and for educational practice', *Educational Research*, 59 (2), pp 209–27.

Campbell, C., Pollock, K., Carr-Harris, S. and Briscoe, P. with Bairos, K. and Malik, S. (2014) *KNAER Final Report.* Knowledge Network for Applied Education Research, University of Toronto and Western University.

Coldwell, M., Greany, T., Higgins, S., Brown, C., Maxwell, B., Stiell, B., Stoll, L., Willis, B. and Burns, H. (2017) *Evidence-informed teaching: an evaluation of progress in England*, London: Department for Education.

Cooper, A. (2014) 'Knowledge mobilisation in education across Canada: a cross-case analysis of 44 research brokering organisations', *Evidence and Policy*, 10 (1), pp 29–59.

Cooper, A.M., Levin, B. and Campbell, C. (2009) 'The growing (but still limited) importance of evidence in education policy and practice', *Journal of Educational Change*, 10 (2–3), pp 159–71.

CUREE (2011) *Report of professional practitioner use of research review: practitioner engagement in and/or with research*, Coventry: CUREE, http://www.curee.co.uk/files/publication/[site-timestamp]/Practitioner%20Use%20of%20Research%20Review%20-%20FINAL%2011_02_11.pdf (accessed 14 January 2014).

Davies, H.T.O, Nutley, S.M. and Smith, P.C. (eds) (2000) *What works: evidence-based policy and practice in public services*, Bristol: Policy Press.

Durbin, B. and Nelson, J. (2014) 'Why effective use of evidence in the classroom needs system-wide change (NFER thinks: what the evidence tells us)', Slough: NFER, http://www.nfer.ac.uk/publications/99942/ (accessed 23 January 2017).

Edwards, A. (2011) 'User engagement and the processes of educational research', in T. Fenwick and L. Farrell (eds), *Knowledge mobilization and educational research: politics, languages and responsibilities*, London: Routledge.

Fitzgibbon, C. (2000) 'Education: realising the potential', in H. Davies, S. Nutley, and P. Smith, (eds), *What works? Evidence-based policy and practice in public services*, Bristol: Policy Press, pp 69–91.

Galdin-O'Shea, H. (2015) 'Leading "disciplined enquiries" in schools', in C. Brown (ed.), *Leading the use of research and evidence in schools*, London: Institute of Education Press.

Gough, D. (2013) 'Knowledge mobilisation in education in England', in B. Levin, J. Qi, H Edelstein and J. Sohn (eds), *The impact of research in education*, Bristol: Policy Press.

Gough, D., Tripney, J., Kenny, C. and Buk-Berge, E. (2011) *Evidence-informed policymaking in education in Europe: EIPEE final project report*, London: EPPI-Centre, Social Science Research Unit, Institute of Education, University of London.

Greany, T. (2015) 'How can evidence inform teaching and decision making across 21,000 autonomous schools? Learning from the journey in England', in C. Brown (ed.), *Leading the use of research and evidence in schools*, London: Institute of Education Press, pp 11–29.

Jones, G. and CEBMa (2016) *Evidence-based practice: a handbook for teachers and school leaders*, Amsterdam: Centre for Evidence Based Management.

Kroll, L. (2006) 'Making inquiry a habit of mind: learning to use inquiry to understand and improve practice', *Studying Teacher Education*, 1 (2), pp 179–93.

LaPointe-McEwan, D., DeLuca, C. and Klinger, D. (2017) 'Supporting evidence use in networked professional learning: the role of the middle leader', *Educational Research*, 59 (2), pp 136–53.

Lord, P., Rabiasz, A., Roy, P., Harland, J., Styles, B. and Fowler, K. (2017a) *Evidence-based literacy support – the 'Literacy Octopus' trial – evaluation report and executive summary*, London: Education Endowment Foundation.

Lord, P., Rabiasz, A. and Styles, B. (2017b) *'Literacy Octopus' dissemination trial: evaluation report and executive summary*, London: Education Endowment Foundation.

Lord, P., Sims, D., White, R. and Roy, P. (2017c) *Evidence for the frontline: evaluation report and executive summary*, London: Education Endowment Foundation.

Mincu, M. (2014) 'Inquiry paper 6: teacher quality and school improvement – what is the role of research?', in British Educational Research Association/The Royal Society for the Encouragement of Arts, Manufactures and Commerce (eds), *The role of research in teacher education: reviewing the evidence*, https://www.bera.ac.uk/wp-content/uploads/2014/02/BERA-RSA-Interim-Report.pdf (accessed 8 November 2015).

Nelson, J. and O'Beirne, C. (2014) *Using evidence in the classroom: what works and why?* Slough: NFER.

Nelson, J. and Sharples, J. (2017) 'How research-engaged are you?', *Impact: Journal of the Chartered College of Teaching*, Interim Issue, May, pp 16–20.

Nelson, J., Mehta, P., Sharples, J. and Davey, C. (2017) *Measuring teachers' research engagement: findings from a pilot study*, London: Education Endowment Foundation, https://educationendowmentfoundation.org.uk/projects-and-evaluation/evaluating-projects/evaluator-resources/research-use-survey/ (accessed 30 November 2017).

Nutley, S., Powell, A. and Davies, H. (2013) *What counts as good evidence?* London: Alliance for Useful Evidence, http://www.alliance4usefulevidence.org/assets/What-Counts-as-Good-Evidence-WEB.pdf (accessed 23 January 2017).

OECD (2014) *New insights from TALIS 2013 – teaching and learning in primary and upper secondary education*, Paris: Organisation for Economic Co-operation and Development.

Ontario Ministry of Education (not dated) *Research and evaluation strategy*, http://www.edu.gov.on.ca/eng/research/.

Parsons, D. and Burkey, S. (2011) *Evaluation of the teaching and learning research programme (second phase).* Horsham: HOST Policy Research, http://www.esrc.ac.uk/_images/TLRP_Impact_Evaluation_tcm8-17373.pdf (accessed 14 January 2014).

Pollard, A. (2011) 'Exploring strategies for impact: riding the wave with the TLRP', in T. Fenwick and L. Farrell (eds), *Knowledge mobilization and educational research: politics, languages and responsibilities*, London: Routledge.

Roberts, C. (2015) 'Impractical research: overcoming the obstacles to becoming an evidence-informed school', in C. Brown (ed.), *Leading the use of research and evidence in schools*, London: Institute of Education Press.

Sharples, J. (2013) *Evidence for the frontline*, London: Alliance for Useful Evidence, http://www.alliance4usefulevidence.org/assets/EVIDENCE-FOR-THE-FRONTLINE-FINAL-5-June-2013.pdf, (accessed 14 January 2014).

Shiell-Davis, K., Wright, A., Seditas, K., Morton, S. and Bland, N. (2015) *Scaling-up innovations. Evidence review*, Scotland: What Works Scotland.

Stoll, L. (2015) 'Using evidence, learning and the role of professional learning communities', in C. Brown (ed.), *Leading the use of research and evidence in schools*, London: Institute of Education Press.

Wilkins, R. (2012) *Research engagement for school development*, London: Institute of Education Press.

8

Using evidence in environmental and sustainability issues

Mark Reed and Laura Meagher

Introduction to evidence use in environmental and sustainability issues

It could be argued that concerns about the environment have become increasingly widespread, even mainstream. The word 'environmentalist' was coined as far back as 1902, and Rachel Carson helped to ignite an environmental movement in 1962 with her book *Silent Spring*, which drew attention to the adverse environmental effects of pesticides. More recently, the United Nations Intergovernmental Panel on Climate Change and Al Gore's winning of the Nobel Peace Prize in 2007 have further highlighted the challenges, and increasing global attention has been paid to climate change. When the internationally agreed Millennium Development Goals were revised into a set of 17 Sustainable Development Goals in 2016, the choice of the word 'sustainable' was telling. Several goals are explicitly environmental in orientation: climate action; life below water; and life on land. In addition, other goals are closely interwoven with environmental issues, such as clean water and sanitation; affordable and clean energy; good health and well-being; and sustainable cities and communities, among others. None of these is a simple challenge.

As individual nations and the international community grapple with increasingly complex and interconnected environmental challenges in a globalised and rapidly changing world, calls for evidence-based policy have grown. However, environmental and sustainability issues present particular challenges for evidence-informed policy and practice (EIPP) for diverse reasons. These include: the political prominence and broad sectoral reach of policies in this area (which often interact with a wide range of other policy areas); tensions arising from policy making at different levels (local, national, international); the wide range of spatial and temporal scales over which environmental processes operate; and the complex, uncertain and often contested nature of the evidence base.

Powerful actors in this field may also seek to shape how problems are conceptualised and addressed. For example, climate change science, painstakingly constructed over decades, has to contend with considerable levels of contestation and outright denial. More insidiously, vested parties may seek to use evidence in partisan ways: purporting to contribute data to scientific debate while nonetheless muddying the waters over what is known and what is still in doubt (Box 8.1 provides a particularly interesting example of how the hydrocarbons industry in the 1980s adopted many of the same obfuscating tactics over anthropogenic climate change, as did the tobacco industry years earlier over the health impacts of smoking).

Politics and vested interests aside, few other policy areas have to consider such a range of spatial scales (for example, from battles over the siting of a local supermarket to global climate change), alongside temporal scales that range from rapid response within hours (for example, to natural disasters) to the pursuit of sustainability goals and targets over generational time-scales (for example, the United Nations Sustainable Development Goals). Policy making in this area needs to address issues that may have global causes beyond the jurisdiction of any given policy maker, but may be felt locally in different ways by

---

Box 8.1: Selective use and non-use of evidence on climate change

A publication in *Environmental Research Letters* (Supran and Oreskes, 2017) used extensive documentary analysis to assess whether the ExxonMobil Corporation had misled the public about the causes and consequences of climate change over an extended period. The authors concluded that as documents from the corporation became more publicly accessible they communicated a greater degree of doubt as to whether climate change was real, human caused, serious and solvable. For example, a large majority of internal documents (80% or more) acknowledged that climate change is real and human caused, whereas only 12% of 'advertorials' did so (such as op-ed pieces in large-circulation newspapers like the *New York Times*), with over 80% of these pieces expressing doubt. The authors conclude that 'ExxonMobil contributed to advancing climate science – by way of its scientists' academic publications – but promoted doubt about it in advertorials. Given this discrepancy, we conclude that ExxonMobil misled the public [about the evidence].'

different social groups. Policies need, therefore, to balance the need to mitigate the causes of environmental degradation (often with very limited budgets) with the need to enable communities to adapt to unavoidable environmental change. They need to provide short-term solutions to avert or cope with challenges such as flooding, while setting in motion longer-term adaptive strategies that can reduce future impacts and tackle underlying drivers of change. All in all, this is a tall order.

Compounding these challenges, evidence from research rarely forms a single, clear-cut line of argument. The evidence base is often highly fractured, for example providing evidence about just one locale or habitat, or describing future environmental impacts based on natural science alone, without considering social, cultural or economic factors. Furthermore, the (developing) evidence base is often uncertain, providing competing claims based on different methods and models. These claims may be promoted in different ways by those with often sharply divergent interests (see, for example, Box 8.1). Few citizens or politicians have sufficient technical understanding of environmental science to be able to critically evaluate competing claims and counter-claims, making it 'relatively easy for a vocal, partisan minority to sow confusion, hoping to justify delay and inaction by amplifying uncertainties' (Pidgeon and Fischhoff, 2011, p 35).

As a result, members of the policy community must interpret often-contradictory research findings, alongside other lines of argument put forward by actors with competing ideological framings (Pidgeon and Fischhoff, 2011). Policies that promote sustainability inevitably involve trade-offs between protecting the natural environment and the social and economic well-being of citizens. Policy makers must therefore consider moral and ideological arguments alongside many and diverse practicalities, such as budget constraints, political expediency and unpredictable external events that change the parameters of decisions.

Bridgman and Davis (2000, p 31) describe this as a dynamic 'policy dance ... [of] seemingly random movements rather than choreographed order'. Others have described the relationship between research and policy in rather more cynical terms: as a way for governments to legitimise policies with reference to evidence from research only when it supports their politically driven priorities (Sanderson, 2002). Indeed, the complex and multifaceted nature of environmental issues, and the rapidly changing and sometimes internally contradictory body of research knowledge, may facilitate picking and choosing by policy makers in their claiming the support of research evidence (see also Chapter Two).

This chapter, then, considers how evidence is created, understood, synthesised and used in environmental and sustainability policy development and implementation. The nature and use of evidence here contrasts somewhat with the other policy and practice areas covered in this section of the book, many of which have mirrored the health sector's trajectory of growing emphasis upon and then nuanced departure from randomised controlled trials (RCTs) as the sine qua non of evidence. In particular, this policy area requires evidence that cuts across multiple systems and sectors, at diverse and sometimes very large scales that are rarely needed in other policy arenas. The nature of evidence ranges from quantitative empirical and modelled data to qualitative and ethnographic accounts, including the 'know-how' of 'what (seems to) work' in practice and the 'know-why' process-based understanding and theory generated by research (including formal evaluations).

In a sense, lines between these types of evidence are becoming blurred (sometimes deliberately so): research-based knowledge is increasingly integrating insights from publics and stakeholders, and synthesising evidence across multiple studies to provide more generalisable lessons for policy making (see also discussions in Chapters Ten and Eleven). There is an increasing move towards more participatory and co-productive forms of evidence production, often in collaboration with boundary organisations and knowledge intermediaries, with the explicit goal of generating beneficial policy outcomes. There are also a number of disparate disciplines providing evidence for policy in this area, and many of these disciplines have distinctive approaches to the generation and use of evidence. In this chapter we bring together insights and approaches from across the range of disciplines and diverse new initiatives that inform environmental and sustainability policy.

The nature of evidence for environmental and sustainability issues

The nature of evidence informing environmental and sustainability policy is particularly broad and increasingly integrated. It cuts across multiple research areas and disciplines, and includes many forms of expert knowledge beyond the academy (ranging from farmers to international non-governmental organisations (NGOs)) as well as lay knowledge such as that from citizen science initiatives. Evidence may be drawn from the natural sciences (for example, climate modelling), economics (for example, deliberative monetary or non-monetary valuation of ecosystem services), social sciences (for example, environmental governance) or the arts and humanities (for example, environmental ethics and aesthetics).

Natural tensions often arise between these research realms – in approaches, methods, premises, foci for investigation, criteria for analysis and even the very questions posed. Researchers from different disciplines may reach quite different conclusions, and such tensions can fracture the evidence base. Hence, policy input from one line of research may not always align readily with input from a different line of research, or indeed with knowledge from other sources, making it all the more difficult for policy makers and practitioners to make decisions.

Knowledge arising from research is explicit (that is, it has been articulated in written or spoken form) and tends to get systematised, decontextualised and presented in forms that are (seen as or purported to be) widely transferable. Thus, this type of knowledge is particularly suited to policy-making processes that typically operate at national scales or beyond (Norgaard, 1984; Ingram, 2008), advancing as it does generalised and somewhat decontextualised arguments. Lundvall and Johnson (1994) refer to this sort of knowledge as 'know-why' knowledge, because research typically attempts to understand the underlying principles and theories that explain phenomena (sometimes through experimental trials of specific interventions). They contrast this with the (often practical, often local) 'know-how' knowledge held by citizens and stakeholders, which may be more tacit, informal, context dependent and rooted in experience and place.

The need to integrate these different knowledge bases has been increasingly recognised by international bodies. For example, there has been the explicit involvement of civil society organisations in representing local knowledge in the development of the United Nations Convention to Combat Desertification (UNCCD), which also enshrined their involvement in its implementation. However, the inclusion of local knowledge in the science–policy interface of the UNCCD, in common with equivalent bodies for the other two Rio Conventions on biological diversity and climate change, is possible only where these perspectives have been codified in peer-reviewed literature. In this respect, then, little has changed since the World Bank explained how it wanted to promote the use of local knowledge in its 'indigenous knowledge for development framework': only after it has been tested and legitimised by formal 'scientific proof' (World Bank, 1998, p 6). This approach has been described by some as 'post-colonial'; or, as Briggs and Sharp (2004, p 667) put it, 'it is still the scientific view, in all its wisdom, that can decide which indigenous knowledge is worthy of serious investigation and dissemination'. There are now calls for a new kind of science in which stakeholders and publics move from being passive recipients of knowledge or objects of study, to being equal partners in the research process (Keeler et al, 2017).

The rationalist epistemological argument is perhaps a more benign explanation for the privileged position given to scientific evidence in many policy-making processes, compared to claims of post-colonialism or the selective use of evidence to legitimise decisions. However, there is a well-rehearsed counter-argument from constructivism that suggests that all knowledge, including scientific knowledge, is socially constructed and influenced by culture, history and context.

The emergence of environmentalism, as it gave rise to many of the policies that now protect our environment, provides a particularly clear demonstration of this perspective. These policies reflect the shift in Western civilisation from utilitarian perceptions of nature as something to be used for human benefit, towards an ethical position that protects nature for its intrinsic value. Much contemporary environmental and sustainability policy can be traced back to Aldo Leopold's (1949) famous 'land ethic', in which he argued for the moral standing we give to other humans to be extended to non-human species and landscapes: 'all ethics so far evolved rest upon a single premise: that the individual is a member of a community of interdependent parts. The land ethic simply enlarges the boundaries of the community to include soils, waters, plants and animals, or collectively the land' (Leopold, 1949, p 203). Viewed in this way, it is clear that both conservation science and policy are based on a normative set of ethics and assumptions that predispose researchers to pose and answer some questions and not others. In this light, different arguments pertaining to the human (typically economic) trade-offs arising from environmental policies may have an equally valid evidence base, but in response to very different questions. The nature of relevant evidence in this field remains, then, very contested.

Production and synthesis of research-based knowledge for environmental and sustainability issues

Despite emerging nuances as to what constitutes 'knowledge', some defend the primacy of scientific knowledge on epistemological grounds as the only way of finding rational argument and universal truth upon which policy can be based. The response to the conflicting accounts often provided by science is to simply seek more and better research, and/or more and better synthesis. This section concentrates on the strategies and structures encouraging the latter.

There is an expanding range of tools available to summarise knowledge, from expert-led, comprehensive meta-analyses and systematic reviews and more time-efficient rapid evidence reviews, to approaches that incorporate the knowledge and perspectives of stakeholders and publics. These engaged synthesis methods range from participatory methods such as citizens' juries to the incorporation of lay knowledge in systems models through Bayesian approaches (that is, where participants' prior beliefs are adjusted by new data placed in front of them).

Initiatives in this area have proliferated. The Collaboration for Environmental Evidence coordinates six centres focused on synthesising evidence on issues relating to environmental policy and practice, based in Australia, Canada, France, South Africa, Sweden and the UK. Each centre secures its own funds and has its own set of interests (such as mining, fisheries or agriculture), but they all contribute to a collective effort at synthesising knowledge for environmental management. In addition, the journal *Conservation Evidence* now produces an annual *What Works in Conservation* publication providing synoptic evidence summaries. Data quality of primary studies is a huge problem for synthesis initiatives, significantly limiting the number of studies that are available for review, but synthesis initiatives are raising awareness in the research community about ways of improving research design and data collection to enable more effective summations to be conducted in future.

The nature of the challenges being tackled by initiatives such as these is typically broad, requiring multi-sectoral and interdisciplinary approaches to the production of evidence. 'Interdisciplinarity' is an approach to producing and synthesising research that has been heralded in many arenas, but it is perhaps most strikingly vital to addressing problems relating to the environment and sustainability. Even what seems to be a singular field, such as environmental science, actually incorporates a wide range of approaches, paradigms and questions. Just one of the disciplines within its umbrella, ecology, has itself been labelled a 'portmanteau field', because when it emerged as a discipline it carried with it a variety of approaches (Phillipson et al, 2009).

Interdisciplinarity beyond the natural sciences is mandated when issues of sustainability arise, with evidence from different fields being needed for crucial elements of societal well-being, the economy, individual behaviours and so on. Many perceive interdisciplinary integration as vital to providing evidence in a form useful to policy makers and practitioners dealing with complex problems (Lowe et al, 2013; O'Brien et al, 2013). Indeed, as well as contributing integrated solutions to problems, effective development of interdisciplinarity shares many of the behaviours of effective knowledge exchange. What works for both processes includes actions such as: joint framing of problems; arriving at some level of reciprocal understanding; building relationships characterised by mutual trust; and development of respect for all roles involved (Lyall et al, 2011). An early and still leading example of what works in combining interdisciplinarity with knowledge exchange and impact generation is the UK Research Council-funded Rural Economy and Land Use programme (RELU, described subsequently in Box 8.4).

Within the UK, research councils, which have long been separated by the cluster of disciplines that each one supports, are being combined into a single entity. Along with economies of scale, there is doubtless a hypothesis (as yet untested, and not yet fully articulated) that this will facilitate interdisciplinary synthesis. Development of capacity for interdisciplinarity among UK researchers takes various forms. Frequently, large-scale research programmes, such as the RELU initiative or the Ecosystem Services for Poverty Alleviation, aim for outcomes from multiple disciplinary inputs and, in so doing, can enable at least some researchers to behave in new ways.

Explicit interdisciplinary attention is also sometimes paid to developing the next generation of researchers, such as the PhD fellowship programme run jointly for several years between the Natural Environment Research Council (NERC) and the Economic and Social Research Council (ESRC). Currently, the two councils are jointly supporting a centre for doctoral training in risk and mitigation, using big data; 'the aim of the consortium is to produce a cohort of researchers who can use large or complex datasets to understand and ease the risks posed by a range of societal and environmental changes' (NERC, 2017). While challenges of inappropriate peer reviewing and obstacles in career pathways still exist, the recognition of the need for interdisciplinary research and research capacity has grown. Taking this further, many countries use the word 'transdisciplinarity' to encompass work that is both interdisciplinary and inclusive of stakeholders. While retaining the two terms of 'interdisciplinarity' and 'stakeholder impact', UK research funders also often seek this combination (Lyall et al, 2015).

Recent decades, then, have seen increasing attention given to the challenges of integrating and synthesising knowledge, leading to a proliferation of approaches with strong interlinking to eventual knowledge use. It is to this latter issue specifically that we now turn.

Encouraging and enabling evidence use in the environmental and sustainability arena

The Impact Case Study Database (created for the 2014 UK Research Excellence Framework) provides many examples of research impact in the environmental and sustainability area. But, despite these documented examples of impact, it is perhaps unsurprising that there remain very real challenges to the use of evidence. One thing is clear: genuine involvement of stakeholders and their knowledge(s) is critical, although the practice of this is challenging and sometimes still contested. Several key approaches to encouraging and enabling evidence use by policy makers and practitioners are discussed in this section. Most of these are seeing increased attention and investment, and they include: knowledge co-production; the development of boundary organisations; the promotion of impact-driven research initiatives; and the use of knowledge intermediaries and relationship building.

Knowledge co-production

In response to the challenges of producing and synthesising research-based knowledge (reviewed in the previous section), there is increasing interest in models of deliberation and co-production for environmental policy (for example, Pohl et al, 2010). The deliberative democracy literature argues for increasing decentralisation of environmental policy to enable greater civic engagement in the development and implementation of policy (for example, Hysing, 2013). Assuming that values are made explicit, there is some evidence that deliberation can alter contextual values (for example, the financial value placed on ecosystem service benefits) over short time-scales (for example, a single workshop), but deeper-held, transcendental values (for example, the non-utilitarian value of ecosystems due to their intrinsic value or the rights of future human generations and non-humans) are likely to require engagement over much longer periods of time (Everard et al, 2016).

More co-productive approaches shift the locus of control from the government to the governed, where new ideas can be developed jointly between members of the research, policy and wider stakeholder communities to tackle highly contested issues (for example, Reed et al, 2017). Increasingly, this is conceived as a nested hierarchy of interacting governance levels, with the institutions of governance in these levels typically differing in the scale of their jurisdiction and level of formality (often referred to as 'multilevel' or 'polycentric' governance; Newig and Fritsch, 2009). Challies et al (2017) describe multilevel governance as a 'governance learning process' through which policy makers draw on evidence and experience to learn about how to design and execute effective participatory decision making. To more effectively co-produce evidence-based policy in these ways, two important research challenges must be addressed; here we will first consider the specific challenge of designing and deploying effective 'boundary organisations', followed by a brief discussion of the power of large-scale, impact-oriented research initiatives and the often diffuse but influential roles played by diverse 'knowledge intermediaries'.

Boundary organisations

It is often proposed that the co-production and practical application of new ideas by researchers and policy actors is coordinated through institutions (often described as boundary organisations) in safe places where these ideas can be tested and refined (often described as 'niches'). It is argued that such 'socio-technical innovations' have the capacity to disrupt stable societal structures and norms, so that society can transition to a new way of doing things (for example, from fossil fuel to renewable energy systems; Geels, 2005). However, there have been limited attempts, to date, to create the sorts of boundary organisations that could be capable of facilitating the co-production of policy innovations at these societal scales.

Real challenges exist in the design of boundary organisations and safe institutional spaces or niches in which evidence-based policy innovations can be co-produced and tested at societal scales. For this to happen, Hanger et al (2013) argue that boundary organisations must facilitate and manage a wide range of complex processes (Box 8.2). These include the creation of suitable boundary objects (such as scenarios, assessments and data models) that can become the focus of dialogue, and the maintenance of multiple lines of accountability and governance (Box 8.2). Limited systematic knowledge regarding the creation of boundary organisations suggests that there may be scope for learning from successful examples (for example, ClimateXChange – described in Box 8.3).

While still in its early stages, ClimateXChange is an example of a new type of boundary organisation that could be used as a model elsewhere to draw on the best available evidence quickly while benefiting from long-term, strategic research. Reflection upon the relevance of its list of identified success factors could be useful to others establishing or leading boundary organisations of various types.

Box 8.2: The role of boundary organisations

Hanger et al (2013) argue that boundary organisations must facilitate the following core processes:

1 **double participation**, that is, people from both or multiple domains need to be involved;
2 **dual accountability**, that is, work needs to conform to both scientific and policy standards;
3 **use of boundary objects**, where discussions can come together, for example scenarios, assessment reports and data modelling;
4 **boundary management/co-production**, that is, communication, translation and mediation between science and policy; and
5 **meta-governance**, that is, orchestration of knowledge across jurisdictional levels.

Box 8.3: The operation of ClimateXChange (CXC) as a boundary organisation

The Scottish Government has pioneered a new model for evidence-based policy that enables policy makers to get high-quality evidence quickly from some of the best researchers in the country, while continuing to support long-term strategic research to tackle complex, global challenges (Wreford et al, 2018).

One of the Scottish Government's new Centres of Expertise, ClimateXChange (CXC), connects a network of government and university researchers across Scotland to get the best possible evidence into policy fast. Some of this is existing evidence, critically reviewed and translated to answer specific questions. Some of the evidence is new primary research, rapidly designed and deployed and then communicated to contribute towards policy development. All of this takes place in the context of a longer-term strategic programme of research (conducted at multiple institutions) to provide long-term datasets and tackle more complex issues.

CXC represents a new type of boundary organisation that can balance short-term evidence needs with the need for longer-term strategic research, integrating knowledge from a large and diverse pool of world-leading expertise. Evidence from interviews with CXC researchers and members of the policy community identified a number of features that were critical to the success of CXC as a boundary organisation.

• There are no magic bullets: the success of an organisation such as this takes time and reinvention, using many different methods. It is highly dependent on the context in which it needs to operate, on the people involved and on changing policy contexts and evidence needs.

• Two-way, trusting and long-term relationships are critical to overcoming barriers between policy makers and scientists.

• The timing of engagement with researchers is critical to ensuring that evidence and expertise are targeted effectively at relevant points in the policy process, where they can provide greatest influence and benefits. Flexibility at project and organisational level, including the ability to draw together different knowledge and skill bases, helps to enable research to remain relevant to evolving policy needs.

• Researchers need incentives to participate: although opportunities for peer-reviewed papers and research funding remain potent, policy impacts are increasingly being rewarded (for example, through the UK's Research Excellence Framework and via promotion criteria).

• Instead of generating knowledge primarily via research push or policy pull, true co-production of knowledge is needed to provide cutting-edge research that has genuine policy relevance. CXC's role in push/pull activities is balanced by sitting within a strategic research framework that is able to advocate more 'blue-skies' innovation to the policy community.

Impact-driven research initiatives

As a more general challenge, including but not limited to boundary organisations, it is necessary to overcome structural barriers to the flows of knowledge so that research initiatives can focus more clearly on impacts. These barriers exist concurrently with increasing trends towards encouraging or demanding impacts among research funders who themselves are finding it necessary to work together in new ways when tackling complex challenges such as sustainability. Increasingly, agencies funding research have encouraged and/or required researchers to propose 'pathways' to impact when bidding for support, and this emphasis is particularly conspicuous in large-scale, often multifunder, interdisciplinary initiatives tackling complex problems.

Relatively early in this trend, a bold initiative relating to the environment was funded with over £26.5 million between 2004 and 2013 by an assembly of research funders. The RELU initiative had interdisciplinarity and (two-way) knowledge exchange as its key interwoven themes. An external evaluation (Meagher, 2012) identified a range of successful impacts stemming both from the programme and from individual projects – but these did not arise spontaneously. Lessons were learned through the RELU that have proved useful not only to research leaders but also to research funders, among whom an increase in confidence in this sort of initiative was identified (Box 8.4).

Knowledge intermediaries and relationship building

Boundary organisations and targeted large-scale initiatives are certainly not the only mechanisms for overcoming structural barriers to the flows of knowledge between members of the policy community, researchers and stakeholders. It is perhaps especially important to note the facilitative role played at a variety of levels in a variety of ways by 'knowledge intermediaries' or 'knowledge brokers'. Notably heterogeneous, and quite often 'under-sung', these are individuals or entities comfortable with the languages and concerns of both researchers and stakeholders, and they frequently act as proactive facilitators of knowledge flows, sometimes with a degree of translation (Reed, 2016).

In the environmental arena as well as elsewhere, people-based processes such as trust building and relationship building have been shown to be key to generating impacts (for example, Jagosh et al, 2015; Reed et al, 2018). This has implications for how research units are run, how intermediaries are supported and the degree to which such 'soft' processes are enabled or rewarded (Greenhalgh and Fahy, 2015;

Meagher and Martin, 2017). Recognising, supporting, incentivising and enabling individuals, units and institutions to play knowledge-intermediary roles can engender the two-way dialogue between researchers and stakeholders that is most likely to lead towards EIPP (Meagher and Lyall, 2013).

Box 8.4: The Rural Environment and Land Use (RELU) initiative: interdisciplinarity and impact

The RELU aimed to foster knowledge exchange and have impact by:
- the requirement that all funded projects should engage in knowledge exchange;
- the organisation of combined researcher and stakeholder events, and the creation of stakeholder advisory forums;
- the creation of cross-boundary work-shadowing and visiting fellowships;
- the expectation of publication of accessible policy and practice briefing notes.

It was clear that the RELU's central goal of interdisciplinarity contributed to its companion goal of knowledge exchange. For example, those involved in the programme (stakeholders and researchers) overwhelmingly agreed that the RELU's emphasis on interdisciplinarity enhanced the capacity of its researchers to deliver integrated understanding relevant to stakeholder problems. When researchers and stakeholders were asked for key lessons learned, they emphasised the importance of:
- leadership;
- requiring early engagement of stakeholders;
- a central pot of discretionary money.

In addition to a suite of impacts arising from constituent projects, the external evaluation identified several overarching legacies of the RELU programme:
- enhanced conceptual and practical understanding of land use;
- influence in the research and science policy arenas, particularly in the growth of acceptance of interdisciplinarity in policy-relevant research and in a shift from a model of one-way knowledge transfer to two-way knowledge exchange;
- evidence of a set of approaches that can deliver research impacts.

Source: Abstracted from Meagher, 2012.

Reflections and conclusions

Environmental issues are complex and multifaceted; approaches to addressing them are no less multilayered. It is increasingly recognised that diverse knowledge claims need to be evaluated as part of environmental policy-making processes (for example, Sanderson, 2006; Crilly et al, 2010). Rather than viewing these competing knowledge claims as a problem, it could be helpful to view different knowledge bases as potentially complementary, and where possible to integrate the 'know-how' of 'what works' in the experience of citizens and stakeholders with the 'know-why' process-based understanding and theory of researchers. There have been some moves in this direction in national and international environmental policy making, but the tension between what is seen as objective knowledge from research and the usually less formalised knowledge from other communities, such as local inhabitants, remains.

Instead of automatically privileging research evidence above other forms of knowledge, a mixed approach weighs knowledge from different sources, recognising the potential for evidence from research to be contradicted or disproved, and the potential for less formal types of knowledge to provide valuable insights upon which more effective and responsive policies can be built. The critical evaluation and synthesis of some knowledges may be more challenging than others, especially those that are tacit (the knowledge we hold but of which we are not consciously aware) or implicit (knowledge that can be, but has not yet been, articulated). There is evidence that implicit knowledge can be useful for managing complex systems if it can be articulated – for example, providing detailed information about how systems work on the basis of many years' experience living and working with a given system or wider context (Olsson et al, 2004; Fazey et al, 2006).

Given the multiplicity of perspectives surrounding what are often emotive issues relating to the environment and sustainability, it is not surprising that explorations of participatory research have taken place, for example, regarding the development and implementation of natural resource management plans (Blackstock et al, 2015) or participatory scenario planning in local communities (Brown et al, 2016). Learning from analysis of this sort of research may become increasingly relevant as complex decisions are made regarding what will inevitably be trade-offs relating to both society and the environment. Indeed, learning continues to emerge from formal impact evaluations of research programmes as well as from critical reflection during complex initiatives (for example, Roux et al, 2010; Spaapen and van Drooge,

2011; Meagher and Lyall, 2013). Capturing such learning should progress our understanding of what works in supporting evidence use.

In sum, then, policy and practice relating to the environment and sustainability face many challenges in using research-based evidence. These challenges include: the inherent complexity of the issues involved; dependence upon integration across multiple fields of evidence, even within the environmental sciences; political considerations, including but not limited to the potential for short-term decisions, avoidance of controversy and/or selective use of agreeable evidence; and the need for multi-way exchange across diverse audiences. However, at the same time, research into the processes through which knowledge is produced and used has spawned a number of practical strategies that have the potential to enhance engagement between the research and policy communities around these complex issues. These include the increased incentives for interdisciplinary integration and the increased emphasis (by governments, research funding agencies, institutions) upon the generation of research-informed impacts beyond academia. Learning from an increasing portfolio of 'experiments' about how to conduct knowledge exchange is also key, alongside a growing appreciation of the need to incorporate different sorts of knowledge along with more formal research-based knowledge (such as the tacit knowledge of practitioners and the experiential knowledge of communities). Taken together, then, and without minimising the weight of scientific, practical and political challenges to addressing issues in the environment and sustainability, these trends show how ambitious initiatives can bring research-based evidence more effectively to the fore.

References

Blackstock, K.L., Dinnie, L., Dilley, R., Marshall, K., Dunglinson, J., Trench, H., Harper, K., Finan, K., MacPherson, J., Johnston, E. and Griffin, A. (2015) 'Participatory research to influence participatory governance: managing relationships with planners', *Area*, 47, pp 254–60.

Bridgman, P. and Davis, G. (2000) *Australian policy handbook*, 2nd edn, St Leonards: Allen and Unwin.

Briggs, J. and Sharp, J. (2004) 'Indigenous knowledges and development: A postcolonial caution', *Third World Quarterly*, 25, pp 661–76.

Brown, I., Martin-Ortega, J., Waylen, K.A. and Blackstock, K.L. (2016) 'Participatory scenario planning for developing innovation in community adaptation responses: three contrasting examples from Latin America', *Regional Environmental Change*, 16: pp 1685–1700.

Challies, E., Newig, J., Kochskämper, E. and Jager, N.W. (2017) 'Governance change and governance learning in Europe: stakeholder participation in environmental policy implementation', *Policy and Society*, 36 (2), pp 288–303.

Crilly, T., Jashapara, A. and Ferlie, E. (2010) *Research utilisation and knowledge mobilisation: a scoping review of the literature. Report for the National Institute for Health Research Service Delivery and Organization*, London: Queen's Printer and Controller of HMSO.

Everard, M., Kenter, J.O. and Reed, M.S. (2016) 'The ripple effect: Institutionalising pro-environmental values to shift societal norms and behaviours', *Ecosystem Services*, 21, pp 230–40.

Fazey, I., Proust, K., Newell, B., Johnson, B. and Fazey J.A. (2006) 'Eliciting the implicit knowledge and perceptions of on-ground conservation managers of the Macquarie Marshes', *Ecology and Society*, 11, art 25.

Geels, F.W. (2005) *Technological transitions and system innovations: a co-evolutionary and socio-technical analysis*, Cheltenham: Edward Elgar Publishing.

Greenhalgh, T. and Fahy, N. (2015) 'Research impact in the community-based health sciences: an analysis of 162 case studies from the 2014 UK Research Excellence Framework', *BMC Medicine*, 13 (1), pp 1–12.

Hanger, S., Pfenninger, S., Dreyfus, M. and Patt, A. (2013) 'Knowledge and information needs of adaptation policy-makers: a European study', *Regional Environmental Change*, 13 (1), pp 91–101.

Hysing, E. (2013) 'Representative democracy, empowered experts, and citizen participation: visions of green governing', *Environmental Politics*, 22, pp 955–74.

Ingram J. (2008) 'Are farmers in England equipped to meet the knowledge challenge of sustainable soil management? An analysis of farmer and advisor views', *Journal of Environmental Management*, 86, pp 214–28.

Jagosh, J., Bush, P.L., Salsberg, J., Macaulay, A., Greenhalgh, T., Wong, G., Cargo, M., Green, L.W., Herbert, C. and Pluye, P. (2015) 'A realist evaluation of community-based participatory research: partnership synergy, trust building and related ripple effects', *BMC Public Health*, 15, p 725.

Keeler, B.L., Chaplin-Kramer, R., Guerry, A., Addison, P.F.E., Bettigole, C., Burke, I.C., Gentry, B., Chambliss, L., Young, C., Travis, A.J., Darimont, C.T., Gordon, D.R., Hellmann, J., Kareiva, P., Monfort, S., Olander, L., Profeta, T., Possingham, H.P., Slotterback, C., Sterling, E., Ticktin, T., and Vira, B. (2017) 'Society is ready for a new kind of science – is academia?', *Bioscience*, 67: pp 591–2.

Leopold, A. (1949) *A sand county almanac*, New York: Oxford University Press.

Lowe, P., Phillipson, J. and Wilkinson, K. (2013) 'Why social scientists should engage with natural scientists', *Contemporary Social Science*, 8, pp 207–22.

Lundvall, B.A. and Johnson, B. (1994) 'The learning economy', *Journal of Industry Studies*, 1, pp 23–42.

Lyall, C., Meagher, L.R. and Bruce, A. (2015) 'A rose by any other name? Transdisciplinarity in the context of UK research policy', *Futures*, 65, pp 150–62.

Lyall, C., Bruce, A., Tait, J., and Meagher, L. (2011) *Interdisciplinary Research Journeys: Practical strategies for capturing creativity*, London: Bloomsbury Academic Press.

Meagher, L. (2012) 'Societal and economic impact evaluation, rural economy and land use initiative', http://www.esrc.ac.uk/files/research/research-and-impact-evaluation/relu-impact-evaluation-part-one/ (accessed 4 June 2017).

Meagher, L. and Lyall, C. (2013) 'The invisible made visible: using impact evaluations to illuminate and inform the role of knowledge intermediaries', *Evidence and Policy*, 9 (3), pp 409–18, doi: 10.1332/174426413X671941.

Meagher, L. and Martin, U. (2017) 'Slightly dirty maths: the richly textured mechanisms of impact', *Research Evaluation*, doi: https://doi.org/10.1093/reseval/rvw024.

NERC (2017) 'Centre for doctoral training in risk and mitigation; using big data', http://www.nerc.ac.uk/funding/available/postgrad/focused/cdt/risk (accessed 28 February 2017).

Newig, J. and Fritsch, O. (2009) 'Environmental governance: participatory, multi-level – and effective?', *Environmental Policy and Governance*, 19, pp 197–214.

Norgaard, R. (1984) 'Traditional agricultural knowledge: past performance, future prospects and institutional implications', *American Agricultural Economics Association*, 66, pp 874–8.

O'Brien, L. Marzano, M. and White, R. (2013) '"Participatory interdisciplinarity": towards the integration of disciplinary diversity with stakeholder engagement for new models of knowledge production', *Science and Public Policy*, 40 (1), pp 51–61.

Olsson, P., Folke, C. and Berkes, F. (2004) 'Adaptive co-management for building resilience in social-ecological systems', *Environmental Management*, 34, pp 75–90.

Phillipson, J., Lowe, P., Bullock, J.M. (2009) 'Navigating the social sciences: interdisciplinarity and ecology', *Journal of Applied Ecology*, 46 (2) pp 261–4.

Pidgeon, N. and Fischhoff, B. (2011) 'The role of social and decision sciences in communicating uncertain climate risks', *Nature Climate Change*, 1 (1), pp 35–41.

Pohl, C., Rist, S., Zimmermann, A., Fry, P., Gurung, G.S., Schneider, F., Speranza, C.I., Kiteme, B., Boillat, S., Serrano, E., Hadorn, G.H. and Wiesmann, U. (2010) 'Researchers' roles in knowledge co-production: experience from sustainability research in Kenya, Switzerland, Bolivia and Nepal', *Science and Public Policy*, 37 (4), pp 267–81.

Reed, M.S. (2016) *The Research Impact Handbook*, Huntly: Fast Track Impact.

Reed, M.S., Bryce, R. and Machen, R. (2018) 'Pathways to policy impact: a new approach for planning and evidencing research impact', *Evidence and Policy* (forthcoming).

Roux, D.J., Stirzaker, R.J., Breen, C.M., Lefroy, E.C. and Cresswell, H.P. (2010) 'Framework for participative reflection on the accomplishment of transdisciplinary research programs', *Environmental Science and Policy*, 13, pp 733–41.

Sanderson, I. (2002) 'Evaluation, policy learning and evidence-based policy making', *Public Administration*, 80 (1), pp 1–22.

Sanderson, I. (2006) 'Complexity, "practical rationality" and evidence-based policy making', *Policy & Politics*, 34, pp 115–32.

Spaapen, J. and van Drooge, L. (2011) 'Introducing "productive interactions", in social impact assessment', *Research Evaluation*, 20 (3), pp 211–18.

Supran, G. and Oreskes, N. (2017) *Environmental Research Letters*, 12, 084019.

World Bank (1998) 'Indigenous knowledge for development: a framework for development. Knowledge and Learning Centre, Africa Region', World Bank, http://www.worldbank.org/afr/ik/ikrept.pdf.

Wreford, A., Martin, S. and Reed, M.S. (2018, in preparation) 'A new model for evidence-based policy that pools expertise and balances rapid evidence generation with strategic research', *Nature Climate Change*.

9

Using evidence in international development

Ruth Stewart

Introduction to evidence use in international development

The field of international development has historically lacked a strong evidence base for both policy and practice (White, 2009; Banerjee and Duflo, 2011; Langer et al, 2015). This is despite the size of the global foreign aid budget, which exceeds $120 billion (about £85 billion) (Glennie and Sumner, 2014). The UK's own foreign aid budget was £13.4 billion in 2016, in line with the legal requirement to spend 0.7% of gross national income on overseas development assistance. However, only a small portion of these public funds are evaluated for the effectiveness of the ways in which they are used. In 2006 the Centre for Global Development published a report, *When Will We Ever Learn?* This highlighted the yawning inconsistency between this considerable financial investment and the relatively small evidence base, and called for an increased application of rigorous impact evaluation of development interventions (Savedoff et al, 2006; Glennie and Sumner, 2014). While evaluations have long been a part of development culture, the incorporation of trial methodology (discussed later) and debates around impact evaluations and generalisability are more recent, as is the language of 'evidence-based' and 'evidence-informed' decisions.

Language also varies around how best to refer to poor countries (Doane, 2017). 'Third world' is no longer considered appropriate and 'developing' is used by some. This chapter uses the World Bank's categorisation of 'low- and middle-income countries', as this terminology is commonly used in the field of development, particularly international development. The chapter also refers to the global North (that is, high-income countries) and global South (that is, low- and middle-income countries), or more generally uses the terms Northern and Southern.

Since 2000 there have been small but significant changes in the field of development. These have included shifts away from the assumption that the donor knows best and an acknowledgement that in a post-colonial world recipients of aid have both experience and expertise that should play a role in decision making. As the UK began to feel the pressure of global recessions in the 1990s and 2000s, so the rhetoric changed from offering support only for poor countries, towards tackling poverty in the UK and greater protection of British interests abroad. Shifts in international politics have seen more emphasis on security and trade, and a concern about helping to secure new and fragile states in order to reduce the impacts of conflict and migration on the UK and to counter terrorism post-2001. The increasing pressure to spend money wisely has given rise to the language of 'aid effectiveness' (which echoes the interests of donors to know that their money is being well used) and 'development effectiveness' (which reflects the broader interests of those affected by development). Alongside the social, political and economic influences on development, has been the growth of a culture of evaluation and of using evidence in development policy and practice in the UK and abroad.

As highlighted at various points in this book (and especially in Chapters Ten and Eleven), the term 'evidence' is used by different people in different ways: for some it is a broad concept, incorporating monitoring and evaluation data, citizens' experiences, financial information and more; for others it refers specifically to systematically reviewed and synthesised evidence from only the most rigorous research designs. In some areas of development, evaluation evidence has long shaped the planning and implementation of policies and practice. However, there has been a gradual shift towards evidence synthesis, although evidence maps and systematic reviews in the development area tend to integrate a broader range of evidence types than is typically the case in, say, health and healthcare evidence reviews (see Chapters Four and Ten).

Whatever the source of evidence, there is an important distinction to be made between the use of evidence in development to inform the policies and practices of development agencies, and the use of evidence as a tool for development when working abroad. To put this into context, the UK's Department for International Development (DFID) aims to utilise evidence within its own organisation, training its staff in how to use evidence to inform their work. Looking outwards, as a department working in 32 countries, it has many tools at its disposal in its work to strengthen peace and security, respond to crises and tackle poverty. One of those tools is promotion of the production and use of research evidence. It is this dual role for evidence in development that makes debates about evidence use so pertinent to the field.

Key players in these debates can be grouped into three broad categories: multinational development bodies; evidence-specialist organisations with an interest in development; and development-specialist organisations with an interest in evidence. Examples of each of these are outlined in Box 9.1.

While there are a number of other international bodies engaging with evidence and its use in policy development and implementation, the UK has arguably been at the forefront of many of these changes (DFID, 2009). DFID leads by example from within government, with public commitments to the use of evidence in its work (see Box 9.2); and UK-based NGOs, such as Oxfam (Walmsley, 2017), are at the forefront of issues of development effectiveness and evidence synthesis. There are also a growing number of university units producing evidence to inform decisions in development. DFID's Research and Evidence Division includes a dedicated Evidence to Action team. Its work has ranged from funding the production of systematic reviews (more on this later) to supporting evidence-informed decision making by governments in low- and middle-income countries.

Box 9.1: Key players with an interest in evidence and development

- Multinational agencies working in this area include the European Commission, the World Bank and the United Nations, global funders such as the Gates and Hewlett Foundations, national governments – particularly those in low- and middle-income countries – and more local agencies such as civil society organisations and universities in the UK and elsewhere.
- Evidence-specific or systematic review-specific organisations have also been pivotal in shifting debates around evidence in development. These include the big systematic review collaborations for health (Cochrane), social policy (the Campbell Collaboration) and the environment (the Collaboration for Environmental Evidence), all of which have included in their priorities the generation of evidence for tackling issues of poverty and inequality.
- Key development-specific agencies supporting the production and use of rigorous evidence include the International Initiative for Impact Evaluation (3ie), the Abdul Latif Jameel Poverty Action Lab, and the International Network for the Availability of Scientific Publications.

Box 9.2: Department for International Development (DFID): a leader in evidence

DFID's commitment to the use of evidence in its own decision making and in the policies it promotes internationally is reflected in a number of key publications. The standards that it has set itself and its application of these standards are reflected clearly in each of the following publicly available documents.

• The 2011 *Multilateral Aid Review* indicates a commitment to considering value for money and aid effectiveness in the department's work (DFID, 2011). It lays out clearly the sources of evidence that DFID draws upon and advocates greater use of evidence to review the impact of its work.
• In 2013, *Research Uptake: A Guide for DFID-Funded Research Programmes* was published, reflecting a clear emphasis in DFID's funding of research on the use of that research to make a difference, essentially promoting evidence-informed decision making (DFID, 2013).
• In 2013 DFID produced a *How to Note* for public servants on 'Assessing the Strength of Evidence', which takes into account both appraisal of individual studies and assessing the strength of a body of evidence. It was updated in 2014 (DFID, 2014a). DFID specifies that the note 'aims to help staff use evidence more judiciously for the benefit of designing and implementing effective policy and programmes' (DFID, 2014a, p 2).

DFID also opened itself up to scrutiny with regard to how it uses evidence to guide its internal decisions, with the 2014 *What Works Review*, which highlights many of its strengths and challenges it to further engage with evidence (DFID, 2014b).

In many ways, influenced by DFID's leadership, both as an organisation that aims to be evidence informed and as an organisation that uses evidence-informed decision making as a tool for development, there has been a considerable expansion of expertise in the sector within the UK. Evidence-specialist organisations have engaged more in development research, and development organisations have engaged more with a broader range of evidence types, going beyond monitoring and evaluation and including randomised trials, systematic reviews and the explicit concept of evidence-informed decision making.

Given the wide range of players in the UK and further afield, it is no surprise that the nature of discussions in this field is wide-ranging, with implications for what constitutes evidence and how evidence is commissioned, produced and used to inform decisions. As the emphasis on evidence in development has grown, innovations have emerged, contributing to the wider field of evidence-informed decision making across the board. Development is by nature an umbrella discipline, both influenced by and influencing other disciplines (there are parallels here with the field of environment and sustainability – see Chapter Eight). It also incorporates a vast geographical scope, raising issues of context and relevance when considering evidence. Finally, development has a challenging history of colonialism and oppression that greatly complicates considerations of knowledge and power. Some of these debates are explored in more detail in the remainder of this chapter.

Development covers the full spectrum of pro-poor policy and practice, from education to health, from economic management to public governance. As such, all those debates that arise in each of these disciplines (as illustrated in Chapters Four to Eight in the book) also apply to development. To give just one example, some education professionals in Malawi will argue, just as some in the UK do, that their schools and students are particular – and therefore the production of generalisable trial and systematic review evidence is simply not useful or applicable to their contexts. Parallel trends to other disciplines can also be seen in international development, for example: shifts towards greater participation of a wide range of stakeholders; discussions of the pros (and cons) of involving a wider group of stakeholders in various aspects of research (a spectrum of activities referred to as 'co-production'); and the conception of a wider evidence 'ecosystem' in which development evidence operates. This is not particularly surprising, given that many of the leaders in evidence for development are also leaders in evidence-informed decision making in sectors such as health and education. Their shared focus on development means that much of the work around development is multidisciplinary, with teams increasingly working across sectors.

The broad geographical scope of the development field adds to critiques of context relevance and policy relevance. Valid questions arise as to the applicability to resource-poor settings of evidence generated in resource-rich settings, both in terms of the environments in which policy and practice are playing out and in terms of the questions, methods and outcomes addressed in this research. In one example from personal experience, doctors working in rural settings in one of the poorest countries in the world requested advice from systematic reviewers about what the most effective treatments were in those settings. The available evidence from a number of Cochrane systematic reviews all pointed to the effectiveness of expensive treatments unavailable to these doctors.

Unique to development are the difficult histories of oppression, slavery, colonialism and apartheid. Without in any way implying that those working in development have poor intentions, these histories bring to the fore issues of power and control (Erasmus et al, 2017). When an organisation such as Save the Children or Oxfam or DFID is promoting the use of evidence in decision making in other countries, challenges therefore arise (Box 9.3). The scandal in 2018 that threatened many in the NGO sector – of sexual exploitation linked to aid work – has only further complicated the relationships. In addition, the tendency to bring to the fore promotion of Northern interests within development policy underlines the delicate balance that must be sought when promoting the production and use of evidence in these contexts. Some of the potential solutions to this challenge are discussed later in this chapter.

The rest of this chapter is structured as follows – first, the nature of evidence in international development is discussed, followed by a section on the production and synthesis of research-based knowledge in international development. The chapter then explores how evidence use is encouraged and enabled in this field, ahead of a short concluding section.

Box 9.3: How evidence-informed decision making may be unwelcome

Evidence-informed decision making is often cited as a Northern approach. Evidence-based policy is sometimes specifically associated with Tony Blair's New Public Management approach to public sector reform. As such, it can be viewed as inappropriate to impose this approach in other countries. In one example, a team was working to support the use of evidence in a government in the global South by providing mentors to senior government officials (Stewart et al, 2017). One of its mentors was advising on the formation of a committee that was to develop a new White Paper. The mentor's advice included broadening the sources of evidence on which the committee was drawing in order to draft its policy paper, helping to search for and critique relevant research, as well as how to select a broad spectrum of stakeholders to ensure that a range of perspectives were taken into account. When the committee met with the evidence-mentor present, members of the committee asked what right this individual, funded as part of a UK government grant, had to seek to change how another government worked. The mentor was asked to leave the meeting and step down from their role of providing advice to the committee.

The nature of evidence in international development

Debates around the nature and use of evidence in development policy and practice are far-reaching. What constitutes evidence, the methods for the generation of useful evidence, whether or not policies and practices across the spectrum are evidence informed, how best to increase the use of evidence and the cost-effectiveness of such initiatives are all being discussed within development agencies within the UK and throughout many of the countries and contexts in which they work. These include some of the world's most pressured, fragile and life-threatening contexts, in which evidence quite literally has the potential to be a life saver. Consequently, the field is forced to innovate and adapt rapidly.

By their very nature, many contexts in which development policy and practice play out are resource poor, with limited technical and administrative structures. This has meant that the collection of even the most basic monitoring data about development programmes can be a challenge. The nature of evidence in this field is broad and, in many countries, starts at the basic level of generating and using local, programme-level monitoring data. Process evaluations, and in some cases impact evaluations, are increasingly promoted, both by development organisations (3ie is a leader in this) and by national governments (for example, through the Evaluation, Research, Knowledge and Data Systems Programme within the Department for Planning, Monitoring and Evaluation in the South African government). The generation of evidence from RCTs in this field is increasing, but remains the exception. The increase is largely driven by Northern institutions promoting the conduct of randomised experiments, initially in the fields of health and development economics (discussed later). The sheer cost of such experiments makes them less likely to be a methodology of choice for Southern researchers, unless backed by Northern expertise and funding.

As with other disciplines, many of the critiques around the nature of evidence in development policy and practice arise from the origins of these approaches in healthcare (see Chapters Four to Seven in this book). That being said, development economics has for many years been tackling issues of data, evidence and impact and has therefore also informed the question of what constitutes rigorous and useful evidence for development. The combination of influences from these two disciplines of health and economics creates interesting debates and some challenges. It is a common critique that approaches developed in the global North for healthcare policy and practice, with an emphasis on

RCTs, the availability of big budgets and the advanced systems linking the production and application of evidence, are simply not transferable to development contexts (White, 2009). There are also suggestions that trials and systematic reviews are insufficiently nuanced for application in real-world settings (Oakley, 2000). While these concerns apply to all disciplines, they are arguably sharper in development, with its wide range of contexts across the globe.

As a result, there have been innovations with regard to stakeholder engagement in evidence production, including not only service users (borrowed from research generation in the field of health) but also the wide range of decision makers as potential users of this evidence. This has in turn led to critical theoretical and practical engagement with how best to do stakeholder engagement (Snilstveit et al, 2012; Oliver and Dickson, 2016; Haddaway et al, 2017), and with what constitutes policy-relevant evidence (Oliver and Dickson, 2016). It is here that ideas of co-production have emerged. This varies in degree and nature, from the inclusion of policy makers on research advisory groups, through to joint research teams from universities and governments working together to produce policy-relevant evidence (Langer et al, 2017). While the latter takes considerable investment from all sides, it has the potential to build champions for the evidence produced within government, making the use of that evidence much more likely.

Methodologically, some development economists support the generation of RCTs (or randomised experiments as they prefer to call them), most notably the international consortium of economists under the Abdul Latif Jameel Poverty Action Lab. These views are by no means universal, however, even within the economists' own discipline, where trial advocates are sometimes referred to as 'the randomistas'. Furthermore, advocacy of RCTs as a mechanism to produce evidence to inform development does not generally extend to support for systematic reviews. The disciplinary silos between economists (who generally reject systematic reviews) and epidemiologists (who largely support them) have led to very public debates about what evidence to trust with regard to the effectiveness of interventions. One such example of these debates has become known as the 'worm wars' and is summarised in Table 9.1. While both sides promote the value of RCTs, the debate illustrates what happens when the findings of one single trial are contradicted by the evidence from a systematic review of several trials.

As both evaluation methods and systematic review methods have been applied to complex development questions, the methodologies themselves have developed (Langer and Stewart, 2014). The DFID-funded Centre of Excellence for Development Impact and Learning describes the need for 'maintaining and strengthening a portfolio of evidence [synthesis] methods capable of responding to any selected problem along the spectrum from simple to complex, with a minimum of loss of credibility' (Oliver et al, 2017, p 7). This portfolio includes production of policy-relevant evidence, more timely evidence and consideration of a broader range of available evidence (Table 9.2). Legitimacy with decision makers has also come to the forefront as one of the key factors shaping ideas about the quality of evidence (Parkhurst, 2016).

As evidence production has adapted to the requirements of development, there has been a greater production of one-off, fit-for-purpose, localised evidence outputs. Rapid reviews to inform specific policy decisions in one country are good examples of this.

Table 9.1: Debates on synthesising evidence from randcmised experiments

An example of a debate that has gone public: deworming primary school children	Cochrane 2012 and 2015 updates of the systematic review on the effects of deworming found that there is a lack of high-quality evidence that community-based deworming programmes improve outcomes (Taylor-Robinson et al, 2012; 2015)	A 2004 study in Kenya found that deworming in schools had a significant impact on children's cognitive learning (Miguel and Kremer, 2004). There has been debate about the data and analysis of this specific study; however, supporters stand by the study as evidence of positive impacts of deworming
What is the debate about?	Support for systematic reviews of all the available research on a given topic	Support for findings of individual trials and synthesis of only selected trials, often conducted by just one organisation
What disciplines tend to support each side?	Primarily epidemiologists	Primarily economists

Table 9.2: Adapting evidence methodologies for development

Challenge	Solution
Generation of policy-relevant evidence	Greater engagement with decision makers in the commissioning, design and production of research
Requirement for timely evidence	Production of rapid reviews, and reviews of reviews Rapid-response services for decision makers
Requirement for legitimacy of evidence for decision making	Inclusion of a wider range of evidence types within evidence maps and syntheses, including government-produced data and reports

As a result, there is an emerging distinction between 'public good research', which is global in scope and generalisable in methodology (Oliver and Dickson, 2016), and locally relevant, rapid research, which is useful immediately for one context but may not be transferable to other environments. The systematic reviews produced by the large international collaborations are an example of the former, while the evidence maps co-produced with government departments to inform a specific policy process are an example of the latter (Langer et al, 2017). So, we see that the nature of evidence required by different stakeholders in international development is strongly related to contextual requirements. Next, we turn to questions around the production and synthesis of evidence.

Production and synthesis of research-based knowledge in international development

The production and synthesis of research-based knowledge for development includes a wide range of evidence and is constantly adapting to meet a broad range of needs. Monitoring and evaluation (M&E) evidence is produced by many, in local, national and international settings. The M&E profession is increasingly recognised through national and regional M&E associations, such as the Tanzania Evaluation Association and the Asia-Pacific Evaluation Association. As the evidence-informed movement (including impact evaluation, evidence mapping and synthesis methodologies) has been adopted within the field in the UK, the structures for evidence production have broadened.

The traditional development agencies (multilateral agencies, NGOs and some government development departments) have continued to commission process evaluations from traditional development researchers. New to the field are the traditional evidence and systematic review organisations (the Cochrane and Campbell Collaborations, the EPPI-Centre and others). Cochrane increasingly considers interventions and outcomes relating to poorer settings. The Campbell Collaboration has an international development coordinating group, largely thanks to investment and drive from the International Initiative for Impact Evaluation (3ie).

New agencies have also emerged *within* low- and middle-income countries, committed to producing evidence that is useful and used in their regions. The Africa Centre for Evidence at the University of Johannesburg in South Africa and the Centre for Rapid Evidence Synthesis at Makerere University in Uganda are just two such examples.

Long-standing evidence organisations are forming new networks (the Global Evidence Synthesis Initiative is one example), and new networks are emerging, such as the Africa Evidence Network (Stewart, 2018). The emergence of these new local agencies is in part due to an anti-colonial, local-is-best drive within the broader field, which is keen to see home-grown solutions, such as the 'Made in Africa' movement championed by the African Evaluation Association. It also reflects greater emphasis on South–South learning, rather than the North–South emphasis that has been typical. This overall strategy is certainly helped by donors' drives to fund collaborations that include Southern partners.

Trends in commissioning can be traced from initial waves of funding for systematic reviews (Box 9.4) to more programmatic thinking around the nature of evidence production and use for development. Good examples of the latter are the DFID-funded Centre of Excellence for Development Impact and Learning and DFID's global programme to Build Capacity to Use Research Evidence (BCURE). In shifting to programmes of longer-term and broader investment, DFID has contributed considerably to the understanding of how to support evidence use, as well as helping to build capacity in its grantees in this area.

Box 9.4: The growth of systematic review evidence in development

In the late 2000s, DFID commissioned an initial tranche of systematic reviews on key issues in development. Since then, multiple waves of reviews have been commissioned, with organisations including 3ie and the EPPI-Centre providing methodological support. Since 2008, 3ie has played a key parallel role in coordinating the commissioning of, first, impact evaluations, and then, systematic reviews in development, and publishing online libraries of both. In doing so it has brought in additional funders and helped to create a critical mass of committed stakeholders and rigorous evidence products within this discipline. Over time, other government development agencies (including in Australia, Canada, Norway and the US) have joined this investment in commissioning rigorous reviews, as well as international agencies (such as UN Women, the World Bank Independent Evaluation Group, the International Fund for Agricultural Development and the Bill and Melinda Gates Foundation). As the number of reviews produced has grown, so methodological expertise has deepened and the pool of experienced researchers and commissioners has broadened.

As one might expect, systems and structures for evidence production for development are international and not purely UK-based. The development field is about the full range of structures and systems, from international systems, through organisations such as 3ie, to national ones (for example, in South Africa – DPME, 2014). UK structures and systems need to relate to these in order to be effective in the field. In line with ideas underlying development, the production of evidence for development was initially largely driven by the global North, and indeed there are still many 'global' initiatives driven from high-income countries for the benefit of low- and middle-income countries. While these can be praised for what they are able to achieve with their access to funding and influence, there has been an increasing drive for greater inclusion of low- and middle-income country researchers and research structures.

Initially, commissioners such as DFID and 3ie encouraged the inclusion of low- and middle-income country researchers within Northern-led research teams, and now, in some cases, this trend has gone further, to supporting more teams and institutions within low- and middle-income countries to produce both locally relevant and globally applicable evidence. These small but significant shifts highlight inherent tensions in the field. The distinction (see Chapter Three) between locally produced evidence (which is often referred to as research *in* practice) and the importation of research findings from elsewhere (known as research *into* practice) does not apply so well in development. Rather, the tensions here relate more to decisions that are made at different levels (global, regional, national, local), who makes these decisions and who decides what evidence is valid at each level.

Multilateral agencies seek information to inform their international (regional or even global) programmes. As such, they tend to value the global evidence base – for example, DFID's commissioning of systematic reviews in 2009/10 on the impact of microfinance on poverty in low- and middle-income countries. Where these international organisations have offices in particular regions, they may also be interested in the synthesis of evidence at regional levels. DFID also commissioned related reviews of the evidence on microfinance from sub-Saharan Africa and Asia. While the findings of these DFID-commissioned global reviews were well received and much discussed at international forums, at a national level decision makers seem to have found the findings of these reviews harder to accept, particularly when the reviews have not included studies from their own countries. For example, one policy maker who was presented with evidence from a global review went straight to the appendix of studies and, on seeing that none of the included studies was from their country, no longer wanted to know the findings (Stewart et al, 2012).

Encouraging and enabling evidence use in international development

Encouraging and enabling the use of evidence in development policy and practice faces a number of challenges. Langer and colleagues (2015) summarise these to include the fact that neither policy makers nor practitioners in development are commonly trained or incentivised to use research evidence, and mechanisms within institutions to improve uptake of evidence in policy and practice are lacking. Measuring impact is also a challenge, as development policies achieve social impact through a large number of incremental changes. Research evidence of the impact of these policies is necessarily confined to, at best, small positive results. However, the celebration of small and context-dependent solutions to challenges of development is out of step with the domain's preference for magic bullets and one-stop blueprints to eradicate global poverty (Barder, 2014; White, 2014).

While these challenges remain, there are a number of approaches that together are beginning to make a difference to the use of evidence in the field, both within development organisations in the UK and in the contexts in which they work. The first area of work focuses on producing more useful evidence and greater engagement with that evidence by development agencies themselves.

Development budgets have been squeezed and there are increasing demands for development agencies to demonstrate effectiveness and value for money. This is reflected in shifts in the evidence-production methodologies commissioned and employed. These changes have led to an increase in the engagement of evidence 'users' in the commissioning and evidence-production processes, the aim being to increase the usefulness of evidence and the probability that it will actually be used. In international development, from the very start, systematic review teams were encouraged to include 'users' in their advisory groups, with clear instructions that these should include national and international policy stakeholders. Indeed teams have been encouraged and at times required to produce detailed policy engagement plans to support uptake of research findings. As noted already, at times these arrangements have gone so far as to include both government and university colleagues on the research teams in full co-production of evidence.

Researchers have also been encouraged to produce different outputs that are more accessible to decision makers. The production of policy briefs, use of plain English and open access publication of outputs, often via online repositories, have all sought to put evidence on decision-makers' desks. Specialist organisations have also emerged to collate and package evidence for specific needs: Evidence Aid, an NGO that aims to support the humanitarian sector to apply an evidence-informed approach, is one such example.

Alongside this increased engagement by research teams with development agency staff, development agencies themselves have increased the evidence literacy of their staff, and indeed have restructured their organisations to reflect the importance of evidence, with the creation of research and evidence units to commission research, conduct research and engage with evidence more broadly.

There are also approaches of an entirely different scale and nature that aim to support decision makers to commission, access, critique and incorporate evidence within their decision making. These fall into the scope of evidence-informed decision making as a strategy for development: supporting low- and middle-income countries to make better decisions. These 'demand side' approaches include training, workshops, mentorships, work-placements and secondments. In the UK, the six BCURE programmes commissioned by DFID in 2013–14 represent one of the biggest investments in support of the use of evidence by low- and middle-income country governments and related agencies (Box 9.5). Outside of the UK, the William and Flora Hewlett Foundation in the US has been offering similar support for

Box 9.5: Building Capacity to Use Research Evidence (BCURE)

Funded by DFID, BCURE was a £16 million programme from 2013 to 2017 that aimed to increase the capacity of decision makers to use research evidence. Six programmes were funded to deliver projects across 12 low- and middle-income countries, with an external evaluation also commissioned.

Activities included workshops and training (online and face to face, in workplace and residential), mentoring, networking activities, development of tailored tools, guidelines and manuals. These were focused at individual, team and organisational levels.

These activities took place in Bangladesh, Ghana, India, Kenya, Liberia, Malawi, Pakistan, Sierra Leone, South Africa, South Sudan, Uganda and Zimbabwe.

think-tanks and other agencies seeking to increase the use of evidence in decision making through its Global Development and Population Programme.

In addition to these 'supply-side' and 'demand-side' activities, there are a number of approaches that encompass the concept of an 'evidence ecosystem': the idea that there are multiple players and roles that need to engage with one another for evidence-informed decision making to become a reality (Tsujimoto et al, 2017; and see Chapter Twelve). Related activities seek to forge closer links between decision makers and research producers, across traditions, sectors and fields. These include activities to improve the nature and content of communications, social networking events, the emergence of knowledge-translator and knowledge-broker professionals and organisations and international meetings focusing on evidence across sectors (that is, including government officials, academics and civil society). While not unlike similar initiatives in other disciplines (see other chapters in this volume), this has by nature included a wide range of fields, with evidence producers and users getting to know one another across pro-poor policy areas. Relationship-building activities within the Africa Evidence Network have, for example, included colleagues from education, health, water and sanitation, social development, finance and tourism, to name just some of the fields involved.

Reflections and conclusions

The development field has made leaps and bounds in both the production of evidence and its support for evidence use. While evidence-informed decision making in development is still relatively young, there is a considerable breadth of activities employed and a large number of countries in which these activities are taking place (both in 'donor' countries such as the UK, and in the low- and middle-income countries in which they work). Development is notable as a field aiming to be evidence informed in the way in which development agencies themselves operate, and in recognising the value of an evidence-based approach as a tool for development to be promoted and supported among the 'developing' communities that these agencies aim to support.

These developments have taken place within a broader shift in the field of development itself, away from donor-knows-best (where power sits within high-income countries alone) and towards greater equality with poorer nations and communities (with stronger voices for low- and middle-income countries, and even a recognition that high-income countries have something to learn from the global South). These changes are part of a wider movement to adjust patronising attitudes and approaches and to begin to rectify historical power imbalances. The emphasis on 'decoloniality' within Southern education systems is just one such example of these global movements. The move towards greater use and application of evidence has also benefited from the wider debates in other fields of application as illustrated across various chapters in this book.

It is in this wider context that there has been a shift towards greater consideration of low- and middle-income country voices in the production and use of evidence, including the voices of decision makers, researchers and citizens. Indeed, Southern-based agencies and governments are beginning not only to have a voice in evidence debates but also to take the lead in aspects of evidence production and use, the co-production of evidence maps for government being one such example. There is a small but growing recognition of this emerging potential for reciprocal learning between North and South in the evidence field. The shift in Southern countries' agency and leadership in their own development agendas is likely to ensure that the use of evidence in decision making for development remains at the cutting edge. While systems for evidence production and use have emerged over much longer periods within sectors such as health, in the field of development rapid change is resulting in on-going adaptation and innovation. As this adaptation and innovation continue to take place, there is a need for on-going consolidation and distillation of learning.

Questions remain as to how to find a balance between locally and globally relevant evidence, between tight timeliness and scientific rigour and between the many competing interests at play in international decision-making contexts. However, it is acknowledged that there is a need for players from low- and middle-income countries to be actively involved in these debates, and for more and deeper relationships to be forged across the wide range of sectors and disciplines involved in development. This is a field of both rapid change and huge potential.

References

Banerjee, A.V. and Duflo, E. (2011) *Poor economics*, New York: Public Affairs.

Barder, O. (2014) 'Evidence and scale', http://www.globalhealthhub.org/2014/05/20/evidence-and-scaling-up/ (accessed 27 June 2017).

DFID (2009) *Building the evidence to reduce poverty. The UK's policy on evaluation for international development*, London: Department for International Development, https://www.oecd.org/development/evaluation/dcdndep/43183649.pdf.

DFID (2011) *Multilateral aid review. Ensuring maximum value for money for UJ aid through multilateral organisations*, London: Department for International Development, https://www.gov.uk/government/uploads/system/uploads/attachment_data/file/67583/multilateral_aid_review.pdf.

DFID (2013) *Research uptake: A guide for DFID-funded research programmes*, London: Department for International Development, https://www.acu.ac.uk/publication/download?publication=691.

DFID (2014a) *How to note: assessing the strength of evidence*, London: Department for International Development, https://www.gov.uk/government/uploads/system/uploads/attachment_data/file/291982/HTN-strength-evidence-march2014.pdf.

DFID (2014b) *What works review of the use of evidence in the department for international development*, London: Department for International Development, https://www.gov.uk/government/uploads/system/uploads/attachment_data/file/340971/What_Works_Review_DFID.pdf.

Doane, D. (2017) 'What's so bad about development? Third world or global south? Pro-poor or pro-wealth? The term 'development' is a minefield that eclipses the real issues', Global Development Blog, *Guardian*, https://www.theguardian.com/global-development/poverty-matters/2014/sep/01/development-ngos-third-world-global-south.

DPME (Department of Planning, Monitoring and Evaluation) (2014) *Overview paper: What is evidence-based policy-making and implementation?* Pretoria: DPME.

Erasmus, Y., Lötter, D., Tannous, N. and Stewart, R. (2017) 'Reflections on per diems in international development projects: Barriers to and enablers of the project cycle', *Development Southern Africa*, pp 1–14.

Glennie, J. and Sumner, A. (2014) 'The $138.5 billion question: when does foreign aid work (and when doesn't it)?', CGD Policy Paper 49, Washington, DC: Center for Global Development.

Haddaway, N.R., Kohl, C., da Silva, N.R., Schiemann, J., Spök, A., Stewart, R., Sweet, J.B. and Wilhelm, R. (2017) 'A framework for stakeholder engagement during systematic reviews and maps in environmental management', *Environmental Evidence*, 6 (1), pp 11.

Langer, L., Erasmus, Y., Tannous, N. and Stewart, R. (2017) 'How stakeholder engagement has led us to reconsider definitions of rigour in systematic reviews', *Environmental Evidence*, 6 (20), pp 1-6.

Langer, L. and Stewart. R. (2014) 'What have we learned from the application of systematic review methodology in international development? – A thematic overview', *Journal of Development Effectiveness*, 6 (3), pp 236–48, doi: 10.1080/19439342.2014.919013.

Langer, L., Stewart, R., Erasmus, Y. and de Wet T. (2015) 'Walking the last mile on the long road to evidence-informed development: building capacity to use research evidence', *Journal of Development Effectiveness*, 7 (4), pp 462–70, doi: 10.1080/19439342.2015.1095783.

Miguel, E. and Kremer, E. (2004) 'Worms: identifying impacts on education and health in the presence of treatment externalities', *Econometrica*, 72 (1), pp 159–217.

Oakley, A. (2000) *Experiments in knowing*, London: Polity Press.

Oliver, S. and Dickson, K. (2016) 'Policy-relevant systematic reviews to strengthen health systems: models and mechanisms to support their production', *Evidence and Policy*, 12 (2), pp 235–59.

Oliver, S., Gough, D. and Copestake, J. (2017) *Approaches to evidence synthesis in international development,* CEDIL: London.

Parkhurst, J. (2016) *The politics of evidence – from evidence-based policy to the good governance of evidence*, Routledge: London.

Savedoff, W.D., Levine, R. and Birdsall, N. (2006) *When will we ever learn? Improving lives through impact evaluation*, Washington, DC: Center for Global Development.

Snilstveit, B., Oliver, S. and Vojtkova, M. (2012) 'Narrative approaches to systematic review and synthesis of evidence for international development policy and practice', *Journal of Development Effectiveness*, 4 (3), pp 409–29.

Stewart, R. (2018) 'Do evidence networks make a difference?', *Journal of Development Effectiveness*, doi: 10.1080/19439342.2018.1425734.

Stewart, R., Erasmus, Y. and the UJ-BCURE team (2017) *Working for solutions: a problem-based and relationship- centred approach to building capacity to use research evidence in Africa*, Johannesburg: Africa Centre for Evidence.

Taylor-Robinson, D.C., Maayan, N., Soares-Weiser, K., Donegan, S. and Garner, P. (2012) 'Deworming drugs for soil-transmitted intestinal worms in children: effects on nutritional indicators, haemoglobin and school performance', *Cochrane Database of Systematic Reviews 2012*, issue 7, art no CD000371, doi: 10.1002/14651858.CD000371.pub4.

Taylor-Robinson, D.C., Maayan, N., Soares-Weiser, K., Donegan, S. and Garner P. (2015) 'Deworming drugs for soil-transmitted intestinal worms in children: effects on nutritional indicators, haemoglobin, and school performance', *Cochrane Database of Systematic Reviews 2015*, issue 7, art no CD000371, doi: 10.1002/14651858.CD000371.pub6.

Tsujimoto, M., Kajikawa, Y., Tomita, J. and Matsumoto, Y. (2017) 'A review of the ecosystem concept – Towards coherent ecosystem design', *Technological Forecasting and Social Change*, https://doi.org/10.1016/j.techfore.2017.06.032.

Walmsley, L. (2017) 'Reviewing humanitarian evidence', *Oxfam Views and Voices Blog*, 25 April, https://views-voices.oxfam.org.uk/humanitarian/2017/04/reviewing-humanitarian-evidence.

White, H. (2009) 'Some reflections in current debates on impact evaluation', 3ie Working Paper 1. New Delhi: 3ie.

White, H. (2014) 'What will it take to get systematic review evidence into policy', keynote address, Campbell Collaboration Colloquium, Queen's University Belfast, Belfast, 16–19 October.

Section Three
Knowing and doing: some cross-cutting themes

Throughout this book we have set out to show that the creation of knowledge for policy and practice – and the labelling of that knowledge as evidence – comprises problem-led, socially mediated and contextually situated *processes* that unfold dynamically. Many and varied types of data, information, existing knowledge, experience, know-how, expertise and wisdom may come together *in context* to create new types of knowledge (and *knowing*) that can influence and impact on policy and practice.

But central to our discussions has been the place of research-based knowledge. While it may be contested, we would argue that there remains a special (and, to some extent, privileged) position for research-based knowledge when considering EIPP. However, in making such a claim we are keen to cast the net widely: research-based knowledge can encompass any systematic and transparent gathering and analysis of empirical data, whether in explicit de novo research studies or through the careful exploitation of existing data sources. Even implicit knowledge, and to some extent tacit knowledge (for example, that held by experts or by service users) can be amenable to systematic extraction and codification – for example, through survey work, in-depth interviews, ethnographic work and Delphi processes.

We promote the role of research (broadly cast) precisely because of the characteristics that help to define it: the careful, explicit, rigorous examination of data; the building on previous knowledge; the use of properly articulated theoretical frameworks both to guide data collection and to aid data analysis; and the transparency and scrutiny that come from clear statements of methods and conscientious peer review. Each of these, we believe, helps to build both the credibility and the value of research for evidence-informed public services.

The characteristics of research set out above are represented not just in formal research studies produced by universities and research institutes. They can also be seen (in full or in part) in work emanating from other bodies, including work found in: policy analytic functions; audit, regulatory and oversight bodies; professional bodies; and consultancy firms, industry analysts and think-tanks, to name just some. So, in labelling specific types of information as research, and in ascribing it a quality level, we should be as mindful of its characteristics as of its provenance.

This view, then, brings into the ambit of 'research' the local production of relevant knowledge – such as service evaluations and audits, performance metrics, stakeholder needs assessments, service user feedback and expert views analysis – where such work abides by some of the principles set out earlier. It also includes the growing area of data analytics, which exploit the vast accumulation of data amassed as part of day-to-day activities and service engagement – so long as such analytics are open to methodological scrutiny.

Taking such an inclusive position on research leads us to focus less on the methodologies of research, in favour of a more rounded assessment of how systematic and cumulative analysis can help to meet the knowledge needs of diverse actors in policy and practice arenas. It also enables us to explore the potential for these systematic analyses to prompt actions, whether in the form of a continuing and evolving dialogue leading to new insights and understandings, or more directly as catalysts for new policy directions, redesigned service configurations or reoriented local practices. It is to these issues that this cross-cutting section of the book is devoted.

The section begins with a chapter exploring systematic approaches to generating evidence in ways that answer important questions for policy makers, practitioners and other interested stakeholders (Chapter Ten). Unusually for an account that emphasises methods, we do not begin with an exposition of the methodological tools available, but open instead with an elaboration of the diverse knowledge needs that arise in policy and practice environments.

The argument is that the diversity of knowledge needs requires a diversity of approaches, both within what might be labelled as research and more broadly in what might be termed information extraction (for example, eliciting consumer preferences; exploring professional consensus; exploiting routinely collected system data). Throughout we point to the different *but complementary* contributions that can be made: from different research traditions; from contrasting methodologies and theoretical conceptualisations; and from varying sources of information. However, integrating knowledge from these divergent methods and sources into coherent, contextually rooted understandings is a challenge: an issue revisited in Chapter Eleven, when addressing the task of assessing and labelling evidence, and in Chapter Twelve, when exploring the mobilisation of knowledge for policy and practice change.

What emerges from the exploration in Chapter Ten is that, while the *source* of knowledge might be important, perhaps as a proxy for rigour, whatever that source is, we still need to attend to the traditional concerns of how well the data have been collected and analysed. Detailed examination of these concerns should never be neglected, even as we pursue a greater inclusivity of knowledge.

We follow this exploration of research-informed knowledge-creation processes with some discussions about the existing arrangements for assessing and labelling evidence for public services; that is, addressing the question of *what counts as good evidence* in what contexts (Chapter Eleven). Our argument is that what begins as a technocratic exercise based on appropriate method choice and checklists for scoring methodological quality stumbles as it encounters the messy world of knowledge needs, prior beliefs and contextual relevance. There is more here than the oft-asserted tension between rigour and relevance: it speaks to how rigour itself can be a function of relevance. That is, if rigour is about assessing the robustness of knowledge, then assessing that robustness decontextualised from prior beliefs, the contexts of generation and the contexts of application begins to look like a limiting and rather unhelpful stance. Rigour and relevance are perhaps more intimately entwined than we might initially suppose.

These arguments, and those of Chapter Ten, push us to think about how research-based knowledge must be combined with other sources and types of knowledge when deciding what counts as good-enough evidence. The arguments developed point to the desirability of a greater inclusivity of different types of knowledge and a more contextually situated idea of building actionable insights from that knowledge. This in turn leads us to consider whether and how evidence is (should, or can be) negotiated and co-created.

Developing the arguments in this direction takes us a long way from the idea that research provides a disinterested way of building a knowledge base to underpin policy and practice. It recognises instead that research – and the use of research-based knowledge – is a political act, with the capacity to disrupt assumptions, destabilise existing power relations and hierarchies, and bring to the fore marginalised interests.

It can be as much about disrupting authority and established interests as it is about building consensus and informing instrumentalist actions.

As such, research data, information, knowledge, evidence – whatever the labels – are *resources* that interested parties can draw on as they advocate positions. They can be democratising forces – allies in rebalancing structural inequalities of knowledge and power in social systems – or they can be powerful weapons to keep those structures in place. There is a lot riding on how evidence is brought into play or is kept at the margins.

The final chapter in this section (Chapter Twelve) picks up this debate by examining the ways in which evidence uptake is shaped, drawing on the burgeoning fields of implementation science and knowledge mobilisation. First, the challenge is to define what we mean by evidence use, influence, uptake or impact: each of these terms has different connotations and draws attention to different things. 'Use' suggests a more singular and instrumental application of evidence (to aid in specific decisions, perhaps, or to direct certain courses of action). In contrast, 'influence' suggests something altogether more processual and percolative, related more to conceptual shifts and problem reframing, for example. In the words of the late Carol Weiss, research (and other evidence) can serve 'an enlightenment function', being used as 'a source of ideas … and orientations to the world' (Weiss, 1977, p 531). Weiss goes on to note that 'although the process is not easily discernible … it may have profound effects' (1977, p 531) – a view that we would endorse.

Many models of policy and practice have emerged that aim to make these processes more understandable. Some models are descriptive, while others have more normative goals concerned with increasing the use and application of evidence. The earlier discussion in Chapter Two, on the misleading nature of some models of the policy cycle, should alert us to the need to consider the veracity (or otherwise) of these models of evidence use. Few have undergone significant empirical testing, and even fewer have become well established.

Yet, possibly the most appropriate issue is not whether these models are accurate representations of the relationship between evidence, policy and practice, but whether they are useful. In Chapter Twelve we set out some of the insights that can be extracted by looking across successive generations of models. In doing so we work through models that emphasise rationality and linearity (that is, taking straight lines from evidence production to evidence use), through those that emphasise the social, situated and entwined nature of knowledge creation/use, and on to more systems-based views, encompassing ideas from complexity theory and pointing to the need for an 'ecological view' of evidence-supporting arrangements.

Drawing out these insights leads us to explore (in Chapter Twelve) the effectiveness of knowledge-mobilisation initiatives and the impacts of specific interventions aimed at increasing the use, influence and uptake of evidence. There is a growing body of work that now examines not just how evidence is used but also to what effect(s). This work too can usefully shape our understandings about evidence use.

The past two decades, then, have created a corpus of both conceptual and empirical work, with many insights and some reasons for optimism that better use of evidence (however defined) can be encouraged. Teasing out these insights hinges on understanding the deeply connected nature of evidence-generating activities, evidence-valuing processes and evidence-use strategies. We have tried to reflect this interconnectedness across the three chapters that follow so as to create an integrated exploration of knowing and doing. Further integration of these cross-sectoral insights is developed in the final chapter of the book (Chapter Eighteen).

Reference

Weiss, C.H. (1977) 'Research for policy's sake: the enlightenment function of social research', *Policy Analysis*, 3 (4), pp 531–45.

10

Systematic approaches to generating evidence

Alec Fraser and Huw Davies

An introduction to generating evidence

Policy makers and practitioners have many questions about what they do and how it could be improved. They also have many different sources of evidence, as well as other forms of data, information and knowledge at their disposal to inform these questions. This chapter outlines some of the challenges faced by policy makers and practitioners in eliciting what they might want or need to know. It asks: how do we generate fresh empirical evidence? And how can this empirically derived evidence be synthesised (across similar studies) and then integrated with other forms of data and information to create new knowledge for application in policy and practice? This latter challenge is explored in two parts: research-based evidence synthesis is covered in this chapter, and broader knowledge integration is examined in more depth in Chapter Eleven.

Often the process by which new knowledge is gleaned from empirical study is referred to as research. But, as already noted in the introduction to this cross-cutting section, we cast the net widely to include any systematic and transparent gathering and analysis of data, whether construed as formal research or not. Such a view opens the door to a consideration of a much wider array of analyses than simply those produced by universities and other research institutes. This has implications for evidence quality, forcing considerations of validity, reliability and bias (see Box 10.1), and places new demands on would-be users to attend carefully to the critical appraisal of the underlying empirical work (again, developed further in Chapter Eleven).

This chapter's focus, then, is on the methodological approaches that can be used to address important empirical questions, alongside an appreciation of the appropriateness or otherwise of these approaches to address specific knowledge questions. An understanding of the varied and sometimes complementary roles of different approaches is a necessary precursor to understanding the quality and labelling of evidence for policy and practice (Chapter Eleven).

Box 10.1: Methodological concerns about quality

The terminology used to discuss methodological concerns about quality can sometimes be a little loose, but nonetheless a constellation of ideas emerge around the following themes:

Validity. At the most basic level, in **quantitative** framings, validity is concerned with measurement issues, sometimes expressed as 'are we measuring what we think we are measuring?'. In more **qualitative** framings, validity relates more to the notion that the methods deployed can access the full range of meanings and narratives associated with a particular phenomenon.

Internal validity. Broader than just measurement, this term is concerned with how well a given study holds together internally in attempting to understand the phenomenon of interest. In *quantitative* studies, this is primarily about issues of bias (see comments in Box 10.4); in *qualitative* work it is more about whether the study has achieved full depth and convincing theorisation. Internal validity is a complement to the following two terms.

External validity. This is more concerned with the extent to which findings from any given study (if internally valid) can be generalised or transferred to other populations, times and places. The alternative term **ecological validity** is sometimes used (almost interchangeably) to refer to the validity of findings in other settings.

Reliability or replicability. In narrow terms these expressions refer to the repeatability of observations (measures or qualitative observations) when nothing underlying has changed; more broadly, these terms relate to the reproducibility of findings between different studies carried out in similar ways.

Triangulation. This is a broad concept that refers to the reinforcing messages that may come from repeated studies using different approaches and methods and in different times and places. Of course, discordance may be as likely as reinforcement, and this may pose significant interpretation difficulties.

Asking the right questions

One attraction of the evidence-informed policy and practice movement has been the development of knowledge strategies that prioritise transparency, comprehensiveness and replicability as values to guide the generation and evaluation of evidence. This has often placed various forms of research at centre stage. At the same time, a common criticism of the evidence movement is that there has tended to be a focus on one type of empirical question, sometimes to the exclusion of others: namely, *what works?* As a result, the methodological approaches prioritised – experimental evaluations – have often been seen to be rather narrow (see debates at various points in this book, but especially in Chapters Four and Five, and Fifteen and Seventeen). This can be to the detriment of both deeper and broader understandings of relevant 'social realities' to which policy and practice actions are directed. It is now widely recognised that there are equally important questions to ask, such as how grave the problem is, and what its wider implications are. Even when addressing policy and practice impacts there are additional important questions beyond what works – to address issues such as how, why and in what ways interventions work, for whom and at what costs?

Box 10.2 provides a fuller exploration of the kinds of questions that policy makers and practitioners might have. The breadth of questions highlights that evidence of general principles is needed (that is, evidence that holds always or across a very wide range of contexts), but alongside more specific and situated knowledge that provides contextualised understanding. This means that we have to attend to both the external validity and the internal validity of empirical findings (see Box 10.1). The case for more inclusive and integrated strategies of evidence generation, often through multiple methodological approaches, is increasingly being recognised (see various chapters across the book).

This chapter explores the many ways in which policy makers and practitioners might draw not only on evaluative or experimental research evidence, but also on other forms of data. These might include: survey data to gauge the size of the problem; administrative and managerial datasets to understand more about how the problem is currently being addressed; interpretive research to explore the meaning and lived experience of the issues; and the know-how of service users and experts in order to see how the problem is understood from diverse perspectives. Different methods drawing on these data sources can offer distinct but complementary insights. For example, panel data analyses offer excellent opportunities to understand changing individual or group behaviour over time; ethnographic approaches aim at understanding the values and meanings attached to real-world phenomena; and Delphi methods can synthesise professional knowledge as to how problems are best managed. Each of these can shed useful light on the questions that policy makers and practitioners have.

Box 10.2: Knowledge requirements for policy makers and practitioners

1 Know-about problems (problem identification in the context of current policy efforts).
- Is there a problem?
- What are its costs and effects?
- Does it impact upon some groups more than others?
- What are the main causal factors?
- Is it getting worse or will it naturally subside over time?
- What is the lived experience of the issue?
- How does it interrelate to other issues of concern?

2 Know-what works (existing knowledge about approaches to remedy problems).
- Does an intervention work?
- How do recipients feel about the processes and outcomes of the intervention?
- When, where and for how long does the intervention work?
- Does it work differentially well or poorly with some groups as compared to others?
- How do we know that it works?
- What do policy makers and practitioners do in other countries when faced with similar issues, and can learning be transferred to local settings?
- Does the intervention do any harm, or have other unintended consequences?

3 Know-how (to put into practice – beyond knowing what works, we need to consider how it works and consider implementation strategies).
- How does it work?
- How can we implement it?
- How does it compare to existing and alternative ways of doing things?
- What are the risks of implementation failure, and how can these risks be mitigated?
- Can the intervention be replicated, spread and scaled up?

---

4   Know-who (to involve – the major stakeholders).
- For whom does it work?
- Is it valued by service users and the public more widely?
- Is it welcomed by practitioners?
- What agencies need to be involved for delivery?
- What capacities and capabilities are needed to make the intervention happen?

5   Know-why (linking policy with politics and values).
- Why does it work?
- Why is it important?
- How much does it cost?
- What are some of the broader implications of the policy?

Source: Adapted from Ekblom, 2002 and Nutley et al, 2007.

Despite the need for these complementary insights, the diversity of relevant approaches and methods uncovers a lurking complexity. The questions posed, and the techniques developed to answer them, have important theoretical underpinnings, and these in turn are linked to certain *epistemological* and *ontological* assumptions bound up in research traditions that have often conflicted historically (Box 10.3). These theoretical tensions and conflicts not only relate to philosophical concerns about the nature of reality and the sources of knowledge, but also draw in issues of power. These concerns include: who sets the questions? Which voices are prioritised or marginalised in answering these questions? Which data are seen as valid, and which as less so? Such questions are not merely technical; they are inherently political (see Chapter Eleven, and related discussion in Chapters Eight and Nine). Moreover, it is neither desirable nor realistic to extract the politics from them: policy makers' and practitioners' questions, as well as the ideas that underpin these, have personal preferences and moral values attached to them (see also Chapter Two).

This chapter is structured as follows. First, we examine some of the ways of differentiating between data, information, knowledge and evidence, and explore the contribution of these different elements to policy makers' and practitioners' understanding. Next, specific research-based approaches to evidence generation are detailed, before the issues linked to combining some of these approaches are discussed. Finally, the promises and challenges of synthesising evidence across studies are highlighted, as single studies alone rarely provide compelling evidence and more comprehensive summations of the evidence are increasingly sought.

Box 10.3: Gaining knowledge of the social world

As we come to know the social world, *two key concepts* shape how we do this. Even though they may be unacknowledged, assumptions in these two areas lie behind all empirical work.

Ontology is the study of what exists. Key questions relate to what constitutes our social 'reality' and how we might understand this. One central divide here is whether this reality is seen as singular, concrete and objective, or multiple, fluid and subjective.

Epistemology is the study of how we might come to know about important social phenomena. Relevant questions here relate to what counts as valid knowledge about the social world, and how we might obtain this. For example, are we primarily interested in objective quantification and measurement, with an emphasis on stability and reproducibility? Or are we more concerned with richer, qualitative understandings built around (inter)subjectivities and personal narratives?

Different research traditions emphasise contrasting approaches for researchers. For example, a positivist ontology seeks objective, verifiable knowledge through facts. In epistemological terms, it draws on deductive methods derived from the natural sciences and quantification. In contrast, an interpretive ontology seeks subjective knowledge through narrative and meaning. In epistemological terms it draws more on inductive methods and interpretation, sometimes combined with broader theoretical inferences.

Data, information, knowledge and evidence

The introduction to these cross-cutting chapters (Ten to Twelve) highlighted that rigorously produced academic research has a privileged position in debates about policy and practice. It is usually seen as producing a verifiable form of knowledge (laying claims to truth), and so it is of high value to most stakeholders, even if (as highlighted in Box 10.3) there are important ontological and epistemological debates about such 'truth claims'. Moreover, when such research-based knowledge is given authoritative approval by influential stakeholders it may come to be labelled as evidence (see Chapter Eleven). Thus, evidence and knowledge are both generated from specific *data* (that is, observations, whether objective quantified 'facts' or more subjective qualitative narratives) as well as more general *information* (that is, data again, but this time more processed, interpreted and contextualised). Data and information can both be seen as the building blocks of knowledge and evidence. The different research methods discussed in this chapter highlight the various ways in which (both existing and new) data and information may be harnessed to produce knowledge and, ultimately, evidence. Although the processes of production and labelling of knowledge as evidence may be contested (see Chapter Eleven), in this chapter we will not make a strong distinction between knowledge and evidence: both are derived from data and information, and both represent resources that have been identified as being in some ways valuable.

There is growing recognition of the importance and democratising potential of early and on-going stakeholder engagement in the identification of important policy and practice questions, as well as from continuing input into the knowledge-building process (Orr and Bennett, 2010). Moreover, there are multiple sources of data and information for all stakeholders to draw upon. These include different stakeholder opinions (both lay and expert), as well as legal sources, reports and data from quasi- and non-governmental organisations, direct reports from public sector organisations (hospitals, schools, local authorities and so on) and input from professional organisations and regulators, as well as think-tanks and other non-academic research organisations.

Expert knowledge about specific policy issues can be sought formally through targeted surveys or more sophisticated Delphi techniques (Hasson et al, 2000). Professional working committees may be tasked to explore and advise on certain issues, and the working practices may range from the wholly informal to highly structured ways of gathering, interpreting and integrating evidence (for example, see the Policy Working Groups in New Zealand, described in Chapter Fourteen). Formal public inquiries into historical policy failure (such as the Independent Inquiry into Child Sexual Abuse, in the UK) and catastrophic incidents (such as the Grenfell Tower Inquiry into the fire in London in 2017) often draw on legal approaches to the production and evaluation of evidence, and they prize expert submissions. Even though it was the recognition of some of the deficiencies of expert summary that gave the evidence movement some of its early impetus (Mulrow, 1987), expertise, in all its diversity, still remains a resource, and this can be explored and exploited in systematic ways.

Independent or quasi-governmental bodies, for example, in the UK, the Institute for Fiscal Studies (IFS) and the National Audit Office

(NAO), also produce important data and information for policy makers, practitioners, researchers and other interested stakeholders. Regular reports provide informational detail in specific areas, for example: on poverty and low pay (IFS, 2018); on the cost burden of diseases such as stroke (NAO, 2005); or on the effectiveness of payment by results (PbR) programmes across the public sector (NAO, 2015). Often, such reports draw on management and administrative performance and audit data. They are extremely useful resources for highlighting important areas for further research, for answering existing questions and for framing current policy issues in new ways.

Finally, there is a vast array of reporting from think-tanks, commercial research institutions, management consultancies, professional bodies, industry organisations and the like. The reports and papers produced from these kinds of sources are often referred to as 'grey literature', and formal peer review is rare. While such information – often *presented* as evidence – may have some value, there are significant dangers around both bias, as reports may support dominant interests, and methodological weaknesses (Head, 2008).

Having highlighted some of the data and information sources from which existing knowledge and evidence for policy and practice may be sought, we now move to explore in more detail the methodological approaches that seek to collect new data, or to provide fresh analyses of old data, for useful knowledge. First we explore the specific contribution of non-experimental quantitative methods before moving to a consideration of experimental designs, with a particular focus on the role of randomisation.

Non-experimental quantitative evidence

Non-experimental quantitative methods such as surveys, case-control methods, cohort studies and panel data are significant for generating evidence to guide policy makers and practitioners (see Box 10.4). Electronic, telephone or paper-based surveys are an important research method used to generate information on a particular topic relatively cheaply and efficiently. For example, we might want to know about specific techniques used by school teachers in the classroom, and one way to generate data on this would be through targeted surveys. A survey would provide us with basic data about the current practices that could in turn be used to inform further questions. It is crucial that researchers use appropriate sampling strategies and achieve adequate response rates for the results of surveys to provide robust data, and considerable attention needs to be paid to measurement issues (to ensure the reliability and validity of any measures deployed). To assist with this, there are quality checklists that may be used for the design and post-hoc assessment of surveys.

Another useful approach is a case control, or *retrospective* study (see Box 10.4), whereby researchers identify individuals displaying a certain characteristic and compare these with others who do not have that feature. An example could be the study of the effects of schooling on future employment experience. Here, a sample of unemployed individuals might be paired with a control group who are

Box 10.4: Quantitative study designs

There are many different terms used to describe aspects of quantitative research. Quantitative research designs may be **cross-sectional** (taking a snap-shot of the situation), **prospective** (collecting data going forwards) or **retrospective** (collecting data by looking backwards).

The following are key research designs:

Surveys are cross-sectional studies of the here and now, although their cross-sectional nature is sometimes muddied by asking about the past and seeking speculations on the future.

Case-control studies are retrospective designs that seek to compare the histories of 'cases' (where something interesting happened) with 'controls' (otherwise similar samples that do not exhibit this interesting feature).

Cohort or panel studies are prospective designs that involve repeated information being gathered from the same sample. These studies are distinct from (and more powerful than) repeated surveys drawn from the same populations but with no continuity of participation.

Natural or quasi experiments are similar to cohort or panel studies in that they involve the (prospective) follow-up on samples, but this is done because subsets of the samples may have had different interventions or may have experienced variable circumstances.

Proper experiments (typically **randomised**) are prospective studies where the researcher has control of the allocation of the intervention or circumstances that are being explored for their effects (see Box 10.6, later).

The core methodological concerns for all of these approaches include the following.

Sampling strategy. A careful sampling strategy can help to ensure the representativeness of study subjects and will aid in making arguments about generalisability (see Box 10.1).

Data completeness. Ensuring adequate response rates is a key challenge if the study is to address both internal and external validity. In particular, 'losses to follow-up' (study drop-outs) can bedevil prospective studies, especially when these run over long time frames.

Measurement issues. Since all quantitative studies hinge on measurement, ensuring adequate validity and reliability of the measures deployed is paramount, but far from straightforward.

Control of confounding. Quantitative studies (especially prospective observational studies and various types of experiment) are often focused on uncovering causality between input and output or stimulus and effect. To do this, we need to be convinced that any correlations between the former and the latter are not due to other extraneous factors (that is, confounding). Observational methods address this through statistical adjustment; the core benefit of proper randomisation is that confounding is addressed through initial group allocations that are (given sufficient numbers) fair and balanced.

in employment. The groups would be matched for many characteristics (age, gender, social class and so on) so that they are as similar as possible, but with the exception of the proposed risk factor being investigated (for example, vocational training received). Such a study would help to elicit understanding about the relationship between training and subsequent employment. However, a problem with such an approach is that a large sample size would be required to generate meaningful results (Hutton and Smith, 2000), and the risk of unexplored confounders is large (as explained in Box 10.4).

Cohort studies follow similar principles, but are done *prospectively*, rather than retrospectively. Large samples of individuals are accumulated, with data being collected on the same individuals through repeated surveys (see Chapter Fourteen for several examples of these). Sometimes called panel surveys, such studies are very valuable for informing policy and practice decisions, and can provide a useful long-term resource. Regular and reliable longitudinal datasets enable researchers to develop secure statistical models of behaviour (Hutton and Smith, 2000). When combined with natural experiments (Box 10.4), where policy and practice changes are made and the consequences can be observed in the data, these datasets can offer powerful and systematic knowledge. So long as researchers have access to reasonably robust outcomes data, they may use natural experiments to explore what works for both individual and programmatic interventions. The major problems with these approaches, however, are those of confounding (separating out the effects of policy and practice changes from other underlying variables) and context (understanding the particular local circumstances that either amplify or attenuate any effects).

The potential to exploit policy divergences – for example, across the devolved administrations of the UK, or between nations of the European Union – is one that researchers, policy makers and practitioners can and do use to increase understanding about underlying problems and potential policy solutions. For instance, comparative analysis of performance in key healthcare indicators across the UK highlights how the different policy trends in the systems across the four countries of the UK may have influenced outcomes since the introduction of devolved responsibilities (Bevan et al, 2014). At the same time, politicians are adept at drawing on such comparative data in order to score political points. For example, a recurring political motif during the Conservative-led administrations from 2010 in the UK was for the Labour Party to criticise the handling of the English NHS by central government, only for Conservative ministers to respond by unfavourably comparing Welsh NHS performance data (where health was devolved to the Labour administration) to that from the English NHS. Politicians (of all stripes) may sometimes seek to strip observational data of their crucially important contextual factors, in the interests of political expediency.

For many reasons, policy makers and practitioners must remain cognisant of context as a potentiating or inhibiting factor in natural experiments. But if used well, such methods offer efficient, fast, cheaper alternatives to controlled experimentation – especially in a world where increasing IT capabilities and 'big data' offer a proliferation of resources that researchers, policy makers and practitioners might draw upon in order to inform their work (Box 10.5). Such studies (or fresh analyses) can also offer superior ecological validity – that is, results generated in real life rather than research settings – with greater reassurances about generalisability and workability (Konnerup and Kongsted, 2012; Benson and Hartz, 2000).

Box 10.5: Exploiting routine data sources

Big data. These are highly complex, massive datasets – often consisting of linked and longitudinal data collected routinely as part of other processes – that challenge the capabilities of traditional analytical processes and data management software. They promise transformative insights into patterns of human behaviour and interactions if analysed effectively by commercial, academic or government actors. There are also extensive ethical as well as technical and methodological concerns with these datasets.

Service delivery data. Modern IT systems can collect real-time individual-level and aggregated service-level data, with analysis provided by management information systems and auditing functions. These developments may be used to link outcomes and service user feedback to payment models (that is, 'payment by results'), as well as providing improved organisational feedback loops through better-informed performance analytics.

Linked data sets. These have the potential to join up data on (for example) hospital admissions, discharges and prescribing decisions, and then link these data with further sources such as census data, housing data and welfare data. Examples of this approach are notable in the UK and New Zealand. Again, there are extensive ethical as well as technical and methodological concerns with these datasets.

Social media data, shopping data and geographical systems. As part of the big data revolution, more data are available on the everyday habits and preferences of individuals, with potential implications that may be both positive and negative in terms of public service responsiveness and individual privacy.

Nevertheless, a central limitation is that observational studies attempt to control through statistical rather than experimental means, and these may sometimes fall short. This particular limitation of observational studies means that policy makers and practitioners can have less confidence that any differences in outcomes between two or more policies or intervention strategies are attributable to any specific interventions. Such findings may be simply due to the presence of uncontrolled confounders, or they may be linked to contextual factors independent of the intervention. Randomised controlled experimental studies continue to offer the most promising option in terms of establishing a causal relationship between an intervention and outcomes. This approach forms the focus of the next section.

Experimental evidence

Different policy sectors and countries have developed contrasting approaches to randomisation in the exploration of what works in public services. For example, in sectoral terms, healthcare internationally has a strong tradition of prioritising randomised controlled trials (RCTs), whereas such approaches have often been resisted in social care (see Chapters Four and Five). Culturally, both within and beyond healthcare, RCTs are seen as particularly salient in policy debates in the US (see Chapter Seventeen), with greater scepticism about the approach in, for example, Scandinavia (see Chapter Fifteen).

There is also a distinction to be made between individualistic and programmatic interventions. The former are aimed at individuals and seek to influence individual outcomes – for example, therapeutic interventions or offender behaviour modification. The latter are aimed at groups or communities and seek to influence both individual and collective outcomes – for example, the testing of new ways of delivering aid, or strategies for shaping recycling. Both types of intervention are influenced by contextual factors that complicate questions of attribution. Classically, the healthcare sector has proved adept at applying RCT techniques to explore the efficacy of therapeutic interventions aimed at individuals in the pursuance of robust data about what works. However, there are individualistic interventions in education (for example, phonics application) and crime and justice (for example, specialised rehabilitation programmes) that might be well suited to randomised testing.

Outside of the US and the healthcare arena, RCTs are less common than might be expected. Partly, this is linked to the fact that interventions at the programme level are considered to be less amenable to randomisation, particularly when context is thought to be a powerful mediating factor. The more complex and contested the context in which a programme takes place, the less confidence we may have in the capacity of studies to deliver results of which policy makers and practitioners can have confidence that they reflect attributable and replicable findings. Box 10.6 explores some of the key reasons for and challenges of randomisation.

Box 10.6: Reasons for and challenges to randomisation

What are some of the main reasons to randomise?

• Randomisation is crucially important in helping us to understand what works in both individualistic and programmatic trials.
• Random allocation will – on average and with increasing certainty with increasing sample size – lead to groups evenly balanced for known and unknown mediating factors.
• Randomised trials can be used to test the efficacy of existing and new interventions. They can be used to compare different approaches against each other or against no intervention.
• Randomisation can take place at the individual level (for example, in testing out a new medical treatment for patients) or at the organisational level (for example, in comparing schools that organise peer tutoring with those that do not). The interventions being tested can be directed at individuals (for example, new strategies for managing substance misuse) or can be programmatic (for example, new ways of rehabilitating offenders).

There are agreed standards and checklists that can help to ensure the robustness of randomised trials.

What are some of the challenges of randomisation?

• It is often claimed that randomisation is more expensive, complicated and time-consuming than other forms of evaluation. However, the exploitation of routine data has in some cases allowed rapid and cheap randomised evaluations.
• Randomisation may be ethically problematic. However, some would claim that *not* randomising when there is genuine uncertainty about intervention benefits is also unethical. Therefore arguments around the ethicality of randomisation often hinge on ideas of equipoise: that is, general uncertainty over which course of action is best.
• Randomisation provides strong *internal* validity (did the intervention work with the study group?) but does not usually provide clear *external* validity (will the intervention work with other groups?). Hence, transferability of findings beyond the controlled context of the trial may be contested.
• Randomised studies provide unbiased estimates of *aggregate* effects in the studied population. This is most appropriate when intervention effects are relatively homogeneous. If intervention effects are thought to be heterogeneous, then aggregation may obscure more than it reveals (Longford, 1999; Davies et al, 2000). It may be that some participants are not helped or are even harmed

by an intervention, yet the mean effect size of the study may still be positive. This poses both ethical problems and challenges for how aggregated results ought to be interpreted.

A good, accessible source on these issues, particularly as applied to the programme level in the UK, is Haynes et al (2012).

It is clear, then, that randomisation offers great promise for policy makers and practitioners in their pursuit of evidence on the specific question of 'what works'. But, important as experimentation and RCTs are, there are many reasons why RCTs may not be adopted in certain settings, or may not be suited to certain questions (see Box 10.6). In particular, the cost or time implications may be prohibitive. Moreover, as important as quantification and causation are as evidential concerns, practitioners and policy makers have questions other than merely 'how many?', 'how much?' and 'what works?' (see Box 10.2). These other questions must also be explored in order to understand the nature and amelioration of social problems more holistically and contextually. In the next section some of the ways that this may be approached are illuminated.

Beyond experimental evidence: realist and qualitative approaches

Systematic enquiry requires policy makers and practitioners to ask questions beyond those to which quantitative research methods alone are capable of responding (see Box 10.2). Such questions include why and how an intervention does (or does not) work in certain settings for certain groups at certain times, what and why people feel about the experiences that they have, and what implications these perceptions have for behaviours, whether of clients or service staff. These questions shift the focus away from quantification alone as a means of exploring impact (in search of causality, efficacy and effectiveness), and towards process and qualitative interpretation, perhaps combined with some measurement. Such approaches draw on the perceptions and interpretations of multiple stakeholders, and they seek insights and contributions from sociology, politics, psychology and broader social science theory.

One approach is through realist evaluation (Pawson and Tilley, 1997) or other forms of theory-led evaluation (Chen, 1990). The realist approach (and theory-led approaches in general) start from the position that randomisation focuses too heavily on the question of whether an intervention *can* work at the expense of knowing *why* it works and in what circumstances (Pawson and Tilley, 1997). Realist evaluation argues for theory-driven approaches that explore the causal mechanisms of interventions on the outcomes sought, and crucially, how these interact with the different contexts in which interventions are delivered. Data generated from realist evaluations can be both quantitative and qualitative, and are potentially more useful to answer the real-world questions of policy makers and practitioners (Monaghan and Boaz, 2018).

Assessing policy or intervention effects in this way is not merely a technical exercise. For example, the outcomes sought from interventions may be highly contested, even politicised, as indeed might be the putative mechanisms by which those outcomes are supposedly achieved. Thus the identification of programme theories through realist and other theory-led approaches may be an unrealistic simplification, or it could itself be politically influenced (that is, unduly shaped by the founding assumptions of the policy or intervention under study). The attribution of causality is also problematic in the absence of randomisation. Hence these approaches are not without their problems or their critics (Jones, 2018). Nonetheless, realist evaluation in particular has been widely applied to explore the impacts of complex and contextually mediated interventions (Greenhalgh et al, 2009).

A key issue with mixed-method data gathering in these kinds of evaluation is the extent to which research traditions with different ontological and epistemological underpinnings may be adequately combined. For example, quantitative research, especially that relying heavily on complex measurements, draws on positivist traditions and assumptions about the nature of knowledge and knowing, while much qualitative research draws on quite different, interpretivist traditions and assumptions (see Box 10.3). This distinction helps to explain why the two research traditions have frequently been dealt with separately and are so often engaged in unproductive 'paradigm wars'. In general, while quantitative research seeks to control for context and exclude extraneous variables, qualitative research seeks to embrace and explore the active role of context (Dopson et al, 2008). It sees the factors embedded in specific contexts as potentially significant in understanding why and how actors do or do not enact interventions, as well as how service users may experience and respond to these interventions. In reality, of course, the questions that policy makers and practitioners pose (not to say those raised by other stakeholders) are not so easily divided into separate categories – hence systematic enquiry often requires both quantitative and qualitative approaches. What follows, then, is some exploration of how interpretative qualitative approaches can aid systematic knowledge.

If researchers wish to understand why and how people behave in the ways that they do, and how they make sense of the world, then a natural place to start is through observing what they do and how they describe everyday activity. Observational approaches in this sense draw on ethnographic techniques that have roots in anthropological enquiry. These approaches aim for what Geertz (1973) labelled 'thick description', aiming to provide sufficient contextual data to convey the cultural significance of action beyond the boundaries of specific settings. Such data (or knowledge) about what goes on are not necessarily evaluative – comparisons or contrasts between behaviour or interpretation in different settings are not usually the explicit aim of such approaches. However, this knowledge is crucial in establishing contextual and symbolic understandings of action and values. If stakeholders want to generate evidence that is relevant to service users, practitioners and others, then such knowledge is essential.

Alongside direct observation, qualitative approaches to knowledge generation include interviewing relevant actors to understand how they articulate (in their own words) their understandings of the world around them, the values they place on actions, and the motivations that may explain their behaviour in certain contexts. Interviews can be more or less evaluative in nature. A distinction is often made in the degree to which interviews are structured – the less structured an interview is, the greater the freedom that informant and researcher have to explore issues that emerge naturally through their interaction. In contrast, more formally structured interviews often maintain an explicit focus on specific questions that policy makers and practitioners may value (Rubin and Rubin, 2011). Different approaches may be more appropriate at different points of the fieldwork, depending on the aims of the research.

Additionally, qualitative approaches may fruitfully draw on written documents as a resource to generate new knowledge. Often, such approaches can be used to (re)interpret an 'official' account (Martin and Learmonth, 2012) through, for example, surfacing the way language is used to construct discourses that make political choices seem natural and inevitable (Fraser et al, 2017). Through the collection of these connected but distinct types of data (that is, observations, interviews and documentary analyses), qualitative approaches can be combined to *triangulate* findings and highlight commonalities and disparities between the 'stated' and the 'unstated' motivations and drivers of actors and organisations (Fulop et al, 2005). These approaches rely heavily on researcher interpretations and dedicated engagement with theory – in both inductive and deductive senses. Hence, rigour is just as important in qualitative research as it is in quantitative research, although it may be harder to provide a convincing account, and more difficult to appraise in published reports (Popay and Williams, 1998).

The processes used in the generation of knowledge through qualitative enquiry – often involving the development and application of theory – must be well described, coherent and transparent. The practice of *reflexivity* is crucial in this regard. Steier (1991) describes reflexivity as 'a turning back on oneself': he focuses on the question of how the language of others and their ways of constructing meaning can be better understood by the researcher, and that requires the researcher knowing and questioning themselves. Qualitative inquiry can be seen as a 'co-constructive process' between the researcher and the researched (Steier, 1991). This conceptualisation lies at the heart of many of the co-production approaches to evidence noted in various chapters in this book and is unpacked further in Chapters Eleven and Twelve. In many ways, it is the depth and quality of such an analytical process that is integral to the generation of robust, relevant, qualitatively derived knowledge for policy makers and practitioners – but this is an iterative, time-consuming and interpretive endeavour (Pope and Mays, 2009).

To summarise, so far this chapter has identified and outlined multiple distinct approaches through which data may be gathered and transformed to inform policy and practice. In the next section we discuss ways in which these distinct approaches can be combined to better address the diverse questions of importance to policy makers and practitioners.

Combining methods

Combining research methods can be difficult, and not just for the philosophical divergences discussed above and noted in Box 10.3. A notable challenge of combining methods is often at the interpretation stage (O'Cathain et al, 2008; Pope and Mays, 2009), when findings from different approaches may lack coherence. This is not helped by disciplinary boundaries and the requirements for different types of research to be published in different academic journals: integrative analysis is often treated with a degree of scepticism. On the other hand, there are various stages of data extraction and handling at which different approaches to research are perceived as being useful and complementary: in shaping study design; in guiding questions; and in informing analysis (O'Cathain et al, 2008; Mays et al, 2005). In Box 10.7, Pope and Mays (2009) highlight four stages of the research process and give examples of how different approaches may be seen to be mutually informative.

At its best, this combined approach draws iteratively on the strengths of the respective techniques to deliver dynamic insights around problem definitions and intervention processes, impacts and wider implications. A useful way to characterise this is to consider how quantitative approaches offer breadth of understanding, while qualitative approaches may offer depth of understanding. While such a characterisation is clearly overly simplistic, the *lack of* breadth or depth when one approach is privileged over another does reveal certain weaknesses of singular approaches.

Combining methods can aid the design and relevance of robust studies. In particular, case studies offer good examples of integrated mixed-methods approaches to relevant questions of policy and practice. Case studies enable researchers to explore particular phenomena in one or more real-life settings and typically draw on multiple methods of data collection (Fraser and Mays, 2019). There is increasing recognition of the importance of mixed-method case studies in policy evaluations

---

Box 10.7: Combining different research methods

Combining qualitative and quantitative approaches can be helpful at various stages of research study.

Design. Early qualitative interviews can be useful in identifying issues for quantitative assessment.

Sampling. Quantitative surveys can be helpful to determine a sampling frame for deeper qualitative study.

Analysis. Qualitative findings may be helpful to inform 'priors' for Bayesian statistical analysis.

Interpretation. Quantitative and qualitative findings may contribute differentially to understanding the 'what' and the 'how' of intervention effects.

Source: Adapted from Pope and Mays, 2009.

− for example, in healthcare research − and it has become relatively common to nest a number of carefully selected local case studies within a larger policy or programme evaluation, perhaps one which also uses quantitative methods such as the analysis of patient surveys or routine activity data (Pope et al, 2008; Robert et al, 2011). Work such as this can be revealing in its own right, but can also act as a precursor to more carefully designed experimental studies. The Medical Research Council Framework for evaluating complex interventions also provides some guidance here (Craig et al, 2008).

Case studies raise important questions about sampling, the validity of the observations made and generalisation. Moreover, there are debates about whether case studies should aim more for internal validity (what Stake (1995) terms 'particularisation' and depth) or more for external validity (the extent to which findings may be generalised to other sites, settings or contexts). Case studies also have different scales: they may involve small-scale, localised, single-site and one-time research, or larger, multiple-site and longitudinal approaches. They may also offer rich, detailed insights: for example, by selecting an atypical or extreme case (such as a positive or negative outlier) the researcher may reveal more about the underlying general processes, procedures and actions than could be gleaned from a larger representative sample of cases (Fraser and Mays, 2019). With respect to study design and sampling, researchers can refine their questions and identify promising cases through scoping interviews − these may be more or less formal in nature and include high-level experts as well as service users and local practitioners. At the same time, quantitative data are often vital in identifying underlying performance trends (for example, crime statistics or exam performance) and where to look to get the richest picture of any phenomena of interest. Finally, mixed-method case studies also offer the opportunity to explore the cost implications of policy interventions. Yet it is the case in the UK that cost data (particularly in terms of comparative analyses) remain limited (NAO, 2015).

In summary, mixed-methods approaches to knowledge generation through integrated research strategies and case studies can offer much to the systematic production of evidence to inform policy and practice. Combining methods prompts questions about the best ways to collate and interpret different forms of newly generated data. Such questions are highly relevant to the following section, which focuses on methods to synthesise existing (usually research-derived) data in a systematic way − so that policy makers and practitioners can be confident that they are drawing on all of the recent, relevant and high-quality data to guide their work.

Synthesising evidence

Knowledge generation draws on a multiplicity of processes and creates many discrete findings from different studies. So far we have outlined the distinct contributions of various research-based approaches, and the challenges of integrating knowledge across these. In this section we examine the role of research synthesis as a key methodology in building new knowledge from existing empirical work.

Some policy or practice issues have many decades' worth of research data, including perhaps hundreds of individual research papers, and sometimes multiple reviews dedicated to exploring what is known. It is neither realistic nor desirable to expect policy makers or practitioners to read all of this existing literature in order to become informed (Sackett and Rosenberg, 1995). For such issues, reviews and overviews of reviews are helpful in bringing all the data together in one place. Reviews and research syntheses can also be updated periodically to reflect the accumulation of new data in a specific domain (the Cochrane and Campbell Collaborations both do this).

The importance of synthesis as a distinct approach is also linked to the position of systematic reviews and meta-analyses (the careful statistical aggregation of effects) at the top of typical hierarchies of evidence – albeit a position somewhat contested in evidence debates (see Chapter Eleven for a full discussion). Box 10.8 describes the classic synthesis approaches of systematic review and meta-analysis, alongside more recent developments, including mixed-method and qualitative approaches such as realist synthesis, critical interpretive synthesis and meta-ethnographies.

Any synthesising approach (sometimes also called 'secondary research', contrasting with the 'primary research' of de novo data collection) needs to adopt similar standards of rigour and transparency to those expected of any research methodology. However, there are also tensions between this demand for rigour and the need to provide rapid reviews that meet the time-scales of policy makers and practitioners. At their best, research syntheses should allow the complete capture of the best and most recent data, analysed in a way that produces new insights. In reality, however, there are trade-offs. For example: the more complete a synthesis, the more likely it is that it will include sub-standard studies; but, on the other hand, the more a synthesis confines itself to the very best studies, the more likely it is that potentially useful information will be discarded (Pawson, 2006). There are also trade-offs around context: reviews that are tightly drawn around studies set in a similar context may have high relevance to policy makers and practitioners in similar settings, but little relevance elsewhere; reviews that neglect the role of context and cast their net widely for original studies may produce average effects of widely heterogeneous findings. It is issues such as these that often see review findings hotly contested when attempts are made to label their findings as evidence.

Box 10.8: Synthesising across research studies

Systematic review. This approach seeks to reduce bias in the production and presentation of research findings by bringing together all available data on a specific topic and identifying what can be said reliably on the basis of that data. Explicit and transparent methods are used, to ensure that reviews are replicable and updatable.

Meta-analysis. This approach uses formal statistical analysis to combine the results from a set of studies identified through systematic review, usually to provide guidance on the overall effect size of an intervention. This requires the studies to have identical or very similar interventions with the same or comparable outcome measures. The approach provides more precise estimates of effects than are available through individual studies.

Realist synthesis. This approach may draw on both quantitative and qualitative data from diverse studies and seeks to identify underlying causal mechanisms, exploring how they work and under what conditions, and so answering the question 'what works for whom under what circumstances?' (Pawson, 2006).

Meta ethnography. This approach is used to review and synthesise findings from qualitative studies. An important facet of this approach is that is should deliver insights beyond those found in the original studies through theoretical engagement (Noblitt and Hare, 1988). Meta ethnography has also influenced the development of new integrative strategies, such as critical interpretive synthesis (Dixon-Woods et al, 2006).

Research mapping. This review method (unlike the others in this box) does not directly discuss findings of other studies. Instead, the approach collates information on data gathering related to a specific review topic such as, where studies were done, how they were designed, where they were published, how they were funded and so on, in order to highlight linkages between studies and the broad characteristics of a research field (Cooper, 2016).

While established policy and practice issues may have substantial collections of (methodologically similar) work that needs to be synthesised, it is often the case that newer concerns may have a much smaller number of quite disparate studies (some empirical, others theoretical; some qualitative, others quantitative; some academic, others 'grey'). For such issues, systematic searching of databases and research depositories can be helpful in bringing the data together in one place, an approach sometimes called 'evidence mapping' (Miake-Lye et al, 2016). In such circumstances – especially where there is a greater reliance on qualitative studies of programmatic interventions – explicitly theory-driven approaches to evidence syntheses may be of real value to policy makers and practitioners. For example, realist reviews (Pawson and Tilley, 1997) highlight the importance of context, and critical interpretive syntheses (Dixon-Woods et al, 2006) draw on meta-ethnography to help summarise the insights from qualitative studies.

Finally, as we have seen (see Chapter Two), windows of opportunity that align problem identification, political will and effective policy solutions are notoriously limited (Kingdon, 1984). This may necessarily encourage a more pragmatic approach to evidence synthesis – for example, rapid reviews, scoping reviews and evidence maps are often sought. It also suggests the need for continuing investment in the infrastructure to support regularly updated, rigorous reviews (such as with the Cochrane and Campbell Collaborations). If decisions are to be informed by research-based knowledge, then it is important that the approaches for appraising and presenting this knowledge are systematic, transparent and theoretically informed. Nonetheless, because of the challenges and complexities already explored we cannot expect the products that emerge to be without contestation and even controversy.

Reflections and concluding remarks

This chapter has explored the kinds of questions that policy makers, practitioners and other stakeholders may have as they reflect on and endeavour to improve policy and practice. We suggest that such questions are frequently complex, multifaceted, value-laden and anchored in deeper debates around ontology and epistemology. Addressing these questions requires careful attention to technical research methods, sometimes singly and at other times combining multiple methods. As policy makers and practitioners are often in search of integrations of knowledge, we have also explored whether and how integrations across methods are possible, and the role of research synthesis in providing cumulative understandings.

In examining the approaches to creating new knowledge from empirical data, we drew attention to the potentially differing perspectives of different stakeholders, and the political implications buried in seemingly technocratic research questions. This suggests that there needs to be much deeper and wider stakeholder involvement in setting (and addressing) research agendas, and it points to the potential value of the co-creation of evidence. This is a theme we return to in the next chapter.

The tension between the production of rigorous and relevant research and the competing demands and time frames of different actors involved in using evidence highlights the need for continuing attention to both the stocks and the flows of usable, empirically sourced knowledge. This may mean greater effort being directed at synthesis activity, while paying careful attention to contextual relevance (for example, bespoke review work), and it also suggests the need to draw on broader synthesis strategies than just systematic review and meta-analysis. Looking to the future, the role of 'big data' and the mining of social media data may increasingly inform policy makers and practitioners, and offer the potential for very quick turnaround times, with regular updating and even some near-real-time analysis of intervention effects. However, ensuring that the creation and analysis of such linked data resources are carried out ethically and rigorously will be a big challenge.

Large-scale RCTs with additional safeguards against bias (such as single-, double- and even triple-blinding) have an important role to play, especially when these feed into high-quality systematic reviews. Yet, there has been something of a 'replication crisis' with these methods, most obviously in medicine (Ioannidis, 2016) and psychology (Martin and Clarke, 2017), and it is unlikely that other fields will escape these concerns. Moreover, EBPP has, since at least the mid-1990s, been criticised for pursuing a broadly positivistic agenda: overly focusing on the question of 'what works', to the detriment of wider, interpretive, contextually informed understandings around how and why policies and practices do (and do not) work for some individuals and groups in certain places. The dangers of such decontextualised understandings of policy and practice are that important questions about what is really going on in complex social realities are not fully explored.

In these debates it is also relevant to consider what types of research attract the interest of major funders, and what kinds of methodological approaches are favoured by publishing outlets. The research production industry (predominantly, but not exclusively, situated in universities) has its own values, preferences and dynamics, and these influence what is produced and how it is funded, validated and communicated

(Walshe and Davies, 2010). We should not be surprised, therefore, that research stocks and flows do not always align with the needs and interests of wider stakeholders.

Any failures of research to provide robust and fully rounded analysis of social problems can be significant. If the knowledge base for policy intervention and public services is constructed from partial or even erroneous understandings, then the strategies pursued by policy makers and practitioners are likely to be suboptimal, at best, and potentially ineffectual or even counter-productive, at worst. This perpetuates dissatisfaction with the seeming inability of policy makers and practitioners to improve social outcomes, which in turn undermines the evidence agenda specifically, and perhaps more importantly subverts support for government intervention and public services more generally. There is thus a great deal riding on the capacity of the system to generate relevant, robust and applicable knowledge.

In sum, it is important that evidence generation is examined not just for its technical virtuosity but also for its capacity to actually deliver better policies and more effective practices. This involves surfacing the often obscured values that lie behind methodological choices, and examining the political and power-related implications of these. The first of these challenges (delivering value from evidence) is the central subject of Chapter Twelve, but first we turn to the value-laden and power-infused processes by which empirical observations and analyses are labelled as evidence (Chapter Eleven, next).

References

Benson, K. and Hartz, A.J. (2000) 'A comparison of observational studies and randomized, controlled trials', *New England Journal of Medicine*, 342 (25), pp 1878–86.

Bevan, G., Karanikolos, M., Exley, J., Nolte, E., Connolly, S. and Mays, N. (2014) *The four health systems of the United Kingdom: how do they compare? Summary report*, https://www.nuffieldtrust.org.uk/files/2017–01/4-countries-report-web-final.pdf

Chen, H.-T. (1990) *Theory-driven evaluations*, Newbury Park, CA: Sage.

Cooper, I.D. (2016) 'What is a "mapping study?"', *Journal of the Medical Library Association: JMLA*, 104 (1), p 76.

Craig, P., Dieppe, P., Macintyre, S., Michie, S., Nazareth, I. and Petticrew, M. (2008) 'Developing and evaluating complex interventions: the new Medical Research Council guidance', *BMJ*, 337, p a1655.

Dixon-Woods, M., Bonas, S., Booth, A., Jones, D.R., Miller, T., Smith, J., Sutton, A.J. and Young, B. (2006) 'How can systematic reviews incorporate qualitative research? A critical perspective', *Qualitative Research*, 6 (1), pp 27–44.

Dopson, S., Fitzgerald, L. and Ferlie, E. (2008) 'Understanding change and innovation in healthcare settings: reconceptualizing the active role of context', *Journal of Change Management*, 8 (3–4), pp 213–31.

Fraser, A., Baeza, J.I. and Boaz, A. (2017) '"Holding the line': a qualitative study of the role of evidence in early phase decision-making in the reconfiguration of stroke services in London', *Health Research Policy and Systems*, 15(1), p 45.

Fraser, A. and Mays, N. (2019) 'Case studies', in Pope, C. and Mays, N. (eds), *Qualitative research in healthcare*, 4th edn, London: Wiley.

Fulop, N., Protopsaltis, G., King, A., Allen, P., Hutchings, A. and Normand, C. (2005) 'Changing organisations: a study of the context and processes of mergers of health care providers in England', *Social Science and Medicine*, 60 (1), pp 119–30.

Geertz, C. (1973) 'Thick description: toward an interpretive theory of culture', in *The interpretation of cultures: selected essays*, New York: Basic Books, pp 3–30.

Greenhalgh, T., Humphrey, C., Hughes, J., Macfarlane, F., Butler, C. and Pawson, R.A.Y. (2009) 'How do you modernize a health service? A realist evaluation of whole-scale transformation in London', *The Milbank Quarterly*, 87 (2), pp 391–416.

Hasson, F., Keeney, S. and McKenna, H. (2000) 'Research guidelines for the Delphi survey technique', *Journal of Advanced Nursing*, 32 (4), pp 1008–15.

Haynes, L., Goldacre, B., and Torgerson, D. (2012) *Test, learn, adapt: Developing public policy with randomised controlled trials*, London: Cabinet Office.

Head, B. W. (2008) 'Three lenses of evidence-based policy', *Australian Journal of Public Administration*, 67 (1), pp 1–11.

Hutton, J. and Smith, P.C. (2000) 'Non-experimental quantitative methods', in H.T.O. Davies, S.M. Nutley, and P.C. Smith (eds), *What works? Evidence-based policy and practice in public services*, Bristol: Policy Press.

IFS (2018) *Poverty and low pay in the UK: the state of play and the challenges ahead*, London: IFS.

Ioannidis, J.P.A. (2016) 'Why most clinical research is not useful', *PLOS Medicine*, 13 (6), e1002049, https://doi.org/10.1371/journal.pmed.1002049

Jones, L. (2018) 'The art and science of non-evaluation evaluation', *Journal of Health Service Research and Policy*, 23(4), pp 262–7.

Kingdon, J.W. (1984) *Agendas, alternatives, and public policies*, Boston, MA: Little, Brown.

Konnerup, M. and Kongsted, H.C. (2012) 'Do Cochrane reviews provide a good model for social science? The role of observational studies in systematic reviews', *Evidence and Policy: A Journal of Research, Debate and Practice*, 8 (1), pp 79–96.

Martin, G.N., Clarke, R.M. (2017) 'Are psychology journals anti-replication?', *Frontiers in Psychology*, 8, p 523.

Martin, G.P. and Learmonth, M. (2012) 'A critical account of the rise and spread of "leadership": the case of UK healthcare', *Social Science and Medicine*, 74 (3), pp 281–8.

Mays, N., Pope, C. and Popay, J. (2005) 'Systematically reviewing qualitative and quantitative evidence to inform management and policy-making in the health field', *Journal of Health Services Research and Policy*, 10 (1_suppl), pp 6–20.

Miake-Lye, I.M., Hempel, S., Shanman, R. and Shekelle, P.G. (2016) 'What is an evidence map? A systematic review of published evidence maps and their definitions, methods, and products', *Systematic Reviews*, 5, p 28.

Monaghan, M. and Boaz, A. (2018) 'The place of realist explanation and review and their impacts on policy', in N. Emmel, J. Greenhalgh, A. Manzano, M. Monaghan and S. Dalkin (eds), *Doing realist research*, London: Sage, pp 167–84.

Mulrow, C.D. (1987) 'The medical review article: state of the science', *Annals of Internal Medicine*, 106, pp 485–8.

NAO (2005) *Reducing brain damage: faster access to better stroke care* London: National Audit Office, https://www.nao.org.uk/wp-content/uploads/2005/11/0506452.pdf.

NAO (2015) 'Outcome-based payment schemes: government's use of payment by results', London: National Audit Office, https://www.nao.org.uk/report/outcome-based-payment-schemes-governments-use-of-payment-by-results/.

Noblitt, G.W. and Hare, R.D. (1988) *Meta-ethnography: Synthesizing qualitative methods*, Newbury Park, CA: Sage.

O'Cathain, A., Murphy, E. and Nicholl, J. (2008) 'The quality of mixed methods studies in health services research', *Journal of Health Services Research and Policy*, 13 (2), pp 92–98.

Orr, K. and Bennett, M. (2010) 'Editorial: The politics of co-produced research', *Public Money and Management*, 30 (4), p 1, doi: 10.1080/09540962.2010.492171.

Pawson, R. (2006) 'Digging for nuggets: how "bad" research can yield "good" evidence', *International Journal of Social Research Methodology*, 9 (2), pp 127–42.

Pawson, R. and Tilley, N. (1997) *Realistic evaluation*, London, Thousand Oaks, CA and New Delhi: Sage.

Popay, J. and Williams, G. (1998) 'Qualitative research and evidence-based healthcare', *Journal of the Royal Society of Medicine*, 91, pp 32–37.

Pope, C. and Mays, N. (2009) 'Critical reflections on the rise of qualitative research', *BMJ*, 339, p b3425.

Robert, G., Morrow, E., Maben, J., Griffiths, P. and Callard, L. (2011) 'The adoption, local implementation and assimilation into routine nursing practice of a national quality improvement programme: the Productive Ward in England', *Journal of Clinical Nursing*, 20, pp 1196–207.

Rubin, H.J. and Rubin, I.S. (2011) *Qualitative interviewing: the art of hearing data*, London: Sage Publications.

Sackett, D.L. and Rosenberg, W.M.C. (1995) 'On the need for evidence-based medicine', *Journal of Public Health*, 17 (3), pp 330–34.

Stake, R.E. (1995) *The art of case study research*, Thousand Oaks, CA: Sage.

Steier, F. (1991) 'Introduction: Research as self-reflexivity, self-reflexivity as social process', *Research and reflexivity*, London: Sage, pp 1–11.

Walshe, K. and Davies, H.T.O. (2010) 'Research, influence and impact: deconstructing the norms of health services research commissioning', *Policy and Society*, 29 (2), pp 103–11.

11

Assessing and labelling evidence

Sandra Nutley, Huw Davies and Judith Hughes

An introduction to assessing and labelling evidence

Given the diversity of approaches to creating evidence described in the previous chapter, an evident challenge is the need for a broadly shared understanding about what forms of evidence provide useful, legitimate or even compelling underpinnings for policy and practice. Yet reaching a workable consensus on appropriate ways of identifying and labelling good evidence is far from straightforward. In this chapter we consider some of the main ways in which evidence-promoting organisations have responded to this challenge, discussing examples of the different evidence standards that have emerged and commenting on their relative merits and implications.

The introduction to Section Three argued that it is appropriate to pay particular attention to research-based evidence when considering these issues, and many promoters of evidence do indeed place research at the centre of their deliberations. This privileging of research is due in part to the transparency and scrutiny that comes from the requirement that research studies should be explicit about their methods and must undergo rigorous peer review. Following on from this, Chapter Ten explored various approaches to gathering and analysing data, many but not all of which may come under the rubric of 'research', and concluded that there is often a need to combine a range of methodologies to answer the many interconnected questions that arise with policy makers and practitioners. However, combining evidence from different sources and different methodological approaches adds another layer of complexity and can be contentious – particularly when the aim is to make an overall judgement on the quality and strength of evidence in support of a novel proposition (such as a policy prescription or a practice innovation). So, how have some of the main organisations concerned with promoting evidence-informed policies and practices gone about this task, and to what extent have they factored in other (non-research-based) forms of knowledge and evidence?

In exploring this issue, we highlight the relevance of both quality assurance processes (such as peer review, and the production of evidence in professionally led research institutes) and post hoc criterion-based assessments that can be applied to completed studies (such as methodological hierarchies and methodological checklists). Each of these has its place in helping us to understand the quality of the data and analysis that can underpin evidence. Ultimately, however, we conclude that both of these approaches are insufficient in and of themselves, and that a more dynamic assessment of evidence in the round is needed: its 'fitness for purpose' in the proposed context of use. This leads us to consider how research-based evidence must be combined with other sources and types of knowledge when deciding what counts as 'good' or 'good enough' evidence. We also consider whether and how understandings about evidence 'quality' can be negotiated and co-created so that the evidence collated is better suited to application and so that these processes of generation and assessment help to create propitious conditions for evidence use.

We begin these discussions by saying something about the sorts of bodies that identify, review and label evidence, before a more lengthy examination of various 'standards of evidence' and the thinking and debates that lie behind such judgements.

Bodies that identify, review and label evidence

There are many bodies in the UK and around the world that aim to inform and guide policy and practice by gathering, sifting and synthesising what is considered to be good evidence in relation to an issue of interest. In the UK, these bodies include government agencies, independent public bodies, professional associations, public service providers from the public and charity sectors, audit and inspection bodies, academic research centres and collaboration networks. Their advice is often focused on particular policy domains (for example, health, education, welfare, crime, social care and so on) and/or specific target groups (for example, patients, children and families, older people, offenders and substance misusers). Many such bodies have been identified earlier in this book, particularly in the domain-specific reviews in Section Two (Chapters Four to Nine), and some are also identified in the international commentaries of Section Four (Chapters Thirteen to Seventeen).

There are some similarities in approach: most of the guidance bodies are concerned with identifying and weighing up the accumulated research base on the effectiveness of specific policy and practice interventions, often with the explicit aim of identifying what works (and, less often, what does not). They sometimes involve practitioners and service users in their judgement processes, but research evidence tends to be privileged over other forms of knowledge. When weighing up research evidence, methodological choices (sometimes rated using hierarchies of method) and methodological quality (often deploying checklists) are paramount.

Alongside these overall similarities, there are important differences in the detailed evidence standards used. This can occur even when bodies are part of the same network, as is the case in the UK What Works Network (see Chapter Thirteen). For instance, the highest 'security of evidence' rating used by the Education Endowment Foundation (EEF; known as five 'padlocks') is based on a different set of criteria to the Early Intervention Foundation's (EIF) highest level of evidence rating (Level 4) (see Box 11.1).

In addition to strength-of-evidence labels, the results of these assessment efforts are often summed up for policy makers and practitioners by labelling practices as promising, good practices, effective practices, proven, evidence-based and so on. While definitions of some of these labels have been enshrined in law for children's mental health and juvenile justice practices in the US (Box 11.2), there is generally no standardised nomenclature that would immediately indicate the evidence standards underpinning such labels, or how confident users should be about their relevance and applicability.

This lack of a standard nomenclature is important because (as we have seen) different evidence-promoting organisations use varied processes and standards when judging the effectiveness of interventions, creating ample scope for uncertainty or even confusion as to the underpinnings of recommendations – even of those clearly labelled as being evidence-based. Moreover, the labels ascribed really do matter: they may influence the viability of certain policy choices; or they may shape the availability, composition and funding of service provision. And, going further, such changes to policy and practice may be for good or ill: service users may benefit from these judgements (because new services and treatments quickly become available as evidence of benefit is effectively marshalled), but there can also sometimes be harmful consequences (for example, if authorities converge too quickly on a singular reading of the evidence, to the exclusion of alternative views; see Box 11.3 for one example of this).

Box 11.1: Evidence rating systems used by two members of the UK What Works Network

Education Endowment Fund. The EEF's Teaching and Learning Toolkit uses a 'padlock' system to rate the security of the evidence underpinning each of the topics/interventions included in the toolkit (for example, phonics and peer tutoring). The highest security of evidence rating is five padlocks.

For evidence on a topic to obtain a rating of five padlocks there needs to be: 'consistent high quality evidence from at least five robust and recent meta-analyses [based on well-controlled experiments] where the majority of the included studies have good ecological validity and where the outcome measures include curriculum measures or standardised test in school subject areas'.

Early Intervention Foundation. The EIF uses a rating system to assess the strength of evidence of impact: the degree to which a programme has been shown to have a positive, causal impact on specific child outcomes. The highest strength of evidence of impact is called Level 4.

For a programme to obtain a Level 4 rating, there needs to be 'evidence from at least two high-quality evaluations [which do not need to be RCTs if a relevant and robust counter-factual can be provided in other ways] demonstrating positive impacts across populations and environments lasting a year or longer. This evidence may include significant adaptations to meet the needs of different target populations.'

Source: EEF and EIF websites (accessed March 2018).

Those who use, or are affected by, the recommendations of evidence-promoting organisations are faced with a dilemma, then: what weight should be attached to different types of recommendation? Does the underpinning evidence need to come from multiple respected sources? What role does and should research methodology play in providing reassurance? Does the evidence need to be compelling, or just good enough? An additional uncertainty is likely to arise about whether a practice that is said to work well in one context will work equally well if applied in another; and such doubts may be compounded by the availability of contradictory advice from different sources. In the light of these uncertainties, the next section considers how at least some of these questions have been addressed in seeking to establish transparent evidence standards.

> **Box 11.2: Legal definitions of evidence labels**
>
> In the US, legal definitions have entered statute, indicating the extent of evidence supporting children's mental health and juvenile justice programmes and practices, as follows.
>
> **Evidence-based.** A programme or practice that has had multiple-site RCTs across heterogeneous populations demonstrating that the programme or practice is effective for the population.
>
> **Research-based.** A programme or practice that has some research demonstrating effectiveness, but does not yet meet the standard of evidence-based practices.
>
> **Promising.** A practice that presents, based upon preliminary information, potential for becoming a research-based or consensus-based practice.
>
> Source: Abstracted from WSIPP (2017), Exhibit 2, p 4 (Note: This exhibit also provides WSIPP's suggested elaborations of these definitions).

Creating standards of evidence

Discussion of evidence standards can be confusing because there is no overall consensus on the definition of terms such as the 'quality' or the 'strength' of evidence, or how these aspects should be translated into evidence standards that set appropriate and demonstrable levels of attainment. The legal force applied to definitions of evidence labels for children's services in the US (see Box 11.2) attests to the importance attached to this issue, but few others have (as yet) followed this lead: while evidence labels proliferate, they generally lack force – and they sometimes lack clarity.

In the UK, DFID (2014) distinguishes between evidence *quality* (where high quality means adherence to the principles of methodological rigour – such as validity and reliability) and evidence *strength* (which is based on an assessment of the size and consistency of a body of evidence, as well is on its quality). In the case of research evidence, quality can be judged indirectly by reference to its source (as a proxy for high-quality processes), as well as more directly by reference to methodological considerations.

Box 11.3: A service-user perspective on the impact of a NICE guideline on the treatment of ME

ME (myalgic encephalomyelitis), or chronic fatigue syndrome (CFS), affects around 250,000 people in the UK. Its symptoms include debilitating exhaustion, muscle pain and weakness and cognitive dysfunction. A 2007 NICE guideline on ME/CFS, based on limited evidence, recommended that graded exercise therapy (GET) and cognitive behaviour therapy (CBT) should be offered to people with mild or moderate ME/CFS.

In 2011 results from the largest clinical trial of ME/CFS treatments were published (PACE – White et al, 2011). This found that GET and CBT were more effective than standard medical care. NICE therefore decided that no change to the existing guideline was needed when it was reviewed the same year. Patient groups were unhappy about this, arguing that, in their experience, graded exercise could do more harm than good. They were also concerned that ME/CFS continued to be treated as a psychological, rather than biological, illness.

I fell sick with ME in 2007 and was prescribed anti-depressants, which failed to help. The findings from the PACE trial in 2011 gave me hope, and I pushed for a referral to an evidence-based service. In 2013 I was offered CBT, but soon after became bedbound. I was told that I could receive CBT only once my symptoms had improved. The specialist experience that NICE recommends for treating those 25% of patients with severe ME wasn't available locally. I felt that although 'gold standard' evidence-based practice (CBT and GET) was being resourced, other forms of practice and expertise were being elbowed out.

The ME/CFS evidence debates raged on. I was too ill to follow them, but in 2016 I spotted an item on an ME web forum that questioned the PACE trial's findings. After years of similar attempts, anonymised PACE trial data had eventually been released following a patient's freedom of information request. A reanalysis of those data concluded that 'the claim that patients can recover as a result of CBT and GET is not justified by the data, and is highly misleading' (Wilshire et al, 2016, p 1). Heated debates about the original analysis and the reanalysis followed.

Patient groups pushed for NICE to review the ME/CFS guideline in the light of Wilshire et al's findings. Initially, NICE decided that there was insufficient new evidence to warrant another review, but further pressure from patients and their supporters prompted a rethink. 'Mutiny by ME sufferers forces a climbdown on exercise treatment' was the headline in *The Times* (Whipple, 2017).

The debacle around the PACE trial has made me more wary of published research findings. I've seen how relations of power shape the way evidence is defined, funded and judged; patients' views on the effectiveness of treatments were quashed for many years.

I'm also concerned that practices labelled as 'evidence-based' can take precedence over other forms of knowledge in an emerging and debated field of medicine. There is knowledge out there about what helps people with ME, it's just not – yet – evidence. These days, I tend to rely on anecdotal evidence of what works for other patients; and on learning, through trial and error, what works for me. I still support the need for good evidence, and am hopeful that recent increases in research funding and studies into the physiological basis of ME/CFS will bear fruit (Maxmen, 2018). However, this will take time: and meanwhile, we need to find ways of accessing and assessing other forms of knowledge about what works for ME.

Source: Contributed by Isabel Walter, one of the co-authors of *Using Evidence* (Nutley et al, 2007), and used with her permission.

Process-based quality assurance: the importance of source

The process whereby research-based evidence is produced is an enduring concern: in consequence, some evidence sources are seen as more credible than others. Peer-reviewed analyses emanating from respectable research institutions (often, but not exclusively, in universities) are generally preferred. Such sources ought to give reassurance about research quality in at least three ways: first, such studies are often peer reviewed prior to inception, for example, to secure funding; second, informal professional standards in research are attended to through collegiate interaction and on-going critical engagement; and third, publication in the better journals is usually accompanied by further significant peer review.

While there are good reasons to be sceptical that these processes *necessarily* provide the reassurances sought (Grayson, 2002), there is still considerable weight given to the distinction between formal peer-reviewed sources and the wider 'grey literature'. Moreover, there is, rightly, considerable suspicion attached to evidence emanating from vested-interest sources, most notoriously the pharmaceutical, tobacco and gambling industries (for example, Moynihan and Bero, 2017), but also other interested parties such as the food and drinks industry

(McCambridge et al, 2013; Livingstone, 2004), governments and consultancy organisations (Head, 2008). Suspicions abound that some evidence sources may be too self-serving to be reliable.

Indirect quality assurance considerations, then, linked to the source of the evidence offered, are relevant and important; but they need to work alongside (more direct) criterion-based assessments, such as methodological checklists and methodological hierarchies, and it is to these that we now turn.

Checklists for study quality: examining the detail of methods

Quality criteria for individual study designs have a long history, especially in healthcare (for example, Crombie, 1996). Indeed, the EQUATOR Network (Enhancing the QUAlity and Transparency Of health Research) has sought to create a robust set of methodology-specific reporting guidelines that incorporate the criteria for legitimacy within each methodology (see also Chapter Four). A detailed exposition of these technical criteria and the methodological considerations that underpin them is beyond the scope of this chapter, but suffice to note that many detailed methodology checklists exist, for all study types, both quantitative and qualitative. These technical standards provide a good starting point for addressing the question 'was this study done well?'. Systematic reviews, especially, are preoccupied with using such quality standards to determine the eligibility for inclusion of individual studies (and this can prove frustrating when stringent quality criteria exclude all but a very few studies, sometimes leading to a loss of relevant insights; Pawson, 2006).

Yet, whether a study was well conducted within the constraints of its own design parameters is a narrower question than whether the chosen design was appropriate or powerful in the first place. This leads us to explore ideas of 'hierarchies of evidence' (usually based on methodological choices) as another means of assessing evidence quality. After noting the proliferation of these hierarchies in the assessment of evidence – and summarising some of the criticisms of the hierarchies approach – we move on to discuss two specific evidence hierarchies that have attempted more nuanced assessments. This is followed by consideration of a broader shift to matrices of evidence levels, where methodological requirements vary according to the question(s) being asked. Finally, we discuss some of the ways in which a broader set of evidence requirements have been expressed, sometimes called evidence principles.

Hierarchies of evidence: quality predicated on study design

When the evidence question is (as it so often is) 'what works?', different research designs are commonly placed in a hierarchy based on an assessment of their relative strengths in determining effectiveness. One of the earliest examples of this dates back fully 40 years, when the Canadian Task Force on the Periodic Health Examination (1979) produced a hierarchy of evidence with systematic reviews and meta-analysis at the apex and expert opinion at the base (sometimes waggishly referred to as the GOBSAT method of evidence generation, or Good Old Boys Sat Around the Table). Even to the present day this hierarchy exists in many arenas, often largely unchanged, as in the Oxford Centre for Evidence-Based Medicine (OCEBM) levels of evidence for assessing intervention effects (Table 11.1).

Table 11.1: Hierarchies of what works evidence, predicated on study design

These two hierarchies both describe evidence in terms of levels. However, rather confusingly, 'level 1' is the *highest* level of evidence in one of these (OCEBM) and the *lowest* level of evidence in the other (the Maryland Scale).

OCEBM levels of evidence when the question is 'Does this intervention help?'	Maryland Scale of Scientific Methods for assessing what works in crime prevention.
Level 1: Systematic review of randomised trials or *n*-of-1 trials. Level 2: Randomised trial or observational study with dramatic effect. Level 3: Non-randomised controlled cohort/ follow-up study. Level 4: Case-series, case-control studies, or historically controlled studies. Level 5: Mechanism-based reasoning. *Source*: Abstracted from OCEBM Levels of Evidence Working Group (2011)	Level 5: Random assignment and analysis of comparable units to program and comparison groups. Level 4: Comparison between multiple units with and without the program, controlling for other factors, or using comparison units that evidence only minor differences. Level 3: A comparison between two or more comparable units of analysis, one with and one without the program. Level 2: Temporal sequence between the program and the crime or risk outcome clearly observed, or the presence of a comparison group without demonstrated comparability to the treatment group. Level 1: Correlation between a crime prevention program and a measure of crime or crime risk factors at a single point in time. Source: Sherman et al, 1998, pp 4–5.

A different and rather more pragmatic hierarchy of evidence is the Maryland Scale of Scientific Methods (see Table 11.1). This was first used to review the effectiveness of state and local crime prevention programmes funded by the US Department of Justice, but it has also seen wider application (for example, it is used by the UK What Works Centre for Local Economic Growth – see Chapter Thirteen). This hierarchy privileges direct comparison over correlation, and sees random assignment as better still. However, it does not presuppose a sufficiency of studies for formal systematic review, far less meta-analysis. Using this scale, crime prevention programmes were categorised as working, not working, promising or unknown, based on the extent and quality of the evidence underpinning them. To be classified as working, programmes needed at least two Level 3 evaluations with statistical significance tests, and the preponderance of all available evidence also needed to show effectiveness.

Evidence hierarchies, such as the Maryland Scale and the OCEBM levels of evidence, have much in common: randomised experiments with clearly defined controls (RCTs) are placed at or near the top of the hierarchy, and case reports, or arguments from basic social or physiological mechanisms, are usually at the bottom. However, there are differences in the numbers of levels in such hierarchies, and the status accorded to systematic reviews and meta-analyses can also vary – often a pragmatic choice when the research base is sparse and/or diverse in the research questions addressed.

Evidence hierarchies are used by many evidence review groups and endorsing bodies around the world, and they are particularly prevalent in healthcare internationally, as well as in other policy areas in the US. Despite their widespread use, the premise, structure and implementation of such hierarchies have been the source of much debate, and they have been heavily criticised (Box 11.4). One response to such criticisms has been to emphasise that evidence hierarchies, such as the Maryland Scale, assess evidence quality only in terms of internal validity, and to assert that other factors need to be taken into consideration when assessing external or ecological validity (Farrington et al, 2002). Nevertheless, in the face of this extensive criticism (Box 11.4) there has been a gradual process of revising earlier hierarchical frameworks in order to make them more inclusive, or to advise more clearly on how they should be applied.

Box 11.4: Sustained critique of methodology-based evidence hierarchies

- Evidence hierarchies often promote systematic reviews and meta-analyses of RCTs as the 'gold standard' of evidence. This focus on carefully controlled trials may be neglectful of the powerful potentiating or inhibitory effects of context (Pawson 2006, and see Chapter Ten).
- Evidence hierarchies may neglect too many important and relevant issues contributing to evidence quality and strength, such as a critical appraisal of how any given study design was implemented, or how its findings fit with other studies on the same issue (Stegenga, 2014).
- Hierarchies tend to underrate the value of study designs that typically appear at the lower levels, particularly the value of observational studies (for example, using administrative data) in estimating the effects on interventions (Cook et al, 2008; Konnerup and Kongsted, 2012; La Caze et al, 2012).
- Evidence syntheses based on hierarchies are sometimes used to exclude all but the highest-ranking studies from consideration, which can lead to the loss of useful evidence (Konnerup and Kongsted, 2012; Pawson, 2006).
- Evidence hierarchies usually pay insufficient attention to the need to understand what works, for whom, in what circumstances and why – that is, programme theory (Ogilvie et al, 2005; Chatterji, 2008).
- Evidence hierarchies in themselves provide an insufficient basis for making recommendations about whether interventions should be adopted, which requires much wider considerations (Bagshaw and Bellomo, 2008).

Revisions to evidence hierarchies and the ways in which they are used

There is a compelling argument that *stronger* bodies of evidence are likely to be characterised by the availability of a wide spectrum of (high quality) evidence that uses (and triangulates) findings from several research designs (DFID, 2014). Revisions to early evidence hierarchies have sought, at least in part, to address these concerns. Two illustrative evidence schemes are discussed here: the GRADE system (Grading of Recommendations Assessment, Development and Evaluation) for healthcare interventions developed in an international collaborative network, and Project Oracle, a UK-registered charity supporting innovation in services for young people.

In healthcare, an informal working group was established in the early 2000s to consider a revised classification system that addressed many of the shortcomings of traditional hierarchies of evidence: the result was the GRADE system (Burford et al, 2012). GRADE defines quality of evidence as the amount of confidence that a clinician may have that any estimate of treatment effect from research evidence is accurate for both beneficial and harmful outcomes. Quality of evidence is graded from 'high' to 'very low', where high reflects a judgement that further research is not likely to change confidence in the estimate(s) of effect(s). In reaching this judgement, GRADE starts by rating the available evidence on the basis of the study designs; it then considers other factors that may affect any initial grading, including: study limitations; inconsistency of results; indirectness of evidence; imprecision of estimates; and potential for reporting bias. In GRADE, although an RCT design is initially rated more highly than other designs in assessing treatment effects, the final rating of the evidence emerging from a group of studies can change when these other factors have been taken into account.

The GRADE working group concluded that there was also a need for a separate 'strength of recommendation' assessment, which indicates the extent to which a practitioner can be confident that adherence to a recommendation will result in greater benefit than harm for any given patient or service user. The strength of recommendation builds on the assessment by incorporating additional factors such as potential target patient populations, baseline risks and individual patients' values and costs (Bagshaw and Bellomo, 2008). Despite these additional considerations, the leap from 'strength of recommendation' to a 'decision to apply' can never be a simple technocratic choice: it will necessarily also involve consideration of local political, financial and other contextual factors.

GRADE is seen as an improvement over traditional evidence hierarchies, and the approach (sometimes modified) has been adopted by many international bodies concerned to set evidence standards. However, critics contend that the single property of randomisation continues to feature too strongly in the assessment of evidence quality, regardless of any subsequent modifications to the level of quality assigned (Stegenga, 2014). Hence there can be a tendency to neglect other forms of study, especially observational studies (Konnerup and Kongsted, 2012; La Caze et al, 2012), and this may, for example, reflect missed opportunities to exploit evidence from large datasets (see Chapter Ten).

For a rather different approach, we turn now to Project Oracle, an initiative that supports youth organisations in measuring and evaluating their own projects so that they can understand how improvements could be made. The Project uses a standards of evidence hierarchy consisting of five levels of increasing confidence that programmes work (Box 11.5). While there is some acknowledgement that not every project will want (or be able) to move through all the levels, each organisation/ project is expected to aim for the highest feasible standard. Project Oracle, then, is a good example of an evidence hierarchy being used to encourage service providers to embark more on an 'evidence journey' than on pursuit of stand-alone standards. That is, practitioners are encouraged to engage with and debate the evidence as it emerges, and to use these engagements to build better evidence sources. However, nearly all of the projects submitted for validation (368 at February 2018) had achieved only standard level 1 or 2, which may suggest that this set of evidence standards, like many others, is still too ambitious and lacking in pragmatism (see Lozano-Casal, 2016).

Box 11.5: Project Oracle standards of evidence

Project Oracle standards consist of five levels of increasing confidence posited from the perspective of an intervention innovator.

1 **We know what we want to achieve.** This entry level requires a sound theory of change or logic model, with clear plans for evaluation.
2 **We have seen that there is a change.** This level requires indication of impact from, say, pre- and post-analyses.
3 **We believe the change is caused by us.** This level requires evidence of impact from at least one rigorous evaluation using a comparison group or other appropriate comparison data.
4 **We know how and why it works, and that it works elsewhere.** This level requires two or more rigorous impact evaluations (using a comparison group or other appropriate comparison data); one of these must be done by an external evaluator.
5 **We know how and why it works, and it works everywhere.** The highest level requires a 'system-ready' intervention that has been subject to multiple independent replication evaluations and cost-benefit analysis.

Submitting organisations undertake a self-assessment of their project(s) against these standards, with the aid of a practitioner guidebook and a support service. Project Oracle staff validate the level achieved and work with the provider to agree a detailed action plan to improve their evidence base.

These two divergent examples illustrate how simple evidence hierarchies have been developed in two distinct ways: first (exemplified by GRADE), building on assessments of research quality to more explicitly address ideas about evidence accumulation, coherence and strength; and, second (illustrated in Project Oracle), creating a more dynamic and interactive assessment process that provides not only a means of assessing evidence but one that also encourages further enhancement of that evidence. Developments from simple hierarchies have evolved in other ways too, creating a mixed landscape of approaches to evidence assessment and revealing a diversity of thinking as to what counts as good evidence.

The development of evidence matrices

Another development in the standard-setting landscape is the emergence of evidence matrices, where types of research design are differentially rated according to the research question being addressed. In taking such an approach, it is argued that, even in relation to the issue of what works, policy makers and practitioners are interested in a range of different questions (Table 11.2), and that RCT designs are inappropriate for answering at least half of these (Petticrew and Roberts, 2003). The approach matches core questions (such as 'how does it work?' and 'does it matter?') to alternative methods, such as observational studies and qualitative work.

In line with these views, the revised version of the Oxford Levels of Evidence for medicine (OCEBM, 2011) is now also expressed as a matrix, rather than as a single simple hierarchy. In addition to outlining the five levels of evidence (research designs) relevant to answering the question about whether an intervention helps (see Box 11.3), the matrix also sets out the levels of evidence (appropriate research designs) relevant to answering a range of other questions, such as: 'how common is the problem?', 'can diagnosis be made accurately?' and 'is early detection worthwhile?' In this way, the primacy of randomised experiments for assessing intervention effects is maintained, while broadening out the range of methodologies seen as appropriate to addressing other relevant issues.

Evidence matrices can certainly help to rebalance the privileging of randomised experiments: a privileging that has seen the marginalising of broader bodies of work, including the exclusion of other types of research. Yet, even evidence matrices still tend to judge evidence quality primarily on the basis of design choice (and adherence to criteria within that choice). This has prompted some to stress the importance of considering a broader set of evidence principles.

Table 11.2: A matrix of evidence to address various aspects of 'does this work?'

Research question	Qualitative research	Survey	Case-control studies	Cohort studies	RCTs	Quasi-experimental studies	Non-experimental studies	Systematic reviews
Does doing this work better than doing that?				+	++	+		+++
How does it work?	++	+					+	+++
Does it matter?	++	++						+++
Will it do more good than harm?	+		+	+	++	+	+	+++
Will service users be willing to or want to take up the service offered?	++	+			+	+	+	+++
Is it the right service for these people?	++	++						++
Are users, providers and other stakeholders satisfied with the service?	++	++	+	+				+

Key: +, ++ and +++ indicate the relevance and relative strength of a method for addressing each question. A blank entry for a method indicates that it is irrelevant for that particular question.

Source: Adapted from Petticrew and Roberts, 2003, Table 1, p 528 and reproduced from Nutley et al, 2013, Box 4, p 16.

The promotion of evidence principles

As with many other evidence-promoting agencies, the Social Care Institute for Excellence (SCIE) has emphasised the importance of valuing different types and sources of knowledge in deciding what should be labelled as a good practice (in this case, for social care). In line with this, SCIE has published a set of six generic standards or principles that can be applied to five different sources of knowledge in social care (Box 11.6). Crucially, the types of knowledge considered include not just that emanating from research communities but also that emerging from service organisations, policy and practitioner communities and, most importantly, user and carer communities. These principles (such as transparency, accessibility and utility) are described as 'a practical way forward for assessing [evidence] quality from those knowledge sources where specific standards are emergent, latent or inappropriate' (Pawson et al, 2003, pp 67–8).

The importance of an inclusive approach is also highlighted by the UK network for organisations working in international development (Bond, 2012), which has produced a checklist of five evidence principles (with 20 associated criteria; Box 11.7). These principles include transparency (for example, about the process of evidence production and sources), appropriateness (which relates to justifiable methods, and so is consistent with earlier approaches to standard

---

Box 11.6: Social Care Institute for Excellence (SCIE): generic evidence principles

A report drawn up for SCIE lists six principles that are applicable across five sources of knowledge (organisational, practitioner, policy community, research and user and carer knowledge).

The evidence principles are:

- **transparency** – is it open to scrutiny?
- **accuracy** – is it well grounded?
- **purposivity** – is it fit for purpose?
- **utility** – is it fit for use?
- **propriety** – is it created and managed with due care to all stakeholders?
- **accessibility** – is it intelligible?

Source: Pawson et al, 2003.

---

setting based on quality) and triangulation (which relates to ideas about the strength of evidence, already discussed). But these principles go further to include such aspects as voice and inclusion (recognising the importance of including wider perspectives, lived experience and lay knowledge) and contribution (seeking to understand how interventions interact with context).

In a similar way, and in the same arena, DFID's (2014) principles of high-quality research also highlight the importance of cultural sensitivity – the local cultural factors that might affect any behaviours and trends observed. These concerns, and the principles of the international development network (see Box 11.7), echo the ideas of valuing diverse epistemologies raised in the reviews of evidence in international development and in the environment and sustainability, as seen earlier in this book (Chapters Eight and Nine).

Overall, then, our review of evidence standards has highlighted their many different forms (from formal, but often narrow, hierarchies, through broader methodological matrices, to a looser collection of principles for inclusion). In doing so, we have sought to tease out ideas of evidence quality and evidence strength, while recognising

---

Box 11.7: Bond's evidence principles

Bond (the UK network for evidence in international development) has enumerated five evidence principles, underpinned by 20 associated criteria. These include the following.

- **Voice and inclusion.** The perspectives of people living in poverty, including the most marginalised, are included in the evidence, and a clear picture is provided of who is affected and how.
- **Appropriateness.** The evidence is generated through methods that are justifiable, given the nature or the purpose of the assessment.
- **Triangulation.** The evidence has been generated using a mix of methods, data sources and perspectives.
- **Contribution.** The evidence explores how change happens, and the contribution of the intervention and factors outside the intervention in explaining change.
- **Transparency.** The evidence discloses the details of the data sources and methods used, the results achieved and any limitation in the data or conclusions.

Source: Bond, 2012.

---

the interconnectedness of these. We have also documented some of the ways in which approaches to evidence standards have evolved over time (becoming somewhat broader in conception and more inclusive in approach). This highlights again the contested nature of evidence, played out in disputes over the legitimacy or otherwise of various schemas. Finally, we have touched on the importance of voice and inclusion, but this and the issue of what is 'good enough' evidence (always a function of contexts of use) are worthy of further attention, and it is to these that we now turn.

'Good enough' evidence at the point of use

We have already emphasised the importance of matching what counts as good evidence to the question being asked, and of expanding the purview of evidence to beyond the realms of research. However, in deciding what is 'good enough' we also need to factor in what the evidence will be used for and in what context. The possibilities here are many and varied and include, for example: top-level policy option generation and appraisal; actual decision making in service organisations (for example, doing something new or stopping doing something already established); on-going learning and development in front-line services; and developing innovative new ways of working prior to formal testing. Each has different requirements for the evidence to underpin actions: for example, the decision to implement a policy or programme at national level typically calls for a stronger and more persuasive base of supporting evidence than when the aim is to develop locally innovative and promising new ways of working.

More generally, there is a need to consider better ways of integrating research-based evidence with other forms of knowledge and knowing. This is partly because research evidence typically provides only partial answers to policy and practice questions, and even when considered alongside other sources of knowledge the picture usually remains uncertain and/or incomplete. But, just as significantly, there are many other factors that are highly influential on key actors: for example, the prior framings of key policy makers (see Chapter Two), or the deeply ingrained tacit knowledge of professional workers (see Chapter Three). Moreover, other types of knowledge or experience should be more influential than they typically are (as has been argued at various places in this book): for example, the views of service users and communities, or the perspectives of non-professional (and hence less powerful) service workers. There is a need, then, to better integrate all of these sources of knowledge as actions unfold, and evidence standards are only a part of this dynamic.

Local and contextual understandings are *negotiated* through complex psychological and social process where power is never far from the surface. Evidence, whatever its quality and strength, and however it is labelled, is only one animator of these dynamics. Coming to shared understandings may be difficult, depending on the context of consideration (for example, whether evidence is considered in a hostile, contentious environment riven with fracture lines, or in a more benign environment where there is already a good deal of consensus). These concerns, especially the role of prior values, interests and preferences, alongside ever-present power relations, draw our attention to a further challenge: evidence standards (like evidence itself) may be deployed for tactical or strategic reasons. The ready availability of methodological checklists and hierarchies provides useful tools for those who wish to discredit inconvenient evidence: methodological niceties may be used as pretexts for side-lining otherwise valuable knowledge. This has been seen in, for example, debates about minimum pricing for alcohol (McCambridge et al, 2013) and the potential harms from advertising to children (Livingstone, 2004).

Despite all these challenges, there are many ways in which the creation, collation, assessment and labelling of evidence can be structured to make it more likely that these concerns are given appropriate attention. Some of these have already been raised in earlier chapters (for example, the collaborative development of new policy framings through policy networks in Chapter Two; the use of Mode 2 knowledge processes in practitioner environments in Chapter Three; and the moves towards knowledge co-production that we have seen in several chapters across many sectors). Further ideas that see closer integration between knowledge creation, sharing and use are explored in the following chapter (Chapter Twelve). Here we see that the effective use, influence and impact of evidence are not readily separable from the contexts of its creation and interpretation: again bringing the assessment and labelling of evidence into the context of use.

Central to all of these approaches is a widening of perspectives at all stages to include more diverse voices and more diverse epistemologies, alongside careful structuring of engagement to attend to power differences (for example, deliberative processes; Jansen et al, 2018). The labelling of evidence then becomes a situated and relational task. This does not mean the jettisoning of methodological concerns or epistemological critiques. However, it does mean a rebalancing between hitherto dominant academic concerns and the pragmatic realities of good-enough knowledge for change.

Reflections and concluding remarks

There is no simple answer to the question of what counts as good evidence. The legitimacy of evidence depends on what decision makers want to know, for what purposes, and in what contexts they envisage that evidence being used. While evidence-promoting bodies may use study design as the hallmark of good evidence, perceptions of evidence legitimacy among a broader group of stakeholders are also likely to be influenced by personal experiences, pre-existing schemas, power relations, politics and emotions. Thus, while there is a need to debate standards of evidence, there should also be caution about attempts to reach widespread consensus on what those standards should be.

Since the late 1990s there has been an evolution of thinking on evidence standards, a broadening out from narrow methodological considerations in labelling evidence, separate from places of use, to more eclectic and interactive evidence principles rooted in the context of application. The drivers of these changes are complex, but certainly include the sustained critiques of evidence hierarchies (see Box 11.4) and the growing user voice in public services. However, we in no way wish to suggest that these debates are over – indeed they can be seen to be as active and contested as ever, and further evolution or distinct fragmentation is to be expected.

This period has also seen a proliferation of new standards and descriptors of evidence quality, many of which have been covered in this chapter. Indeed, one recent review (Puttick, 2018) uncovered 18 evidence frameworks for UK social policy and noted that while there were commonalities, such as the goal of improving decision making, there were also wide variations in such aspects as the audiences anticipated, the questions addressed and the uses expected. Here again we can expect to see on-going developments as these debates mature.

Debates about evidence validity are also spilling out from the professional domains and into a wider public view. A plethora of organisations, such as Sense about Science, the Science Media Centre and Full Fact, aim to check facts, challenge evidence misrepresentations and offer independent assessments of the state of evidence on important topics of public interest. While such services are generally to be welcomed, they do not obviate the need for on-going examination of evidence claims and counter-claims. Deciding what counts as good evidence is far from straightforward and is highly dependent on underlying assumptions and inclusion criteria. In addition, claims of independence should not necessarily be taken at face value: given the potential for bias due to vested interests, there is a need to consider the funding sources and governance structures of evidence assessors as well as of evidence providers. In that sense, then, 'fact checkers' and other evidence assessors differ little from think-tanks and other intermediaries: they have interests, preferences, ideologies and stakeholders, and their claims too need to be given proper scrutiny.

The ways in which evidence is assessed and labelled can have important ramifications. Recommendations (such as with those from NICE) can quickly become mandatory once given the imprimatur of 'evidence-based'. This may be important in driving rational policy and practice, but, as we have seen at various points through this book, it may also lead to inappropriate narrowing of practices, to the detriment of services (such as synthetic phonics in teaching, see Chapter Three; or treatment recommendations for ME, see Box 11.3). Moreover, a privileging of technical standards, such as method choice or the details of method design, may invite the cynical rejection of evidence by vested parties – evidence that might otherwise have been good enough for policy change (perhaps with subsequent evaluation). Counsels of perfection in evidence standards are necessarily conservative, and sometimes even reactionary. Furthermore, it has become clear at many points in this book that evidence application is more easily accomplished when there is a closer degree of integration between knowledge and use, and this provokes a tension with those who would seek stand-alone assessments and labelling.

We also need to be mindful about how evidence standards can affect the nature of evidence generation. Over the two decades since the late 1990s, evidence hierarchies have been used to argue for more experimental studies (particularly RCTs) when assessing the effectiveness of social policy interventions. While advocacy for more experimentation continues apace (Goldacre, 2015), more recent reviews of evidence standards have led to calls for a greater focus on the production of 'system-wide evidence': evidence that considers impacts on communities and people in the round rather than focusing on impacts within an individual sector or programme (Coutts and Brotchie, 2017). As discussed in Chapter Ten, there is on-going work on ways of factoring in the importance of context, the complexity of many interventions and the need to consider multiple impacts. However, reorienting researchers and research funders to focus on these issues will not be straightforward, especially given the likely resources and time scales involved in producing system-wide impact evidence.

A related issue is the role – and assessment – of research used less for instrumentalist purposes and more for reframing and reproblematising policy and practice concerns. This type of research – more conceptual, more exploratory and often qualitative – necessitates different ways of thinking about standards of evidence. Quality appraisal is more complex for such studies, which may or may not have much in the way of empirical underpinnings, and which rarely slot neatly into pre-existing evidence hierarchies and schemas. Such research is also likely to emphasise different ways of producing evidence: for example, through engaged scholarship, on-going dialogue and iterative co–production processes (see Chapter Ten). These situated ways of producing evidence add to the challenges of assessing the quality of the evidence so produced. In particular, a commitment to a participatory approach to service development (which involves service users, practitioners and evaluators working together) emphasises research designs that would typically score low on traditional hierarchies of evidence. As attention is paid to formal evidence standards, care must be taken that these kinds of approaches are not neglected, devalued or marginalised.

Finally, there is a need to be realistic about the extent to which evidence-informed (or even evidence-based) recommendations will be compelling for policy makers and practitioners: their tacit hierarchies of evidence may look very different to the formal hierarchies discussed earlier in this chapter (Davies, 2007), and their preoccupations with acceptability, feasibility and expedience all need to be factored in. Studies of the actual use of guidelines, even those strongly underpinned by evidence such as that produced by NICE, suggest that the extent of their use is not determined by the strength of evidence: other factors are much more influential (Grove et al, 2016). Perhaps, then, one neglected criterion for the quality of evidence is the extent to which it can garner attention, be engaged with and influence change. This and other issues related to our understanding of the use of evidence and how this might be improved are the subjects of the next chapter.

References

Bagshaw, S. and Bellomo, R. (2008) 'The need to reform our assessment of evidence from clinical trials: A commentary', *Philosophy, Ethics, and Humanities in Medicine*, 3 (23), doi: 10.1186/1747-5341-3-23.
Bond (2012) *An introduction to the principles for assessing the quality of evidence*, London: Bond (the UK Network for organisations working in international development), https://www.bond.org.uk/data/files/Effectiveness_Programme/120828Full_Bond_checklist_and_guide.pdf.

Burford, B.J., Rehfuess, E., Schünemann, H.J., Akl, E.A. Waters, E., Armstrong, R., Thomson, H., Doyle, J. and Pettman, T. (2012) 'Assessing evidence in public health: the added value of GRADE', *Journal of Public Health*, 34 (4), pp 631–5.

Canadian Task Force on the Periodic Health Examination (1979) 'The periodic health examination', *Canadian Medical Association Journal*, 121, pp 1193–254.

Chatterji, M. (2008) 'Synthesizing evidence from impact evaluations in education to inform action', *Education Researcher*, 37 (1), pp 23–6.

Cook, T., Shadish, W. and Wong, V. (2008) 'Three conditions under which experiments and observational studies produce comparable causal estimates: new findings from within-study comparisons', *Journal of Policy Analysis and Management*, 27, pp 724–50.

Coutts, P. and Brotchie, J. (2017) *The Scottish approach to evidence: a discussion paper*, Dunfermline: Carnegie UK Trust.

Crombie, I.K. (1996) *The pocket guide to critical appraisal*, London: BMJ Publishing Group.

Davies, P. (2007) 'Types of knowledge for evidence-based policy', Presentation to NORFACE Seminar on Evidence and Policy, University of Edinburgh, 26 November .

DFID (2014) *Assessing the strength of evidence*, How to Note, London: Department for International Development.

Farrington, D.P., Gottfredson, D.C., Sherman, L.W. and Welsh, B.C. (2002) 'The Maryland scientific methods scale', in L.W. Sherman, D.P. Farrington, B.C. Wels, and D.L. MacKenzie (eds), *Evidence-based crime prevention*, New York: Routledge, pp 13–21.

Goldacre, B. (2015) 'Commentary: randomized trials of controversial social interventions: slow progress in 50 years', *International Journal of Epidemiology*, 44, pp 19–22, doi: 10.1093/ije/dyv005.

Grayson, L. (2002) *Evidence based policy and the quality of evidence: rethinking peer review*, ESRC UK Centre for Evidence Based Policy and Practice, Queen Mary, London University, Working Paper 7.

Grove, A.L., Johnson, R.E., Clarke, A. and Currie, G. (2016) 'Evidence and the drivers of variation in orthopaedic surgical work: a mixed method systematic review', *Health Systems and Policy Research*, 3 (1), pp 1-14.

Head, B.W. (2008) 'Three lenses of evidence-based policy', *Australian Journal of Public Administration*, 67 (1), pp 1–11.

Jansen, M.P., Baltussen, R., Mikkelsen, E. et al (2018) 'Evidence-informed deliberative processes – early dialogue, broad focus and relevance: a response to recent commentaries', *International Journal of Health Policy Management*, 7 (1), pp 96–7.

Livingstone, S. (2004) *A commentary on the research evidence regarding the effects of food promotion on children*. Prepared for the research department of the Office of Communications, London: Media@LSE.

Konnerup, M. and Kongsted, H. (2012) 'Do Cochrane reviews provide a good model for social science? The role of observational studies in systematic reviews', *Evidence and Policy*, 8 (1), pp 79–86.

La Caze, A., Djulbegovic, B. and Senn, S. (2012) 'What does randomisation achieve ?', *Evidence-Based Medicine*, 17 (1), pp 1–2, doi: 10.1136/ebm.2011.100061.

Lozano-Casal, P. (2016) 'Let's stop chasing unicorns', Blog, Edinburgh: Evaluation Support Scotland, 22 June, http://www.evaluationsupportscotland.org.uk/news/2016/Jun/22/blog-lets-stop-chasing-unicorns/.

McCambridge, J., Hawkins, B. and Holden, C. (2013) 'Industry use of evidence to influence alcohol policy: a case study of submissions to the 2008 Scottish Government consultation', *PLOS Medicine*, 10 (4), e1001431.

Maxmen, A. (2018) 'A reboot for chronic fatigue syndrome research', *Nature*, 3 January.

Moynihan, R. and Bero, L. (2017) 'Toward a healthier patient voice: more independence, less industry funding', *JAMA Internal Medicine*, 17 January.

OCEBM Levels of Evidence Working Group (2011) *The Oxford 2011 Levels of Evidence*, Oxford: Oxford Centre for Evidence-Based Medicine, http://www.cebm.net/index.aspx?o=5653.

Ogilvie, D., Egan, M., Hamilton, V. and Petticrew, M. (2005) 'Sytematic review of health effects of social interventions: 2. Best available evidence: how low should you go?', *Journal of Epidemiology and Community Health*, 59, pp 886–92.

Pawson, R. (2006) 'Digging for nuggets: how "bad" research can yield "good" evidence', *International Journal of Social Research Methodology*, 9 (2), pp 127–42.

Petticrew, M. and Roberts, H. (2003) 'Evidence, hierarchies, and typologies: horses for courses', *Journal of Epidemiology and Community Health*, 57, pp 527–9.

Puttick, R. (2018) *Mapping the standards of evidence used in UK social policy*, London: Alliance for Useful Evidence.

Sherman, L.W., Gottfredson, D.C., MacKenzie, D.L., Eck, J., Reuter, P. and Bushway, S.D. (1998) *Preventing crime: what works, what doesn't, what's promising*, Research in brief, Washington, DC: U.S. Department of Justice, National Institute of Justice.

Stegenga, J. (2014) 'Down with the hierarchies', *Topoi*, 33 (2), pp 313–22, doi: 10.1007/s11245-013-9189-4.

Whipple, T. (2017) 'Mutiny by ME sufferers forces a climbdown on exercise treatment', *The Times*, 25 September.

White, P.D., Goldsmith, K.A., Johnson, A.L. et al (2011) 'Comparison of adaptive pacing therapy, cognitive behaviour therapy, graded exercise therapy, and specialist medical care for chronic fatigue syndrome (PACE): a randomised trial', *Lancet*, 377 (9768), pp 823–36.

Wilshire, C., Kindlon, T., Matthees, A. and McGrath, S. (2016) 'Can patients with chronic fatigue syndrome really recover after graded exercise or cognitive behavioural therapy? A critical commentary and preliminary re-analysis of the PACE trial', *Fatigue: Biomedicine, Health and Behavior*, doi: 10.1080/21641846.2017.1259724.

WSIPP (Washington State Institute for Public Policy) (2017) *Updated inventory of evidence-based, research-based, and promising practices: for prevention and intervention services for children and juveniles in the child welfare, juvenile justice, and mental health system*, Olympia, WA: Washington State Institute for Public Policy, http://www.wsipp. wa.gov/ReportFile/1672/.

12

Using evidence

Annette Boaz and Sandra Nutley

Introduction to using research-based evidence

In exploring the role of evidence in policy and practice we have drawn attention to the very wide range of types of knowledge that can inform policy makers, practitioners and other stakeholders, while also highlighting the special and sometimes privileged role of research-based evidence. Our argument has been that research-based knowledge only rarely stands alone, and needs to be integrated into wider understandings through being incorporated with other forms and types of knowledge. However, such incorporation of research findings has often been disappointing and, in the face of this, efforts to encourage research use have grown in number and ambition over the two decades since the late 1990s. Many examples are documented throughout the book (particularly in Sections Two and Four). It is to this issue that we turn in this chapter.

Initiatives to increase the uptake of research range from national centres/clearing houses that produce, synthesise and disseminate research evidence to local initiatives that encourage researchers and practitioners to work together in knowledge co-producing partnerships. There has been a partial move away from any 'one size fits all' solution to promoting the use of research evidence, perhaps prompted by growing recognition that evidence use is situated, and that efforts to promote research use need to respond to differences in policy and practice contexts. There is also increasing acknowledgement that research use is not a single event but a complex process that unfolds over time and involves many actors. Different approaches to encouraging and enabling research use are likely to be more or less helpful at various points in this process (for example, there may be a need for both national clearing houses and local partnerships). This has led to an interest in identifying and developing the key features of an 'evidence ecosystem': a system of interconnected elements that interact in the process of evidence generation, synthesis and use (for example, Shepherd, 2014). An effective ecosystem would seem to need a 'requisite variety' of initiatives to encourage and enable evidence use – that is, the repertoire of initiatives to promote evidence use needs to be (at least) as varied and nuanced as the policy and practice contexts that are being targeted.

This chapter considers whether our understanding of research use has progressed to a point where it is possible to identify, with confidence, the key features of an effective evidence ecosystem. We do this by taking stock of progress in four main areas: defining and recognising research use and research users; framing and modelling the research-use process (including ecosystem models); identifying promising approaches to promoting research use; and assessing research use and impact. As already signalled in these opening paragraphs, and in line with the other chapters in this section of the book, our main focus is on the use of research evidence. We conclude that, while we know much more than we did 20 years ago, there is still some way to go in understanding how to optimise research use in policy and practice. This conclusion prompts consideration of where the field might go next, identifying themes that will be further developed in the final chapter of the book.

Defining research use and research users

It is important to be clear about what we mean when we talk about the use and influence of research, because of the way this shapes initiatives aimed at encouraging and enabling evidence application, and impacts on the criteria used to assess the effectiveness of these initiatives. The different terms themselves have different connotations and implications for how we understand and explore this area. For example, 'use' typically implies an instrumental application of evidence (to aid in specific decisions, perhaps, or to direct certain courses of action). In contrast, 'influence' suggests something softer, even nebulous, often relating to more gradual conceptual shifts and problem reframing. We also need to be clear about who might be considered as the potential users of research, as this is another critical element in promoting and assessing evidence use.

A key distinction is often made between 'instrumental' and 'conceptual' uses of research, where the former refers to the direct impact of research on policy and practice decisions, while the latter captures the often indirect ways in which research can influence the knowledge, understanding and attitudes of policy makers and practitioners (Caplan, 1979). One of the most commonly cited elaborations of this distinction was provided by Carol Weiss (1979).

She described seven different types of use: knowledge driven, problem solving, interactive, political, tactical, enlightenment, and as part of the intellectual enterprise of society (Box 12.1). Knowledge-driven and problem-solving uses can be characterised as forms of instrumental use. Interactive, enlightenment and intellectual enterprise uses represent more conceptual uses of research. Weiss adds a third category of 'strategic' use to the instrumental/conceptual distinction, which encompasses political and tactical uses of research. In policy contexts, Weiss found that the instrumental use of research was relatively rare and that conceptual and strategic uses are much more common. Despite this finding, many initiatives aimed at improving evidence use focus on increasing the instrumental use of research, and the effectiveness of these initiatives is often judged on the extent to which they have achieved these instrumental aims.

Although Weiss developed her typology from empirical work on policy makers' use of research, it has influenced accounts of research use in practice contexts too. While it continues to provide an influential framing of different types of research use, more recent empirical studies (for example, Haynes et al, 2011; Monaghan, 2011) have suggested that further work needs to be done to develop the categories if they are to be applied as analytical tools. In a study of UK drugs policy, Monaghan (2011) argued that the Weiss categories are at too high a level of abstraction to capture the nuanced nature of political uses of evidence. Haynes and colleagues (2011) studied public health policy makers in Australia and found that policy makers used research and researchers as galvanisers, guides, champions and shields. That is to say, researchers were able to generate ideas, offer clarification and advice, help to persuade different audiences and provide policy makers with evidence to justify and defend policies. They concluded that these four uses are not well captured by Weiss's typology (or those produced by others).

In addition to these concerns, it can be misleading to treat the different types of research use as discrete and static categories (Nutley et al, 2007). A set of research findings may be used in different ways over time and by different groups. For example, it is possible to imagine a relatively rapid uptake of research for political or tactical purposes, but this may be followed by a more gradual percolation of research findings and ideas into policy and practice thinking, possibly helping to reshape and reframe a policy problem. Because research use may move between different types over time, categorisations should be treated as dynamic rather than static.

Box 12.1: Seven types of research use

Knowledge driven. This assumes that once research has been produced it will be developed, applied and used.

Problem solving. This assumes the direct application of research to a policy problem. Research provides solutions and resolution to policy problems.

Interactive. Research knowledge enters into the policy arena through the interactions of researchers and policy makers. It forms part of the web of knowledge and opinion that support decision making.

Political. Research is used to support policy decisions that have already been made. This type of use occurs where research aligns with and supports a particular decision or a predetermined position.

Tactical. Research can be used more generically for tactical purposes, to deflect attention or delay action around a particular issue. For example, governments might claim that more research is needed before action can be taken.

Enlightenment. Research enters into the policy domain in the form of concepts and ideas (as opposed to findings from individual studies or bodies of research). Over time it changes the way that people think about a policy issue.

Research as part of the intellectual enterprise of society. Research production is embedded within a wider system. Research responds to changes in the landscape (political priorities, the media, the law and so on) and adjusts accordingly.

Source: Weiss, 1979.

Another popular way of defining research use is to conceptualise different types of use as a series of stages. For example, Knott and Wildavsky (1980) identify seven forms of evidence use that are likely to occur in the order of: receiving evidence, understanding it, making reference to it, making an effort to adopt it, adopting evidence, implementing it and achieving impact in terms of changes to policy and/or practice. Despite concerns about the linear and instrumental nature of this framing of evidence use, it has had considerable traction in shaping the design of evidence-use initiatives, in evaluating the effectiveness of these initiatives and in assessing research impact more generally (Monaghan, 2011). However, many initiatives aimed at promoting research use have mainly focused on the first of these stages – 'receiving evidence' – that is, getting findings into the hands of potential research users, even though, according to this model, this is only the very start of a research-use journey.

Another strand of debate concerns distinguishing between legitimate and illegitimate uses of research evidence. Weiss (1979) concluded that all seven of the uses she identified were potentially legitimate and beneficial, arguing, for example, that 'when research is available to all participants in the policy process, research as political ammunition can be a worthy model of utilisation' (Weiss, 1979, p 429). For her, research use was illegitimate only when findings were distorted or misinterpreted. Others have been more extensive in their categorisation of evidence misuse. For example, the Social Care Institute for Excellence (SCIE) identifies a range of ways in which research can be misused, including: using findings out of context, stretching findings, distorting findings and rejecting or ignoring findings (SCIE, 2012). In a similar vein, McCambridge and colleagues (2014) highlight many examples of what they consider to be misuses of evidence in their analysis of industry submissions of evidence on minimum pricing of alcohol to the Scottish Parliament. Over-use, as well as misuse, has also been identified as an issue, especially where tentative findings are taken up too zealously or are implemented wholesale (Nutley et al, 2007).

Many initiatives aimed at improving research use have conceptualised the challenge as a need to address the under-use of research, while at the same time guarding against the misuse and over-use of research findings. However, what counts as misuse and over-use tends to be situationally defined, with plenty of scope for disagreement (Patton, 1997). While it may seem self-evident that poor-quality findings should not be used, there is still considerable debate about what constitutes good or adequate evidence for policy and practice (see Chapter Eleven). Research knowledge is also likely to be actively interpreted and negotiated within the contexts of its use, and this raises a question about when such negotiation moves from being legitimate adaptation to being evidence misuse (possibly due to stretching, reinterpreting and potentially distorting findings).

Typologies of research use also surface the importance of clarifying what is meant by users of evidence. Typically, the literature proposes two categories of evidence users: policy makers and practitioners. The terms reflect an initial orientation in the literature towards identifying those developing policy for the public sector and those putting the policy into practice. However, these categories in and of themselves are not unproblematic. 'Policy maker' and 'practitioner' are not terms that individuals readily use to describe themselves. Furthermore, the diversity of activities under these broad umbrella terms needs to be acknowledged in efforts to promote evidence use. A further development in understanding evidence users has been the recognition that they are not always situated in central and local government. There are a vast array of organisations with the potential to use evidence and to influence how others use evidence, including voluntary organisations, audit bodies and think-tanks. These organisations are often producers as well as consumers of evidence. In recent years there has been growing acknowledgement that service users and the public more widely have an interest in evidence and should be seen as important groups of potential evidence users. Finally, Concannon and colleagues (2012) remind us that other researchers are a key group of evidence users.

Research users are often described as individuals and organisations with a potential 'stake' in research (stakeholders). The nature, timing and intensity of their engagement are likely to vary from one study to another. Stakeholders have a range of potential contributions to make, including helping to set research priorities, shaping research and supporting dissemination. They can be engaged as advisors, co-applicants and co-researchers. Identifying potential stakeholders is often described as an iterative and on-going process. It can be helpful to distinguish between those stakeholders who are in a position to act on the results of a research study and those who are able to influence those who are in a position to act.

Taken together, the typologies of research use discussed in this section already point to different ways of modelling the research–use process (for example, as a problem-solving or political process). We have also highlighted the diversity of potential users of evidence, which can again point to greater clarity over intended audiences and channels of communication. The next section elaborates on these ideas by considering the main ways in which the research-use process has been framed and modelled.

Framing and modelling research use

Models of the research-use process vary according to whether their core aim is simply to describe this process or to offer a more normative picture of how the process could or should be improved. Chapters Two and Three have already provided examples of these differences. For example, Chapter Two contrasts the idealised models of comprehensive rationality and the policy cycle with more descriptive models of bounded rationality and policy networks. In general, descriptive models of the research-use process tend to be less simple than prescriptive models, although there are exceptions and there has also been a movement toward developing more nuanced prescriptive framings of research use.

Best and Holmes (2010) have captured this movement by describing three waves or generations of 'knowledge-to-action thinking': ways of modelling the process for improving research use (Box 12.2). They argue that first-generation models are mainly linear and involve producing evidence and disseminating it to potential users. Second-generation models emphasise the importance of dialogue between the producers and users of evidence, and factor in the need to consider and value other forms of knowledge that interact with research in the process of its use. Finally, in third-generation thinking greater

---

Box 12.2: Three generations of thinking on evidence use

First-generation thinking: rational-linear models and dissemination
Linear models suggest a one-way process from production to use. Researchers produce evidence, which gets disseminated to end-users and then incorporated into policy and practice. In linear models, evidence is often viewed as a product to be moved through a series of stages towards (rational) use.

Second-generation thinking: relational approaches
Relationship models incorporate the linear-model principles for dissemination and diffusion, and then focus on the interactions among people creating and using evidence. The emphasis is on the sharing of evidence, the development of partnerships and the fostering of networks of stakeholders with common interests.

Third-generation thinking: systems-wide approaches
Systems models build on linear and relationship thinking, incorporating learning from a systems approach. These models recognise that diffusion and dissemination processes and relationships themselves are shaped, embedded and organised through structures that mediate the types of interaction that occur among multiple agents. Individuals are tied together by a system that requires activation if its various parts are to be linked together.

Source: Adapted from Best and Holmes, 2010.

---

attention is paid to systems theory, with an emphasis on identifying system elements and their complex interactions.

We use this generational framing to discuss some of the main models of the research process. Our focus is on describing the overall character of models from each generation of knowledge-to-action thinking – a more extensive picture of the wealth of models and frameworks in this field is provided by Ward et al (2009), Nilsen (2015) and Davies et al (2015). The idea of successive generations of thinking might suggest that third-generation thinking has supplanted first- and second-generation ideas and models. However, Best and Holmes argue that this is not the case in practice, nor should it be, because some aspects of first- and second-generation thinking (for example, dissemination and relationship building) remain critical to the research-use process. We end this section by considering where the idea of evidence ecosystems sits in relation to these three generations of knowledge-to-action thinking.

First-generation thinking: linear models and dissemination

The evidence-based medicine (EBM) literature has played a dominant role in informing thinking about the research-use process. As noted in Chapter Four, the initial focus of EBM was on producing and curating reliable evidence, making it more available and usable. Although there was interest in the use of this evidence, there was a tendency to assume that improved dissemination would stimulate use, due to a general receptiveness to implementing effective practices.

The term 'knowledge transfer' is often associated with a linear conceptualisation of the research-to-practice journey. It is characterised by a focus on single-element interventions (such as the implementation of a guideline), evidence as a product and the privileging of particular forms of research knowledge as being most appropriate for use (particularly, systematic reviews and RCTs). Its influence has been, and remains, extensive. For example, it has shaped the 'what works' agenda in the US (see Chapter Seventeen) and underpins many of the activities of the What Works Centres in the UK (see Chapter Thirteen). However, there is now broad acceptance that knowledge-push alone is rarely a sufficient way of stimulating EIPP, and elements of a more relational approach often feature alongside a knowledge-push strategy.

Even with knowledge-push, there is greater recognition now that the knowledge being pushed is not necessarily stand-alone or static. For example, Majone (1989) discusses the role of *argumentation* in the application of evidence, which emphasises how evidence is shaped and crafted beyond its initial production, in the form of research reports, academic papers and web resources. Similarly, Smith (2013) focuses on the influential nature of *ideas*, and identifies different types, including: critical ideas (challenging the status quo while not promoting an alternative); and charismatic ideas (persuasive visions of how things might be different). The notions of evidence as argument and evidence as ideas offer a way to move beyond a focus on evidence as a static product, bringing in a consideration of the interplay between evidence, values, politics and advocacy as part of the dissemination process. Such considerations also point to the importance of interaction and dialogue in the process of evidence use.

Second-generation thinking: relational approaches

The 'two communities' thesis has influenced the way in which the relationship between researchers and research users is understood (Caplan, 1979). The argument is that researchers and research users live in different worlds and have different goals, priorities and motivations, which limits their mutual understanding and disrupts communication between them. The proposed answer to this problem is to stimulate greater interaction between the two groups and enhance their two-way communication. For this reason, the term 'knowledge exchange' is often associated with relational approaches to improving research use.

An influential model that has its roots in the two-communities thesis is the 'linkage and exchange' model of the research–policy–practice relationship (Lomas, 2000). This model focuses on communication and interaction as the key to research use, but also offers a more complex and contextualised theorisation of the connections between research, policy and practice. Linkage and exchange portrays research use as a process that involves multiple actors operating within a wider political context, with an emphasis on the interfaces and interaction between four main groups: researchers, decision makers, research funders and knowledge purveyors. The model suggests that research use happens when the links between all four groups are mutual and strong. It represents a significant shift away from first-generation models, which tend to portray research use as a single and relatively simple interaction between researchers and research users. It also has many features that are further enhanced in third-generation thinking.

Third-generation thinking: system-wide approaches

The importance of context has already been noted when discussing second-generation thinking about research use. While many models of the research–use process mention the importance of context, what is actually meant by context is often poorly developed. Third-generation thinking seeks to remedy this by using ideas drawn from complexity theory and the notion of complex adaptive systems (see Box 2.3, Chapter Two). Such an approach treats context as an integral element within the research–use process, rather than as a somewhat separate backdrop (Holmes et al, 2017). The term 'knowledge mobilisation' is sometimes used to refer to third-generation ideas about improving research use.

The potential relevance of complexity theory and systems thinking to framing and improving research use is illustrated in Chapter Five's discussion of evidence use in social care. There is increasing support for the idea that systems need to be viewed as complex assemblages of interlocking networks that cannot be understood in terms of linear and rational relationships but are instead conditional, contextual and relational (Davies et al, 2015). However, a lack of associated practical tools and detailed guidance means that it has been difficult to operationalise these ideas into innovative strategies aimed at improving research use (Davies et al, 2015).

In developing third-generation models, researchers have sought to draw in learning from a variety of disciplines such as science and technology studies and policy studies. For example, there is a large literature on policy implementation that is of potential relevance to those seeking to promote evidence use, especially as this field has considered the complexity of change processes and the interdependency of factors likely to influence change (Nilsen et al, 2013). The literatures relating to individual and organisational learning, knowledge management and the diffusion of innovations also have much to tell us about how knowledge is acquired, processed and applied (Nutley et al, 2007). Nilsen (2015) has collated and categorised some of the frameworks and models that have potential in this regard. He identifies five categories: process models, which aim to map out the steps from research to practice; determinant frameworks, which try to surface the factors that lead to change; classic theories, drawn from various fields that help to explain implementation; implementation theories, developed specifically from within the field of implementation studies; and, finally, evaluation models, which focus on what and how to learn from the implementation studies. By drawing on knowledge from these literatures, new models and frameworks have emerged that seek to capture the complexity of change and provide greater insights into research-use processes. Examples include the diffusion of innovation models (Greenhalgh et al, 2004) and the SPIRIT action framework (Redman et al, 2015).

The growing interest in the idea of evidence ecosystems seems like a promising development and one that ought to fit well with third-generation thinking. However, thus far, the operationalisation of these ideas in prescriptive models of evidence ecosystems tends not to live up to the promise. For example, rooted in an analysis of the early years of the UK What Works Centres, Shepherd (2014) proposed a model of a generic evidence ecosystem using the analogy of the petrochemical industry. The main elements are arranged in a linear progression from raw evidence generation, through evidence pumps (and storage) and then to evidence synthesis and guideline production and more pumps, before reaching evidence users. Push and pull forces are noted at the beginning and end of this continuum. For evidence ecology models to make a useful contribution to the field, they will need to embrace the nuanced, interactive and multifaceted nature of the relationship between evidence, policy and practice: they are unlikely to look like linear pipelines.

In summary, a wide variety of frameworks and models exist to support our understanding of the research-use process. Many of these models mainly describe research-use processes and tend not to be explicit about the configurations, actions or resources required to support successful research use. That is, they do not readily provide prescriptions for improving research use. In addition, with a few notable exceptions, most models have received only limited empirical testing (Davies et al, 2015). As such, they provide more of a starting point than an end point in developing strategies and initiatives to support research use (Boaz et al, 2016). To augment these models, there is a need to consider what is happening 'on the ground' to promote research use and the effectiveness of these activities. Such initiatives are the focus of the next section.

Identifying promising approaches to promoting research use

There is a diverse landscape of initiatives designed to promote evidence use (see Chapters Four to Nine and Thirteen for largely UK examples; Chapters Fourteen to Seventeen for international examples). However, while there has been a considerable increase in activity designed to promote research use since the late 1990s, much of this is not systematically documented, and even less has been evaluated with regard to its effectiveness. Here, ironies abound in how the promoters of evidence often struggle to be evidenced based themselves (Powell et al, 2018). There also continues to be a prevalence of 'push' strategies (focusing on dissemination of research) rather than activities designed to increase capacity for research use, build engagement in research and change systems in order to support evidence use (Powell et al, 2017). This section considers some of the prominent and potentially promising interventions and approaches (with some generic examples from this book highlighted in Box 12.3).

These prominent and/or promising approaches can be aligned with the three generations of thinking about evidence use outlined in the previous section (Best and Holmes, 2010). For example, there continues to be significant investment in the generation and dissemination of evidence. With the introduction of Evidence Clearing Houses in the US and What Works Centres in the UK, this approach retains a dominant place in the landscape. Often these initiatives invest considerable resources in the dissemination of the results of systematic reviews, including the production of online toolkits to support evidence use by practitioners (see, for example, the EEF toolkits discussed in Chapters Seven and Thirteen). This is seen particularly in the field of healthcare, where the production and dissemination of systematic reviews has proved to be a key approach to promoting evidence use.

However, in healthcare and more recently in other sectors such as criminal justice, efforts to synthesise and disseminate have been accompanied by capacity-building programmes for practitioners, aimed at equipping practitioners with the skills to use research. There has also been investment in developing hybrid roles in which practitioners can conduct research alongside their professional role as part of a joint practitioner-academic career. While much of the effort to build capacity for evidence use has focused on practitioners, there have also been some developments designed to build capacity for evidence use by policy makers (Redman et al, 2015). Related to this, in the UK, analysis and use of evidence is one of the core pillars of the 2016 standards for policy professionals.

Much of the work associated with the generation, dissemination and use of evidence in the first-generation model retains a conceptualisation of evidence as a product to be transferred from producers to users. However, there are also a wide range of interventions and approaches that tap into the importance of relationships in promoting evidence use. This theme fits closely with Best and Holmes's (2010) second generation of knowledge exchange, in which building relationships is a high priority in promoting evidence use. Previous chapters have included examples of interventions and approaches that involve closer

Box 12.3: Examples of initiatives designed to promote research use

Communities of practice bring together groups of people to participate in a process of collective learning around a shared area of interest.

Embedded researchers co-locate with practitioners to work together on practical problems in a service-orientated environment.

Evidence-synthesis centres, such as Clearing Houses and What Works Centres, are funded to produce and disseminate high-quality syntheses of evidence.

Knowledge brokers connect research producers and end-users to identify areas where research might be of help, to encourage interactions, to support the use of research in practice and to develop mutual understanding among research producers and users.

Research champions are individuals who provide leadership to support the use of research within different environments, including organisations, disciplines or service domains.

Research networks provide opportunities for knowledge exchange and facilitate research-related interactions between individuals and organisations.

Research–practice partnerships are long-term collaborations between researchers and practitioners. The collaborations work together to identify problems that require research, to conduct studies and to apply the findings in practice settings.

Research training programmes for policy makers and practitioners to build capacity to do and/or use research. Typically, this involves formal training programmes (ranging from masters programmes to tailored short courses), but might also employ other approaches such as peer support, mentoring and coaching.

Source: The examples are drawn from other chapters in this book.

working with stakeholders. In the US, education researchers are currently developing lasting research–practice partnerships (RPPs) as a potentially promising approach to promote the production of more useful and usable research (see Chapter Seventeen; Coburn and Penuel, 2016). Although temporary partnerships between researchers and practitioners are relatively common, the US examples point to a newer breed of long-term collaborations (beyond single studies) that have shared ways of working (involving explicit rules and procedures) and are intended to focus the partnership on practice-based problems (as opposed to research-led agendas). A further related development in the field is the introduction of embedded researchers or 'researchers in residence'. Here researchers co-locate with practitioners to work together on practical problems in a service-orientated environment (Marshall et al, 2014).

There are a number of similar initiatives emerging elsewhere. For example, in Canada, healthcare researchers have developed the concept of integrated knowledge translation (iKT), an approach to collaborative research in which researchers work with potential research users who can both identify a problem *and* have the influence and sometimes authority to implement the knowledge generated through research (McCutcheon et al, 2017 and Chapter Sixteen). RPPs and iKT share some common characteristics with a wider body of activity currently labelled as research co-production (see below). For example, they favour sustained interactions and joint working throughout the process of research production, with shared follow-through into research application.

There are fewer examples of more whole-system thinking in the design of approaches and interventions to promote evidence use. However, some interesting examples have been drawn out in previous chapters of the book. For example, in the UK a programme of NIHR-funded Collaborations for Leadership in Applied Health Research and Care (CLAHRCs, subsequently relabelled as Applied Research Collaborations, or ARCs) were designed to build multifaceted collaborations between academic institutions and NHS Trusts (see Chapter Four). In Canada, the province of Ontario developed a systems approach to supporting evidence use in education policy and practice (see Chapter Seven). There have also been some efforts to understand the contribution of inter-organisational structures such as research networks, which are often cited as promising approaches to building learning (Boaz et al, 2015). For example, Chapter Seven discusses the Research Schools Network, which shares evidence-based guidance, provides training and supports innovation in hundreds of schools in England; and Chapter Nine discusses the role of research networks in international development, citing the example of the Africa Evidence Network, established in part to promote more local learning between countries in the global South (that is, low- and middle-income countries).

There is, of course, also a long tradition of action research, whereby researchers and practitioners embark together upon a journey of discovery. However, action research challenges what we mean by evidence, how it fits within a wider system of knowledge production and how we might assess its impact (Campbell and Vanderhoven, 2016). As such, action research potentially offers a more whole-systems approach, advocating an alternative mode of evidence production. Yet, until recently, action research was often considered a marginal activity within the research community, and publication of findings from such activity is also problematic. In very recent years, perhaps spurred on by the drive to identify promising approaches to promoting research use (see also Chapter Three), methods that promote co-production have come to occupy a more central role in the research debate. These are described in Chapter Three as 'inside out' approaches to knowledge production, where locally sensitive knowledge is co-produced in situ. While offering the promise of a more whole-systems approach to evidence production, the extent to which researchers are keen to embark upon a true process of co-production with shared agendas and an even distribution of power has been questioned in the literature (Pinfold et al, 2015).

Taken together, then, these experiences give us a wide range of insights on which to draw, and Nutley et al (2007) distilled a set of guiding principles to support the use of research in practice, based on what was known at that time (Box 12.4). These still offer appropriate practical guidance for those interested in increasing the application and use of research in these settings. However, the state of the empirical research base that underpins this guidance is rather limited and in need of further development.

Early studies of approaches to promoting research use focused on evaluating single-mechanism approaches (for example, tailored dissemination; audit and feedback; incentives). Subsequent reviews of these studies concluded that the most promising interventions did not rely on single approaches but were multifaceted interventions employing a range of approaches to promoting change (Grol and Grimshaw, 2003; Boaz et al, 2011). A recent systematic review found a wide range of interventions in place to promote the use of research (Langer et al, 2016). It reviewed the evidence relating to six mechanisms for increasing research impact and three intermediary outcomes (Box 12.5). The review confirmed a general lack of systematic empirical evidence on many of the mechanisms and associated outcomes, although the promising nature of multifaceted interventions was again reported.

Box 12.4: Ten guiding principles to support the use of research in practice

1 **Research must be translated.** To be used, research needs to be adapted for or reconstructed with local practice contexts. Simply providing the findings is not enough. Tailoring might involve enabling debate about the implications, adapting the research to fit the local context or developing research-based programmes or tools.

2 **Ownership is key.** Ownership of the actual research, of the research-based programmes or tools, or of projects to implement the research, is preferable to implementation that is considered to be coercive.

3 **Enthusiasts are needed.** Individual enthusiasts or 'champions' can help to carry the process of getting research used. They are crucial to promoting new ideas and practices. Personal contact is often particularly effective.

4 **Consider the local context.** Analyse the local context for research implementation and target specific barriers and enablers of change.

5 **Ensure credibility.** The credibility of research, those producing it and those promoting it (such as opinion leaders) are essential.

6 **Provide leadership.** Strong and visible leadership at both management and project levels can help to provide resources, motivation, authority and organisational integration.

7 **Give adequate support.** On-going support for those implementing change is important. It can involve financial, technical, organisational, emotional and motivational support.

8 **Develop integration.** Activities need to be integrated within existing organisational systems and practices.

9 **Engage key stakeholders.** Stakeholders need to be involved, preferably from an early stage in the research process.

10 **Capture learning.** Identify what worked well in supporting the use of research to support future projects.

Source: Adapted from Nutley et al, 2007.

Box 12.5: Reviewing the evidence on effective mechanisms to promote research use

A review of the efficacy of interventions applied to increase decision makers' use of research was conducted by Langer and colleagues (2016). Interventions were grouped according to six mechanisms of change, described as the processes by which increased use of research might be achieved:

1 **awareness** (of the importance and role of evidence);
2 **agreement** (building an understanding between researchers and decision makers on policy-relevant questions and the type of evidence needed);
3 **communication and access** (of research results to potential decision makers);
4 **interaction** (between researchers and decision makers to build trust, relationships and collaborations and so on);
5 **skills** (decision-maker skills to access and use evidence);
6 **structure and processes** (psychological, social and environmental structures and processes that influence decision makers).

The review examined the relationship between the mechanisms and three intermediary behavioural outcomes (capability, motivation, and opportunity). It considered the existing evidence relating to each of these mechanisms and intermediary outcomes (where evidence exists). For example, the review found an absence of evidence on the awareness and agreement mechanisms. In relation to structures and processes, the review found reliable evidence that multifaceted interventions that included changes to decision-making structures such as supervision and formal access to evidence were effective in increasing both the opportunity and motivation to use evidence.

Source: Langer et al, 2016.

The lack of a strong evidence base on effective approaches to promoting research use is not surprising, given the complexity and contextually sensitive nature of the research-use process. Identifying effective approaches is not a straightforward task, and we now turn to a discussion of this methodological challenge, alongside other issues relating to assessing research use and impact.

Assessing research use and impact

In this section we explore methods employed to study how research is actually used. We then discuss the relatively few attempts to evaluate the effectiveness of research-use interventions and consider some of the reasons why this might be the case. Recently, there has been a renewed focus on assessing the impact of research in terms of actual changes in policy and practice, rather than simply looking at changes in the processes of research consideration. In the final part of this section we consider why assessing impact is important, and examine some of the methodological challenges of impact assessment.

Research on understanding research use

Research on describing and explaining the research-use process has expanded considerably over the past 20 years. A wide range of research methods have been used, with semi-structured interviews, case studies and documentary analysis (often in combination with each other) most commonly cited (Boaz et al, 2009). Initially, studies tended to focus on understanding research-use barriers and facilitators, using mainly qualitative methods. These studies have been collated in systematic reviews, generating a consistent set of barriers and facilitators that seem stable over time (Greenhalgh et al, 2004; Oliver et al, 2014). They include factors associated with the nature of the intervention, the process of implementing the intervention and the local and wider context within which this occurs. Barriers and facilitators have also been explored to a lesser extent in survey-based studies (Landry et al, 2001). The results of studies of barriers and facilitators have generated models, frameworks, theories of change or logistic models that map out how the research is likely to bring about impact (see above in this chapter).

There is growing acknowledgement that researching and explaining research use involves drawing on concepts and methods from a range of social science disciplines, including psychology, sociology, policy studies, organisational and management studies and economics. For example, as noted in Chapter Three, research by Gabbay and Le May (2004) and Currie and Suhomlinova (2006) in healthcare demonstrates the potential of social science methods and theories in contributing to our understanding of research use. Gabbay and Le May (2004) conducted rich ethnographic research to explore how GPs meld various sources of information with tacit knowledge drawn from their experience. Currie and Suhomlinova (2006) drew on institutional theory from organisational sociology to explain the limited success of knowledge-sharing initiatives in the English NHS.

Given the complexity of research use in policy and practice, it has been argued that there is a need to develop research-use strategies and assessment methods that fully capture the nuanced contribution of research to policy and practice (Riley et al, 2018). Perhaps a failure to do so to date explains the limited insights so far garnered – at least in terms of turning descriptive accounts into prescriptive guidance for improved use. Such approaches need to use and build on the different types of research use considered above in this chapter; Spaapen and van Drooge's (2011) 'productive interactions' assessment method for learning about the use and impact of research is a step in this direction.

Evaluating the effectiveness of research-use interventions

The increase in research on research use has not been matched by a similar growth in studies that evaluate interventions designed to promote research use. One consistent observation is that studies of such interventions are in their infancy (Davies et al, 2015). There are only a small number of studies of the implementation of specific knowledge-mobilisation mechanisms, and many of these are of poor quality. For example, many studies fail to define what they mean by research use or to define outcome measures clearly; the validity and reliability of the outcome measures are rarely reported; subjective measures of research use are commonly used; and many studies are retrospective, thus risking recall bias and incomplete data. The outcome measures used to measure research use have been varied but tend to emphasise instrumental use and downplay the importance of other uses (such as conceptual use). There is, therefore, a lack of robust empirical evidence on many of the likely components of effective knowledge-mobilisation strategies.

RCTs have been viewed as the ideal method for evaluating the effectiveness of knowledge-mobilisation interventions in healthcare and, more recently, in education (see, for example, the description of the work of the EEF in Chapter Seven). However, given the limitations of RCTs in situations where context is thought to be a powerful mediating factor (see Chapter Ten), it unsurprising that, even where they are used, RCTs are increasingly just one part of a multi-method evaluation strategy. For example, in Canada, Maureen Dobbins and colleagues conducted an experimental trial as part of a multi-method study of knowledge brokering (Dobbins et al, 2009); and in Australia a random-allocation stepped-wedge design is just one component of an investigation of a multifaceted programme designed to build organisational capacity for the use of research evidence in policy and programme development (The CIPHER Investigators, 2014).

Assessing research impact

There are a number of reasons why researchers might set out to assess the impact of their research. The two most prominent reasons are for accountability purposes and for learning. In recent years, much effort has been devoted to assessing impact for accountability purposes. This has often been focused on assessing the impact of individual pieces of research, individual researchers and their institutions, usually initiated by governments and other research funders. Perhaps the most developed agenda around assessing impact is the UK Research Excellence Framework (REF), a system for assessing the quality of research conducted in UK higher education institutions. There are similar systems in place in other countries, most notably Australia. In 2014 the REF assessments included 'impact case studies' alongside conventional research-quality metrics (particularly on the quality of research publications). In the impact case studies, institutions told the story of impact successes relating to individual research studies conducted in their organisations. The results of the assessment have a direct impact on the allocation of government funding to universities, as well as indirect impacts in terms of institutional rankings and reputations. Research funders also increasingly ask research grant applicants to consider the potential impact of their work, with some funders asking for applicants to map the anticipated pathway to impact for their proposed studies.

These activities remain a critical element of the research landscape and have an enduring influence on researchers and their host organisations. However, most efforts to assess research impact continue to be underpinned by a rational, linear model of the relationship between evidence, policy and practice. They also attract criticism as costly and bureaucratic exercises (Sivertsen, 2017). On the positive side, the introduction of impact case studies and pathways to impact has positioned research impact as a mainstream academic concern and increased discussion and debate about what counts as impact.

Assessments of research impact can also be orientated towards learning (as well as, or instead of, accountability). In this scenario the focus is on understanding how research has been used in order to inform future efforts to promote the impact of research. Much of this can be informal and cumulative: learning from experience throughout a research career. While individuals learn through trial and error in promoting their research, such learning is rarely captured in formal studies of research impact. Where studies have been conducted to assess impact for learning purposes they have run up against a number of methodological challenges. For example, there is an option to either track forward from a piece of research to see when and how it influences policy or practice, or to track backwards from a policy or practice change or document to see what research was used in its development. Sometimes these decisions will be pragmatic (such as availability of data) or relate to the timing of a study (when a policy change has occurred). Studies might be undertaken retrospectively or in 'real time'. For example, Hanney and colleagues conducted a retrospective analysis of a completed programme of research funded by Asthma UK, to inform the future research strategy of the organisation (Hanney et al, 2013), and Boaz et al (2018) conducted a prospective study of stakeholder engagement in research, tracking in real time the nature and impact of research engagement.

Whatever the approach, measures of research use and impact are often poorly developed and are rarely standardised. They have typically ranged from the presence of citations in policy documents to changes in outcomes for service users (Box 12.6). Furthermore, the extent to which it is possible to study research impact is, to some extent, determined by the conceptualisation of impact. For example, if the results of a research study aim to shift the way in which a particular problem is understood (an enlightenment use of research), it is unlikely that evidence of this shift would be easy to identify and measure. In particular, shifts in thinking take time, and it might be some years before the research has diffused sufficiently through multiple and potentially circuitous routes to bring about the anticipated change. In contrast, if a researcher is working with a linear model of research-into-practice (and an instrumental use of research), it is likely that getting the findings

Box 12.6: Five examples of measures of research use

1 Where research has been accessed or considered.
2 The presence of citations in documents.
3 Changes in knowledge, understanding and attitudes.
4 Direct applications of research in policy or practice.
5 Changes in ultimate outcomes for services users.

Source: Adapted from Nutley et al, 2007.

of a study into a policy document or guideline will be considered to offer a promising indicator of impact.

The key challenges associated with assessing research impact relate to timing and attribution (Nutley et al, 2007; Morton, 2015). Timing refers to identifying the best point to capture impact. While it is widely acknowledged that research impact can take a considerable amount of time to achieve, impact assessments typically occur at a fairly early point in time. Attribution refers to the difficulty in demonstrating that it was a particular piece of research (and not something else) that brought about a specific change. The challenge of attribution is compounded by the complexities of the context or setting in which research is seeking to make a difference. These challenges are familiar territory for evaluators, as most complex interventions take some time to show an impact and present challenges in terms of attribution. In response, Morton (2015) has developed a framework for applying contribution analysis as a tool for assessing research use and impact.

In 2007, Nutley et al concluded that 'research impact then is a somewhat elusive concept, difficult to operationalise, political in essence and hard to assess in a robust and widely accepted manner' (Nutley et al, 2007, p 295). The challenges involved in assessing research impact (whether it is for reasons of accountability or for learning) go some way to explaining why practice in this field still remains in its infancy.

Reflections and concluding remarks

Research on using evidence is often ambiguous about what is actually meant by evidence, with many studies focusing rather more narrowly on the use of research-derived findings. This chapter has largely followed the tradition of concentrating on the use of research evidence, while recognising that such use always happens in the context of other forms and types of knowledge that may need to be integrated into contextually based understandings.

We have considered the importance of defining research use and research users, as a precursor to exploring what we know about the use of research evidence, including how to retrospectively analyse this and how to prospectively promote it. In some respects, we now know a lot more about using research than we did in the late 1990s. In particular, we have gathered considerable knowledge on the barriers and facilitators to evidence use, and we have used them to generate complex conceptual models and frameworks to capture the key features of the research-use process. There are a growing number of empirical studies that help to shed light on elements of the evidence, policy and practice environments and the interaction between them. However, in general, robust empirical studies of research-use processes and evaluations of strategies and interventions aimed at promoting research use are still relatively scarce. In part, this is due to the methodological challenges involved in undertaking such studies, but it is also symptomatic of the very limited funding available for research on research use. This has led to the paradox that those advocating greater research use often struggle to practise in research-informed ways themselves (Powell et al, 2018).

However, the field is not devoid of relevant and helpful knowledge. More is now known about what helps to encourage evidence use (and what does not) than was known two decades ago, and, although progress has been relatively slow and patchy, there are examples of innovation and development on which others can build, as demonstrated in this book. Many stakeholders (particularly researchers, practitioners, policy makers and knowledge-mobilisation intermediaries) have learned a lot by doing and by being involved in initiatives to promote evidence use. There is a need to articulate, unpack and evaluate these tacit understandings.

The next step is to build a stronger evidence base for seemingly promising interventions to promote evidence use, including on their strengths, weaknesses and costs. For example, what is it about knowledge-brokering individuals and organisations that seems to support evidence use? Under what circumstances does a research-active organisation achieve better outcomes for service users, and what mechanisms are at play? Building such an evidence base is no small task, given the complexity of change processes and our increasing appreciation of evidence use as a systems issue. In our efforts, it is important to value the many different ways of defining and understanding evidence and evidence use, and to respect the different approaches to promoting and evaluating evidence use. These differences should be seen as sources of learning rather than as part of the problem (especially as the latter can result in diverting much-needed time and effort towards critiquing approaches and conceptualisations rather than seeking more productive accommodations). This is a field that is likely to benefit from greater interdisciplinary and cross-sector working by academics and external stakeholders than has hitherto tended to be the case.

In closing, our hope is that over the next two decades the field will develop into a stronger position to support research producers and intermediaries as they seek to promote evidence use. Greater research investment in this area now should also mean that in the future research funders will be able to draw on a stronger evidence base when deciding how to invest their money to support the use and impact of the research they commission.

References

Best, A. and Holmes, B. (2010) 'Systems thinking, knowledge and action: towards better models and methods', *Evidence and Policy*, 6 (2), pp 145–59.

Boaz, A., Baeza, J. and Fraser, A. (2016) 'Does the "diffusion of innovations" model enrich understanding of research use? Case studies of the implementation of thrombolysis services for stroke', *Journal of Health Services Research and Policy*, 21 (4), pp 229-34.

Boaz, A., Hanney, S., Jones, T. and Soper, B. (2015) 'Does the engagement of clinicians and organisations in research improve healthcare performance: a three-stage review', *BMJ Open*, 5 (12).

Boaz, A., Hanney, S., Borst, R., O'Shea, A., and Kok, M. (2018) 'How to engage stakeholders in research: design principles to support inprovement', *Health Research Policy and Systems* (Epub ahead of print).

Campbell, H. and Vanderhoven D. (2016) 'N8/ESRC research programme Knowledge That Matters: Realising the Potential of Co-Production', Manchester: N8 Research Partnership, http://www.n8research.org.uk/research-focus/urban-and-community-transformation/co-production/.

Caplan, N. (1979) 'The two communities theory and knowledge utilization', *American Behavioural Scientist*, 22 (3), pp 459–70.

Coburn, C. and Penuel, W. (2016) 'Research–practice partnerships in education: outcomes, dynamics, and open questions', *Educational Researcher*, 45 (1), pp 48–54.

Concannon, T.W., Meissner, P., Grunbaum, J.A., McElwee, N., Guise, J.M., Santa, J., Conway, P.H., Daudelin, D., Morrato, E.H. and Leslie, L.K. (2012) 'A new taxonomy for stakeholder engagement in patient centered outcomes research', *Journal of General Internal Medicine*, 27, pp 985–91.

Currie, G. and Suhomlinova, O. (2006) 'The impact of institutional forces upon knowledge sharing in the UK NHS: the triumph of professional power and the inconsistency of policy', *Public Administration*, 84 (1), pp 1–30.

Davies, H.T.O., Powell, A.E. and Nutley, S.M. (2015) *Mobilising knowledge to improve UK health care: learning from other countries and other sectors – a multimethod mapping study.* Southampton: NIHR Journals Library, *Health Services and Delivery Research*, 3 (27).

Dobbins, M., Robeson, P., Ciliska, D. et al (2009) 'A description of a knowledge broker role implemented as part of a randomized controlled trial evaluating three knowledge translation strategies', *Implementation Science,* 4, p 23.

Gabbay, J. and Le May, A. (2004) 'Evidence based guidelines or collectively constructed "mindlines"? Ethnographic study of knowledge management in primary care', *British Medical Journal,* 329, 7473, pp 1013–16A.

Greenhalgh, T., Robert, G., Macpharlane, F. et al (2004) 'Diffusion of innovations in service organizations: systematic review and recommendations', *The Milbank Quarterly,* 82, p 4.

Grol, R. and Grimshaw, J. (2003) 'From best evidence to best practice: effective implementation of change in patients' care', *Lancet* 362, pp 1225–30, doi: 10.1016/.

Hanney, S., Watt, A., Jones, T. and Metcalf, L. (2013) 'Conducting retrospective impact analysis to inform a medical research charity's funding strategies: the case of Asthma UK', *Allergy Asthma and Clinical Immunology,* 9 (1), p 17, doi: 10.1186/1710-1492-9-17.

Haynes, A.S., Gillespie, J.A., Derrick, G.E., Hall, W.D., Redman, S., Chapman, S. and Sturk, H. (2011) 'Galvanizers, guides, champions, and shields: the many ways that policymakers use public health researchers', *Milbank Quarterly,* 89 (4), pp 564–98, doi: 10.1111/j.1468–0009.2011.00643.x.

Holmes, B., Best, A., Davies, H., Hunter, D., Kelly, M., Marshall, M. and Rycroft-Malone, J. (2017) 'Mobilising knowledge in complex health systems: a call to action', *Evidence and Policy,* 13 (3), pp 539–60.

Knott, J. and Wildavsky, A. (1980) 'If dissemination is the solution, what is the problem?', *Knowledge,* 1 (4), pp 537–74.

Landry, R., Amara, N. and Lamari, M. (2001) 'Utilization of social science research knowledge in Canada', *Research Policy,* 30(2001), pp 333–49.

Langer, L., Tripney, J. and Gough, D. (2016) *The science of using science: researching the use of research evidence in decision-making,* London: EPPI-Centre, Social Science Research Unit, UCL Institute of Education, University College London.

Lomas, J. (2000) 'Using "linkage and exchange" to move research into policy at a Canadian foundation', *Health Affairs,* 19 (1), pp 236–40.

McCambridge, J., Hawkins, B. and Holden, C. (2014) 'Vested interests in addiction research and policy. The challenge corporate lobbying poses to reducing society's alcohol problems: insights from UK evidence on minimum unit pricing', *Addiction,* 109: 199–205nSet full point in roman.

McCutcheon, C., Graham, I.D. and Kothari, A. (2017) 'Defining integrated knowledge translation and moving forward: a response to recent commentaries', *International Journal of Health Policy and Management*, 6 (5), pp 299–300.

Majone, G. (1989) *Evidence, argument and persuasion in the policy process*, New Haven, CT: Yale University Press.

Marshall, M., Pagel, C., French, C., Utley, M., Allwood, D., Fulop, N., Pope, C., Banks, V. and Goldmann, A. (2014) 'Moving improvement research closer to practice: the researcher-in-residence model', *BMJ Quality Safety*, 23, pp 801–5.

Monaghan, M. (2011) *Evidence versus politics: exploiting research in UK drug policy making?* Bristol: Policy Press.

Morton, S. (2015) 'Progressing research impact assessment: A "contributions" approach', *Research Evaluation*, 24 (4), pp 405–19.

Nilsen, P. (2015) 'Making sense of implementation theories, models and frameworks', *Implementation Science*, 10 (53) doi: 10.1186/s13012-015-0242-0.

Nilsen, P., Ståhl, C., Roback, K., and Cairney, P. (2013) 'Never the twain shall meet? - a comparison of implementation science and policy implementation research', *Implementation Science*, 8 (63) http://doi.org/10.1186/1748-5908-8-63

Nutley, S., Walter, I. and Davies, H.T.O. (2007) *Using evidence: how research can inform public services*, Bristol: Policy Press.

Oliver, K., Innvar, S., Lorenc, T., Woodman, J. and Thomas, J. (2014) 'A systematic review of barriers to and facilitators of the use of evidence by policymakers', *BMC Health Service Research*, 14 (1), p 2.

Patton, M.Q. (1997) *Utilization-focused evaluation: the new century text*, Thousand Oaks, CA: Sage Publications.

Pinfold, V., Szymczynska, P., Hamilton, S., Peacocke, R., Dean, S., Clewett, N., Manthorpe, J. and Larsen, J. (2015) 'Co-production in mental health research: reflections from the People Study', *Mental Health Review Journal*, 20 (4), pp 220–31.

Powell, A.E., Davies, H.T.O. and Nutley, S.M. (2018) 'Facing the challenges of research-informed knowledge mobilization: 'practising what we preach', *Public Administration*, 96 (1), pp 36–52.

Powell, A.E., Davies, H.T.O. and Nutley, S.M. (2017) 'Missing in action? The role of the knowledge mobilisation literature in developing knowledge mobilisation practices', *Evidence and Policy*, 13 (2), pp 201–23.

Redman, S., Turner, T., Davies, H., Williamson, A., Haynes, A., Brennan, S., Milat, A., O'Connor, D., Blyth, F., Jorm, L. and Green, S. (2015) 'The SPIRIT action framework: a structured approach to selecting and testing strategies to increase the use of research in policy', *Social Science and Medicine*, 136–7, pp 147–55.

Riley, B., Kernoghan, A., Stockton, L., Montague, S. and Yessis, J. (2018) 'Using contribution analysis to evaluate the impacts of research on policy: Getting to "good enough"', *Research Evaluation*, 27 (1), pp 16–27, doi: 10.1093/reseval/rvx037.

SCIE research mindedness resource (2012) https://www.scie.org. uk/publications/researchmindedness/makingsenseofresearch/ misuseofresearch/index.asp.

Shepherd, J. (2014) *How to achieve more effective services: the evidence ecosystem*. Cardiff: What Works Network/Cardiff University, https://www.scie-socialcareonline.org.uk/how-to-achieve-more-effective-services-the-evidence-ecosystem/r/ a11G0000006z7vXIAQ

Sivertsen, G. (2017) 'Unique, but still best practice? The Research Excellence Framework (REF) from an international perspective', *Palgrave Communications*, 3, art no 17078, doi: 10.1057/ palcomms.2017.78.

Spaapen, J. and van Drooge, L. (2011) 'Introducing "productive interactions", in social impact assessment', *Research Evaluation*, 20 (3), pp 211–18, doi: 10.3152/095820211X12941371876742.

The CIPHER Investigators (2014) 'Supporting policy in health with research: an intervention trial (SPIRIT) – protocol for a stepped wedge trial', *BMJ Open*, e005293, doi: 10.1136/bmjopen-2014-005293.

Ward, V., House, A. and Hamer, S. (2009) 'Developing a framework for transferring knowledge into action: a thematic analysis of the literature', *Journal of Health Services Research and Policy*, 14 (3), 156–64.

Weiss, C. (1979) 'The many meanings of research utilisation', *Public Administration Review*, 39, pp 426–31.

Section Four
International comparison and commentary

The aim of this section is to reflect on some of the international experiences of EIPP, exploring how debates have developed over recent decades in five distinct geographic areas. The section provides an opportunity to build on the broad ideas introduced in Section One and consider their particularities in different country contexts. It also encourages reflection from an international perspective on the predominantly UK analysis of different fields of policy and practice intervention introduced in Section Two, helping us to see where debates internationally have developed in sync with UK experience and where they have diverged. Such reflections also allow us to explore how experiences in one place may have influenced developments elsewhere. Contributions to this section consider the similarities and differences in evidence generation, evidence appraisal and evidence use (explored in Section Three) across different jurisdictions.

This section contains five international commentary chapters from: the UK; Australia and New Zealand; Scandinavia (covering Sweden, Denmark and Norway); Canada; and the US. These five jurisdictions have been selected primarily for their prominence in the debates about evidence, policy and practice, as well as for the ease of access to these debates as they play out in English. While some focus on individual countries, others draw learning from across a wider regional area. We acknowledge that these countries are predominantly anglophone and high income; however, each of the countries covered has experienced lively discussion and debate within its policy and practice communities about the role of evidence. They have also experienced many evidence-related developments, including: infrastructural developments on the supply side; developments on the demand side; adoption of high-profile, 'evidence-based' interventions; and the emergence of large numbers of intermediary bodies that seek to 'bridge the gap' between evidence supply and evidence demand. Academics in these countries have also often taken an active role in national and international debates through contributions to journals, seminars and conferences.

The chapters in this section each consider the extent to which the use of evidence is a prominent concern and aim in each country, before discussing views about the nature of evidence, the structures and systems for evidence production and the key approaches to encouraging and enabling evidence use. Necessarily, given their relative brevity, each chapter presents a selective and somewhat idiosyncratic exploration, rather than being comprehensive, drawing on a variety of policy sectors to reflect national or regional preoccupations. The accounts also reflect the specific interests and expertise of the chapter authors, many of whom have been active players in some of the developments described: some develop broad, multi-sectoral narratives, while others pursue more focused, sector-specific accounts. By design, these lively and diverse contributions offer the possibility for reflection on others' experiences and touchpoints, rather than systematic comparisons for analytical purposes.

Perhaps surprisingly, given the UK focus of much of Section Two, this international section opens with an exploration of the evidence debates in the UK (Chapter Thirteen). But the focus of this new piece is on highlighting the political and governmental backdrop against which the sector-specific accounts of Section Two played out. As such, it provides a useful contextualisation of some of the finer-grained analyses laid out in Chapters Four to Nine. The following chapter, on Australia and New Zealand (Chapter Fourteen), takes a similar tack, offering an illuminating, macro-level account of the historical drivers behind the moves towards evidence-informed policy in those two countries.

The Scandinavian contribution (Chapter Fifteen) signals a move more towards an exploration of practice. It examines what the authors term the 'evidence idea' as it developed in Norway, Denmark and Sweden across health and social care, as well as (a little) in education. Taking a cluster of countries and looking across sectors allows for an interesting comparative angle, highlighting similarity and difference. The remaining chapters provide analyses homing in on evidence utilisation in healthcare in Canada (Chapter Sixteen) and in education policy and practice in the US (Chapter Seventeen). These two chapters offer readers the opportunity for detailed comparisons with Chapters Four and Seven, on healthcare and education in the UK, allowing us to see how the evidence idea sometimes unfolds quite differently in different jurisdictions, and also how ideas formulated and articulated in one place may go on to have much wider reach.

Some significant cross-cutting themes emerge from these five chapters. Universally, there has been a clear increase in the discourse of evidence in both policy making and practice across all these countries. Insights from Australia and New Zealand in particular (Chapter Fourteen) suggest that this increase may be seen to have occurred through two broad temporal waves. First, in the half-century following the end of the Second World War, many governments gradually developed an increasingly sophisticated bureaucratic apparatus to attend to the health and social needs of their populations in more systematic and coordinated ways than had traditionally been the case. These bureaucratic institutions produced and relied upon more data and information about policy and practice issues. These were amenable to use by social scientists to develop further insights and evidence about social issues and policy making.

Recognition of the limitations of the application of much of this evidence – most obviously in the healthcare setting – led to the second wave of activity, from the mid-1990s onwards. This was inspired by the EBM movement, emerging most obviously in Canada, the US and the UK, but spreading quickly across parts of Europe as well as to Australia and New Zealand – a spread helped by the emergence of new epistemic communities and burgeoning transnational institutions (such as the Cochrane Collaboration). The centrality of measurement, standardisation and a reframing of professional power structures inherent in EBM were closely aligned with the broader trends towards public sector efficiency and effectiveness, value for money and managerial control of the New Public Management movement (NPM) that swept through these countries (to different degrees) at around the same time. Many of the NPM principles remain deeply embedded in policy and practice across these countries and are closely aligned with the discourse of evidence and rational forms of policy making.

A further cross-cutting theme is linked to the epistemic dominance of EBM as the original model influencing ideas about how evidence should inform policy and practice from the mid-1990s across these different countries. The centrality of the positivist approach of the early proponents of EBM, and their favouring of RCTs and hierarchies of knowledge, have impacted on how other sectors have structured their own approaches to evidence use in support of, or sometimes in opposition to, these positivistic principles (see also Chapters Ten and Eleven). These debates are discernible across the different countries, reflecting the varying ways in which knowledge is understood and valued within and across different sectors. While it is the case that the debates about research paradigms appear to be less confrontational now than they used to be, it is apparent that these debates have shaped the ways in which different sectors and practitioners define their relationships with evidence – with consequent impacts upon professional relations, policy and practice.

Perhaps in recognition of the historical impacts of these epistemic debates, and representing a move towards more pluralistic approaches to evidence generation and interpretation, an increasing interest in knowledge 'co-production' is discernible across the countries covered in this section. Yet, just what co-production actually is and how it might be achieved are by no means universally understood or defined. Another important finding across these five chapters is the active roles (often collaboratively) played by government and academia in the development of structures for evidence production, use and evaluation.

There are also some important differences between the countries covered in this section. For example, the dominance of RCT methodologies in education debates in the US reflects a cultural preference among policy makers there for quantitative data, randomised experimentation and positivist modes of knowledge, allied with more coercive forms of practitioner behaviour change. This even goes so far as the codification of such preferences in legal statutes. Such strong preferences are seemingly not replicated by policy makers in other countries to the same degree, although healthcare as a whole has privileged such ways of knowing for a long time, albeit usually without legal back-up and with softer modes of encouraging front-line change.

Differences in population size (which influence connectivity across policy and professional worlds) and diversity of politico-institutional arrangements may be significant in shaping how EIPP unfolds in different jurisdictions, and this is hinted at in these accounts. Such factors influence, for example, whether governments are able to develop their own architecture for evidence production and use, or are more often forced to rely on other countries' research outputs or international syntheses. This then has implications for the transferability and acceptability of findings (see, for example, the debates in Scandinavia, Chapter Fifteen). A related issue is the cross-national influence of ideas *about* evidence, separate from the evidence itself. For example, when newly formed, the international Cochrane Collaboration was highly influential in parts of Scandinavia (see Chapter Fifteen), and Canadian ideas about the links between research and practice (and integrated knowledge translation) have impacted upon debates in many other countries (see Chapter Sixteen).

Notwithstanding some differences between jurisdictions, the international commentaries in the next five chapters highlight much convergence across quite different countries in terms of the long-term development of EIPP, albeit with concurrent contextual and sectoral distinctions. In this sense, we see a parallel between Section Two (comparison across fields of application in the UK) and this section (comparison across distinct geographical jurisdictions). What is striking is the familiarity of the arguments about how and when evidence might inform policy and practice that are encountered across the different countries (and sectors), yet how in each country (and sector) these arguments have to be replayed anew in order to win converts. We see, for example (in Chapter Fifteen), that evidence created outside of national contexts in Scandinavia requires local contextualisation in order to garner acceptance (in a similar way to that highlighted in Chapter Nine, on international development). Thus, the local resolution of arguments and contestation with respect to evidence is enduringly important. Reflecting on how these issues are framed, contested and resolved in different (national and sectoral) jurisdictions may be of practical interest and may, ultimately, be of some help to those exploring similar issues elsewhere.

13

Using evidence
in the UK

Jonathan Breckon and David Gough

Introduction to evidence use in the UK

There have been ups and downs in the history of evidence use in the UK. After the Second World War an appetite for evidence-informed policy gave way to scepticism and a more ideologically driven approach during the 1970s and 1980s, only to be followed by renewed enthusiasm for evidence use again from the mid-1990s (Nutley et al, 2007). Alongside these general trends, there have also been highs and lows in the use of evidence to inform specific policy debates. An obvious low point was the debate surrounding the UK referendum on membership of the European Union (EU) in 2016. That debate was characterised by ambiguous evidence claims, some active misuse of evidence and quite a few unsavoury attacks on those who provided evidence. An iconic moment during the referendum campaign was the appearance of a big red bus with the slogan 'We send the EU £350m a week'. This was a gross figure that did not take into account the rebate or other flows from the EU to the UK, and its use was criticised by many respected bodies, including the UK Statistics Authority.

However, specific events, such as the referendum campaign, should not overshadow a generally encouraging history of evidence use in the UK since the late 1990s, especially when it comes to developing the architecture for the creation and sharing of robust evidence. Throughout this period, politicians on all sides have broadly backed the idea of government based on learning and knowledge, at least in theory if not always in practice. The UK has initiated or supported a large number of initiatives on evidence use over this time-frame. For example, in 1999 NICE was formed to develop evidence-based guidance for clinical health (and more recently for public health and social care services too). NICE has since proved to be an influential model for many other sectors and countries (see Chapter Eleven). More generally, as noted across Chapters Four to Nine, political support and professional leadership in the UK have spawned many other evidence-promoting initiatives.

The way in which the evidence agenda has developed over the last two decades can be described chronologically, starting from 1997 with the development of specific policies and much fanfare for the use of research evidence by the New Labour government, under the banner of 'what counts is what works'. There was then a broad continuation of these evidence policies by the Coalition government from 2010, and the Conservative government installed since 2015 has largely sustained this approach thereafter. Initially, the evidence agenda was pursued alongside a major increase in investment in public services (especially healthcare). However, following the 2008 global financial crisis, financial austerity rather than growth has characterised the public services environment within which evidence use has been pursued. Nonetheless, since 2010 there has been an expansion of a network of What Works Centres, which act as intermediaries between research production and use across many areas of social policy.

While there has generally been support for the idea of more EIPP, there has also been considerable debate and contestation about what this idea means in practice. For example, within the education sector many researchers saw early investments in EIPP as a means to exercise managerial control over education research, to limit its independence from government and to prioritise a simplistic, naive and overly rational 'what works' research agenda (Ball, 2001). Such concerns about the aims of evidence may have been heightened further by discussion about the cost-effectiveness of research, such as the National Audit Office (NAO, 2003) report on the management of, and the return on, government investment in research aimed at informing policy making.

Changes to the way in which university research is assessed may also be shifting the academy further in the direction of applied work. Since 2014 universities have been rewarded for contributing to policy and practice through the government's UK-wide REF, which incorporates societal impact alongside research quality as a core component of the assessment. While this framework has been the subject of much criticism, it can be argued that it has brought policy engagement and research impact up the agendas of individual academics and their institutions. Nevertheless, there are concerns about overly simplistic views of the research-impact process and evidence-informed policy making, particularly those that assume comprehensive rationality and an orderly policy cycle (as discussed in Chapter Two). There are also critiques of a top-down approach to defining and implementing evidence-informed practices (as discussed in Chapter Three).

This chapter draws on our experience in brokering relationships between decision makers and researchers (Breckon), and in studying research synthesis and research use (Gough). It provides a thematic commentary on the development of the evidence agenda in the UK, structured around three key aspects: the nature of relevant evidence; structures for producing and synthesising evidence; and approaches to encouraging and enabling evidence use. The aim is to provide a national-level overview that complements and contextualises the sector-specific accounts already provided in Section Two of this book. As many of the concerns about the evidence agenda have hinged on what counts as good evidence, it is fitting that we turn first to this issue.

The nature of evidence

From the outset there has tended to be an inclusive view of what counts as relevant evidence for policy and practice development in the UK. For example, an early Cabinet Office document talks of high-quality information ('the raw ingredient of evidence') being derived from a variety of sources, including domestic and international research, expert knowledge, practitioner knowledge, statistics and stakeholder consultations (Cabinet Office, 1999, paras 7.1 and 7.22). Subsequently, the Cabinet Office and the Treasury provided further guidance on the nature of good evaluation evidence (Box 13.1), and interest in experimentation gained ground.

Increased use of experimentation

There has not been much of a tradition of using experimental methods to evaluate social policies and practices in the UK. However, interest in experimentation for social policies grew during the late 1990s and early 2000s (John, 2013). There was early enthusiasm for using policy pilots as public policy experiments, although a review of the use of these pilots noted that too often they were not allowed to run their course and produce their findings before decisions on policy roll-outs were made (Cabinet Office, 2000b).

In healthcare research, RCTs have historically been seen as the standard method for evaluating impact (see Chapters Four and Ten and the detailed critiques covered in Chapter Eleven). Yet, despite guidance from the 2003 edition of UK Treasury's *Magenta Book* (see Box 13.1), which set randomised experiments as the strongest method for demonstrating impact, RCTs have not generally been used to evaluate the effectiveness of social policy pilots. The early 2000s did see some government investment in a small number of randomised trials in criminal justice and employment, such as the Employment, Retention and Advancement Demonstration between 2003 and 2007 (Blundell et al, 2003). However, a lack of understanding of RCTs and perceptions of practical and ethical difficulties in using them in these arenas have sometimes created insurmountable barriers.

Calls for more experimentation were renewed with the election of the Coalition government in 2010, and there has been much more activity in this area since then. For example, the Education Endowment Foundation (EEF), established in 2011, identified a lack of experimental data to inform education practice, and in response it developed and funded a large programme of RCTs. The Behavioural

Box 13.1: UK Treasury guidance on evaluation

Various Treasury documents have emphasised the importance of policy, programme and project evaluations as an essential component of effective decision making (for example, *Managing Public Money*, HM Treasury, 2013). The Treasury has also produced two complementary guide books on the evaluation process and recommended evaluation methods.

The Treasury *Green Book* (HM Treasury, 2018) recommends an evaluation framework, which is based on the idea of a policy cycle (see Chapter Two for a critical discussion of policy-cycle models). The framework sets out the key stages in the development of a proposal: from the articulation of the rationale for intervention and the setting of objectives, through to options appraisal and, eventually, implementation and evaluation (including the feeding back of evaluation evidence into the policy cycle). Various editions have been produced by the Treasury over 40 years. The most recent version has been updated to include more on environmental and well-being approaches. Greater emphasis is also placed on building monitoring and evaluation throughout policy development – before, during and after implementation.

The *Magenta Book* (HM Treasury, 2011) complements the *Green Book* by providing detailed guidance on evaluation methods. It sets out what needs to be considered when designing an evaluation. It explains how results can be interpreted and presented, and what should be taken into account in this process.

Insights Team (sometimes called 'the nudge unit') has also expanded the use of randomised experiments by setting up 46 individual 'nudge' RCTs across government. The team has also produced a popular short guide to RCTs, advocating their wider use (Sanders et al, 2018). More broadly, a cross-government Trial Advice Panel was set up in 2015 to provide Whitehall departments with technical support in designing and implementing RCTs.

Supporting trials with routine data

A common criticism aimed at RCTs is the difficulty of collecting robust data regarding impacts (see, for example, Gibbons et al, 2013). However, the 'nudge' experiments have demonstrated that RCTs do not always require resource-intensive investments when applying and evaluating the impact of novel interventions. These experiments can make small adjustments to normal practice for random subgroups and then use routine administrative data to assess impact (see Chapter Ten). For example, the nudge trials implemented in conjunction with Her Majesty's Revenue and Customs (the UK's tax authority) considered different ways to encourage people to submit their tax returns. A modest investment in these trials is credited with delivering over £200 million in additional tax income (Cabinet Office Behavioural Insights Team, 2012).

Improvements in the availability of administrative data in the UK have increased the potential for trials by sometimes dispensing with the need for a separate, expensive data-collection exercise. Related initiatives have focused on encouraging more research use of data that is collected by government. A Justice Data Lab was piloted in 2012 at the Ministry of Justice, and it provided information for charities to enable them to conduct quasi-experimental research (Adler and Coulson, 2016). The Department for Education provides access to the National Pupil Database so that researchers, including those funded by the EEF, can obtain attainment scores to use as outcome measures when evaluating interventions. Finally, the Administrative Data Research Partnership launched in 2018 takes forward the work undertaken by the Administrative Data Research Network since 2013 to create a secure environment for researchers who use government data.

Resistance to randomised experiments

It is too early to tell whether these developments are helping to create a sustained appetite for experimentation. There remains a considerable degree of resistance and contestation around the presumed superiority of experimental methods (see Chapters Ten and Eleven). Trials remain 'the exception and not the rule', according to a 2013 report on *Evaluation in Government* (NAO, 2013). Furthermore, interest in RCTs has not taken hold across all of the UK, and has been predominantly located in England. There is certainly considerable scepticism on the part of the Scottish Government about the use of RCTs in social policy: it has been argued that the small size of the country, and an interest in co-production and localism, go against an ethos of randomly selecting unknowing participants for trials (Cairney, 2017).

While debates about appropriate approaches to identifying what works for whom and in what circumstances continue (see Chapter Ten), the so-called 'paradigm wars' between experimental and qualitative researchers in the UK have perhaps entered a rather quiet phase. Experimentalists have become more interested in the role of theory in understanding the complexity of social interventions; there has also been increased use of mixed-methods strategies, combining the power of both more aggregative and configuring conceptual approaches to research (again, see Chapter Ten). Many of these methodological developments have been forged or harnessed by the various bodies that produce and synthesise evidence for policy and practice.

Structures for the production and synthesis of evidence

There are a wide range of centres and institutions that produce and synthesise evidence for policy makers and practitioners in the UK. Each of the sector-specific chapters (in Section Two of this book) outlines and discusses some of the main centres working in their fields (such as the Cochrane Collaboration, the Campbell Collaboration and the EPPI-Centre). Many of these bodies focus on synthesising evidence for public service practitioners and service-delivery organisations. There are also some high-profile and long-standing institutions that aim more broadly to inform public debate and policy making (for example, the Institute for Fiscal Studies – Box 13.2).

An important infrastructure development has been the growth of a network of What Works Centres. The 2012 Civil Service Reform Plan committed the UK government to setting up a 'what works' institution that could 'test and trial approaches and assess what works in major social policy areas, so that commissioners in central or local government do not waste time and money on programmes that are unlikely to offer value for money' (HM Government, 2012, p 17).

Box 13.2: The Institute for Fiscal Studies (IFS): informing public debate

The IFS was founded in 1969 as an independent, non-profit and non-political research institute. It aims to inform public debate on economics and promote the development of effective fiscal policy. Its research remit is broad, covering subjects from tax and benefits to education policy, and from labour supply to corporate taxation. The institute works to influence policy and practice at national and international levels. It provides advice to policy makers in the UK, Europe and developing countries, and disseminates its research findings globally through the press, media and the web. All publications are available free of charge for the public to read.

IFS hosts or is a partner in three major research centres, including two ESRC research centres. It receives funding from a range of sources, including the ESRC, UK government departments, foundations, international organisations, companies and other non-profit organisations. It does not accept funding that would compromise its independence and neutrality.

In the event not one but eight institutions were set up or retrospectively branded as What Works Centres (Table 13.1), with two additional 'affiliate members' in Wales and Scotland (Rutter and Gold, 2015). Some of these centres are wholly funded by government (for example, NICE), others are part-funded by government in partnership with others (for example, the Early Intervention Foundation), and one is independently funded by the Big Lottery Fund (the Centre for Ageing Better). Although most receive funding from government, all are described as being independent: some are established as charities, while others are based in universities or non-departmental bodies. Although they operate as independent bodies, the Cabinet Office has a cross-centre coordinating role. For a more detailed overview of these centres see a recent Cabinet Office publication: What Works Network, 2018.

By far the most investment and activity around producing and synthesising evidence has been in the health sector (see Chapter Four), with NICE sitting at the centre of this activity. NICE inspired the creation of the other centres, but each centre has developed its own way of working. All centres are dedicated to evidence synthesis, generation, transmission and adoption, but there is no rigid blueprint for the way in which they work, and each employs somewhat different standards of evidence systems (see Table 13.1).

Table 13.1: An overview of the UK What Works Centres

What Works Centre	Policy area	Status	Budget and core staff	Main funder(s)	Standards of evidence system for quantitative evidence of impact
NICE (established 1999 and rebranded as a What Works Centre in 2013)	Health and social care	Operationally independent. Non-departmental public body of the Department of Health	£71.3 million gross expenditure for 2016/17; 617 staff, including 595 permanent	Department of Health and Social Care	Methods handbook that includes adapted use of the GRADE system (see Chapter Eleven)
Education Endowment Foundation (EEF) (established 2011 and rebranded as a What Works Centre in 2013)	Educational attainment	Independent charity. Founded by parent charities the Sutton Trust and Impetus-PEF, and funded by a Department for Education (DfE) grant	£125 million endowment (£12 million expenditure in 2016); 25 staff	DfE, Sutton Trust and others	The Teaching and Learning Toolkit combines impact estimates from high-quality research studies into a single average for a topic area, such as 'one-to-one tuition' or 'classroom assistants'
Early Intervention Foundation (EIF) (established 2013)	Early intervention	Independent charity	Planned £1.5 million expenditure in 2018; 20 staff	DfE and Department for Work and Pensions, Ministry of Housing, Communities and Local Government and Public Health England	The Evidence Standards rating system distinguishes five levels of strength of evidence of impact. This is not a rating of the scale of impact but of the degree to which a programme has been shown to have a positive, causal impact on specific child outcomes

What Works Centre	Policy area	Status	Budget and core staff	Main funder(s)	Standards of evidence system for quantitative evidence of impact
What Works Centre for Crime Reduction (established 2013)	Crime	Hosted by the College of Policing	£1.5 million (approximately) for 2017/18; 20 staff	College of Policing, Home Office and ESRC	The EMMIE framework summarises the best available research evidence on what works to reduce crime and rates each intervention against the following five dimensions: Effect, Mechanism, Moderators, Implementation, and Economic cost
What Works Centre for Local Economic Growth (established 2013)	Local economic growth	Collaboration between the London School of Economics, Centre for Cities and Arup	Approximately £1.25 million per year; 9 staff	ESRC and HM Government	Based on the Maryland Scale (see Chapter Eleven, Box 11.3)
What Works Centre for Well-being (established 2014)	Well-being	Community Interest Company (applying to be a charity)	Around £3.9 million over the first three years (2014–17); 6 staff	ESRC, Arts and Humanities Research Council, 12 government departments/agencies, four businesses and the Big Lottery Fund	It uses CERQual (Confidence in the Evidence from Reviews of Qualitative research) to grade the evidence of qualitative data in systematic reviews. It is conceptually like GRADE but is tailored to suit qualitative evidence
Centre for Ageing Better (established 2015)	Ageing	Independent charity	£5.3 million for 2017; 27 staff	£50 million endowment from the Big Lottery Fund	No formal evidence standards as yet

What Works Centre	Policy area	Status	Budget and core staff	Main funder(s)	Standards of evidence system for quantitative evidence of impact
What Works Centre for Children's Social Care (forthcoming)	Children's social care	To be confirmed, but will be independent of government	About £10 million (to be split between an 'incubation' centre and the research consortium)	Department for Education	To be confirmed
What Works Scotland (established 2014 and an affiliate What Works Centre)	Scottish local services	A 'co-funded research based initiative' with the core funding grant from ESRC and the Scottish Government awarded to the University of Glasgow (charity)	Approximately £1 million; 11 staff	ESRC, Scottish Government and the Universities of Glasgow and Edinburgh	No formal evidence standards
Wales Centre for Public Policy (relaunched June 2017 and an affiliate What Works Centre)	Welsh public services	Externally funded institute within Cardiff University (charity)	Annual budget £450,000; 7 staff (as of July 2017)	ESRC and Welsh Government	No formal evidence standards

Note: Information correct as of 26 June 2017, but is subject to change.

Source: Adapted from What Works Network, 2014, Annex A; information on Standards of Evidence system for quantitative evidence of impact taken from https://www.alliance4usefulevidence.org/assets/2018/05/Mapping-Standards-of-Evidence-A4UE-final.pdf.

The What Works Centres are primarily focused on supporting the evidence needs of practitioners and service-delivery organisations, but some of their outputs are useful for and aimed at policy makers too. More specifically, the What Works Centre for Wales has provided Welsh ministers with an on-demand evidence service. All of the centres can be understood as evidence intermediaries. Many see their role not only as supplying relevant evidence to policy makers and practitioners but also as encouraging and enabling evidence use: for example, by interpreting research findings to provide actionable evidence; and sometimes by offering implementation advice and support. The What Works Centres are complemented in their endeavours by a wide range of other initiatives aimed at encouraging evidence use.

Key approaches to encouraging and enabling evidence use

Alongside the many supply-side initiatives to produce actionable evidence, there have been activities to encourage evidence 'pull' among potential users of evidence. These have included: initiatives that link spending decisions and payments to evidence of effectiveness (such as spending reviews and payment-by-results schemes); helping policy makers to understand and use evidence; motivating and supporting evidence use in front-line service delivery; and increasing user involvement in research and service delivery. Moreover, these specific initiatives have been supported by a growth in research on research use and general advocacy of the evidence agenda. The remainder of this section briefly discusses each of these developments.

Linking spending decisions and payments to evidence of effectiveness

The UK Treasury has over the years promoted and encouraged evidence use in various ways (which go beyond just providing guidance on evaluation methods). In 2002, a Treasury Spending Review required evidence of the effectiveness of funded programmes to be provided by government departments. However, some of those advocating greater evidence use in policy have argued that the Treasury could do more. For example, Rutter (2012) argues that there is scope to further incentivise the use of research and evaluation by more explicitly linking spending decisions to evidence.

The Payment by Results (PbR) model of delivering public services is viewed as another way of incentivising evaluation and evidence use by linking funding with results. Under this model, the government and other commissioners of public services pay service providers for the outcomes they achieve. This is in contrast to the more traditional model of service delivery whereby government either provides services itself or has a contract that pays providers regardless of success. PbR is used across government in the UK and is a cornerstone of the Open Public Services agenda initiated during the 2010 Coalition government (Cabinet Office, 2011).

Under PbR, the commissioner pays only for those results demonstrably achieved. So, in theory, the PbR contract should require evidence of impact. The desire is to pay for success and avoid paying for what is called 'deadweight': outcomes that would have happened anyway. The NAO and others recommend that commissioners ensure that they include a counterfactual in the form of a control group to measure the impact of any PbR scheme (NAO, 2015). However, counterfactuals for PbR schemes are relatively rare, although quasi-experimental designs have been used, as, for example, in the Peterborough Prison Reoffending Social Impact Bond intervention (Ministry of Justice, 2015) as well as in the drug recovery pilots (Mason et al, 2015).

A second way that PbR might encourage evidence use is due to an appetite to learn from others through an increased role for evaluation. However, it is unclear if this is happening in practice: indeed, an Audit Commission (2012, p 3) study concluded there is little evidence that PbR is driving any improvement in delivering services. Nevertheless, the ethos of seeking results is still a strong theme in the delivery of public services across the UK. Even where services are not tendered out to external bodies via PbR, governments in Scotland, Wales and Northern Ireland frequently call for more 'outcomes-based services'.

Developing the skills and knowledge of policy makers

An important aspect of encouraging evidence use is to have 'intelligent customers'. In other words, decision makers need to know what to ask for, and how to critically interrogate research and evaluation findings and other evidence. Despite many UK civil servants having degrees in social sciences and science subjects, many struggle with basic statistics. In 2000 the Cabinet Office launched Adding it Up, a strategy for developing greater quantitative ability in the UK Civil Service (Cabinet Office, 2000a). The aim was to embed the demand for and supply of good quantitative analysis across government.

These skills have since become a core part of the curriculum for policy professionals. One of the core pillars of the 2016 standards for policy professionals is 'analysis and use of evidence' (with the other two pillars relating to 'politics' and 'delivery'). Policy professionals are expected to have an understanding of statistics and data analysis, policy framing, economics, science and technology and horizon scanning. A new Executive Master of Public Policy for future leaders of the civil service teaches empirical methods for public policy, economic policy analysis and a refresher course on statistics (Civil Service Learning, 2017). However, it is worth noting that attempts to embed and institutionalise quantitative approaches to evidence reflect only part of a 'high quality evidence' agenda (as discussed in Chapters Ten and Eleven).

Motivating and supporting evidence use by professionals and service managers

As seen in many of the earlier chapters in this book, an important audience for evidence has been front-line practitioners and commissioners of services. Bottom-up campaigns organised by practitioner networks (such as the Society for Evidence-Based Policing, researchED, and Evidence for the Frontline) have focused on increasing interest in evidence use. Professional bodies are also increasingly supporting evidence use as part of their remit. As an indicator of their commitment to the evidence agenda, a number of professional bodies (including the College of Policing and the Chartered College of Teachers) signed an Evidence Declaration at the Royal Society in 2017.

In parallel, the devolution of services, particularly in England, has given opportunities for more evidence-informed decision making at a local level. Schools, for example, have increased autonomy, which means that they have scope to decide how they spend their budgets and choose their teaching approaches. In theory at least, school leaders and teachers can make local decisions based on evidence of what has been found to work in classrooms (as, for example, summarised in the EEF's Teaching and Learning Toolkit). This and many other field-specific initiatives are fleshed out in Chapters Four to Nine.

Increasing user involvement in research and service delivery

An important theme in the evidence agenda has been public participation and user involvement in research, service policy and delivery. Different groups in society have a variety of perspectives, values and priorities that are not necessarily shared by those developing or studying policy and practice (see Chapters Ten and Eleven). For this reason, participation in research has been seen as a democratic issue (Gough and Elbourne, 2002; Oliver et al, 2004). User voice has been particularly strong in health research: in 1996 INVOLVE was established with government funding to support public involvement in health and social care research; and in 2004 the James Lind Alliance was formed to bring patients, carers and clinicians together to form Priority Setting Partnerships in research. More broadly, in 2008 the National Co-ordinating Centre for Public Engagement was established by major research funders to increase public engagement in research.

User involvement has also been a key theme of some of the What Works Centres. For example, What Works Scotland has adopted a co-construction approach to evidence generation and use (involving policy makers and practitioners). The Wales Centre for Public Policy also assists the Welsh government in producing research evidence relevant to its policy needs. Moreover, while NICE has a number of top-down characteristics (as explained in Chapters Three and Four), it also has elements of a stakeholder demand-driven approach to developing guidance for practice.

Advocating and researching research use

There has been increased financial support for the promotion of evidence use. One example of this is the investment (by Nesta, the ESRC and the Big Lottery Fund) in the Alliance for Useful Evidence, which acts as an advocacy and catalyst organisation designed to promote the evidence-use agenda in the UK (and is directed by one of the authors – Breckon). A further important component of increasing research uptake has been the development of research on the production and use of research. Since the pioneering work of the Research Unit for Research Utilisation (reported in Nutley et al, 2007; www.ruru. ac.uk), there has been a gradual growth in research use as a programme of study in its own right. Not surprisingly, this has been most evident in the area of health but it is slowly broadening to other areas of social policy, including education, social care and science and technology.

Although this overview of approaches to encouraging evidence use is not exhaustive, it does illustrate a rich array of initiatives that aim to increase evidence 'pull'. Whether these initiatives have actually increased the demand for and use of evidence is an issue that we consider in drawing this account to a conclusion.

Concluding remarks

There have been many developments in the UK to help evidence use since the late 1990s. There is greater acceptance that, notwithstanding the dangers of an over-simplistic rational model of decision making (see Chapter Two), social research has an important role in policy making and service delivery. However, the question remains whether there has been an increase in the use of research and evaluation. There has been no systematic and regular monitoring of evidence take-up by government or practitioners, so it is hard to know for sure. The picture has certainly been obscured during the Brexit debates that have dominated since 2016, with polarised positions often divorced from evidence of any kind. Other high-profile political issues, as diverse as badger culling and grammar schools, can seem similarly somewhat disconnected from dispassionate analysis of the evidence. However, we do have surveys and interview-based studies that reflect an appetite for evidence among civil servants and politicians (Institute for Government, 2011), although it is not clear whether, or to what extent, this appetite translates into action. More positively, the five-year review of the What Works Network (2018) provides some self-reported examples of the impact of its outputs and activities, and the investment across these centres certainly reflects sustained investment in capacity, if not yet full institutionalisation of the approach.

The NAO (2013) analysed the use of evaluation by government between 2006 and 2012. They found only a handful of examples where departments were able to say that evidence had made any difference to policy. Indeed, only 15% of departments referred to evaluations in regulatory impact assessments. This was also true of spending review documentation, with a very limited proportion of the resources sought from the Treasury in the 2010 Spending Review including any reference to evaluation evidence. The House of Commons Public Accounts Committee has also highlighted poor practice and a lack of evaluation across many government departments.

Although there have been many initiatives in the UK to promote the evidence agenda, and particularly the use of research evidence, the traditional system persists of expert committees as the standard providers of evidence to government. The UK government also maintains its very broad definition of evidence that goes well beyond evaluation or academic research. For instance, the official curriculum for the policy profession in the civil service defines evidence as including 'relevant facts, figures, ideas, analysis and research' (Civil Service Learning, 2013, p 12). In the UK Parliament, 'evidence' submitted to House of

Commons Select Committees can be any views or opinions given by interested parties. A report on the use of evidence in the UK Parliament found that the university sector was one of the least frequent submitters of evidence to Select Committees (Kenny et al, 2017).

One potentially promising development is a campaign on evidence transparency. Sense about Science (a UK charity that promotes the public understanding of science) has been looking at how easy it is to find clear thinking and evidence behind government policies. Between 2015 and 2016 it sifted through 593 policies, covering 13 domestic departments – and used volunteers to score how transparent the policies were about evidence. While this was not an attempt to measure research uptake, it provides a model for comparing and contrasting the evidence claims behind policies. Without transparency, outsiders will never be able to find and check claims behind government policies.

In summary, there seems to be a more positive attitude towards, and stronger infrastructure for, evidence use in the UK than was the case before 1997, even if high-level politics often belie this. The experiences between 1997 and 2010 were especially important in developing ideas and an openness to evidence use. Since then there has been significant additional investment in an evidence infrastructure. There has been growing recognition that evidence use requires multiple changes and complex interventions, rather than one-off initiatives. A next step would be to collect evidence on whether and how these changes in attitudes and infrastructure translate into better use of evidence in policy and practice.

References

Adler, J.R. and Coulson, M. (2016) *The Justice Data Lab synthesis and review of findings*, Department of Psychology, School of Science and Technology, Middlesex University.

Audit Commission (2012) *Local payment by results briefing: payment by results for local services*, London: Audit Commission.

Ball, S.J. (2001) 'You've been NERFed! Dumbing down the academy. National Educational Research Forum "a national strategy – consultation paper": a brief and bilious response', *Journal of Education Policy*, 16 (3), pp 265–8.

Blundell, R., Green, H., Greenberg, D., Lissenburg, S., Morris, S.T., Mittra, B. and Riccio, J. (2003) *The United Kingdom Employment Retention and Advancement demonstration design phase: an evaluation design*, GCSRO Occasional Papers Series No 1, London: Cabinet Office.

Cabinet Office (1999) *Professional policy making for the twenty first century*, London: Cabinet Office, Strategic Policy Making Team.

Cabinet Office (2000a) *Adding it up: improving analysis and modelling in central government*, London: HMSO.

Cabinet Office (2000b) *Trying it out: The role of 'pilots', in policy making: Report of the review of government pilots*, London: Cabinet Office, Government Chief Social Researcher's Office.

Cabinet Office (2011) *Open Public Services White Paper*, Cm 8145, London: HM Government.

Cabinet Office Behavioural Insights Team (2012) *Applying behavioural insights to reduce fraud, error and debt*, London: Cabinet Office.

Cairney, P. (2017) 'Evidence-based best practice is more political than it looks: a case study of the "Scottish Approach"', *Evidence and Policy*, 1 3 (3), pp 499–515.

Civil Service Learning (2013) 'Policy profession skills and knowledge framework', *Civil Service Learning*, January.

Civil Service Learning (2017) *Policy profession standards; a framework for professional development*, Civil Service Learning/Policy Profession, https://civilservicelearning.civilservice.gov.uk/sites/default/files/2016–12–21_policy_profession_standards_v3.3.pdf.

Gibbons, S., McNally, S. and Overman, H. (2013) *Review of government evaluations: a report for the NAO*, London: LSE Enterprise.

Gough, D. and Elbourne, D. (2002) 'Systematic research synthesis to inform policy, practice and democratic debate, *Social Policy and Society*, 1, pp 1–12.

HM Government (2012) *The Civil Service Reform Plan*, London: HM Government.

HM Treasury (2013) *Managing public money*, London: HM Treasury.

HM Treasury (2018) *The Green Book; central government guidance on appraisal and evaluations*, London: The Stationery Office.

Institute for Government (2011) *Policy making in the real world; evidence and analysis*, London: Institute for Government.

John, P. (2013) 'Experimentation, behaviour change and public policy', *The Political Quarterly*, 84(2), pp 238–46.

Kenny, C., Rose, D.C., Hobbs, A., Tyler, C., Blackstock, J. (2017) *The role of research in the UK Parliament volume one*, London: Houses of Parliament.

Mason, T., Whittaker, W., McSweeney, T., Millar, T., Donmall, M., Jones, A. and Pierce, M. (2015) 'The impact of paying treatment providers for outcomes: difference-in-differences analysis of the payment by results the drugs recovery pilot', *Addiction*, 110, pp 1120–28.

Ministry of Justice (2015) *Annex A Interim reconviction figures for Peterborough payment by results pilot*, London: Ministry of Justice Statistics Bulletin, 29 October 2015.

NAO (2003) *Getting the evidence: using research in policy making*, London: National Audit Office.

NAO (2013) *Evaluation in government*, London: National Audit Office.

NAO (2015) *Outcome-based payment schemes: government's use of payment by results*, London: HC 86, Session 2015–16.

Nutley, S.M., Walter, I. and Davies, H.T.O. (2007) *Using evidence: how research can inform public services*, Bristol: Policy Press.

Oliver, S., Clarke-Jones, L., Rees, R., Milne, R., Buchanan, P., Gabbay, J., Gyte, G., Oakley, A. and Stein K. (2004) 'Involving consumers in research and development agenda setting for the NHS: developing an evidence-based approach', *Health Technology Assessment*, 8 (15), pp 1–148.

Rutter, J. (2012) *Evidence and evaluation in policy making. A problem of supply or demand?* London: Institute for Government.

Rutter, J. and Gold, J. (2015) *Show your workings. Assessing how government uses evidence to make policy*, London: Institute for Government.

Sanders, M., Snijders, V. and Hallsworth, M. (2018) 'Behavioural science and policy – where are we now and where are we going?', *Behavioural Public Policy Journal*.

What Works Network (2014) *What works? Evidence for decision makers*, London: Cabinet Office.

What Works Network (2018) *What Works Network: five years on*, London: Cabinet Office.

14

Using evidence in Australia and New Zealand

Brian Head and Michael Di Francesco

Introduction to evidence use in Australia and New Zealand

This chapter examines the growth and the future prospects of evidence-informed approaches to policy making and policy evaluation in Australia and New Zealand. It focuses on an exploration of these concerns at a macro level, examining the rhetoric and actions of government rather than looking more deeply into policy and practice in specific fields of application (for example, healthcare, education and so on). Public leaders and officials in these two countries regularly proclaim their commitment to the use of rigorous evidence in policy decision making and programme review, and so it is worth examining how this rhetoric plays out. But the achievements are uneven and there are many gaps between the rhetoric of evidence utilisation and the realities of policy making (for some of the reasons for this, see the discussion in Chapter Two).

In terms of governmental roles and responsibilities, both countries have a parliamentary system of government, but Australia is a federation, whereas New Zealand is a centralised unitary state. In Australia the national government has responsibility for external relations (for example, trade, defence, immigration) and for social security payments, while the eight state and territory governments have primary responsibility for human services delivery (that is, education, healthcare, justice services and so on). Because of intergovernmental financial transfers and strategy agreements, human services policy has become embroiled in federal/state bargaining.

In New Zealand, key governmental service responsibilities are delivered principally at the central government level, with a range of specific functions provided by two tiers of sub-national government, such as environmental management (run by regional councils) and public transport and municipal services (run by city councils).

Australia and New Zealand were in the forefront of Organisation for Economic Co-operation and Development (OECD) countries that embraced key aspects of the New Public Management (NPM) agenda for policy reform and governmental restructuring in the 1980s and 1990s (Bell and Head, 1994; Boston et al, 1996). A central feature of NPM was the intensive use of performance information, especially for driving the efficient delivery and management of client services (Pollitt and Bouckaert, 2017). Achievement of performance milestones and continuous improvement in service delivery became institutionalised as operating norms. Steered by treasury and finance departments, this emphasis on using performance metrics underpinned priority setting for policy reform, including asset privatisation, the outsourcing of service delivery and tighter social security objectives. Another important theme, although with different accents in each country, was the evaluation of programme effectiveness to improve programme design and the use of new policy instruments.

The NPM reform process also pursued greater contestability in the provision of policy advice. The quasi-monopoly in the provision of expert advice to ministers – traditionally enjoyed by the public (civil) service in Australia and New Zealand up to the 1980s – was challenged within government by ministerial advisors, and externally by the increasing influence of consultancy firms, think-tanks and industry lobby groups (Vromen and Hurley, 2015). Widening the market in policy advice generated new expectations that non-state actors would and could provide evidence-informed arguments in order to participate seriously in policy debates.

Political support for evidence

In 2008 the Australian prime minister announced that his new Labor government – echoing the rhetoric of the Blair government in the UK a decade earlier – saw a strong link between good governance, policy innovation and 'evidence-based policy' (Rudd, 2008). These sentiments were initially well received (Head, 2014), but no clarity emerged as to whether new investments would be needed to strengthen evidence-based policy capability (Productivity Commission, 2010). In practice, these issues were rapidly overtaken by the onset of the global financial crisis later the same year, especially given the need for new and different public investments to counter the looming global recession. Successfully avoiding a severe recession in Australia, the Labor government was later able to refocus on major social reforms, taking a strongly evidence-informed approach.

Following the 2013 election, a conservative government placed greater emphasis on tighter welfare targeting, 'conditional' social security payments and fiscal restraint, but these too needed evidence underpinnings. An increasing focus on programme performance and market contestability – to obtain 'best value' (value for money) and to fund 'what works best' – was underpinned by commitments to gather systematic performance information through specialised governmental bodies (for example, the Australian Institute of Family Studies, established in 1980) and non-state organisations dedicated to data analysis, policy development and issue advocacy (for example, the Australian Council for Education Research, created as far back as 1930). However, in areas characterised by strong values and diverse viewpoints, evidence was often used more to justify than to shape decision making.

In New Zealand, the pattern of recent institutional developments in policy capacity and evidence utilisation materialised as 'paradoxical consequences' of NPM-inspired reforms (Boston and Eichbaum, 2014). The pace and scope of market-based restructuring, made possible by a political system that routinely delivered 'unbridled' executive government, triggered a backlash in the form of a new proportional representation electoral system. Since its introduction in 1996, minority governments, dependent on 'confidence and supply' agreements between major and minor parties, have become commonplace. This has altered the complexion of government – and the policy process – within New Zealand's Westminster system of government. For example, multiparty governments now require more frequent and open interaction between the public service and governing minor parties.

Against this reform background, the government sector in New Zealand has exhibited fluctuating preferences for data and evidence. These correspond with three reform phases and the steady 'correction' of their unintended consequences for public service policy capacity and system performance (Gill, 2011). The first phase – from 1987 to 1996 – put in place systemic underpinnings such as separated policy and delivery functions and the creation of quasi-markets in health and social services. During this phase, administrative performance data, especially on cost and quantity, was prized in the contract-based system. Its nemesis was the Schick Report (Schick, 1996), an independent review highly critical of the system's 'slavish' adherence to disaggregation and prescriptive output specification.

The second phase – between 1996 and 2008 – saw the rollback of NPM reforms in response to Schick. It emphasised a greater focus on outcomes and citizen needs (Advisory Group on the Review of the Centre, 2001). The performance metrics designed for the annual budget process were seen to neglect the effectiveness of, and need for, government-funded services over time. In this phase, new strategic planning processes that mapped outputs to outcomes were instituted, along with efforts to develop public service capacity to apply programme evaluation methodologies.

The third and most recent phase – which coincides with the conservative National Party government of 2008-17 – was characterised by an agenda for cost containment, demonstrable improvement in service outcomes and structural incentives for collaborative working across organisations. Signature whole-of-government initiatives included the Better Public Services (BPS) Results programme, combining new system-level shared accountabilities with a small number of priority policy targets, and a 'social investment approach' to social services that utilises sophisticated data analysis to better correlate high-risk welfare recipients and costs (see Box 14.2 later). Although the BPS policy targets were abandoned abruptly in early 2018 by a newly elected minority Labour Party government, both initiatives are noteworthy for their focus on creating systemic demand for data, analysis and evidence.

Thus, political support for evidence to inform policy has been an enduring theme in both countries, but exactly what is meant by evidence and how that evidence is produced, synthesised and used are being reshaped over time.

The nature of evidence

The policy-making culture in Australia is a mix of pragmatic, ideological and technical streams, reflecting the issue-specific patterns of engagement between the political, managerial and research-oriented sectors. Economic analysis has been central to the national reform agenda and notions of evidence: in accordance with the efficiency and effectiveness agendas of NPM, the capacity to undertake detailed cost modelling of intervention options has been highly prized.

In 1995 the Council of Australian Governments – the peak intergovernmental forum in Australia – commissioned a long-term project, steered by central agencies in all jurisdictions, to publish nationally consistent data on human services in a format allowing comparisons of cost-efficiency across jurisdictions and policy fields (COAG, 2011). This regularly updated information is used widely to improve the understanding and management of public services. In social security, federal agencies have developed extensive databases and strong internal capacity to model the potential impacts of proposed changes in benefits; they also commission specialised analysis from university research centres (such as the National Centre for Social and Economic Modelling) and from the large consultancy firms.

The evidence bases for human services policies are very diverse. Their depth and quality have generally improved, owing to the relative independence of research and reporting bodies. For healthcare and clinical interventions, international models of the 'evidence hierarchy' are well entrenched (see Chapter Eleven) and the Cochrane Collaboration networks are robust. However, there continue to be lively debates about the practical utility of RCTs in a range of related programme areas, and there is increasing support for recognising the value of robust qualitative evidence, especially for the evaluation of community health and social programmes.

As in its neighbour, the institutions and culture of policy-making in New Zealand came of age in the post-war period, with the embrace of Keynesianism and its conviction that economic and social development could be underwritten by technical capacity in the bureaucracy. But the small size of the country has meant that the state sector has played the main role in economic development, and hence in policy-making (Mulgan, 2004). In particular, the public service has traditionally been the pre-eminent source of data and expertise, but with policy capacity either highly concentrated (as in the case of the Treasury) or distributed thinly across many departments and special advisory bodies.

Overall, New Zealand policy workers display similar evidentiary preferences to their counterparts in other Westminster-based systems. When appraising academic research, policy workers place comparable weightings on qualitative (for example, case study) and quantitative (for example, evaluation) research; and when identifying key factors that constrain their use of research, low policy relevance ranks highly: overseas research is largely seen as not applicable to the local context (Lofgren and Cavagnoli, 2015).

However, there are signs that attitudes towards the value of research-based evidence are being reshaped over time. One domain is the meshing of basic research and administrative data analysis in social policy: New Zealand has emerged as a pioneer in applying longitudinal health and social data, particularly through Otago University's globally recognised Dunedin Multidisciplinary Health and Development Study. Established in the early 1970s, this research programme follows a cohort of New Zealanders from birth and has generated a massive range of findings on the prevalence, causes and consequences of health and development problems. It neatly illustrates the change in engagement between researchers and policy makers, one cultivated by the researchers themselves who recognised the data's policy potential (Poulton, Moffitt and Silva, 2015). The use of other longitudinal datasets – such as the Survey of Family Income and Employment – has also increased in the health and housing policy domains, principally through the role played by Statistics New Zealand, the country's independent statistics office.

In both countries, then, there is real interest in exploiting both home-grown research and local administrative datasets. While there is a degree of methodological inclusivity, costing data remain important, as would be expected from an emphasis on efficiency and cost control. Integrating across diverse sources of knowledge remains a challenge.

Structures for the production and synthesis of evidence

In Australia, specialised governmental bodies devoted to systematic data collection, information analysis and the evaluation of policy options have grown in size and capability since the 1970s. Important examples include the Australian Law Reform Commission, the Australian Bureau of Agricultural and Resource Economics, the Productivity Commission (Box 14.1) and the Commonwealth Grants Commission (which provides expert advice on fiscal redistribution across the Australian states and territories).

In terms of building capacity to use evidence for social policy and human services, a very significant feature has been the growing series of government investments in longitudinal research, such as the Household Income and Labour Dynamics survey since 2001, followed by several other important panel studies like the Longitudinal Study of Australian Children from 2004 and the Longitudinal Study of Indigenous Children from 2008. These panel data – and the research studies derived from them – have been heavily used in policy debates and they have been crucial in consolidating an evidence-informed approach.

Performance-oriented assessment exercises have also become attractive to government. In schooling, for example, skills testing is seen as a proxy for measuring the effectiveness of service delivery. However, critics claim that the creation of league tables from the test results has led to shaming rather than learning opportunities (there are parallels here with some of the concerns laid out in Chapter Three).

Inquiry mechanisms have also become an important channel for eliciting and synthesising expert research and stakeholder information. The development of the National Disability Insurance Scheme from 2010, and its staged implementation in 2013–16, for example,

Box 14.1: Evidence-based inquiries: the Australian Productivity Commission

According to the Australian government's semi-autonomous policy advice body (the Productivity Commission), the capacity to undertake evidence-based policy making requires specific practices and institutional conditions (Productivity Commission, 2010). These include: gathering and disseminating accurate and comprehensive data; deploying professional analytical skills in key organisations; and providing political support for the production of evidence-based analysis to advise ministers and to inform public debate. The work programme and methodology of the Productivity Commission are instructive. Its terms of reference for each inquiry are provided by the federal government, but its inquiry process includes seeking submissions on an issues paper, further submissions on a draft report and making a final report to government that sets a framework for governmental policy responses. This provides numerous opportunities to harvest best available evidence from a range of experts and stakeholders in an iterative manner. In the two decades since 1998, when its mandate was expanded to include social and environmental issues (as well as economic and industry issues), the Productivity Commission has undertaken well over 100 inquiries. Significant areas of social and educational policy have included childcare and early learning, disability services reform, health system efficiency, intellectual property, international education services, workforce training, regulation of the gambling industry, the education evidence base and public investment in research.

were put in train by the impact of a formal inquiry (Productivity Commission, 2011). This major reform of disability services required an intergovernmental agreement to ensure nation-wide coverage and sufficient funding. In other cases, public inquiries (such as those by parliamentary committees) and special inquiries (such as Royal Commissions: Prasser and Tracey, 2014) have considered such matters as domestic violence, sexual abuse of children in institutional care, and the incarceration of indigenous youth. The inquiry process typically calls for evidence-informed submissions about problems, trends, causes and solutions, and makes recommendations to the relevant government.

New Zealand's efforts to develop policy research are shaped by a number of contextual features. First, policy capacity is concentrated in a few powerful government agencies and is spread only thinly elsewhere. This has consequences for receptiveness to evidence and the influence of policy advice. Second, research-based policy knowledge outside government is highly fragmented across the not-for-profit sector and universities. Thus, despite the competition-oriented intent of NPM reforms, the notion of a critical-mass 'policy market' remains elusive, with significant gaps in policy domain coverage.

The New Zealand Treasury is widely regarded as the policy powerhouse of government: it is rivalled in numbers only by the giant social service ministries of Social Development and Education (REPA, 2010). However, this policy strength is a relatively recent development. Spurred by New Zealand's precipitous economic decline in the 1970s, the Treasury purposefully transformed itself into an 'internal economic think tank' by recruiting the most able – often US-trained – PhD graduates. There followed a 'rapid diffusion' of institutional economics as the dominant analytical frame for public policy (Christensen, 2017).

Outside the Treasury, the highly dispersed nature of policy capacity in New Zealand public services has been identified as a significant impediment to evidence utilisation (Gluckman, 2013). From a ministerial perspective, departmental policy advice is often not sufficiently proactive in scanning for new approaches and the evidence of their effectiveness. And there are simply too many small advisory units delivering high variability in advice quality. The remedy, as recommended by an influential review (REPA, 2010), included instituting a 'cluster' approach in order to achieve economies of scale and cross-portfolio perspectives. The review also called for 'professionalising policy advice' by creating a 'head of profession', and lifting the overall quality of analysis by strengthening supporting infrastructure, such as the sharing of administrative data, and improving access channels to external research and expertise. This agenda has served as a template for current initiatives to rebuild policy analysis capacity (see below).

The uneven quality of policy capability within the New Zealand public service is matched by the generally 'poor record' of durable government-initiated strategic policy institutions (Scobie, 2010). The New Zealand Institute of Economic Research (established in 1958) is perhaps the exception, being one of the few policy think-tanks to endure, having done so by maintaining strategic partnerships with government departments. A more recent creation is the New Zealand Productivity Commission, established in 2010 as an independent advisory body. Emulating its highly regarded Australian counterpart (see Box 14.1), the New Zealand Productivity Commission uses in-house analysis to conduct inquiries into topics referred by government. Its remit is wide, and recent inquiries have examined social services delivery, tertiary education and housing affordability. In the university sector, the Institute for Governance and Policy Studies at Victoria

University of Wellington (VUW) is perhaps the only example of a broad-based, long-lasting, university-based think-tank in New Zealand (formerly the Institute of Policy Studies, established back in 1983).

Working within these capacity constraints, a recent New Zealand development is the government's use of 'policy working groups' (Christensen, 2017). Endorsed by government, yet formally independent, these university-hosted mechanisms tap both public service and non-government expertise and utilise novel methods, including carefully constructed consultations and evidence-based options development. Several of these working groups have proved influential. For example, the VUW-based Welfare Working Group in 2010–11 provided the analytical impetus for the social investment approach discussed in the next section and in Box 14.2.

Developing the capacity for evidence creation and integration has been an enduring challenge in both countries, and there are concerns that significant headroom remains. But it is in getting policy-relevant evidence *used* that we have seen most innovation.

Key approaches to encouraging and enabling evidence use

The need for detailed analysis of evidence in departmental documents is widely recognised by all players in the policy process, and in both countries. But much of the actual use of evidence for policy and programme development occurs under conditions of confidentiality within government agencies and inside ministerial offices. Fortunately, there are other channels of research-informed policy discussion that are more visible, especially at the intersections between the governmental, research and community sectors.

In Australia, there has been significant growth in recent years in knowledge translation and brokering, and the rise of intermediary organisations to perform these roles. Prominent examples include the Australian Housing and Urban Research Institute, the Australian Research Alliance for Children and Youth, and the Sax Institute for public health research translation. There have also been several changes in research funding arrangements to facilitate collaboration. Some national competitive funding schemes have been designed specifically to require linkages to industry, government and the community sector, in the expectation that joint research agendas and greater research utilisation will emerge (for example, Australian Research Council Linkage grants, Cooperative Research Centre grants). Moreover, Centres of Excellence and research centres have been funded to undertake contract research and address urgent areas of concern, with a mandate for translation and dissemination. The Australia and New Zealand School of Government (ANZSOG), a network school created by national and state governments, promotes evidence-informed research and training and publishes *Evidence Base*, a journal dedicated to systematic reviews of policy interventions.

Australia has also seen recent changes in the incentive structures for academic researchers to develop closer relationships with other sectors, including in government, industry and the community. Universities are now being funded for research 'engagement', measured through the extent of external research funding. Moreover, research quality will now be assessed in terms of 'impacts', alongside traditional peer-review quality (a direction influenced by the UK experience of the REF; see also Chapter Thirteen).

In New Zealand policy making, the period since 2012 has seen a concerted effort to leverage new technologies and institutionalise evidence use. In part, this was permitted by continuity in government that allowed the pursuit of two sets of institutional reforms: the systemic creation and application of evidence to increase its *supply* across government; and whole-of-government structural reforms to build *demand* for evidence and to renew policy capabilities. Alongside this, there is commitment to improve the shared use of social research and administrative data, especially large datasets. Interestingly, while central agencies, particularly the Treasury, play a lead role, there is increasingly a distributed network of expertise.

These reforms do not sit alone. Since 2012 the New Zealand government has been constructing what can be called an 'evidence ecosystem' (Superu, 2016, p 13). The core asset is the Integrated Data Infrastructure (IDI), a longitudinal dataset (housed at Statistics New Zealand) linking economic, education, justice and health data. As the first generation of linked longitudinal data – which permits reuse of information about disadvantaged households and individuals – the dataset has been subjected to intense scrutiny to protect privacy and confidentiality (Giles, 2014). The IDI provides a common data resource to support various analytical activities for policy-making. Two initiatives stand out: the 'social investment' approach to public service provision (see the example set out in Box 14.2); and the Social Policy Evaluation and Research Unit (known as Superu; Box 14.3).

The welfare valuation methodology (as exemplified in Box 14.2) has received a mixed assessment. It has, for instance, been used to identify at-risk (and potentially high-cost) teenage sole parents and to tailor individualised support (such as schooling, training or life-skills supervision), and has also been credited with reducing the projected

Box 14.2: Social investment: using data analysis to link risk factors and problems

The 'social investment approach' is the signature initiative of recent evidence-based policy making in New Zealand. Its origins can be traced to the 2010–11 Welfare Working Group – itself a novel evidentiary mechanism (noted in the main text) – which focused on reducing long-term benefit dependency. Learning from data-modelling practices prevalent in the insurance industry, the working group recommended actuarial assessment to measure the performance of welfare programmes and develop a risk-based assessment tool – the 'Likelihood of Long Term Benefit Receipt' Score. This score was then used as a means of streaming client needs and benefits (Welfare Working Group, 2011). In the context of fiscally sustainable redesign of social services, the then Ministers for Social Development and Finance became joint advocates for 'social investment' as a policy approach.

In 2012 the Ministry of Social Development (MSD) developed ways to predict the likelihood of welfare dependency, and so to identify ways to intervene earlier (that is, 'invest') to improve outcomes for high-cost beneficiaries impacted by multiple high-risk factors (MSD, 2016). One observation, made by the then finance minister (English, 2015), was that

> '[We] know that around 6 per cent of children still spend their whole childhood in benefit-dependent households. This matters because data shows that these children are at very high risk of not achieving at school, become dependent on a benefit themselves and spend time in prison. In fact, there is a group of one per cent of five year olds –that's about 600 children each year – for whom we can expect that ... a quarter will have been in prison by the time they are 35 ... [and] each of these children will cost taxpayers an average of NZ$320,000 by the time they are 35, and some will cost more than a million dollars. And we know this at age five.'

NZ$78 billion (about £40 billion or US$57 billion) social welfare liability (English, 2015). Critics, on the other hand, contend that social investment is first and foremost about removing people from benefits, and is fundamentally flawed because it treats income redistribution solely as a future liability (Chapple, 2013); others claim that it expands data availability, but without incentives to innovate outside of existing services (NZIER, 2016).

To coordinate a system-wide application, the government moved to institutionalise the approach, initially in 2015 by creating a cross-

> ### Box 14.3: The Social Policy Evaluation and Research Unit (Superu)
>
> Superu, an independent New Zealand Crown Entity, was created in 2014 from the Families Commission to broaden that entity's original social research purpose of advocating for the interests of families and whanau (a Maori term for an extended family or community). Superu expands the use of evidence in the social sector by informing public debate on key policy issues and strengthening New Zealand's social research infrastructure to create and use evidence. For example, it conducts programme evaluations, works with other government agencies to distil evidence for policy development and hosts The Hub, a clearing house for all government-funded social research (Superu, 2016).

agency entity – the Social Investment Unit – and in July 2017 by establishing a dedicated Social Investment Agency. The evidence about the impact of social investment is contested (Boston and Gill, 2017), but its experimentation with longitudinal data analytics and policy engagement structures represents a serious effort to embed the type of 'commitment devices' that are said to promote evidence use in long-term policy-making (Boston, 2016).

These 'supply-side' efforts to strengthen evidence availability in New Zealand have been accompanied by whole-of-government reforms to build policy *demand* and to strengthen public service policy capabilities. The best known is the BPS Results Program, initiated in 2012 (Scott and Boyd, 2017). Ten high-priority areas with intractable issues (such as long-term benefit dependency and criminal reoffending) were subject to new collaborative governance arrangements (such as changes to legislation and cabinet structures to enable cross-agency working, and the assignment of service-wide 'functional' leaders). These innovations were complemented by the Policy Project, a system-wide approach to leadership and capability development, including the creation in 2014 of a 'head of policy profession' (Davison, 2016).

Taken together, both Australia and New Zealand have invested considerably not only in the evidence resources to address pressing needs but also in revised structures and processes to encourage application of those evidence resources to policy and practice. Evident in this has been considerable innovation and some diversity of approach (for example, see the contrasting approaches to supporting policy for indigenous peoples, Box 14.4). Learning about the success or otherwise of these innovations, and gleaning insights from the diversity, remain on-going tasks.

Box 14.4: Contrasting evidence approaches to indigenous peoples

The most distinctive policy field in Australia is the provision of services for indigenous citizens. Stemming from a disturbing history of colonial occupation and dispersal of indigenous populations, the cumulative inequalities endured by Indigenous Australians have been profound. Governmental responses to the stark indications of persistent disadvantage culminated in a strategic overview of available evidence in 2003 and identification of seven key areas to target improvements. This led to an intergovernmental commitment to 'close the gap' between indigenous and other Australians, together with a series of new programmes and annual performance reporting (Australian Government, 2016).

Many aspects of these policy initiatives remain controversial and politically contested, largely because indigenous stakeholder knowledge and experience have been seen as less important than bureaucratic expertise (see also the debates in Chapters Eight, Nine and Eleven). Nonetheless, one area of significant achievement has been in indigenous healthcare, with a very promising initiative being the expansion of indigenous-managed primary healthcare facilities. The main explanation for the relative success of this initiative is the importance given to trust-building and self-management. Many of the failed programmes in the past have been designed and delivered 'top down', through external contractors; however, by emphasising indigenous capacity building, there has been a gradual turnaround in health service provision and health outcomes (Lowitja Institute, 2017).

Social policy for indigenous people in New Zealand is a contrast point with Australia. In Aotearoa (the official indigenous name for New Zealand) the relationship between government and Maori is framed by the 1840 Treaty of Waitangi, the Maori version of which guarantees tino rangatiratanga ('absolute sovereignty'). While over time the formation of indigenous social policy has been buffeted by conflict, paternalism and, more latterly, the ill-effects of NPM's market orientation, a range of 'by Maori, for Maori' approaches have progressively shaped social policy and services (Moewake Barnes, 2012, p 156). The latter have been institutionalised in important ways. Entities such as the Waitangi Tribunal (established in 1975 to redress unlawful confiscation of Maori lands) and Te Puni Kokiri (established in 1992 to ensure the adequacy of state sector services to Maori) have provided important and systematic advisory and monitorial roles. Policy development is also increasingly informed by distinct Maori approaches, such as the focus on whanau ('extended family'), which has been embedded in programmes and official guidelines (for example, Whanau Ora, introduced in 2010).

Concluding remarks

The advocates of evidence-informed policy since the 1980s have urged the incorporation of rigorous research evidence into public policy debates, policy advising, processes for public policy evaluation, and actions to improve programmes (Banks, 2009; Head, 2008; 2016; Gluckman, 2013). This review of aspirations and experience in Australia and New Zealand suggests that public agencies in these countries have built relatively high levels of relevant policy skills and institutional stability to support evidence-informed approaches. They have participated actively in OECD reviews and initiatives to strengthen evidence-informed policy improvement. They have supported, at least in principle, the concepts of 'open government' and making government information more accessible to businesses, researchers and citizens.

There are numerous examples of policies and programmes in Australia and New Zealand that are well grounded in evidence supplied from many quarters: community engagement processes, lobby groups, think-tanks, policy inquiries, programme reviews and internal analysis of administrative information concerning performance. The evidence-informed policy movement has been strong in Australia and New Zealand, in part because these countries have continued to invest heavily in health, education and social services, where value-for-money arguments are crucial. Moreover, these governments have also invested in performance information and advisory systems supporting a rigorous approach to policy design and evaluation.

The overall picture, then, is one of considerable investment and innovation, with an equal focus on the application of evidence in reformed policy processes, as in the careful creation and synthesis of evidence addressing relevant policy needs. This is not to suggest that progress has always been smooth, but it is to assert that progress has been made.

References

Advisory Group on the Review of the Centre (2001) *Report of the advisory group on the review of the centre*, Wellington: State Services Commission.

Australian Government (2016) *Closing the gap: prime minister's report*, Canberra: Department of Prime Minister and Cabinet.

Banks, G. (2009) *Evidence-based policy making: what is it? How do we get it?* ANU public lecture series presented by ANZSOG, 4 February, Canberra: Productivity Commission.

Bell, S. and Head, B.W. (eds) (1994) *State, economy and public policy in Australia*, Melbourne: Oxford University Press.

Boston, J. (2016) 'Anticipatory governance: how well is New Zealand safeguarding the future', *Policy Quarterly*, 12 (13), pp 11–24.

Boston, J. and Eichbaum, C. (2014) 'New Zealand's neoliberal reforms: half a revolution', *Governance*, 27 (3), pp 373–6.

Boston, J. and Gill, D. (eds) (2017) *Social investment: A New Zealand policy experiment*, Wellington: Bridget Williams Books.

Boston, J., Martin, J., Pallot, J. and Walsh, P. (1996) *Public management: the New Zealand model*, New York: Oxford University Press.

Chapple, S. (2013) 'Forward liability and welfare reform in New Zealand', *Policy Quarterly*, 9 (2), pp 56–62.

Christensen, J. (2017) *The power of economists within the state,* Stanford, CA: Stanford University Press.

COAG (Council of Australian Governments) (2011) *Intergovernmental agreement on federal financial relations*, Canberra: Council on Federal Financial Relations.

Davison, N. (2016) *Whole-of-government reforms in New Zealand: the case of the Policy Project*, London: Institute for Government.

English, B. (2015) 'Speech to the Treasury guest lecture series on social investment', 17 September.

Giles, P. (2014) *Meeting longitudinal information needs: recommendations for Statistics New Zealand*, Wellington: Statistics New Zealand.

Gill, D. (ed) (2011) *The iron cage revisited: the performance management of state organisations in New Zealand*, Wellington: Institute of Policy Studies.

Gluckman, P. (2013) *The role of evidence in policy formation and implementation: A report from the Prime Minister's Chief Science Advisor*, Auckland: Office of the Prime Minister's Science Advisory Committee.

Head, B.W. (2008) 'Three lenses of evidence-based policy', *Australian Journal of Public Administration*, 67 (1), pp 1–11.

Head, B.W. (2014) 'Public administration and the promise of evidence-based policy: experience in and beyond Australia', *Asia Pacific Journal of Public Administration*, 36 (1), pp 48–59.

Head, B.W. (2016) 'Toward more "evidence-informed" policy-making?', *Public Administration Review*, 76 (3), pp 472–84.

Lofgren, K. and Cavagnoli, D. (2015) 'The policy worker and the professor: understanding how New Zealand policy workers utilise academic research', *Policy Quarterly*, 11 (3), pp 64–72.

Lowitja Institute (2017) *Changing the narrative in Aboriginal and Torres Strait Islander health research*, Melbourne: Lowitja Institute.

Moewake Barnes, H. (2012) 'Better indigenous policies: an Aotearoa New Zealand perspective on the role of evaluation', in Productivity Commission, *Better indigenous policies: the role of evaluation*, Canberra: Productivity Commission, pp 155–81.

MSD (2016) *2015 Benefits system performance report for the year ended 30 June 2015*, Wellington: Ministry of Social Development.

Mulgan, R. (2004) *Politics in New Zealand*, 3rd edn, Auckland: Auckland University Press.

NZIER (New Zealand Institute of Economic Research) (2016) *Defining social investment, Kiwi-style*, NZIER Discussion Paper Working Paper 2016/5, Wellington: NZIER.

Pollitt, C. and Bouckaert, G. (2017) *Public management reform: a comparative analysis – into the age of austerity*, 4th edn, Oxford: Oxford University Press.

Poulton, R., Moffitt, T.E. and Silva, P.A. (2015) 'The Dunedin multidisciplinary health and development study', *Social Psychiatry and Psychiatric Epidemiology*, 50 (5), pp 679–93.

Prasser, S. and Tracey, H. (eds) (2014) *Royal Commissions and public inquiries*, Canberra: Connor Court.

Productivity Commission (2010) *Strengthening evidence-based policy in the Australian federation, Roundtable Proceedings*, Canberra: Productivity Commission.

Productivity Commission (2011) *Disability care and support. Inquiry report*, Canberra: Productivity Commission.

REPA (Review of Expenditure on Policy Advice) (2010) *Improving the value and quality of policy advice: findings of the committee appointed by the government to review expenditure on policy advice*, Wellington: The Treasury.

Rudd, K.R. (2008) 'Prime Minister: Address to heads of agencies and members of senior executive service', 30 April.

Schick, A. (1996) *The spirit of reform: Managing the New Zealand state sector in a time of change*, Wellington: State Services Commission.

Scobie, G. (2010) 'Evidence-based policy: reflections from New Zealand', in Productivity Commission, *Strengthening evidence based policy in the Australian federation, Proceedings*, Canberra: Productivity Commission, Vol 1, pp 169–83.

Scott, R. and Boyd, R. (2017) *Interagency performance targets: a case study of New Zealand's results programme*, Washington, DC: IBM Center for the Business of Government.

Superu (Social Policy Evaluation and Research Unit) (2016) *Annual Report 2015–16*, Wellington: Superu.

Vromen, A. and Hurley, P. (2015) 'Consultants, think tanks and public policy', in B.W. Head and K. Crowley (eds), *Policy analysis in Australia*, Bristol: Policy Press, pp 167–82.

Welfare Working Group (2011) *Long-term welfare dependency: Recommendations*, February, Wellington: Welfare Working Group.

15

Using evidence in Scandinavia

*Anne Mette Møller, Kari Tove Elvbakken
and Hanne Foss Hansen*

Introduction to evidence use in Scandinavia

The use of evidence is a prominent concern in all the Scandinavian countries. Scandinavian observers have described the development as an 'evidence movement' (Hansen and Rieper, 2009) and as 'the fourth wave of evaluation' (Vedung, 2010). Evidence-based policy and practice (EBPP) has also been characterised as a 'master idea' – that is, an idea that has obtained a high degree of prevalence and legitimacy, but one without a great deal of specificity, and so it can be used to argue in favour of often disparate policies and reforms (Røvik and Pettersen, 2014).

This chapter focuses on developments concerning the use of evidence in policy and practice in three countries: Denmark, Norway and Sweden. All three Scandinavian countries are relatively small, social democratic states, with high public spending, elaborate social safety nets, free education and universal healthcare – in combination with free market capitalism. Public services are decentralised, with most services being delivered by local governments.

With regard to developments in EBPP, Sweden has been the frontrunner among the three countries. In Sweden, a health technology assessment (HTA) agency was established in 1987. When the international Cochrane Collaboration was founded in 1992/93, the Swedish agency was one of the early supporters; Danish researchers were also involved, and Denmark became the host of the Nordic Cochrane Centre in 1993. The evidence movement also spread to Norway, and an HTA centre was established there in 1997. Later, the evidence agenda spread to other policy fields, especially social care and education.

Within health and social care, entrepreneurs promoting evidence collaborated closely across the three countries, and with the international Cochrane Collaboration and/or the Campbell Collaboration. This linkage meant that as the production of systematic reviews became institutionalised, so the methodological approach of choice was firmly anchored in ideas of an 'evidence hierarchy' (see Chapter Eleven). This was broadly accepted in healthcare, but highly contested in the field of social care, especially in Denmark and Sweden. When the production and use of evidence later became an equal concern in the field of education, critical voices increased (Moos et al, 2005). In all three countries, debates on the nature of evidence and its relevance and use in policy and practice have led to changes in both the approaches used and the rhetoric of leading actors.

This chapter elaborates on this story by exploring differences in approaches, structures and systems between the three countries. We focus primarily on the fields of health and social care, with some mention of developments in education. We have chosen these fields as they have become highly politicised in Scandinavia, where several decades of neoliberalistic, New Public Management (NPM)-inspired public sector reforms (Hansen, 2011) have confronted the historically strong Nordic welfare model, most especially in Denmark and in Sweden.

In this account of evidence use in Scandinavia we examine first the key forms of knowledge that are seen as providing relevant evidence for policy and practice, before next looking at the organisational structures that are in place to facilitate the production and synthesis of such evidence. Finally we cover the approaches deployed to encourage and enable evidence use in the three countries.

Similarities and differences across countries and policy areas are highlighted throughout the chapter. The chapter is primarily based on findings from national empirical studies of the adoption and institutionalisation of the evidence agenda, as well as on documentary material such as policy documents, reports and guidelines from the evidence-producing organisations. In addition, the authors have all been involved in empirical projects studying institutionalisation processes concerning the production and use of evidence, and have attended several practitioner-focused conferences and seminars over the past decade.

The nature of evidence

In all three countries, the views on which forms and sources of knowledge are seen as providing relevant evidence for policy and practice have been subject to debate and change over time. Much of this debate has focused on synthesis of the 'what works' type of knowledge. When the evidence agenda came to prominence in Scandinavia and spread across policy sectors, linkages to the Cochrane Collaboration, and later the Campbell Collaboration, were very tight. As both collaborations at that time were dedicated to the 'evidence hierarchy', giving priority to research-based evidence and meta-analyses of randomised controlled trials (RCTs), the pioneering organisations in Scandinavia also took this methodological position.

One prominent example was the Nordic Campbell Centre (NC2). NC2 was established in Copenhagen in 2002 as a regional representation of the international Campbell Collaboration, focusing mainly on social policy and practice. The centre had an ambition to unite policy makers, researchers and professionals in all the Nordic countries around evidence, through the production and dissemination of systematic reviews and by the promotion of the ideal (or ideology) of EBPP. However, efforts to promote EBPP were strongly contested, especially by professional associations, first in the field of social care (notably in Denmark and Sweden) and later even more strongly in the field of education (Krejsler, 2013).

The critique of this evidence agenda was based on several arguments (Rieper and Hansen, 2007). First, the number of RCTs of social interventions was (and is) limited and these are mostly carried out outside Scandinavia. Systematic reviews, in particular, were often primarily based on studies conducted in the US. The transferability of the results to a Scandinavian welfare-state context was seen as limited. Second, critics argued that RCTs were both unethical and unfit for the field of social care, due to the context-dependent nature of social problems. Hence, efforts to carry out RCTs faced many practical obstacles. Third, the evidence agenda in general was viewed as managerial and technocratic in nature, signifying an attack on professional autonomy and discretion (see related arguments in Chapter Three). Today, methodological positions on what counts as good evidence in social care are more nuanced, and debates focus more on how to move forward (see also Chapters Five and Eleven).

Given the methodological critiques outlined above, Table 15.1 presents an overview of which forms of knowledge the organisations

Table 15.1: Forms of knowledge given priority in synthesising activities

	Health	Social care
Denmark	RCT research-based evidence. Strength of evidence assessed using GRADE (Sundhedsstyrelsen, 2017).	Transition from RCT research-based approach to a more inclusive approach.
Norway	RCT research-based evidence. Strength of evidence assessed using GRADE (Kunnskapssenteret, 2015).	
Sweden	HTA approach giving priority to RCT research-based designs. Strength of evidence assessed using GRADE (SBU, 2017).	Transition from RCT research-based approach to a multifaceted approach that also includes user experience and professional expertise. Lack of RCTs no longer accepted as a 'knowledge gap'.

that are responsible for producing reviews in health and social care currently include and prioritise in their synthesising activities.

The general picture is that in the field of healthcare evidence from RCTs is still given priority when assessing the effects of interventions. In healthcare, principles and practices for synthesising evidence are very similar across the three countries, and they all refer to the Cochrane Collaboration's guidelines and the GRADE scale (explored further in Chapter Eleven). However, when other types of questions besides the effects of interventions are addressed, there is openness to including other forms of knowledge, including qualitative studies addressing user experiences.

In the field of social care, there has been a transition from an RCT-based approach to a much broader strategy, especially in Denmark and in Sweden. In Sweden, declaring a 'knowledge gap' due simply to a lack of RCTs is no longer accepted, and it is clearly stated in policy documents that user experience and professional expertise also constitute relevant evidence (SOU 2008:18). However, observers note that the transition may be more evident on paper than in practice, as the responsible agency (Swedish Agency for Health Technology Assessment and Assessment of Social Services, SBU) is challenged with handling the increased complexity of its task that follows from a more inclusive approach (Johansson et al, 2015).

In Denmark, the National Board of Social Services published a policy for the production and use of evidence in 2013, which highlighted issues of costs and implementation as well as the effect of interventions (Socialstyrelsen, 2013). Recently, the Danish National Centre for Social Research (SFI) and the National Board of Social Services published a report titled *Promising Practice* (Box 15.1). Here, they argue that there

Box 15.1: Documenting promising practices

'Promising practice' is an initiative based on the realisation that robust research evidence concerning the effects of social care interventions is scarce. The aim of the project has been to develop a tool to assess those practices that are likely to produce good results for the client and for society. The tool assesses the extent to which the practice may be characterised as 'promising', by exploring 11 key elements:

1. Theory and knowledge underpinning the practice;
2. Studies demonstrating likelihood of positive effect;
3. Systematic description (for example, of target groups, activities and goals);
4. Clear and relevant goals;
5. Transferability;
6. Economy (that is, cost-effectiveness);
7. Support of professional reflection;
8. Support of the development of relational competencies among professionals and between professionals and clients;
9. Individual client-focused approach;
10. Monitoring of progress;
11. Evaluation and feedback-informed adjustments.

Source: Based on SFI and Socialstyrelsen, 2016.

is a need to develop a typology for assessing practices in areas where effective evaluations are not possible or have not yet been carried out. With the proper caveats, such practices could be labelled 'promising', even if it was not yet possible to fully document their effects.

Turning to the field of education, conceptualisations of what counts as good evidence have been broad from the beginning. In Scandinavia, there are no experimental traditions in educational research. In addition, linkages to international RCT-based evidence-synthesising organisations are loose. In this case, the evidence-synthesis approach of the EPPI Centre in London seems to have been the model organisation (see Chapter Seven).

Notably, some evidence-producing or disseminating organisations in education and social care seem to have chosen to avoid – or even abandon – the term 'evidence'. Again, explanations are at least twofold. First, some political actors explicitly argue that using the term 'evidence' has proved counter-productive to efforts aimed at encouraging evidence use, as the controversies around it tend to stifle all dialogue. Others argue that, due to methodological disputes, the term 'evidence' is at risk of being watered down: they want to reserve it for those cases where evidence exists in the form of robust RCTs and systematic reviews of these. Box 15.2 illustrates examples of this.

Box 15.2: The evolving terminology around evidence

The following are examples of the different ways in which evidence-producing and disseminating organisations have chosen to respond to criticism of the concept of evidence.

The Swedish Institute for Educational Research has defined the concept of evidence on its website. Here, it says that evidence means 'research-based support – not proof'. So, evidence-informed teaching means that the teacher weaves together the best research-based knowledge with his/her own experienced-based knowledge as well as pupils' views, needs and choices.

The Norwegian Knowledge Centre for Education has chosen not to use the concept of evidence – instead it uses terminology such as 'how knowledge from research meets practitioners' experiences and becomes relevant for educational practice'.

The Danish National Board for Social Services changed its website in 2015. What were previously labelled 'evidence-based methods' are now labelled 'documented methods'. In recent publications and conference invitations, it has used the expression 'knowledge-based' rather than 'evidence-based'.

Structures for the production and synthesis of evidence

All the Scandinavian countries have publicly funded systems in place for the production and synthesis of knowledge, with the emphasis more on the latter than on the former. As we have seen, there are some differences across policy fields – but mostly similarities across countries – regarding concepts of evidence. However, when it comes to the structures for the production and synthesis of evidence, differences across countries and policy fields are large. This goes for both structures and resources, with Table 15.2 providing an overview of the main organisations.

Table 15.2: Structures for the synthesis of knowledge

	Health	Social care	Education
Denmark	Several units at hospitals, most importantly the Nordic Cochrane Centre.	Unit at the Danish National Centre for Social Research (SFI), closely linked to the Campbell Collaboration.	Danish Clearinghouse for Educational Research, located at Aarhus University.
Norway	Norwegian Knowledge Centre merged into the Norwegian Institute of Public Health (NIPH) in 2016. One unit in the Institute produces knowledge syntheses. One section within this unit focuses on social welfare research and hosts the Campbell Collaboration's headquarters. The field of child protection is organised separately in the Norwegian Centre for Child Behavioral Development (NUBU) and regional knowledge centres.		The Knowledge Centre for Education located as a unit in the Research Council of Norway.
Sweden	Swedish Agency for Health Technology Assessment and Assessment of Social Services (SBU).		The Swedish Institute for Educational Research.

In relation to structures, there are separate synthesising organisations in each policy field in Denmark. In Sweden, efforts within health and social care have been organised together since 2015. Norway also has a united structure synthesising evidence within health and social care, but here, since the 1990s, the field of child protection has been organised separately (Vindegg, 2009). In Denmark the synthesising organisations are located at hospitals (healthcare), at a governmental research organisation (social care) and at a university (education), all at arm's length from the relevant ministries. Contrary to this, the organisations in Sweden are public agencies. In Norway, we find both public agencies and organisations more at arm's length.

The number of staff occupied with producing and synthesising evidence differs. At one end of the scale, the Danish Clearinghouse for Educational Research has only one permanent staff member. Other staff members are hired on a project basis and the number of projects is limited. At the other end of the scale, in Norway the Norwegian Institute of Public Health (NIPH) has about 100 staff members working on synthesising activities (but only seven working on social care), and in Sweden the SBU has about 80 staff members. These numbers can be taken to reflect differences between policy fields (with the healthcare sector having substantially more resources, as well as a research tradition that is more 'compatible' with the evidence agenda), as well as differences between the three countries concerning the prevalence of the evidence agenda at the policy level.

Especially in Norway and Sweden, organisational reforms within and around the organisations have been frequent. In Norway, the Knowledge Centre was established in 2004 as a merger of several former units working with evidence and evaluation in the field of healthcare (Malterud et al, 2016). From the beginning, the Centre took up knowledge-producing activities in the field of social care, from 2008 in a separate section. The NUBU (see Table 15.2) dates back to 1999 and started out as a project with the tasks of implementing and evaluating programmes such as Parent Management Training – Oregon and Multisystemic Therapy. In 2003 the project was turned into a centre, Atferdssenteret, and in 2017 into the NUBU (Ogden et al, 2010).

In Sweden, the SBU (see Table 15.2) was specialised within the health field until 2015, when it was expanded to encompass activities within social care. Prior to that, synthesising activities within social care services were organised first in the Centre for Evaluation of Social Services, established 1994 as a counterpart to the SBU (Soydan, 2010; Sundell et al, 2010), and later, from 2004 to 2010, in Sweden's Institute for Evidence-Based Social Work Practice (IMS). In 2010 the IMS was merged into the National Board of Health and Welfare, perhaps because activities developed slowly, even though considerable resources were allocated (Bergmark and Lundstrøm, 2011, p 171).

In Denmark, there has been more organisational stability, but the Danish units are small in terms of resources and depend on unstable project funding. However, the unit at the SFI has undergone several internal reorganisations, and recently, in 2017, the SFI as a whole was merged with the Danish Institute for Local and Regional Government Research (known as KORA) under the common name VIVE – The Danish Center for Social Science Research.

It seems important to note therefore that, apart from the Swedish SBU, the evidence-synthesising organisations are vulnerable both structurally and, in some contexts also, in terms of resource allocation.

Key approaches to encouraging and enabling evidence use

There are interesting differences between the synthesising organisations in relation to which approaches they use to encourage evidence use, including which audiences they address. Whereas the SBU in Sweden primarily addresses professionals working with health and social care in local government, the main target groups for the Norwegian

Knowledge Centre have been ministries and other governmental organisations. Likewise, whereas the Swedish Institute for Educational Research operates in a fashion similar to the SBU, addressing professionals in the educational sector, the Norwegian Knowledge Centre for Education both addresses professionals in the educational sector and provides advice to the ministry.

Differences in approaches and audiences partly reflect variation in the way problems are conceptualised, and partly they reflect organisational variation. For example, the activities in both the SBU and the Swedish Institute for Educational Research seem to be mostly based on the 'research-based practitioner model', where professional education and training are seen as the main factors enabling research use (Nutley et al, 2007, p 205). In contrast, the activities of the Norwegian knowledge centres are to a much larger degree anchored in the 'embedded research model', where responsibility for ensuring research use lies primarily with policy makers and efforts revolve around the development of standards, guidelines and programmes (Nutley et al, 2007, p 210). However, one should be cautious in relation to interpreting this along national lines, because in both countries there are other organisations whose activities reflect other models. In Sweden, for example, the National Board of Health and Welfare works out national guidelines using the evidence syntheses produced by the SBU. Thus, the practice of the Board reflects the embedded research model. In Norway, regional knowledge centres train professionals in child protection in this approach. Thus, activities at the regional centres seem to rely primarily on the research-based practitioner model.

In Denmark, there is a sort of division of labour between the organisations responsible for synthesising research and the agencies responsible for producing guidelines from those syntheses. The fact that guideline producers are closer to government sometimes initiates discussions about whether guidelines are evidence based or perhaps more policy based, or at least policy influenced. An example from healthcare is shown in Box 15.3.

In social care, in both Sweden and Denmark the introduction of the evidence agenda was initially rooted in the embedded research model. In child protection services (especially) this saw the importation of evidence based standardised treatment programmes (often called 'manualised' programmes); these had primarily been developed and tested in the US, and had then taken root in Norway. However, these initiatives were often accompanied by harsh criticism of the apparent non-use of empirical research among front-line social workers. For example, traditional practice was described as 'opinion based' rather than evidence based (Sundell et al, 2010), and this caused considerable dissent and discontent in the field (Krogstrup, 2011; Bergmark et al, 2012).

Box 15.3: Evidence-based or policy-based guidelines?

In the field of healthcare, approaches to encouraging evidence use focus mainly on the production and dissemination of guidelines. In general, there is separation between the organisations producing and synthesising evidence, and those producing the guidelines. For example, the Danish Health Authority has since 2012 been responsible for the development of National Clinical Guidelines, which function as 'evidence-based decision-support tools aimed at clinicians' (Sundhedsstyrelsen, 2017).

However, the fact that these guidelines are drafted by a government agency means that not only evidence but also political considerations may find their way into the guideline recommendations. This was demonstrated in regard to the National Clinical Guidelines for bariatric (weight loss) surgery, where experts from the Cochrane Centre publicly accused the Health Authority of dismissing clear recommendations based on systematic Cochrane reviews. The Cochrane recommendations had stated that people with lower body mass index than those who had previously had access to this type of (publicly funded) surgery might also benefit. Meanwhile, it had long been a political priority to cut public spending on this particular service. Hence, the Health Authority had to navigate opposing concerns in producing its guidelines.

The introduction of guidelines and standardised programmes also ran counter to strong normative ideals of professional discretion, and the conceptualisation of evidence was strongly criticised (as described above). In relation to the evidence-based programmes, many questioned whether these were really compatible with the Scandinavian context in terms of different social-pedagogical traditions. There was also much debate as to whether the evidence base for the programmes was transferable across contexts: since the programmes were developed and evaluated in the US, many doubted that the US 'treatment as usual' was a relevant comparison to 'treatment as usual' in the Scandinavian welfare states, which was perceived to be of a much higher standard.

Despite these cross-country similarities in social care, there are also some significant differences in developments between countries, partly due to differences in governance structures. In Denmark, for example, local government enjoys a high degree of autonomy. As a result, apart from a few frontrunner municipalities that were very much inspired by the widespread use of standardised treatment programmes in Norway and went to Norway to get trained in these, most of the Danish municipalities were reluctant to embrace the evidence agenda. Even by 2017 only around half of municipalities had implemented one or more 'documented methods', as they were then labelled.

Over the years, calls for locally produced, context-sensitive evidence have intensified, especially in Denmark. This has led to a focus on the development of local evaluation capacity and the documentation of 'promising practices' as described above (see Box 15.1). Both strategies are viewed by the National Board of Social Services and other policy actors as necessary antecedents to developing a more rigorous evidence-informed practice in the field of social care. Concurrently, the Ministry of Social Affairs has been developing a national data strategy where the term 'evidence' is increasingly used as synonymous with administrative data (Møller, 2018).

The Swedish government has recently initiated a new national coordination initiative in the continuous effort to promote evidence-based practice. Since 2015 Sweden has aimed at developing a national knowledge-based governance system within the fields of health and social services through the Ministry of Health and Social Affairs (DS 2014:9). Nine authorities are collaborating in this work in the Committee for Knowledge-Based Guidance. The National Board of Health and Welfare directs the work. Further, a group with representatives from national authorities, municipalities and counties, tasked with keeping the Committee informed of knowledge needs, has been established. This development reflects an aim to transform the former top-down knowledge-based governance system into a more distributed, dialogue-based system (Statskontoret, 2016). Future developments in the Norwegian context, after the merging of evidence production into the NIPH, are not yet fully clear, but may parallel some of those noted above.

Following the early focus on evidence-based methods and guidelines, then, the issue of implementation has received increasing attention across several policy fields, including healthcare, social care and education. In Denmark, an Implementation Network was established in 2012 with the aim of bridging research-based knowledge and professional practice. In 2013, the Nordic Implementation Interest Group was established and Linköping University in Sweden hosted the first Nordic Conference on the Implementation of Evidence-Based Practice, which is now a recurring event.

Finally, it is worth noting that non-state actors generally do not play a strong role in promoting either the ideology or practice of evidence use in the Scandinavian countries. In all countries, however, private consultancies do play a major role in carrying out analyses and evaluations, including research syntheses, and often for government agencies, and thus potentially they have an important part to play. In Norway there is strong engagement by professionals in evidence-based practice in the field of nursing and several options for further education in this regard. A Danish Society for Evidence-Based Practice was established in late 2016 by a group of heterogeneous actors, funded by a private foundation. Private foundations are also major funders of both research and intervention programmes in social care and education and could potentially become important players. Time will tell whether they choose to take on a more active and strategic role.

Concluding remarks

To sum up, the analysis of the Scandinavian case concerning what forms of knowledge are seen as providing relevant evidence for policy and practice has uncovered mostly similarities across countries, but differences across policy fields. However, conceptions in the field of social care in Norway seem to be more similar to conceptions in the medical field, as compared to Denmark and Sweden, where more inclusive approaches have developed.

When it comes to the organisation of 'what works' initiatives, we find variety across both countries and fields. When the evidence agenda travelled into Scandinavia, national initiatives were implemented in specific and different contexts in each country. Whereas the Nordic Cochrane Centre in Denmark is a foundation, organisations in Norway and Sweden are public agencies or parts of such, and the same is true for the Danish organisations in education and social care. National public sector reform agendas have influenced organisational development.

Vulnerability, structural as well as resource-wise, seems to be an organisational condition for Scandinavian evidence-producing organisations, although more so in Denmark and Norway than in Sweden. This leads one to question whether this is because research expertise is more highly recognised in Sweden, while often questioned in Denmark, for example; or whether it is instead the result of the more pragmatic culture of the Danish public sector, as compared to the more rationalistic Swedish culture. Teasing out these differences has yet to be achieved.

One can also wonder why the linkages to the Cochrane and Campbell Collaborations have been so important in the Scandinavian countries, as compared to other jurisdictions. Apart from being sources for inspiration, and very relevant in shaping methodological debates, the international networks have been used to seek legitimation for national initiatives. Key Scandinavian actors in national evidence-producing organisations have also played prominent roles in the international networks.

Finally, our analysis has shown that initiatives in Scandinavia are anchored both in the 'embedded research model' and the 'research-based practitioner model' (Nutley et al, 2007). However – apart from in Sweden – there is not much discussion of the models as such. Discussions have instead focused on the term 'evidence', and how narrow or broadly this should be defined (see also arguments in Chapter Eleven). Therefore, it is especially interesting that some of the evidence-producing or knowledge-brokering organisations have chosen to abandon the very term 'evidence' in favour of looser expressions such as 'knowledge' or 'research' (or even 'documented'). In our view, this indicates that the level of controversy that the evidence movement generated in some professional fields and research communities is perhaps now diminishing, signalling a move towards increasing inclusivity and some consensus. How such developments will play out from here is a story we wait to see unfold.

Acknowledgement
The authors would like to thank Professor Verner Denvall, Department of Social Work, Linnæus University, Sweden for his valuable and insightful comments on a draft version of this chapter, especially concerning the Swedish case.

References
Bergmark, A. and Lundstrøm, T. (2011) 'Evidensbaserad praktik i svensk socialt arbete. Om ett programs mottagande, förändring och möjligheter i en ny omgivning', in I. Bohlin and M. Sager (eds), *Evidensens många ansikten,* Lund: Arkiv förlag, pp 163–83.
DS 2014:9 (2014) Regeringskansliet: Socialdepartementet. *En samlad kunskapsstyrning för hälso- och sjukvård och socialtjänst.* Stockholm.
Hansen, H.F. (2011) 'NPM in Scandinavia', in T. Christensen and P. Lægreid (eds), *The Ashgate research companion to new public management,* Farnham: Ashgate Publishing Limited, pp 113–29.

Hansen, H.F. and Rieper, O. (2009) 'The evidence movement: the development and consequences of methodologies in review practices', *Evaluation*, 15 (2), pp 141–63.

Johansson, K., Denval, V. and Vedung, E. (2015) 'After the NPM wave. Evidence-based practice and the vanishing client', *Scandinavian Journal of Public Administration*, 19 (2) pp 69–88.

Krejsler, J.B. (2013) 'What works in education and social welfare? A mapping of the evidence discourse and reflections upon consequences for professionals', *Scandinavian Journal of Educational Research*, 57 (1), pp 16–32.

Krogstrup, H.K. (2011) *Kampen om evidens*, Copenhagen: Hans Reitzels Forlag.

Malterud, K., Bjelland, A.K. and Elvbakken, K.T. (2016) 'Evidence-based medicine – an appropriate tool for evidence-based health policy? A case study from Norway', *Health Research Policy and Systems*, 14, pp 1–9.

Møller, A.M. (2018) 'Organizing knowledge and decision-making in street-level professional practice: a practice-based study of Danish child protective services', PhD thesis. University of Copenhagen.

Moos, L., Krejsler, J., Hjort, K., Laursen, P.F., and Bønløkke Braad, K. (2005) *Evidens i uddannelse?* (1st ed) København: Danmarks Pædagogiske Universitetsforlag.

Nutley, S., Walter, I. and Davies, H.T.O. (2007) *Using evidence. How research can inform public services*, Bristol: Policy Press.

Ogden, T., Kärki, F.U. and Teigen, K.S. (2010) 'Linking research, policy and practice in welfare services and education in Norway', *Evidence and Policy*, 6 (2), pp 161–77.

Rieper, O. and Hansen, H.F. (2007) *Metodedebatten om evidens*. Copenhagen: AKF Forlaget.

Røvik, K.A. and Pettersen, H.M. (2014) 'Masterideer', in K.A. Røvik; T.V. Eilertsen and E.M. Furu (eds), *Reformideer i norsk skole. Spredning, oversettelse og implementering*, Oslo: Cappelen Damm Akademisk, pp 53–86.

SBU (Swedish Agency for Health Technology Assessment and Assessment of Social Services) (2017) *Assessment of methods in health care. A handbook*, Stockholm: SBU.

SFI (Det Nationale Forskningscenter for Velfærd) and Socialstyrelsen (2016) *Lovende praksis på det specialiserede socialområde*, Copenhagen: SFI – Det Nationale Forskningscenter for Velfærd.

Socialstyrelsen (2013) *Viden til gavn – politik for udarbejdelse og anvendelse af evidens*, Odense: Socialstyrelsen.

SOU 2008:18 (2018) *Evidensbaserad praktik inom socialtjänsten – till nytta för brukaren. Betänkande av utredningen för kunskapsbaserad socialtjänst,* Stockholm: Statens Offentliga Utredningar, Socialdepartementet.

Soydan, H. (2010) 'Evidence and policy: the case of social care services in Sweden', *Evidence and Policy,* 6 (2), pp 179–93.

Statskontoret (2016) *Utvärdering av en samlad styrning med kunskap för hälso- och sjukvård og socialtjänst,* Stockholm: Statskontoret.

Sundell, K., Soydan, H., Tengvald, K. and Anttila, S. (2010) From opinion-based to evidence-based social work: the Swedish case, *Research on Social Work Practice,* 20 (6), pp 714–22.

Sundhedsstyrelsen (2017) *Metodehåndbog for udarbejdelse af Nationale Kliniske Retningslinjer for puljeprojekter 2017–2020* Copenhagen: Sundhedsstyrelsen.

Vedung, E. (2010) 'Four waves of evaluation diffusion', *Evaluation,* 16 (3), pp 263–77.

Vindegg, J. (2009) 'Evidensbasert sosialt arbeid', in H. Grimen and I. Terum (eds), *Evidensbasert profesjonsutøvelse,* Oslo: Abstrakt forlag, pp 63–85.

16

Using evidence in Canada

Bev Holmes and Sharon Straus

Introduction to evidence use in Canada

Scientific integrity was a prominent issue in the Canadian federal election of 2015, with incumbent Conservative Party prime minister Stephen Harper being increasingly criticised for appearing to dismiss evidence that did not support his agenda. In the lead-up to the election, Liberal Party leader Justin Trudeau focused on this issue, committing to a number of actions to strengthen evidence-based decision making in Canada. Many believe this played a role in his successful election as prime minister.

Of course, Canada's federal government is not the only, or even the ultimate, authority on evidence production and use within Canada. Provincial, territorial and municipal governments, as well as individual public sector organisations, also hold various policy- and decision-making powers. However, it is the case that the value placed on evidence by the highest level of government – and the ways in which that value is enacted, for example, through funding – is without doubt influential, and it provides an important context for this chapter.

Although evidence – the available body of information indicating whether a proposition is valid – is produced and used in many sectors, in this chapter we draw on our experiences as a clinician/researcher (Straus) and a researcher/funder (Holmes) to focus primarily on Canada's healthcare system. Under this system, which serves a culturally diverse population of 36 million people across a largely rural and remote landscape (apart from a few major cities), all Canadian residents have access to medically necessary services without charge.

Federally, the government sets national standards for the healthcare system and supports healthcare for specific groups (for example, indigenous populations, serving members of the Canadian Forces, inmates of federal penitentiaries and some refugee claimants). The federal government also regulates pharmaceuticals and medical devices, and oversees the Patented Medicines Price Review Board, the Canadian Food Inspection Agency, and the Public Health Agency of Canada. Provincial and territorial governments deliver healthcare through hospitals, community care and public health services, both with their own funding and through federal transfers, across a network of 13 provincial and territorial health insurance plans. These governments partner with, and in some cases fund, a diverse range of non-government care providers and community organisations in an extension of the services offered to citizens. These providers include primary and specialty care physicians, whose payment models vary widely across the country and who are largely independent operators. What exists, then, is a complex tapestry of healthcare policy, healthcare funding, service delivery organisations and service delivery practices. Evidence of various kinds is integral to these multilevel and multiform arrangements.

What follows is an account – necessarily partial and idiosyncratic – that explores views on the nature of evidence in healthcare in Canada, examines the structures for its production and synthesis and describes recent initiatives aimed at enabling greater use. At various points we will draw attention to the shaping role played by federal agencies, but much of the action unfolds in a more distributed manner.

The nature of evidence

Evidence has not, to our knowledge, been defined at the highest federal level. Trudeau's government has followed through on some evidence promises (for example, reinstating the mandatory long-form census that can inform policy making; appointing a chief science advisor; commissioning a fundamental science review (Investing in Canada's Future, 2017) and has taken criticism for not acting on others (particularly those related to the environment). But in politics, and in general perhaps, it seems that the word 'evidence' does not need defining. It appears to speak for itself as a positive thing: unbiased, objective, untainted by ideology. Yet, as the debates in this book show (see, especially, Chapters Two and Eleven), there are significant doubts as to whether truly independent, value-free evidence is ever possible, or even desirable.

Historically, healthcare in Canada has been seen as somewhat disconnected from research (Barnes et al, 2015), at least outside of academic teaching hospitals. Research has been viewed by some as a costly and even unethical diversion from patient care; initiatives to improve care are often referred to as quality improvement or evaluation, as opposed to research; and many are undertaken in local clinical settings without adequate control or comparison sites. This often frustrates researchers, who see missed opportunities to improve care at a system level, looking across programmes and jurisdictions.

The separation of evidence from what it is meant to improve has spawned a major effort in Canada aimed at closing the 'know–do gap'. The term predominantly used in health in Canada for actions aimed at closing this gap is *knowledge translation*, whereas the natural sciences and engineering disciplines tend to favour ideas of *innovation*, and the social science and humanities use *knowledge exchange* (Box 16.1). More recently, a number of sectors in Canada seem to have adopted the term *knowledge mobilisation*. A further trend is that many major granting councils for health-related research no longer feature dedicated sections on knowledge translation (whatever the terminology deployed), but instead are asking for more integration of these activities throughout funded projects (see below). Sometimes regardless of, and sometimes driven by, the debates on terminology, there have been productive and evolving conversations since the late 1990s within all sectors in Canada about what counts as evidence; what types of evidence are needed and when; and how and by whom evidence should be generated and applied.

In healthcare, for example, the evidence-based medicine (EBM) movement has featured prominently, and Canadian voices such as Gordon Guyatt, David Sackett, Deborah Cook, Jonathan Lomas and David Davis were important in driving this agenda (see also discussion in Chapter Four). The importance of evidence generated from robust research studies (focused on clinical epidemiology and health services

Box 16.1: Federal granting agencies in Canada

Canada has three federal granting agencies: the Natural Sciences and Engineering Research Council, the Canadian Institutes of Health Research and the Social Sciences and Humanities Research Council. These agencies support research in a wide variety of disciplines and areas. They tend to use different terminology for the 'know-do gap': in science and engineering, much of the discourse is around ideas of *innovation*; in health research, the talk is often of *knowledge translation*; and in the social sciences and humanities, more common is the use of ideas around *knowledge exchange*. The term *knowledge mobilisation* is also gaining currency across sectors.

research) became widely acknowledged, although this often emphasised experimental trials (see Chapters Four and Eleven). Further work highlighted gaps in knowledge on how to change physician behaviour (Davis et al, 1995) and catalysed important efforts around continuing professional development. Others were exploring how to bring into the dialogue a broader range of stakeholders, as reflected in the establishment of the Canadian Health Services Research Foundation in the 1990s, led by Jonathan Lomas. The Foundation promoted collaborations between researchers and research users of various types, establishing the concept of 'linkage and exchange' (Lomas, 2000) – a more dynamic set of relationship-based processes between sources of evidence and places of use. The literature and practice on evidence use at the organisational and health system levels also evolved, moving beyond a focus on stakeholders in isolation to consider more fully the context(s) in which they operate (Ellen et al, 2013).

In areas such as population health and the social determinants of health, evidence had always been seen as more multifaceted, perhaps due to the broad social and political situations in which it was produced and used (Petticrew and Roberts, 2003). Decades-old traditions, such as community-based and participatory action-oriented inquiry, largely evolved separately from biomedical and clinical research, with their more circumscribed definitions of evidence: much as the efforts in health and other sectors such as the environment, justice and education systems remain separate in Canada today. In our view, however, the health evidence movement came together to a great extent around 2000, with the establishment of the federal funding agency the Canadian Institutes of Health Research (CIHR). The CIHR created a stand-alone portfolio for knowledge translation (KT) and distinguished between end-of-grant and integrated KT (iKT) – the latter drawing on participatory action-research principles to engage research users throughout a project (see later). This approach ensured relevance across the four pillars of health-related research: clinical, health services and policy, and population health, as discussed above, and also biomedical research (which seeks to understand human functioning at the molecular, cellular and organ system levels). Through this integration, efforts to increase evidence use have moved beyond mere dissemination through journal publications and commercialisation, to more interactive and inclusive sharing and discussion of results with the public through, for example, Cafés Scientifique (informal debates about science in café settings) and via various social media strategies.

CIHR is not the final authority on evidence use in Canada. However, it is the country's major funder of health research, with an annual budget (in 2018) of approximately one billion Canadian dollars (about £600 million or US$800 million). With a mandate to create new scientific knowledge across the spectrum of health research and enable its translation into improved health, the organisation must respond to the health evidence needs of Canadian society. By virtue of this role and its considerable financial influence, CIHR has furthered the sharing of KT strategies among a diverse range of evidence producers and users – many working in this area long before CIHR was established – who are now learning from each other and are collectively advancing knowledge about 'what works in KT' as well as 'what works' for health improvement.

Despite progress on evidence production and use in healthcare, there are several areas that need to advance further. For example, although recent work on learning health systems has been welcome (Reid, 2016), there remains too much simplistic thinking about how evidence moves into practice (Holmes et al, 2016). This may be related to unrealistic expectations of impact held by some stakeholders, including some funders and researchers, but also healthcare decision makers and even the public. Although work is underway nationally on common measures for advancing and applying knowledge, researchers are under great pressure to demonstrate results more quickly than is typically feasible. It seems perhaps that Canada's progressive ideas about evidence are not matched by realism about what it takes to produce and use high-quality evidence, nor how to scale and sustain that use.

Another area for advancement is how best to be guided by patients, public and community groups in the development of evidence important to them (Holmes et al, 2018). A patient-oriented research movement and increasing respect and support for Indigenous ways of knowing are steps in the right direction (ideas explored in other chapters, especially Chapters Eight and Nine). In particular, there is now much focus on Indigenous ways of knowing, following the 2015 Truth and Reconciliation Commission that reported on the legacy of residential schools (Truth and Reconciliation Commission of Canada, 2015; Box 16.2). Despite these advances, however, areas outside the traditional academic research culture are often expected to fit into the dominant scientific paradigm, as opposed to being seen as legitimate and credible in their own right (Boivin et al, 2014).

Finally, debates about the nature of evidence are inseparable from the environment in which they take place (see Chapter Eleven). As we write, with healthcare costs on the increase, there are more calls for commissioned research on specific topics. At the same time, the federal government-commissioned science review mentioned above

Box 16.2: Bringing Indigenous voices into the research process

The Indian Residential Schools Settlement Agreement, the largest class action settlement in Canadian history, began implementation in 2007. It aimed to recognise the harms inflicted on native Canadians who had been enrolled as children in the Canadian Indian Residential School system. Former students of the residential schools decided to settle out of court with the federal government and four national churches. The launch of a Truth and Reconciliation Commission (TRC) was part of the terms of settlement: the former students wanted to ensure that their stories were not lost by settling out of court. The commission's mandate was to gather the written and oral history of residential schools and to work toward reconciliation between former students and the rest of Canada.

The TRC spent six years travelling to all parts of Canada, and in 2015 presented findings in a multi-volume report. Many organisations are responding to the report's 94 'calls-to-action' in partnership with Indigenous groups. For example, CIHR's Institute of Indigenous Peoples' Health is supporting Indigenous peoples and communities to share their traditions with researchers through study designs; implementation and evaluation of policies and interventions; and coordinated efforts of health and non-health partners in remote, rural and urban communities.

– which covers sectors beyond health – advocates for more funding for researcher-driven projects. Therein lies a tension not unique to Canada: that of balancing the need for research relevant to urgent and emerging issues (thus prioritised by policy makers) with researcher-led, curiosity-driven research whose impacts are harder to quantify in advance and likely much further away. The question currently, then, is less about the nature of evidence and more about what evidence is most important, and how and by whom it should be produced.

Structures for the production and synthesis of evidence

Because of Canada's complex federal and provincial structure, research evidence is needed to inform practice and policy at multiple levels. Some of this analytic work takes place within these levels of government itself, where researchers and policy analysts conduct primary and secondary studies. However, federal and provincial governments also work with external agencies, some of them purpose-built. With regard to health, there is the Canadian Task Force on Preventive Health Care, whose approach involves researchers in two provinces who conduct systematic reviews to inform guidelines developed by a national panel. Similarly, the Canadian Agency for Drugs and Technology in Health was created in 1989 by both levels of government to provide evidence about drugs, diagnostic tests and devices. There are many research production and synthesis agencies external to the government and broader than health that declare themselves non-partisan but are often at odds with each other in terms of their views on evidence. For example, the national Fraser Institute, which produces research on taxation, healthcare, Indigenous issues and education (among others) is seen as more conservative than the Canadian Centre for Policy Alternatives, despite an overlap in domains of research interest.

Most provinces and territories create specific agencies to meet their additional evidence needs. For example, in each province and territory cancer care is typically provided by an agency that may also conduct primary and secondary research. Many health authorities and healthcare organisations also have their own research institutes, some in partnership with universities, and these increasingly focus on evidence use as well as production.

Largely outside the formal healthcare system, and focused on a broad range of research, are the national and provincial funding agencies and universities. At the national level, the federal minister of health is responsible for CIHR, discussed in the previous section. CIHR has offered various funding programmes related to evidence use since 2000, although some have been terminated as the agency shifts priorities in response to budget constraints. Funding agencies exist in most provinces, primarily funded by these local governments. These range from solely health-focused agencies to those supporting a wider range of research. Finally, universities are of course the major generators of health research activity across the country and are increasingly important as funders: in 2015 almost 50% of higher education expenditure on research and development in Canada was funded by universities and colleges themselves and only 23% was funded by the federal government – a highly anomalous situation internationally (Investing in Canada's Future, 2017).

The above description, while demonstrating the breadth and depth of Canada's evidence-production infrastructure, also points to some failings: while there is a lot of activity, there is much disconnection and duplication. One approach to streamlining evidence production and synthesis in health would be a pan-Canadian strategy aimed at answering research questions for federal and provincial/territorial policy makers in a timely fashion using advanced methods. In that sense, a national guideline enterprise such as NICE in the UK would be useful (see Chapter Four), with an additional focus on work to inform contextualised use of evidence across Canada. Harmonised approaches to data collection and use would also alleviate many challenges: a 2015 Council of Canadian Academies' report on access to health and social data for research (Council of Canadian Academies, 2015) found large variation across the country. While strategies specific to guidelines development and data access would be helpful, they would likely not be fully effective without an overall coordinated science policy at all provincial and territorial levels, which is currently lacking. Commenting on this gap, the Council of Canadian Academies (2015) is unequivocal about the benefits of science policy: it increases transparency, clarifies resource distribution and both leverages and complements federal support for science.

There is much yet to be done, then, before Canada can be said to have a fully coherent approach to the production and synthesis of evidence, even in the singular field of healthcare and public health policy and practice. Meantime, in parallel to the developments outlined above, the challenges of encouraging and enabling research use have also received sustained attention.

Key approaches to encouraging and enabling evidence use

Not all are comfortable embracing multiple views of evidence, and many reject the need for a distinct focus on evidence use. Indeed, even those involved in applied health research are debating the relative merits of knowledge translation as a stand-alone or as a fully integrated enterprise (Greenhalgh and Wieringa, 2011). Regardless of these debates, the focus on evidence use in Canada since the late 1990s has been valuable, generating activity that will help to increase the impact of health research for citizens' benefit in the future. Here we briefly comment on three on-going areas of activity: using evidence; measuring evidence use; and supporting evidence use. Again, we focus primarily on the healthcare arena.

Using evidence

Efforts to date on health research evidence use in Canada have generated a much greater respect for different types of knowledge: there is now much more awareness of the importance of including diverse types of knowledge (see Chapter Eleven). This goes further than just a methodological inclusiveness, to a growing recognition that other sources of knowledge and expertise are important: clinicians, policy makers, patients, the public and specific cultural, regional or other sub-populations (see Box 16.2).

The field of iKT, a growing area of practice and research in Canada, embodies this respect for various types of knowledge. Sometimes called co-production or co-creation, iKT draws on older traditions originating in disciplines other than health research, but with aligned principles (such as action research, appreciative enquiry and engaged scholarship). iKT is a model of collaborative research, then, where researchers work with research users (perhaps policy makers, healthcare managers or front-line practitioners) who identify a problem and have the authority to implement the research recommendations. The research itself involves a collaborative effort between those with methodological expertise and those affected by the research implications (Kothari et al, 2017).

Canada is also seeing increasing interest in patients' knowledge through engaging patients as active partners in health research (Holmes et al, 2018). A major initiative in this area is Canada's Strategy for Patient-Oriented Research (SPOR), which defines patient engagement as meaningful and active collaboration in research governance, priority setting, conduct and knowledge translation. SPOR is a federal and provincial/territorial partnership and so has very wide reach. One element of this initiative is Support for People and Patient-Oriented Research and Trials Units. Ten of these units across Canada provide services to individuals and teams doing research that involves patient engagement. In this way we are beginning to see some institutional embedding of the priority now being given to more diverse voices in the research process.

Measuring evidence use

Measuring evidence use has always been challenging, in part due to the time it takes to realise the benefits of research and the lack of availability of comprehensive, accurate and timely data for its measurement (see also Chapter Twelve). It may be especially difficult in health services, policy and population health research, given the number of factors that inform and affect decision making, and the complexity of the underlying issues.

Although work has been underway for years on health research impact measurement, our view is that too much focus has been placed on demonstrating the impact of individual researchers and organisations, usually in support of funding requests. Rather than being critical of these stakeholders, we recognise that they are working in a system that rewards competition rather than collaboration: demonstrating individual impact is important to academic survival in the current paradigm.

Fortunately, however, the movement that has increased respect for different types of knowledge (as described above) has also highlighted important differences between demonstrating the impact of health research for reputational, marketing and social media purposes and understanding impact so that we can achieve more. In turn, it has catalysed collective work across the country on indicators and metrics to measure health research use and assess the diversity of impacts. Categories in which these are being developed – from a framework developed by Canadian Academy of Health Sciences (CAHS, 2009) – include: capacity building; advancing knowledge; informing decision making; health impacts; and broader social and economic impacts.

Thus, although researchers and organisations will always need to promote their own work, we are hopeful that the debates outlined so far in this chapter will further societal awareness and understanding of the complexities of using evidence in practice and policy.

Supporting evidence use

The use of evidence – especially evidence aimed at changing individual, organisational and system behaviour – requires many kinds of support. Funding agencies are one obvious group to provide some of this support, and many are adapting their programmes with evidence use in mind (Holmes et al, 2014). Grant competitions have changed dramatically since the early 2000s based on learning from early attempts to encourage evidence use and to support co-produced research.

Most funders now recognise that expecting all researchers to translate the evidence they generate is neither feasible nor helpful, and that evidence use is not guaranteed by simply requiring co-application by a researcher and research user. Acknowledging that complex health issues require a team approach (Council of Canadian Academies, 2017), including researchers from different disciplines as well as research users, funders are designing more appropriate types of grants that in turn demand new ways of thinking about application processes and review criteria. Grant-assessment processes, which historically have been based on narrow views of excellence (Scarrow et al, 2017), are undergoing reform in many agencies, with the inclusion of research users on peer review panels. Finally, many funders have identified the critical need to build capacity in both the practice and science of evidence use (Straus et al, 2011), through training, and also through specific research funding to advance knowledge about knowledge use.

Of course, funding agencies are only one piece of a complex system that involves many other influential individuals and organisations. Increasingly, conversations are taking place across the country about the need to collectively support evidence use through a range of actions beyond single initiatives. A few of the issues to address, going forward, include aligning mismatched incentives, changing restrictive policies and building leadership capabilities. Leaders and members of academic centres, government ministries, professional organisations, charities and community groups have all, to some extent, joined the effort to maximise evidence use in Canada, but there is still considerable work to be done.

Concluding remarks

Much of what is presented in this chapter is not unique to Canada, including the evolution of how evidence is framed, the opportunities and challenges that new framings present and the associated institutional responses across the many layers of policy and practice. However, Canada has been at the forefront of a number of developments. These include: the development of the global EBM movement seeded from McMaster University (see also Chapter Four); the creation of novel methods to synthesise, package and deliver evidence; the advancement of the science and practice of knowledge translation and exchange; and a growing recognition of the need to understand complex systems for evidence-informed public health and healthcare improvement.

Despite these developments, there are still challenges when it comes to evidence production and use in Canada. The causes and the symptoms of these challenges, many noted in this chapter, are myriad and difficult to disentangle. They include uncertainty and over-competition among the research community; a serious lack of funding, leading to a decline in grant funding per researcher since 2008 (Investing in Canada's Future, 2017); differences of opinion on what types of evidence are most important; and an unfortunate and insupportable duplication of effort across provinces and territories. At the time of writing, we are hopeful that the renewed interest in evidence on the part of our federal government – that will ideally last long beyond the tenure of one administration – will lead to increased funding for research and research use, as well as incentives for provinces and territories to better coordinate these important activities. Finally, we hope that the Canadian public's high level of support for health research (Canada Speaks, 2015) will lead to its increased understanding, involvement and calls for accountability by the federal government and others involved in Canada's research enterprise.

References

Barnes, R.O., Holmes, B.J., Lindstrom, R.T., Trytten, C. and Wale, M.J.C. (2015) 'Evidence-informed healthcare through integration of health research', *Healthcare Management Forum*, 28, p 2.

Boivin, A., Lehoux, P., Burgers, J. and Grol, R. (2014) 'What are the key ingredients for effective public involvement in health care improvement and policy decisions? A randomized trial process evaluation', *The Milbank Quarterly*, 92 (2), pp 319–50.

Canada Speaks (2015) 'A national public opinion poll on health and medical research', https://rc-rc.ca/6206-2/

CAHS (Canadian Academy of Health Sciences) (2009) 'Panel on return on investment in health research. Making an impact, a preferred framework and indicators to measure returns on investment in health research', https://www.cahs-acss.ca/wp-content/uploads/2011/09/ROI_FullReport.pdf

Council of Canadian Academies (2015) Accessing health and health-related data in Canada, Ottawa (ON): The Expert Panel on Timely Access to Health and Social Data for Health Research and Health, Council of Canadian Academies.

Council of Canadian Academies (2017) *Science Policy: Considerations for Subnational Governments*, https://www.scienceadvice.ca/wp-content/uploads/2018/08/subnatlscipol_fullreport_en.pdf.

Davis, D.A. et al (1995) 'Changing physician performance – a systematic review of the effect of continuing medical education strategies', *JAMA*, 274 (9), pp 700–705.

Ellen, M.E. et al (2013) 'What supports do health system organizations have in place to facilitate evidence-informed decision-making? A qualitative study', *Implementation Science*, 8 (1), p 84.

Greenhalgh, T. and Wieringa, S. (2011) 'Is it time to drop the "knowledge translation" metaphor? A critical literature review', *Journal of the Royal Society of Medicine*, 104 (12), pp 501–09.

Holmes, B.J., Schellenberg, M., Schell, K. and Scarrow, G. (2014) 'How funding agencies can support research use in healthcare: an online province-wide survey to determine knowledge translation training needs', *Implementation Science*, 9, p 71.

Holmes, B.J., Best, A., Davies, H., Hunter, D., Kelly, M., Marshall, M. and Rycroft-Malone, J. (2016) 'Mobilising knowledge in complex health systems: a call to action', *Evidence & Policy*, 13 (3), pp 539–60.

Holmes, B.J., Bryan, S., Ho, K. and McGavin, C. (2018) 'Engaging patients as partners in health research: lessons from BC, Canada', *Healthcare Management Forum*, 31(2), pp 41–4.

Investing in Canada's Future: Strengthening the Foundations of Canadian Research. Canada's Fundamental Science Review (2017) Government of Canada.

Kothari, A., McCutcheon, C. and Graham, I.D. (2017) 'Defining integrated knowledge translation and moving forward: a response to recent commentaries', *International Journal of Health Policy and Management*, 6 (5), pp 299.

Lomas, J. (2000) 'Using "linkage and exchange" to move research into policy at a Canadian foundation, encouraging partnerships between researchers and policymakers is the goal of a promising new Canadian initiative. *Health Affairs*, 19 p 3.

Petticrew, M. and Roberts, H. (2003) 'Evidence, hierarchies, and typologies: horses for courses', *Journal of Epidemiology and Community Health*, 57, pp 527–9.

Reid, R.J. (2016) 'Embedding research in the learning health system', *Healthcare Papers*, 16, 30–35.

Scarrow, G., Angus, D. and Holmes, B.J. (2017) 'Reviewer training to assess knowledge translation in funding applications is long overdue', *Research Integrity and Peer Review*, 2, p 13.

Straus, S.E. et al (2011) 'KT Canada Strategic Training Initiative in Health Research (STIHR). Core competencies in the science and practice of knowledge translation: description of a Canadian strategic training initiative', *Implementation Science*, 9 (6), p 127.

Truth and Reconciliation Commission of Canada (2015) *Calls to Action*, Ottawa: Government of Canada.

17

Using evidence
in the US

Vivian Tseng and Cynthia Coburn

Introduction to evidence use in the US

Research-based evidence has an important role to play in many sectors in the US, including healthcare, mental health, child welfare, employment, environmental management and criminal justice. However, it is in education that many of the evidence debates are sharpest. In this chapter we focus on the use of evidence to shape public education in the US.

In many ways, we are at an inflection point in the use of evidence in US education. Since the early 2000s the 'what works' agenda (more often capitalised as What Works) has been the dominant framework for driving the use of research and data in education policy making. Unlike in most countries, the agenda has been characterised by a strikingly narrow focus on evidence of the impact of interventions (that is, did it work?), and has neglected a broader set of concerns including the need for interventions and wider system issues. In contrast, the evidence-based education agenda in the UK (see Chapters Seven and Thirteen) has focused on a wider range of issues, such as addressing cost and implementation concerns, as well as seeking to engage teachers and school leaders at all stages of research development, synthesis and use.

In this chapter, we take stock of where we are in the what works agenda in the US, and provide some reflections on future developments if our goal is to create more research-informed education policy. Although the narrow agenda since the early 2000s has left an indelible footprint, other developments have risen to the fore in national conversations: developments in the learning sciences (a new subfield at the intersection of learning and cognition), alongside broader insights from the continuous improvement movement and from studies of research use. As these various streams of work come together, the possibility emerges of building more robust mechanisms and infrastructure for producing and using research evidence to address a range of pressing problems of practice and policy, and to do so in ways that promote local ownership. This melding of influences also raises the potential for evidence-building and evidence-use efforts to be more collaborative – bringing research, practice and policy communities into closer alignment around a shared goal of educational improvement.

In what follows, we explore the evolving debates about what counts as evidence, how such evidence is produced and synthesised and which strategies are showing promise for encouraging and enabling more ready use of evidence.

The nature of evidence

What counts as evidence in US education has been hotly contested, but definitions built into federal policy have had a strong influence. Soon after the turn of the millennium, two major pieces of federal legislation shaped the debate about what constituted evidence, and created the influential Institute of Education Sciences (IES).

The No Child Left Behind (NCLB) Act

The NCLB Act (2001) ushered in a new era for the use of research and data in US education. More than ever, data and research were elevated as key levers for educational improvement (Honig and Coburn, 2008). Schools and districts would be held accountable for student- and school-level performance on standardised tests in reading and math. Furthermore, weighty stakes would be attached to schools' performance: failure to meet performance targets would result in an escalating series of sanctions, from being placed on a watch-list to wholesale restructuring of schools.

In the NCLB Act, Congress introduced the term *scientifically based research*, defining it as 'research that involves the application of rigorous, systematic, and objective procedures to obtain reliable and valid knowledge relevant to education activities and programs'. Although the definition included 'methods that draw on observation or experiment', the law also called out a preference for random-assignment experiments. Thus, not only were legislators defining what constituted rigorous research, but they were also singling out a particular research design (see Chapter Eleven for a broader account of what counts as evidence). In addition, the Act linked the use of federal funds to the selection of programmes that were 'scientifically based'. Reading First (Box 17.1), a competitive state grant programme intended to assist low-income, low-performing schools in raising reading achievement, was an early example of this linkage. So potent were this legislation and the administrative actions that followed that in subsequent years the term 'evidence' would become synonymous with RCTs in some education policy and practice circles.

In the NCLB era, the what works agenda was grafted onto a top-down accountability framework. This most recent push for accountability, as in past versions, was characterised by a drive towards centralisation, standardisation and control as the rational means for bringing order, effectiveness and efficiency to the 'soft and undisciplined field' of education (Mehta, 2013, p 5). Data and research evidence were seen as key tools to accomplish these aims.

The Education Sciences Reform Act and the Institute of Education Sciences

In short order, Congress also passed the Education Sciences Reform Act (ESRA) of 2002, signed into law by President George W. Bush. As with NCLB, evidence-based policy advocates found much to celebrate, and President Bush described ESRA as 'an important complement' to NCLB that would 'substantially strengthen the scientific basis' of classroom teaching (Rudalevige, 2009). The Act also created the Institute of Education Sciences (IES), a research arm

Box 17.1: The Reading First programme

The Reading First programme was part of the NCLB Act. It was a leading example of the promotion of programmes identified as research based. To receive funds under this programme, states had to develop plans for increasing teachers' use of scientifically based instructional approaches by adopting scientifically based curricular materials. Reading First invested heavily in monitoring teachers' use of these materials and approaches, requiring that states provide guidance for teachers and monitor their practice to ensure fidelity of implementation. Teachers in many states experienced this approach as an assault on their professional judgement, leading to resistance (Achinstein and Ogawa, 2006; Kersten, 2006; Kersten and Pardo, 2007). There were also widespread complaints about the 'Open Court police' – those who monitored the implementation of a widely adopted programme in support of Reading First called Open Court. The approach to scientifically based research in Reading First was particularly intense, but similar approaches were built into a range of federal policies.

of the Department of Education, which was to become influential in shaping what counted as robust research in US education.

While the ESRA legislation left room for research priorities 'focused on understanding and solving particular education problems and issues', the IES evolved to concentrate on evaluation questions (ESRA, 2002, s115(a)), and RCTs were heralded as the 'gold standard' for assessing intervention impacts. While it is not entirely clear why what works evidence gained such prominence, one potent influence came from medicine (Haskins and Margolis, 2015). A common narrative among evidence-based policy advocates was that the widespread use of experiments was what enabled medicine to become an evidence-based field, and, if other fields were to become evidence-based, then they too should embrace experimental methods. Like analogous agencies in human services, justice and labour, the IES's focus on what works questions and RCTs was codified in agency funding priorities and programmes. For example, the IES structured its funding scheme as staged models that resembled the phases of clinical drug trials. The first step involved exploratory research; in the second stage, the findings would be used to develop interventions to improve student outcomes; and subsequent stages then tested the efficacy and effectiveness of the interventions in increasingly larger experimental trials, in more sites and under less controlled conditions.

Structures for the production and synthesis of evidence

In support of this emphasis on a particular type of research question and the associated research design, the IES championed focused capacity building. It provided large-scale investments in training pre- and post-doctoral students to conduct RCTs. Moreover, the agency launched the What Works Clearinghouse, a web-based repository to synthesise and report evidence on the effectiveness of educational interventions. Other government agencies also developed clearinghouses, including: the Department of Justice (Crime Solutions); the Substance Abuse and Mental Health Services Administration (National Registry of Evidence-based Programs and Practices); the Office of Juvenile Justice and Delinquency Prevention (Blueprints for Violence Prevention); and the California Clearinghouse for Evidence-Based Practice in Child Welfare. The IES's work was a leader in a nation-wide effort to document and promote experimentally 'proven' interventions.

Professional associations also supported this movement. The Society for Research on Educational Effectiveness (SREE) and its *Journal of Research on Educational Effectiveness* were established to further the cause of more rigorous (read: experimental) evaluations in education. The Society for Prevention Research – a professional association of researchers 'committed to identifying and disseminating the most effective ways of preventing problems of human behavior' – established standards of evidence for identifying interventions that fit the stages of *efficacy*, *effectiveness* and *dissemination* (Flay et al, 2005: p 152) and, for a time, conference presentations were organised by these stages at the organisation's meetings.

Given the intensely partisan politics in the US, it is significant that the what works agenda enjoyed considerable support in both the Republican Bush administration and the subsequent Democratic Obama administration. Under Bush, the Office of Management and Budget (OMB) created the Program Assessment Rating Tool (PART; Box 17.2) and required that federal agencies use it to gauge the effectiveness of government programmes. In support of this, and amid concerns about lack of rigour in assessing effectiveness in this process, the Coalition for Evidence-Based Policy developed additional guidance for federal agencies identifying RCTs as the strongest method for assessing effectiveness (Owen and Larson, 2017). The Coalition went on to conduct reviews of programme evaluations in various areas and organised training workshops on RCTs. Language that prioritised random assignment evaluations increasingly appeared in OMB policy, regulations and guidance on budget scoring, as well as in congressional appropriations (Gueron and Rolston, 2013; Owen and Larson, 2017).

Building on that work, the Obama administration furthered the what works agenda by linking evidence of intervention effectiveness directly with funding decisions. Under Obama, the OMB expanded its work with PART and called for rigorous evaluations that could focus government funding on what works. The financial crisis of 2008, and the period of austerity that followed, allowed policy makers to attach stronger incentives to evaluation evidence. In laws passed during and after the recession, the federal government invested over US$6 billion in 'tiered evidence grant making initiatives' (Box 17.2). In a tiered evidence design, interventions with more rigorous evidence of impact were eligible for the largest grants, while those with less rigorous or emerging evidence were eligible for smaller grants (Haskins and Margolis, 2015).

Over this period, then, the evidence agenda was advanced nationally by legislative reforms, government agencies and professional organisations. At the heart of these shifts lay ideas about the primacy of what works questions, RCTs as the strongest research design for

> ### Box 17.2: Federal programmes to encourage what works
>
> **The Program Assessment Rating Tool (PART)**
> PART was developed under the US Office of Management and Budget (OMB)
> to assess and improve programme performance. PART reviews were intended
> to identify programme strengths and weaknesses so as to inform funding and
> management decisions aimed at making the programme more effective. The PART
> tool deployed 25 to 30 questions across four categories: programme purpose
> and design; strategic planning; programme management; and programme results.
>
> **Tiered-evidence grant making**
> 'Tiered-evidence grant making' was a strategy designed to direct federal
> funding to states, localities and non-profits to support effective interventions.
> Larger funds were awarded as the rigour and extent of evidence on programme
> effectiveness was established, and smaller pots of money were available to
> those having less rigorous evidence (Haskins and Margolis, 2015). This strategy
> was used not only in education, but also for community-based programmes,
> workforce development and international assistance.

producing evidence on those questions and the need for strong push efforts to disseminate evidence-based interventions across the nation.

Early and on-going critiques

While the what works movement greatly increased the rigour of research on the effectiveness of education programmes and practices, the movement has not lacked critical friends or even dissidents. The approach generated controversy among researchers who were concerned that the movement privileged a narrow range of research questions and designs. Early critics argued that a narrow focus on causal inference excluded other methodological approaches that can inform educational improvement. Erickson and Gutierrez (2002) contended that efficacy studies in the absence of studies of implementation provide little information on how or why an approach is successful, and little guidance for implementing programmes at scale. Bryk and colleagues (2015) maintained that it was unlikely that efficacious programmes would be widely implemented without the structures and processes that enable practitioners to learn how to implement them in local contexts, problem-solve issues that arise and share knowledge across sites. Others expressed concern that questions about staffing, costs and funding were also left largely unanswered (arguments that are echoed in Chapters Ten and Eleven).

Practitioners too raised concerns. Programme adoption decisions are relatively rare, and many practitioners regarded research on ways to improve existing systems and practices as being more valuable (Yohalem and Tseng, 2015). In addition, local decision makers were interested in knowing whether interventions would work in their contexts and with their students, and experimental trials too rarely provided that information. Moreover, some worried that a focus on adopting programme models contributed to a search for 'silver bullet' solutions, at the expense of steady incremental improvement. Perhaps the most significant tension arose with teachers, who felt at the mercy of federal policy makers in Washington, DC – actors far removed from the day-to-day work of schools. Consequently, teachers and service providers sometimes perceived evidence as something done *to* them, and not *with* them.

Supporters of the what works agenda also called for course corrections as the field matured. In an address to the SREE, Hedges (2018) noted the lack of information on the generalisability of intervention impacts and called for more research examining variation in intervention effects, as well as better matching of the research approaches to the intervention complexity. Others, responding to the expense of large-scale experiments or the frequency of null findings, argued for different approaches: lower-cost experiments that capitalise on administrative data (Coalition for Evidence-based Policy, 2012), mechanism experiments (Knowles and Ludwig, 2013), designing descriptive and experimental research in novel ways (Hill et al, 2013).

Fractious debates over evidence often pivoted around the centrality of RCTs and top-down policy directives. But, over time, there has been a gradual softening of some of these divisions and a widening acknowledgement of the need to address a greater diversity of questions, which in turn call for other research designs and methods. There has also gradually been recognition that getting evidence used remains an enduring challenge.

Key approaches to encouraging and enabling evidence use

As the what works agenda was ascending in federal policy, other efforts were brewing to reconfigure the relationship between research and practice. Whereas the what works policy framework was undergirded by the centralising forces of the federal government (Mehta, 2013; Haskins and Margolis, 2015), other approaches were initially more bottom-up and organic. Advances in studies of research use (for example, Nutley et al, 2007), progress within the learning sciences and new continuous improvement research and research–practice partnerships all provide the inspiration for a new framework for building an evidence-informed education system.

To be clear, a new framework does not entail abandoning evaluation and the significant progress made in developing and testing interventions. However, it does suggest a different starting point for bridging research, practice and policy: one that is rooted in the pressing questions of practice (which include – but are not limited to – understanding what works). The framework also encompasses the varied research designs and methods that are needed to address the wide array of practice-relevant questions (see Chapter Ten) and the need to forge more productive relationships between researchers, practitioners and policy makers (see Chapter Twelve).

Using research for policy and practice

The stimulus for an alternative framework can be found first in empirical studies of research use. Conceptual and empirical work on research and knowledge utilisation initially reached a zenith in the late 1970s and early 1980s, when academics such Weiss, Caplan, Cohen, Patton and others produced a spate of publications on the relationship between social science and public policy. That work waned in the 1980s, but in the late 2000s the William T. Grant Foundation (a philanthropic agency supporting research on children and youth) sought to reinvigorate the field by launching an initiative to support studies of the use of research evidence in policy and practice (Tseng, 2008; Granger, 2014). In 2014 the IES also jumped into this field by funding two national Research and Development Centers on Knowledge Utilization. The National Academies have also produced two reports (National Academies of Sciences, Engineering, and Medicine, 2012; 2017) to stimulate empirical study of the communication and use of research evidence: *Using Science as Evidence in Public Policy* (2012) and *Communicating Science Effectively: A Research Agenda* (2017).

In contrast to the narrow evidence definition propagated by what works proponents, studies of research use consistently find that education policy makers and practitioners define evidence more widely. For many, evidence includes social science research as well as administrative data, expert testimony, experience and parent and community input (Honig and Coburn, 2008; Asen et al, 2011). In addition, the what works schema presumes a rational, linear model of policy making and practice change, whereby decision makers have a choice to make (whether to adopt a programme or practice) and seek information to make that choice (using what works evidence). But research on the use of research highlights the more variable, contingent and contested nature of policy making (Nutley et al, 2007; and see Chapter Two) and the situated complexities of practice (see Chapter Three). Research use requires consideration of various types of evidence and a grappling with the more complex ways in which research can inform, alongside other types of evidence, considerations and interests (McDonnell and Weatherford, 2013; Mosley and Gibson, 2017; see Chapter Twelve).

In addition, studies of the use of research reveal multiple pathways through which research is used in policy or impacts on practice. Research is sometimes used instrumentally to make a decision, such as which programme to adopt, but it also plays an important role by informing understandings of problems and orienting decision makers towards certain types of solutions. This form of research use, termed conceptual use by Carol Weiss (1977; and discussed more in Chapter Twelve), has been shown to be quite consequential, able in the longer term to reshape basic understandings, framings and cognitive models, and thus to open up new directions for innovative policy and programmes. For example, in a large-scale survey, district leaders and school principals reported that research provided a common language, a set of ideas and a framework for guiding reform efforts, in addition to information on programme adoption (Penuel et al, 2016). In-depth observational and interview data reveal that research can enable district administrators to see a problem that had not previously been visible and thereby shift the solutions that are considered (Farrell and Coburn, 2016).

Research–practice partnerships (RPPs)

Recent studies also suggest that the use of research evidence can be encouraged by direct and sustained interaction with research partners (Farrell et al, 2018). The burgeoning field of RPPs can be traced to ideas from the educational and improvement sciences, and the collaboration model pioneered by the Chicago Consortium on School Research. Collectively, partnerships around the country are testing out an alternative framework to bridge research and practice.

In the late 1980s researchers began developing design-based approaches to scholarship with the aim of creating closer connections with – and greater impacts on – practice. The approaches call on researchers to work closely with practitioners to design new curricula, pedagogical approaches, tools and systems that support educational improvement. The innovations are then tested in classrooms, schools and districts, and are studied by researchers, with the findings used to enhance the innovations iteratively (Brown, 1992; Collins, 1992). The work is often small scale, involving a small number of classrooms or schools, but a few researchers have focused on design and implementation work in entire districts (Penuel et al, 2011; Cobb and Jackson, 2012). Design-based research became part of the national discussion of the research–practice relationship through reports from the National Academy of Education and the National Research Council (Donovan et al, 2003). While design-based research did not gain traction in federal policies such as NCLB, it did influence the National Science Foundation, a key public funder. The reports also inspired doctoral training programmes to train novice researchers to work in design research partnerships with schools and districts.

At the same time, researchers at the University of Chicago were developing what has come to be known as a Research Alliance (Coburn et al, 2013). The Chicago Consortium on School Research (CCSR) was established as early as 1990 to produce independent research on Chicago Public Schools (Roderick et al, 2009). Over the years, CCSR evolved towards a closer collaboration with the district in order to jointly define research questions, produce independent findings on those questions and share findings in ways that would inform the district's and other stakeholders' work. By the mid-2000s, researchers inspired by CCSR began forging long-term partnerships with the districts in their cities. The Baltimore Education Research Consortium was launched in 2006, the Research Alliance for New York City Schools in 2008, the Los Angeles Education Research Institute in 2009, San Diego Education Research Alliance in 2010 and the Houston Education Research Consortium in 2011.

A third partnership approach emerged in the early 2010s. Anthony Bryk, a founder of CCSR and a veteran of design-based research, became president of the Carnegie Foundation for the Advancement of Teaching. Bryk and colleagues united improvement science concepts and methods from healthcare with the idea that networks can be leveraged to accelerate learning across sites, and began forming Networked Improvement Communities (Bryk et al, 2015). Networks varied, but they shared a focus on rapidly designing, testing and reshaping education practices in order to improve education systems and outcomes.

Coburn and colleagues (2013) examined these three strands of work and identified a set of cross-cutting principles for RPPs (Box 17.3). They defined these partnerships as 'long-term, mutualistic collaborations between practitioners and researchers that are intentionally organised to investigate problems of practice and [develop] solutions for improving district outcomes' (ibid, p 2). RPPs are guided by a set of principles that contrast with the what works framework. What works approaches place a high premium on researcher independence: researchers should work with detachment from practitioners, so that they can objectively assess intervention impacts and report findings without bias. Moreover, researchers' involvement with a programme is often short-lived, lasting only as long as the specific evaluation contract or grant. In contrast, RPPs emphasise long-term commitments from researchers and are designed to build relational trust and deep knowledge of the interventions or systems under study. The thinking is that, with greater trust and engagement, practitioners are more likely to use the research. Trust also enables partners to continue to collaborate, even when research findings are disappointing – such as when evaluations yield null effects or show that a policy is potentially harmful to students. With more knowledge of the system and its context, researchers can study topics that are rooted in educators' needs, draw more accurate inferences from the data and offer recommendations that fit the local context.

Proponents of RPPs argue that these long-term collaborations shift researchers' and practitioners' focus from one of *proving impact* to that of *improving services*. Under the what works agenda, practitioners were often pressed to prove that their interventions were effective and worth further dissemination and funding; RPPs, in contrast, focus on creating

---

Box 17.3: Key features of Research–Practice Partnerships (RPPs)

Research–Practice Partnerships:

1 are long-term;
2 focus on problems of practice;
3 are committed to mutualism;
4 use intentional strategies to foster partnerships; and
5 produce original analyses.

Source: Coburn et al, 2013.

---

and using knowledge to serve local improvement goals (Henrick et al, 2017). In addition, under what works, the focus on disseminating and scaling up evidence-based programmes meant that research was often being pushed into districts with a one-size-fits-all approach. With RPPs, however, research is intended to be co-developed with districts and tailored to the local context. Lastly, because RPP agendas stem from the interests of districts, a broader range of research questions arise and a more diverse array of research designs and methods are used. While some RPPs conduct evaluation studies (including RCTs), those studies sit alongside other types of study in the partnership portfolio.

RPPs grew in the 1990s and 2000s but did not catapult onto the national stage until John Q. Easton became the second director of the IES in 2009. Bringing his experience of leading CCSR to the federal agency, Easton established a grants programme to support the development of new RPPs. While they are promising, RPPs are not a panacea: they represent useful strategies for connecting research and practice in local communities, but critics say they face limits to the generalisability of findings and ability to inform improvement in other contexts (Kelly, 2004). Moreover, many RPPs have sprung up in urban communities where research universities are available to partner with districts; and partnerships have had limited reach into rural communities. In those places, it may be more fruitful to forge partnerships between a network of rural districts, or a regional or state agency, and researchers. Other critics argue that, by working closely with practitioners, researchers lose their objectivity (Kelly, 2004; Anderson and Shattuck, 2012), a concern that some types of RPP grapple with more than others.

A loosening policy landscape

The policy context for research use in US education is shifting. The Every Student Succeeds Act (ESSA), the successor to the NCLB, was signed into law in late 2015. Legislators maintained a focus on evaluation evidence but responded to the political backlash against federal law makers by devolving greater authority to state governments. This devolution shifted the political and policy discourse away from getting states to comply with federal policy, and towards supporting states and localities in improving schools.

ESSA largely operates within the what works agenda by promoting the adoption of evidence-based interventions. The legislation defines 'evidence-based' using a hierarchy based on research designs to assess intervention effectiveness (see also Chapter Eleven). Because of widespread concerns that the evidence base was too sparse, the legislation includes room for interventions that lack empirical evidence but for which there exists 'a rationale that is based on high-quality research findings' that will be subjected to 'ongoing efforts to examine the effects'. Referred to as the 'evidence building' or 'under evaluation' level, it provides an access point for new interventions to get onto the evidence ladder (West, 2016).

The on-going tensions between centralised top-down approaches (driving research *into* practice) and more decentralised bottom-up strategies (connecting research *and* practice) reflect tensions seen elsewhere in this book (see Chapter Three). For now, the pendulum seems to be swinging towards more pluralistic approaches in US education, but it remains to be seen if this trend will continue and take hold.

Concluding remarks

Shifting political times may open a window for more fundamental transformations in the relationships between research, practice and policy. Here, we have offered three recommendations for rethinking the role of research evidence in the future.

First and foremost, policy makers need to focus more on *evidence use* rather than *evidence products*. Recent policy documents, such as *The Promise of Evidence-Based Policymaking* (Commission on Evidence-Based Policymaking, 2017), produced by a bipartisan commission, still focus largely on evidence production. Building an infrastructure to support meaningful and routine use of evidence is a more difficult challenge, and requires drawing on the emerging research knowledge about how to support research use and deploying political leadership to take this work to the next level.

Second, RPPs and similar efforts should play a more central role in research use. Through these long-term collaborations, researchers assist decision makers in answering high-priority questions, thereby drawing tighter connections between research and real-world dilemmas. But there is more that partnerships can do to promote use of the research that is produced (Tseng, 2017). The ESSA legislation provides opportunities for RPPs to better support school improvement: they can help state and local agencies to meet the requirements for evidence-based programmes and strategies under the new law by supporting districts to adapt their existing programmes, develop new ones and test both old and new (Penuel and Farrell, 2017; Penuel et al, 2017). In addition, RPPs can aid states, districts and schools in identifying measures of school quality for their accountability systems. To be successful, however, researchers and leaders of education agencies will need to build their capacity to work together productively to foster more substantive and meaningful research use.

Third, the work of building and using research should be rooted in democratic principles and include more bottom-up strategies. In a chapter on 'democratizing evidence in education', Tseng et al (2018) argue for 'a more engaged and evidence-informed citizenry' in which different stakeholders can meaningfully shape the production and use of research to inform educational improvement. In a more democratic evidence movement, the power to define research agendas would be shared among researchers, practitioners, policy makers and communities. This has many echoes with the arguments laid out in Chapters Ten to Twelve. Rather than research questions arising from researchers' discussions with each other or from policy makers' accountability demands, questions would stem from vibrant back-and-forth exchanges between researchers, educators, parents, students, policy makers and community stakeholders. The demand for evaluation would come not just from policy makers or foundations seeking to make funding decisions, but also from practitioners seeking to improve their work and parents concerned about their children's education. Setting research priorities would become less an academic exercise and more a matter of deliberation, negotiation and compromise among diverse stakeholders.

In addition, research and data would not serve as monitoring and evaluation tools only for managers and policy makers. Evidence would also be accessible to community organisations, parents, students and the broader public as they seek to drive improvements in education. There would be a stronger focus on developing a shared understanding of what the research says and its implications for practice and policy. Of course, disagreements will remain about values, the proper role of government in education and where to direct resources. As we know from studies of research use, data and research evidence alone cannot resolve those debates. However, research and data can be tools for forging consensus about the scope and nature of the problems at hand and the likely outcomes of moving in particular policy directions.

To be clear, we should not throw out the proverbial baby with the bath water. Much has been gained in education from the what works agenda, including the strengthening of doctoral training in research on causal inference and the accumulation of evidence on the efficacy of curricula, instructional approaches and programmes. Rather, we suggest a shift in our understanding of decision making itself: moving from the established focus on rational, technocratic and top-down models of decision making to other approaches that acknowledge decision making as interpretive, social, situated and more bottom-up (see also Chapter Three). In the new framework, we advocate for different research methods to address a range of local problems and questions that include but are not limited to questions about what works. We need greater participation from a range of stakeholders to set research priorities; we need capacity-building efforts that support researchers in developing skills to work with diverse stakeholders in new ways; and we need government agencies and communities to use research to support their improvement efforts over the long term.

References

Achinstein, B. and Ogawa, R.T. (2006) '(In)fidelity: what the resistance of new teachers reveals about professional principles and prescriptive educational policies', *Harvard Educational Review*, 76 (1), pp 30–63.

Anderson, T. and Shattuck, J. (2012) 'Design-based research: a decade of progress in education research?', *Educational Researcher*, 41 (1), pp 16–25.

Asen, R., Gurke, D., Solomon, R., Conners, P. and Gumm, E. (2011) '"The research says": definitions and uses of a key policy term in federal law and local school board deliberations', *Argumentation and Advocacy*, 47 (4), pp 195–213.

Brown, A.L. (1992) 'Design experiments: theoretical and methodological challenges in creating complex interventions in classroom settings', *The Journal of Learning Sciences*, 2 (2), pp 141–78.

Bryk, A., Gomez, L., Grunow, A. and LeMahieu, P. (2015) *Learning to improve: how America's schools can get better at getting better*, Cambridge, MA: Harvard Education Press.

Coalition for Evidence-based Policy (2012) *Rigorous program evaluations on a budget: how low-cost randomized controlled trials are possible in many areas of social policy*, Washington, DC: Coalition for Evidence-Based Policy.

Coburn, C., Penuel, W.R. and Geil, K.E. (2013) *Research-practice partnerships a strategy for leveraging research for educational improvement in school districts*, New York: William T. Grant Foundation.

Cobb, P. and Jackson, K. (2012) 'Analyzing educational policies: a learning design perspective', *Journal of Learning Sciences*, 21 (4), pp 487–521.

Collins, A.M. (1992) 'Toward a design science of education', in E. Scanlon and T. O'Shea (eds), *New directions in educational technology*, New York: Springer-Verlag, pp 15–22.

Commission on Evidence-Based Policymaking (2017) *The promise of evidence-based policymaking: a report by the commission on evidence-based policymaking*, Washington, DC: Commission on Evidence-Based Policymaking.

Donovan, M.S., Wigdor, A.K. and Snow, C.E. (2003) *Strategic Education Research Partnership*, Washington DC: National Research Council.

Erickson, F. and Gutierrez, K. (2002) 'Culture, rigor and science in educational research', *Educational Researcher*, 31 (8), pp 21–4.

Farrell, C.C. and Coburn, C.E. (2016) 'What is conceptual use of research and why is it important?', William T. Grant Foundation blog, April, http://wtgrantfoundation.org/conceptual-use-research-important.

Farrell, C., Coburn, C.E., and Chong, S. (2018) 'Under what conditions do school districts learn from external partners: The role of absorptive capacity', *American Educational Research Journal*.

Flay, B.R., Biglan, A., Boruch, R.F., Castro, F.G., Gottfredson, D., Kellam, S., Moscicki, E.K., Schinke, S., Valentine, J.C. and Ji, P. (2005) 'Standards of evidence: criteria for efficacy, effectiveness and dissemination', *Prevention Science*, 6 (3), pp 151–75.

Granger, R.C. (2014) Foreword. In K.S. Finnigan and A.J. Daly (eds), *Using research evidence in education: from the schoolhouse door to Capitol Hill*, Heidelberg: Springer.

Gueron, J.M. and Rolston, H. (2013) *Fighting for reliable evidence*, New York: Russell Sage Foundation.

Haskins, R. and Margolis, G. (2015) *Show me the evidence*, Washington, DC: Brookings Institution Press.

Hedges, L. (2018) 'Challenges in Building usable knowledge in education', *Journal of Research on Educational Effectiveness*, 11(1), pp 1-21.

Henrick, E.C., Cobb, P., Penuel, W.R., Jackson, K. and Clark, T. (2017) *Assessing research-practice partnerships: five dimensions of effectiveness*, New York: William T. Grant Foundation.

Hill, H.C., Beisiegel, M. and Jacob, R. (2013) 'Professional development research: consensus, crossroads, and challenges', *Educational Researcher*, 42 (9), pp 476–87.

Honig, M.I. and Coburn, C.E. (2008) 'Evidence-based decision making in school district central offices: toward a policy and research agenda', *Educational Policy*, 22 (4), pp 578–608.

Kelly, A.E. (2004) 'Design research in education: yes, but is it methodological?', *The Journal of the Learning Sciences*, 13 (1), pp 113–28.

Kersten, J. (2006) 'Hybridization, resistance, and compliance: negotiating policies to support literacy achievement', *The New Educator*, 2 (2), pp 103–21.

Kersten, J. and Pardo, L. (2007) 'Finessing and hybridizing: Innovative literacy practices in Reading First classrooms', *The Reading Teacher*, 61 (2), pp 146–54.

Knowles, T. and Ludwig, J. (2013) 'Strengthening Education Sciences Reform Act: fostering innovation and efficiency through mechanism experiments', in *Leveraging learning: the evolving role of federal policy in education research*, Washington, DC: The Aspen Institute.

McDonnell, L.M. and Weatherford, M.S. (2013) 'Evidence use and the Common Core State Standards Movement: from policy definition to policy adoption', *American Journal of Education*, 120 (1), pp 1–25.

Mehta, J. (2013) *The allure of order*, New York: Oxford University Press.

Mosley, J.E., and Gibson, K. (2017) 'Strategic use of evidence in state-level policymaking: matching evidence type to legislative stage', *Policy Sciences*, 50(4), 697–719.

National Academies of Sciences, Engineering, and Medicine (2012) *Using science as evidence in public policy*, Washington, DC: The National Academies Press.

National Academies of Sciences, Engineering, and Medicine (2017) *Communicating science effectively: a research agenda*, Washington, DC: The National Academies Press.

Nutley, S., Walter, I. and Davies, H.T.O. (2007) *Using evidence: how research can inform public services*, Bristol: Policy Press.

Owen, J.W. and Larson, A.M. (2017) *Researcher–policymaker partnerships*, New York: Routledge.

Penuel, W.R., Allen, A.-R. and Finnigan, K.S. (2017) *How research-practice partnerships can support ESSA implementation for educational improvement and equity: a guide for school districts, state education leaders, and researchers*, Boulder, CO: Research+Practice Collaboratory.

Penuel, W.R., Farrell, C.C., Allen, A-R, Toyama, Y. and Coburn, C.E. (2016) 'How district leaders use research: comparing differences within and across districts', *Educational Policy*, 32(4), pp 540–68.

Penuel, W.R. and Farrell, C. (2017) 'Research-practice partnerships and ESSA: a learning agenda for the coming decade', in E. Quintero (ed.), *Teaching in context: the social side of reform*, Cambridge, MA: Harvard Education Press, pp 181–200.

Penuel, B., Fishman, B., Cheng, B.H. and Sabelli, N. (2011) 'Organizing research and development at the intersection of learning, implementation and design', *Educational Researcher*, 40 (7), pp 331–7.

Roderick, M., Easton, J.Q. and Sebring, P.B. (2009) *The consortium on Chicago school research: A new model for the role of research in supporting urban school reform*, Chicago, IL: Consortium of Chicago Schools Research.

Rudalevige, A. (2009,) 'Juggling act: the politics of education science', *Education Next*, 9 (1), www.educationnext.org/juggling-act/

Tseng, V. and the Senior Program Team (2008) *Studying the use of research evidence in policy and practice. William T. Grant Foundation 2007 annual report*, New York: William T. Grant Foundation.

Tseng, V. (2017) *The next big leap for research-practice partnerships: building and testing theories to improve research use*, New York: William T. Grant Foundation.

Tseng, V., Fleischman, S. and Quintero, E. (2018) 'Democratizing evidence in education', in B. Bevan and W.R. Penuel (eds), *Connecting research and practice for educational improvement: ethical and equitable approaches*, New York: Routledge.

Weiss, C.H. (1977) 'Research for policy's sake: the enlightenment function of social research', *Policy Analysis*, 3 (4), pp 531–45.

West, M. (2016) *From evidence-based programs to an evidence-based system: opportunities under the Every Student Succeeds Act*, Washington, DC: Brookings Institute.

Yohalem, N. and Tseng, V. (2015) 'Commentary: moving from practice to research, and back', *Applied Developmental Science*, 19 (2), pp 117–20.

18

Conclusions: lessons from the past, prospects for the future

Huw Davies, Annette Boaz, Sandra Nutley and Alec Fraser

Evidence-informed policy and practice revisited

This book is a revisiting of the evolution of the evidence agenda over the past two decades. In 2000 we published the first comprehensive cross-sectoral review of the burgeoning activity around evidence (Davies et al, 2000), and this revealed a fascinating diversity of practices, tensions and debates, but also many overlaps and convergences of concern. In 2007 we developed a more focused review of strategies for increasing the use and influence of evidence (Nutley et al, 2007), paying particular attention to research-based knowledge, seeing this as the area most in need of illumination (a view reinforced by this current collection). The intervening years have done nothing to lessen our interest in these concerns, or to dim our view that the use of evidence of all kinds, but especially research-based knowledge, is deserving of intense study.

The political and economic context has shifted considerably since the previous volumes were published, with implications for the debate about the role of evidence in policy and practice. There is now much talk of a post-truth world – highlighted by the election of Donald Trump to the presidency in the US in 2016, and also by the UK's EU membership referendum campaign of the same year (Brexit). Both these events may be seen to align with other global moves towards populist ideologies, and both Trump and those campaigning for the UK to leave the EU belittled the role of experts – the Conservative MP Michael Gove most famously so ('people in this country have had enough of experts'). Moreover, the role of expertise, and especially economic expertise and forecasting, had already been deeply questioned following the financial crash of 2008 and the ensuing recession – even prompting the British monarch, Queen Elizabeth II, to ask why no experts had foreseen the crisis.

The period of secure economic growth across many Western democracies from the mid-1990s up until that banking crisis accompanied the rise in post-ideological, evidence-based policy making, and the rise and rise of technocratic solutions to political dilemmas. Indeed, there are parallels between technocracy and populism: technocracy seeks to identify an optimally 'correct' solution to any defined problem, while populism asserts that there is only one authentic will of the people (Müller, 2017). It is through these assertions of singularity that both approaches downplay the importance of pluralism, contestation and political debate: 'hence it is plausible to assume that one might pave the way for the other, because each legitimizes the belief that there is no room for disagreement' (Müller, 2017, p 97).

However, in the professional environments that underpin many public services (the realms of doctors, social workers, teachers and managers, for example) we see no real diminution in the strong underpinning appetites for a better-informed world, especially around the day-to-day work of making policy and that of delivering services. The shift in this volume to an evidence-*informed* as opposed to an evidence-*based* discourse is also significant in highlighting a less deterministic, ambitious and hierarchical view of evidence generation and use. In its place there is recognition of the importance of difference, dialogue and debate in policy making, and there are more realistic assumptions about the contribution of expertise alongside the importance of democratic choices fleshed out with public and user engagement. Taken together, the accounts curated in this book demonstrate a range of important features around evidence use: continuing interest and energy across many fields of application; international resonance of the ideas and challenges; significant investments in infrastructure and projects; lively and engaged debates with increasing nuance; and a seriousness of purpose about the overall enterprise.

Evidence use, in our current framing, is about the improvement of public policy and public services for public benefit – while not neglecting that it can, at the same time, be about many other things, such as sustaining power, supporting vested interests and enhancing professional prestige. Indeed, it seems to us that there is still great potential for societal good from evidence, both directly and more indirectly: directly, through improved policies that better address social needs, as well as by the improvement of services to meet these needs; and indirectly, through using knowledge to challenge established interests, authorities and hierarchies. The overarching endeavour of understanding when and how evidence can play these roles – and how to enable it to do so more effectively – therefore remains worthwhile.

Clearly, then, evidence-informed policy and practice (EIPP) remains an enduring area of concern across many countries and services, within many professional and non-professional groupings and across diverse research disciplines. This interest in evidence was certainly given fresh impetus by wider implementation of the ideas associated with new public management (NPM) (Head, 2008), ideas that came to such prominence either side of the millennium. Yet, while the tide of NPM may be receding in some areas (Dunleavy et al, 2006; Osborne, 2006), it does not appear to be taking the evidence agenda with it. To the contrary, we see in the debates played out in this book a desire to disentangle ideas of evidence from some of the more contentious aspects of NPM and to reshape them for a less technocratic and more multivocal world. So, while not wishing to minimise the importance of managerialism in institutionalising evidence use (through, for example, guidelines and targets), we would argue that the evidence agenda has broadened out considerably from its founding focus on 'effectiveness and efficiency' (Cochrane, 1972).

The evidence agenda is also playing out somewhat differently in various fields of application (see Section Two) and in different jurisdictions (see Section Four), but the commonality of concerns is striking. Where there are differences, these are often of degree, or emphasis or terminology. Some of these differences between sectors may be rooted in the different scientific bases underpinning knowledge for key professional groups (for example, the natural science basis for medical knowledge versus a more socially oriented science seen in social work and criminal justice). Other differences may be more about certain path dependencies, or may reflect variations in the degree of borrowing or importation of ideas from other sectors (the influence of an evidence-based framing drawn from medicine, for example).

One striking feature of the accounts from across different fields of application (Section Two) is the assertion that the area under consideration has 'unique challenges', such as multiple actors, complex and/or 'wicked' problems, challenging contexts, divergent research traditions, parallel competing epistemologies and so on. Overall, we are not wholly persuaded by such claims of exceptionalism. Commonality rather than distinctiveness of challenge is far more evident. This suggests that there is much that we can learn from this kind of cross-sector and international review, and this is the focus of our intent. Indeed, it may be that fault lines and incongruities, as well as insights and opportunities, are more readily discernible when looking outside one's area of specialist experience than they are when looking within, so that too is a goal of this work: to prompt reflection and learning across the widest field.

In this chapter we reflect on the contributions of these collected insights. First, we draw (relatively brief) attention to a series of recurrent themes from across the book, before highlighting (more fully) some recurring responses to these themes. By expressing these themes generically (although all are exemplified in the contributed chapters, sometimes many times over) we hope that the contours of debate and opportunities for new angles on those debates may be seen more clearly. The reflections on the state of EIPP gathered here are designed to complement the cross-cutting analyses of evidence generation, valuing and use laid out in Section Three. In that section we focused on the lifeblood of the issue (evidence), whereas here we focus more on the thinking supporting the evidence agenda; the ways in which that thinking is expressed in actions and initiatives; and the concomitant tensions, challenges and debates that then arise. Necessarily, these issues are not readily separable, and so some of the recurrent themes noted here can be followed into various chapters in Section Three for a fuller treatment. Where that is so, appropriate links are noted in the text.

Recurring themes

Across the six fields of policy and practice (Section Two) and the five jurisdictional accounts (Section Four), four recurrent themes stand out: the dominance of 'what works' thinking; which in turn feeds directly into disputations around what counts as evidence; the challenges of getting evidence used; and the importance of contextual considerations in these debates. Each of these is now taken in turn.

The 'what works' agenda remains dominant

The discourse around what works still seems dominant in many areas, and it is support for, or a reaction against, this that drives many of the debates. Crucially, addressing what works is the site of much organisational effort and investment, both nationally in the UK (for example, NICE, SCIE and the other What Works Centres) and internationally (for example, the Cochrane and the Campbell Collaborations; and the international efforts aimed at coordinating health technology assessment). These initiatives have focused attention on evidence generation and dissemination, albeit evidence of a particular kind. While this 'knowledge push' approach has an important role to play, on its own it is unlikely to transform the use of evidence in policy and practice. Of course, arguments about effectiveness (and hence efficiency) can drive policy makers' attention and galvanise delivery efforts, and so a focus on what works is highly relevant. Indeed, payment-by-results (PbR), early intervention arguments, life-course analyses and social investment approaches all attest to the importance and enduring nature of cost-effectiveness concerns in the delivery of public services. Yet discontent at the narrowness of this agenda has fuelled sustained critique of the dominance of what works and randomised experiments, their underlying positivistic precepts and the accompanying linear 'evidence-into-practice' models. This in turn has led to much broader debates about what does – or should – count as evidence, and on whose authority.

What counts as evidence is still disputed

Arguments about the value of randomised controlled trials (RCTs), specifically, and evidence hierarchies more generally, have animated the evidence debates in many fields. While initially these were characterised as relatively unproductive 'paradigm wars', the careful articulation of more nuanced positions and critiques has allowed for a proliferation of insights and developments. These debates, while starting in methodological concerns (see Chapter Ten), quickly become rooted in ideas of power and privilege (see Chapter Eleven). One consequence has been much more careful use of terminology (for example, a change from evidence-based to evidence-*informed*, and from knowledge transfer to knowledge *interaction* and *exchange*). Another has been a widening of the types of voices admitted to the debates about policy and practice, alongside a grappling with the ways by which different types of knowledge can be accommodated. In turn we have seen a diversification of the questions asked of and addressed by evidence, and even direct questions of evaluation are now often examined by looking at processes as well as impacts, and by examining the lived experience of interventions as well as their objective outcomes. Taken together, many of these accounts attest to the view that discerning knowledge and becoming knowledgeable are complex and sometimes fraught processes. From this it should be unsurprising that acting on knowledge is similarly problematic.

Getting evidence used is enduringly difficult

Broadly, there is enduring disquiet at how few of the actions across public services (whether policies or practices) are ever properly underpinned by evidence or exposed to much in the way of formal evaluation. Such concerns have resonated internationally. A related concern is the difficulty in securing disinvestment in activities when these are thought to be ineffective. Even in areas where evidence has been accumulating, leading to some relatively robust evidence-informed recommendations, actually *using* that evidence remains a key challenge sadly undiminished by several decades of work on just this issue (Nutley et al, 2007, and see Chapter Twelve). Hence, securing a more impactful relationship between evidence and policy and evidence and practice is of abiding interest.

Contemporary understandings of policy making have clarified that overly rational and idealised policy-cycle models offer neither a good description of the process nor a reasonable prescription for how to intervene. Yet, as Chapter Two suggests and as many accounts in this book attest, evidence and policy can indeed have productive engagement, so long as craft (and sometimes cunning) are deployed by those seeking to influence or be influenced. It is in part to inform these crafted practices that this book is aimed.

With respect to practice change there are perennial tensions between evidence being used to drive specific changes (for example, by mandate) or to influence improvement (for example, through local learning). These tensions manifest through a variety of dichotomies: top-down versus bottom-up implementation; central direction working with or against local autonomy; external, decontextualised evidence as compared with contextually situated understandings; and standardised delivery ('high fidelity') versus local adaptation ('tinkering'). While the temptation, as ever, is to call for balanced and/or blended approaches, such recommendations gloss over the deep-seated fractures that underlie these dichotomies: concerns about power, knowledge and autonomy, for example (see Chapter Three). The challenges of getting things done with evidence cannot easily be separated from these deeper concerns, which in turn are influenced by the setting – or context – within which actions play out.

Contextual considerations are still key

All of the accounts presented in the book draw attention to some of the specific and distinctive characteristics of their macro, meso and micro contexts as being important for evidence (of various types) to get a hearing and to have influence. Yet, beyond quite general statements that 'context matters', it seems that we do not yet have a sufficiently shared vocabulary or sufficiently useful organising frameworks to make full sense of the context(s) for evidence use.

It is clear that some contexts can be favourably disposed to evidence, while others inhibit its use. Some of these are integral to the field of application, such as poor availability of evidence, contested and ambiguous goals and processes, and fragmented and disputatious occupational groups. Others are more temporary phenomena, such as budget cuts or top-down, politically driven demands. Whatever the particular circumstances that pertain, distilling a clearer understanding of these dynamics and building shared understandings about the nature and value of evidence are central concerns. Overall, however, this area – the contextual mediation of evidence use – remains poorly understood and analytically neglected.

The themes noted above represent some of the foci of attention for evidence debates in public services and beyond. Untangling these and securing productive actions – rather than unproductive clashes – has been a painstaking process in many of the settings explored across the book. But real progress has been made, and from this we can identify a number of positive developments and responses.

Recurring responses

The recurring themes in the accounts presented in this book (noted above) are also accompanied by some recurring responses. Running across these responses are ideas of breadth, plurality and inclusivity as regards evidence, with the concomitant challenges then of contestation, trade-offs and integration. While we elaborate on a number of these separately below, it is clear that there is a strong degree of interconnectedness between them.

Broader expectations about the nature of evidence use

The contemporary visions of evidence use apparent in the various accounts across the book may pivot around ideas of what works (that is, making instrumental choices), but sustained critique and counter-claim have brought to the fore many other ways in which evidence may be used. First, evidence (however derived) can contribute to conceptual reframing and reproblematisation, thus opening up new ways to talk about policy and practice concerns, and potentially new ways to address these. Over time, these slower, more percolative uses of evidence – sometimes cast more as arguments or ideas, than evidence as such – can have profound long-term impact (for example, the recognition of informal carers as key to social support; the identification of hospitals as unsafe places, leading to a strong patient safety movement; and the recasting of many social ills such as substance misuse, domestic violence and prostitution as public health rather than judicial concerns). Evidence, then, can be *about* policy and practice – its value drivers, its underlying goals, ideals and conceptualisations, and its concealment of power – as well as *for* policy and practice, to inform choices and shape services.

Evidence use has also been construed more widely in other ways: instead of the traditional rational and reasoned consideration of evidence as the mainstay of formal decision making, evidence can be seen more as just another resource, co-opted in support of persuasion (Cairney and Oliver, 2017). Hence, evidence has become part of the rhetorical arsenal of a wide range of players, used both for opening up new sites of action and for defending established positions. Moreover, the critique of evidence quality – often appropriate, but sometimes based on self-interested and potentially specious grounds (see Chapter Eleven) – is often just another part of that arsenal. Although sometimes cast as evidence *mis*use, we can at least see how acknowledging these varied tactics provides many more avenues for knowledge to enter debates. It also brings to the fore not just what knowledge but also whose knowledge is at play.

A greater inclusivity around types of knowledge

A core observation about the past two decades of evidence use across diverse fields of application is the willingness and urgency around seeking a greater degree of inclusivity of the types of knowledge admitted to debates about policy and practice. This concern is not just with multi-methods and a plurality of research underpinnings (for example, balancing positivistic trials with process analysis and more interpretivist accounts of lived experience; see also Chapter Ten). It is also about drawing in a much wider array of non-research data and information. For example, as we enter the era of 'big data' there are many opportunities to build information architectures that allow the exploitation of such routinely collected data (both within service systems and much more widely). Data linkage, especially, has the capacity to highlight life-course and social investment approaches (see Chapter Fourteen), with rich possibilities for better understanding, and real-time data processing by institutions can allow ready testing of modifications to interventions (for example, the 'nudge trials' noted in Chapter Ten). However, the technical, practical and ethical implications of these approaches should not be under-estimated, nor should we neglect the hidden politics of such analyses. For example, exploiting existing service data necessarily reinforces prior framings about appropriate interventions, where these should happen and with what goals, and so precludes more radical reorientations to achieving (perhaps quite different) social aims through alternative means.

A greater inclusivity around evidence also extends to embracing very different kinds of knowledge: the expertise and practice wisdom of service providers; the experiential knowledge of service users and carers; lay and indigenous knowledge of population subgroups drawing on different epistemologies; and the differing values and moral framings that underpin the preferences of stakeholders. One consequence of this greater inclusivity is the need for more effective knowledge integration *processes*. While systematic review and synthesis will still have their place, the greater challenge lies in creating integrated and situated *knowing*, rather than emphasising the production of knowledge products. Hence, a consequence of embracing wider types of knowledge is the need to pay far greater attention than hitherto to deliberative and inclusive processes.

Increasing expectations around lay participation

Many of the accounts in this book recognise that for too long debates about evidence have been firmly focused on professional domains: behind the closed doors of policy making; or within managerial and professional hierarchies. But, as public services have gradually been opened up to greater participation and scrutiny, there have been changes in the processes around evidence production and use aimed, if somewhat patchily and haphazardly, at increasing openness and inclusivity. There is a greater acceptance now that the public and service users have a right to be partners in how evidence is interpreted and then used to shape policy and practice. Moreover, since there is no expectation that any participant in evidence considerations necessarily comes to the table as a blank sheet, this wider engagement brings into play other forms of lay and tacit knowledge.

A greater inclusivity of knowledge and stakeholders suggests that, when considering evidence, more situated and dialogical processes are needed: situated, because of the essential interplay between knowledge and context, and dialogical because sense making is essentially an interactional process. Managing these processes is clearly a challenge, not least because power imbalances are pervasive. This remains an area where sustained and focused work is still needed to explore what kinds of processes can lead to more productive engagements around knowledge. Too often, considerations of knowledge can stall on unspoken professional rivalries, implicit power hierarchies or the divergent epistemological bases of knowing.

Related to these concerns are the issues of partnership working. Commentators in many domains have called for sustained and deeper partnerships to support enhanced user voice, increased knowledge integration and improved receptivity to change. While we would endorse this direction of travel, it is clear that to be sustained there is a need for more structural embedding of partnership working, rather than piecemeal and project-based approaches. It is also clear from the accounts in this book that, for the most part, such embedding of partnerships has not yet been achieved. This too is an area deserving of further attention.

Closer integration of the generation and use of evidence

The drive towards knowledge interaction and integration, with a keen eye on situatedness, has shed further light on the need for closer integration between the ways in which knowledge is generated, valued and used (see Chapters Ten to Twelve). Such insights come from a growing awareness of the importance of context as a mediator of policy and practice interventions. While some interventions (such as drug therapies) may be relatively little affected by context, others (such as offender-rehabilitation programmes, violence-reduction strategies or poverty-alleviation work) manifestly are. Thus there are clear needs not only to search for 'portable knowledge' (insights into causal pathways and dependencies that travel well across widely different contexts) but to balance these with insights into what happens during context-specific implementation. All of this suggests the need for deeper and earlier involvement of those who will be affected by evidence in the production of that evidence: and this means those who have to deliver evidence-informed policies and practices as well as those upon whom they impact.

Moreover, there are other reasons why the evidence agenda is aided by closer involvement from downstream stakeholders (whether service providers or service recipients), it is more likely, then, that local perspectives, priorities and concerns will be factored into empirical work, so producing work that is relevant and valued by those stakeholders. Finally, there are reasons to believe that those actively involved in prioritising and producing knowledge are more likely to be influenced subsequently by its messages. Recognition of these arguments has led (in some fields) to a growing emphasis on knowledge co-production processes, further dissolving distinctions between researchers/researched and evidence generation/evidence use. Of course, there are many ways in which such collaborative processes can be arranged, embedded and enacted, and this has become an exciting field of study, albeit one requiring a great deal of further definition, investigation and testing.

A worthwhile counterpoint to this renewed emphasis on situated knowledge is that we must not lose sight of the benefits of research undertaken *separately* from the contexts of application. In the rush to embrace user-led research, partnerships, co-production and impact, there are possibilities of loss as well as gain. For example, 'blue skies' research (work without immediate application) and paradigm-breaking research (research that seeks to undercut existing modes of thought) both have a role to play in any open, critical and pluralist society. We must ensure that well-founded moves to increase the applicability and use of research-based knowledge do not lead to a withering of other important endeavours (Cribb, 2018).

Actions at all levels and on many fronts

The major lesson from this analysis is that there is a requirement for actions at many levels, and on many fronts, by diverse actors. As the complexity of approaches has become apparent, with their attendant strengths and weakness, it becomes imperative that we do not simply replace one set of (partially useful) approaches with another set of (still only partially useful) approaches. For example, the evolution of thinking (Best and Holmes, 2010) from rational and linear models of research uptake through relational models ('linkage and exchange') to more embracing systems models should not lead us to jettison earlier approaches. Instead we should seek a judicious mix of 'requisite variety', while remaining fully cognisant of the tensions and incongruities built in to such an approach.

In the policy arena, this means a range of new ways of working – for example, enhanced influencing across diverse networks; drawing on ideas and narratives as much as numbers; and searching for propitious windows of opportunity (see Chapter Two). All of this requires the softer skills of networking, persuasion, story-telling and alliance building, alongside the harder technical skills of data analysis and evidence appraisal.

In practice arenas we have to learn to better connect the evidence-use agenda with the organisation studies and organisational behaviour literatures, so that we can see that evidence use sits within – not outside – an understanding of organisational dynamics. In doing so, we can more readily see the advantages, disadvantages and unintended consequences of various approaches to evidence application, such as those emphasising 'outside in' or 'inside out' strategies (see Chapter Three). The elaboration of these approaches around archetypes of evidence-based practice, embedded research and organisational excellence (Nutley et al, 2007; and see Chapters Six and Fifteen) highlights fresh ways of describing and supporting evidence-informed practice change. Newer ideas such as embedded researchers (different from embedding *research*; Marshall et al, 2014) and co-constructing knowledge (Pinfold et al, 2015) also offer many new avenues for designing innovative local arrangements.

Taken together, then, there are many and varied strategies open to those seeking to strengthen the role of evidence, whether in policy or in practice. There is also a strong need to ensure that any strategies enacted are examined and tested if we are to avoid the irony that the EIPP movement lacks much of an evidence base (Powell et al, 2018).

Conclusions and reflections

Since the late 1990s the profile and importance of the relationship between evidence and policy have fluctuated at national levels. These fluctuations are linked to political events and agendas. In the UK context, while there have been notable low points, such as the invasion of Iraq and the debates around the 2016 EU membership referendum, there have also been high points, such as the establishment of NICE and the institutionalised architecture of the What Works Centres. Additionally, at an organisational level, a more consistent relationship between evidence, policy and practice has endured. Moreover, it is the case in the UK, and increasingly internationally, that a greater awareness of the perils of simplistic assumptions (for example, over policy-cycle models; or of rational-linear models of research implementation) has opened up many new possibilities for more effective engagements around evidence. The field as a whole is now displaying much greater energy and diversity as we see the arguments break out from the hegemony of evidence-based medicine (EBM) framings (for example, in education, social care and criminal justice services; perhaps even in healthcare too). In addition, in some arenas, we are seeing the arguments develop somewhat disconnected from the dominant discourses in health and healthcare (for example, in ideas about the environment and sustainability, and in international development). Such novelty, energy and diversity provide many opportunities to build cycles of virtuous learning rather than unreflective copying or negative reactivity.

Understanding in detail the drivers and shapers of how the agenda plays out in different sectors and different jurisdictions is a longer-term project beyond the scope of this book. Yet there are fascinating glimpses here into the intricate relationships between local political and governmental contexts, academic activities, professional service dynamics and wider stakeholder interactions. While there are increasingly familiar patterns in how these dynamics play out, there are also always local contingencies and, it seems, core tensions, arguments and debates that must be considered anew in each setting.

In gathering together and exemplifying these arguments there are implications here for all kinds of actors: research funders; research producers; knowledge mobilisers of all kinds; policy architects; and service designers. Lessons too for the many and diverse interested parties who wish to have more influence and more impact on policy processes and service delivery.

Twenty years on from our first foray into cross-sectoral and cross-national comparisons we are reaffirmed in our belief that evidence matters. While many of the themes discussed here will be enduring, there will be further developments and opportunities. For example, looking forward, it appears increasingly apparent that technological advances and the uses of 'big data' have the potential to further extend and enrich, and maybe even reshape, evidence use in policy making and service delivery. We need to work with this potential while also addressing the myriad practical and ethical challenges associated with these advances, such as cyber-attacks, security breaches and ensuing data misuse. The more we understand the challenges and subtleties of evidence use (past, present and future), the better placed we will be to identify opportunities and enable various types of evidence to come to the fore. We hope this book will assist with that process.

References

Best, A. and Holmes, B. (2010) 'Systems thinking, knowledge and action: towards better models and methods', *Evidence and Policy*, 6 (2), pp 145–59.

Cairney, P. and Oliver, K. (2017) 'Evidence-based policymaking is not like evidence-based medicine, so how far should you go to bridge the divide between evidence and policy?', *Health Research Policy and Systems*, 15, p 35.

Cochrane, A. (1972) *Effectiveness and efficiency: random reflections on health services*, London: Nuffield Trust.

Cribb, C. (2018) 'Improvement science meets improvement scholarship: reframing research for better healthcare', *Health Care Analysis*, 26 (2), pp 109–23.

Davies, H.T.O, Nutley, S.M. and Smith, P.C. (eds) (2000) *What Works: evidence-based policy and practice in public services*, Bristol: Policy Press.

Dunleavy, P., Margetts, H., Bastow, S. and Tinkler, J. (2006) 'New public management is dead – long live digital-era governance', *Journal of Public Administration Research and Theory*, 16 (3), pp 467–94.

Head, B.W. (2008) 'Three lenses of evidence-based policy', *Australian Journal of Public Administration*, 67 (1), pp 1–11.

Marshall, M., Pagel, C., French, C., Utley, M., Allwood, D., Fulop, N., Pope, C Banks, V. and Goldmann, A. (2014) 'Moving improvement research closer to practice: the Researcher-in-Residence model', *BMJ Quality and Safety*, 23, pp 801–5.

Müller, J.W. (2017) *What is populism?* Harmondsworth: Penguin.

Nutley, S., Walter, I. and Davies, H.T.O. (2007) *Using evidence: how research can inform public services*, Bristol: Policy Press.

Osborne, S. (2006) 'The new public governance?', *Public Management Review*, 8 (3), pp 377–87.

Pinfold, V., Szymczynska, P., Hamilton, S., Peacocke, R., Dean, S., Clewett, N., Manthorpe, J. and Larsen, J. (2015) 'Co-production in mental health research: reflections from the People Study', *Mental Health Review Journal*, 20 (4), pp 220–31.

Powell, A., Davies, H.T.O. and Nutley, S.M. (2018) 'Facing the challenges of research-informed knowledge mobilization: "practising what we preach"?', *Public Administration*, 96 (1), pp 36–52.

Index

References to boxes that are separate from the relevant text are in *italics*.

References to organisations/schemes that are not British or global have their country of origin in brackets after.